To Aaron
Happy Birthday
Mom + Jim

Jan 2020

DAVE CAMPBELL'S FAVORITE TEXAS COLLEGE FOOTBALL STORIES

Swaim-Paup Sports Series
Sponsored by James C. '74 & Debra Parchman Swaim and
T. Edgar '74 & Nancy Paup

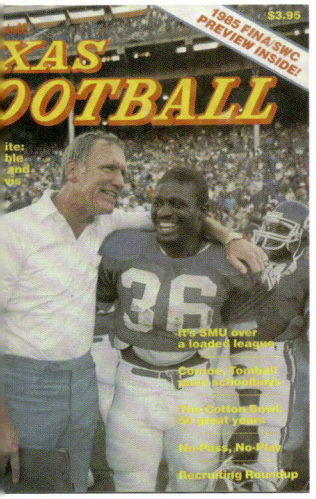
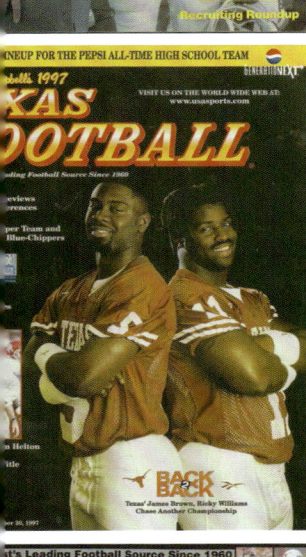

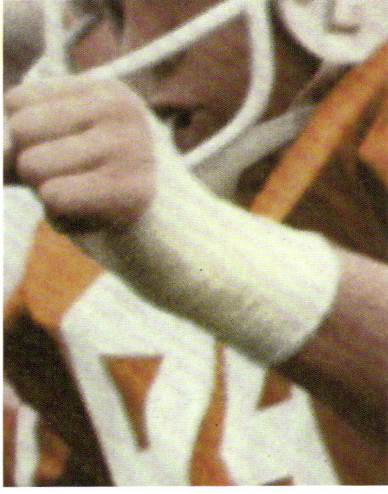

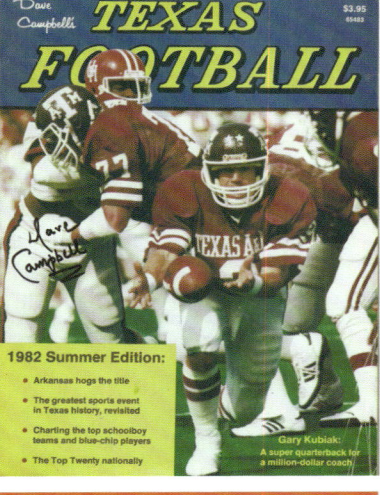
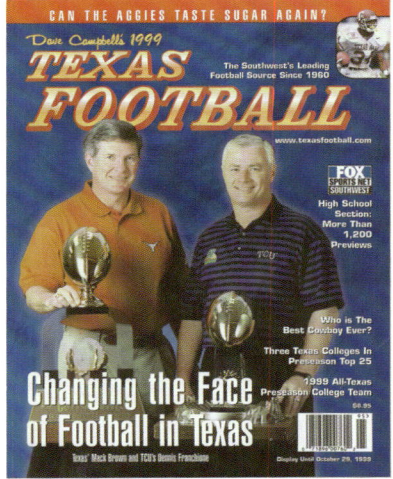
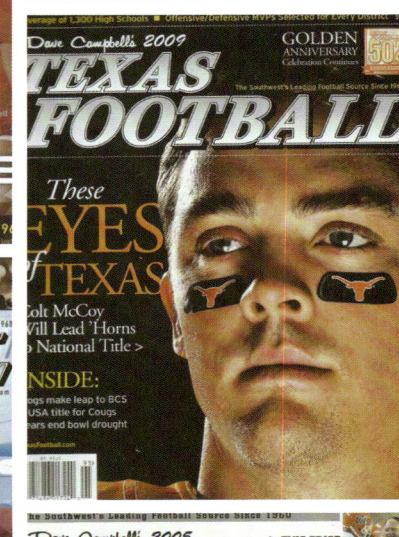

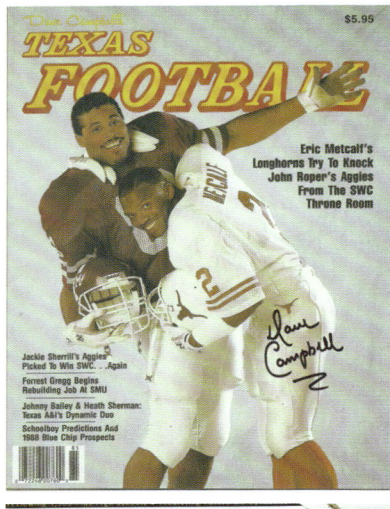
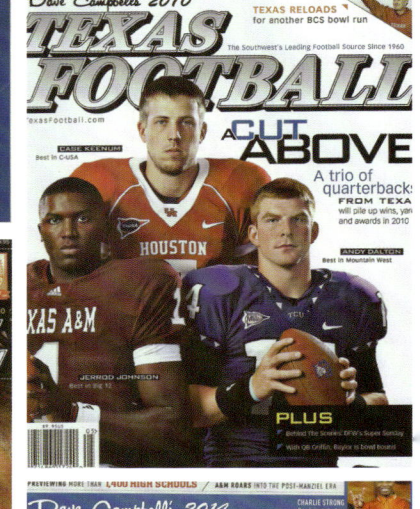

Dave Campbell's FAVORITE TEXAS COLLEGE FOOTBALL STORIES

Dave Campbell

Foreword by Mickey Herskowitz

Texas A&M University Press
College Station

Copyright © 2019 by Dave Campbell
All rights reserved
First edition

This paper meets the requirements of ANSI/NISO Z39.48-1992 (Permanence of Paper).
Binding materials have been chosen for durability.
Manufactured in China through Four Color Print Group
∞

Library of Congress Cataloging-in-Publication Data

Names: Campbell, Dave (Sports journalist), author.
Title: Dave Campbell's favorite Texas college football stories / Dave Campbell.
Other titles: Favorite Texas college football stories
Description: First edition. | College Station: Texas A&M University Press, [2018] | Series: Swaim-Paup sports series |
Identifiers: LCCN 2018037114 (print) | LCCN 2018041610 (ebook) | ISBN 9781623497262 (ebook) |
    ISBN 9781623497255 | ISBN 9781623497255 (cloth : alk. paper)
Subjects: LCSH: Football—Texas. | College sports—Texas.
Classification: LCC GV959.52.T4 (ebook) | LCC GV959.52.T4 C36 2018 (print) | DDC 796.332/6309764—dc23
LC record available at https://lccn.loc.gov/2018037114

CONTENTS

Foreword, by Mickey Herskowitz — vii

Preface — ix

1. In the Beginning . . . : 1953–1959 — 1

2. A Royal Arrival, a Junction Boy Makes Good, and the "Big Shootout" in Arkansas: 1960–1969 — 65

3. The Tyler Rose and the Houston Veer: 1970–1979 — 135

4. New Faces, Changing Times: 1980–1989 — 197

5. Good-Bye to the Southwest Conference: From the 1990s to the New Millennium — 231

Index — 273

FOREWORD

MICKEY HERSKOWITZ

This is being written from memory, which may or may not hold up in court. The story has to do with a night in the early fall of 1960 in Lubbock, Texas.

The details are not entirely clear, but they were a little vague that night as well, so there is no point in blaming the passage of time. I am no longer sure how the three of us wound up together, but Dave Campbell and I had a grand time that night talking over dinner and drinks with DeWitt Weaver, then the head football coach at Texas Tech.

I don't believe Dave or I knew Weaver all that well, but it did not take many rounds of whatever we were drinking to plunge the three of us into an extremely mellow state.

And as the drinks came, Weaver began to take us into his confidence. The Red Raiders had been admitted into the Southwest Conference not long before, and Coach Weaver began describing the long campaign that won them their objective.

Much of what we heard that night had been unreported. Weaver talked about the political pressures that had been applied in Austin, plus the consumer boycott that led thousands of Lubbock families to mail back their charge cards to the Neiman Marcus store in Dallas.

Dee Weaver was warm and funny and totally candid with us. Dave and I kept trading glances across the table, knowing we were onto something good.

Weaver sounded like a man who was thinking about retirement, and though much of what he said was off the record and no notes were taken, we knew that at the appropriate time, we would be free to write it.

I want to be careful how I say this, but both Dave and I were drinking out of our class. Campbell was not then, or ever, one of those people who gets 100 miles out of Waco and turns into Richard Burton.

It must have been pushing two o'clock in the morning when we staggered off to our rooms, Dave and I supporting each other as we walked down a long hotel corridor. As we parted, we agreed that in time, we were going to have a helluva story.

What I remember with absolute clarity is standing in the wire room, watching the Associated Press copy move across the teletype machine. This was a day or two after the season had ended, and I jumped a little when a Lubbock dateline appeared, followed by a story that said DeWitt Weaver had resigned as head coach at Texas Tech.

By the time I walked the few feet to my desk in the sports department of the *Houston Post*, my phone was ringing. It was Dave.

He asked me if I had seen the wire story. I said I had. He asked me if I remembered the night we had dinner and drinks with Weaver in Lubbock. I said I did.

There was a very meaningful pause, and then Dave asked, "Do you remember all those stories he told us?"

And I said, "Not a damned word of it."

"Neither do I," said Dave, and we both laughed. Our special insider story was locked away in our minds, which for most writers is the worst possible place.

Few stories escaped Dave Campbell in those years, or the years to follow, in his sports column in Waco or in the slicker pages of his creation, *Texas Football*.

I don't want to suggest that Dave Campbell invented the concept of the regional magazine, but his product certainly helped it along and created a model outside of sports for city magazines across the land and such quality publications as *Texas Monthly*.

Dave has been a fine, thoughtful, and honest writer and the best kind of editor—one who sets high standards, who has a reverence for the words on the page and sets his own good example of it.

I never got around to asking Dave what inspired him to publish a football magazine—and out of Waco, at that. But he made it work. The magazine, and the several spin-offs that came along behind it, found a loyal and admiring audience well beyond the borders of Texas.

Dave recruited wonderful writers over the years, starting with the likes of Blackie Sherrod, Al Ward, Steve Perkins, and Jack Gallagher. They did not require much actual recruiting; they were his friends.

The writing business has changed since the 1960s. So has the sports business. A lot of the camaraderie is missing, the gabfests the night before and the day after a big game. On those occasions, to share a table with Dave and his bright, charming wife, Reba, was to be in the best of company.

Did any group of writers have so much fun on so little money as we did in the late '50s and '60s? "Underpaid and overprivileged" was the popular phrase. You identified a city by its best-known sports columnist. Orville Henry owned Arkansas, as Blackie did Dallas. Waco was Dave Campbell's.

To read Dave was almost like having a conversation with him. He never overwrote. I know he cared deeply about his hometown team, the Baylor Bears, but in his columns there was little bias, the mark of a quality reporter.

There were, of course, years of frustration waiting for the Bears to win a championship. On the morning of a game that decided the Southwest Conference title in 1963, Dave and I followed the Baylor team through the Texas players' dining room. Bowls of fruit and cold cuts had been set for a pregame snack.

We overheard one of the players say, "Gee, even their apples are bigger than ours." I decided right then that Baylor would not end its drought that day. They did not. Duke Carlisle saved the game with an interception in the end zone. Texas won and went on to a national championship. The Longhorns shut out Baylor's lethal combination, Don Trull to Lawrence Elkins.

There is a story in these pages about that '63 Texas team. All the teams, the games, the great coaches and players—all passed through the pages of *Dave Campbell's Texas Football*.

PREFACE

As I will mention a bit later in this book, the very first issue of *Dave Campbell's Texas Football* was put together on my kitchen table, using somewhat different methods than publishers now use. Back in 1960, we wrote all our stories on typewriters, the kind with keys striking an ink ribbon and making marks on real paper. When we "cut and pasted," we used actual scissors and glue.

All these years down the line from that first issue, a lot of things have changed, both in the world of publishing and in the world of football. Computers have had a lot to do with alterations in both areas. Not only is almost everything in books and magazines written, transmitted, composed, and printed using computers, but coaches and players now have access to the kind of technology that they could only have dreamed about in the early days of my career. To scout an upcoming opponent, for example, coaches used to have to get someone to film the game, then get the film developed, then watch it with their players on grainy screens while crammed into a dark room. If you wanted to study a play, you had to keep rewinding the film over and over. Nowadays, you can get a digital video of the game that you can scrutinize millisecond by millisecond. You can freeze a play, isolate a blocker, zoom in on a formation—all with the touch of a few keys. You can send it to your players wirelessly, and they can watch it on their smartphones. Yes, things are pretty different now.

But a lot is still the same. I'm getting on up in years, 93 at this writing, but I still get excited when the calendar starts to turn toward late summer and early fall—the time when two-a-days start on practice fields all across Texas. When I catch the sound of marching bands rehearsing, I get a feeling of anticipation. I know, like everybody else, that football season is about to start, and I can hardly wait.

Football, like all sports, is a great leveler. No matter how much technology has changed certain aspects of the game, the players must still get on the field every week and play the game until a winner is declared. They must match their strength, their skills, their understanding of the game, and their strategy against that of their opponents. It doesn't matter which team is favored or who supposedly has the most star athletes—they must still play the game to decide the outcome. I suppose that's what I like the most about it. And that is also probably why, even after more than 60 years of watching, thinking about, and getting paid to write columns on Texas college football, I'm still not tired of it.

As you read this book, I hope you'll see what I'm talking about.

DAVE CAMPBELL'S
FAVORITE TEXAS
COLLEGE FOOTBALL STORIES

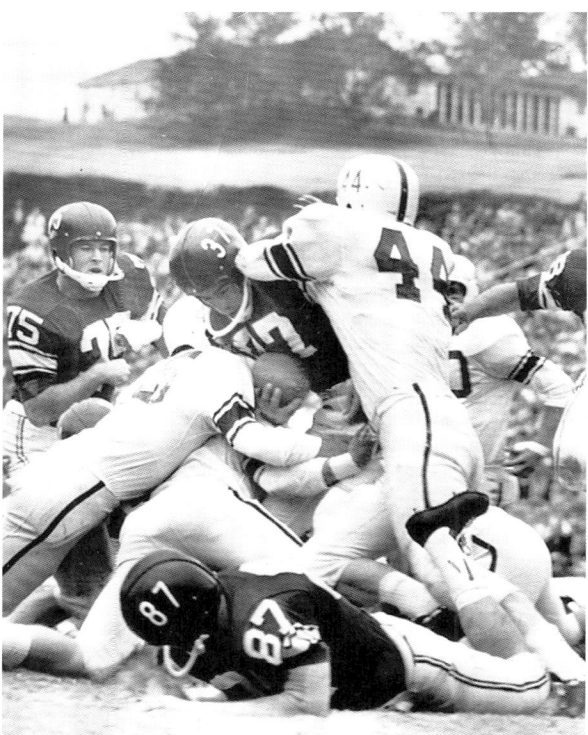

1
IN THE BEGINNING . . .
1953–1959

I covered my first college football game on September 19, 1953, when I flew from Texas out to California to report on the Baylor Bears' 25–0 thrashing of the University of California (now the University of California, Berkeley). I wasn't supposed to go; at the time, I was the junior sports reporter for the *Waco Tribune-Herald*. But Jinx Tucker, the senior sportswriter, had heart trouble and his doctor told him not to go, so I was tapped to make the trip out to the West Coast with the team and the Baylor fans, along with other sportswriters. Not too long after that, Tucker passed away, and I was put in charge of the sports coverage at the newspaper.

I had started at the newspaper as copyboy in 1942, when I was 17 years old. I thought that old newspaper office on South Sixth Street in Waco was the most exciting place in the world back then. World War II was going on, and if some major event happened, five bells would ring on the Associated Press teletype machine when the story would start to come across. I was hooked on the newspaper business from that point on. So when I returned home after the war and got the opportunity to begin covering high school and college football, it was a tremendous thrill.

It still is.

George Sauer, Baylor head coach, 1950–55. Courtesy of Baylor University Athletics.

James Ray Smith. Courtesy of Baylor University Athletics.

SEPTEMBER 20, 1953

INSPIRED BAYLOR DISMAYS COAST FANS

BERKELEY, Calif.—Poised and tricky Baylor ruthlessly blew down California's gridiron house of cards here Saturday, grinding out a 25–0 victory before 34,000.

The victory came with surprising ease. A touchdown underdog at game time, the veteran Baylor wrecking crew ran over, around, and through the vaunted California defense in scoring in each period.

Playing their first game under the new one-platoon rule, the Bears used just 25 men in handing the Cal team its lacing.

The Baylor romp came as an eye-opener to the Golden State's dismayed and unbelieving fans. It was the first opener lost by coach Lynn Waldorf since he arrived at California in 1947, and the defeat equaled a loss at the hands of Southern California as the worst setback for Waldorf while at Berkeley.

Above all today, this inspired Baylor team had poise. Nothing rattled it; nothing fazed it. It scorned temporary setbacks with the air of a champion, and indeed, that's what it was today.

The Baylor offense was sharp and clean—surprisingly clean for so early in the season—but it was the defense that stunned the fans. Only twice did the Berkeley Bears seriously menace the Baylor goal, and each time, George Sauer's charges mercilessly pinned them down.

The game's showdown came early in the second quarter. Baylor had just tacked its first seven points on the scoreboard. Rolling against the green and gold second team, Cal surged to the Baylor 9-yard line, with first down and goal to go. Here Sauer inserted his first team, and the Cal drive shriveled and died. Four times the men of Berkeley crashed into the Baylor line, and when the fourth whistle had blown, the ball was resting on the Baylor 8.

Cal didn't know it, but that was the ball game.

Leading the way in this greatest of all Baylor opening-season victories was the dazzling Bruin backfield, plus brilliant tackle James Ray Smith.

How good was Smith today? In the first period when Cal still had fire and fight, Smith recovered a fumble on the Baylor 34 to stop a threatening drive. When Cal was knocking at the goal line from the Baylor 8,

Smith nailed the runner on two of four thrusts. In the fourth period, a Baylor handoff went astray and Smith pounced on the bouncing ball. In addition, he three times boomed the kickoff to the goal line and once put it into the end zone. And his blocking was devastating.

Smith, of course, was not alone in that surprising Baylor line. Clarence Dierking, Pete Erben, Robert Knowles, and Bill Lucky riddled Cal's defensive veterans. The middle of the Baylor line was seldom fooled on defense, and indeed, when the chips were down, it was invulnerable.

Baylor's end play on defense—a matter of concern in pregame workouts—was only fair at the start of the game, but it improved rapidly as the game progressed. And what Charley Smith and Wayne Hopkins did to the rival Bears on offense was something to behold.

That good old Baylor line blasted the way as Baylor's dazzling quartet of Jerry Coody, Allen Jones, Cotton Davidson, and L. G. Dupre went about its tasks. Their play was no surprise, of course. Veterans of many an offensive thriller, they chewed up Cal's defense with brisk precision. When Coody was stopped, Dupre broke loose, and when both were slowed, Jones dashed ahead, averaging 3.6 yards per carry for his afternoon's work. Dupre's average was 4.3, and Coody's was the same.

They were the boys who got the cheers, but the superstar of that driving backfield was Davidson, that sharp-shouldered Gatesville product. Starting his final year, he quarterbacked Baylor with an uncanny skill that constantly exposed Cal's weak spots. He was the game's most rugged performer, going 59½ minutes before being relieved just before the final gun. And when he trotted off the field, even the California fans joined Baylorites in a stirring tribute.

And his passing? That's where he broke Cal's heart.

Eight of 15 aerials found their mark for an amazing 236 yards. Cotton's aerials, principally to speedy Hopkins, were of the killer variety. In the second period,

Clarence Dierking. Courtesy of Baylor University Athletics.

Jerry Coody. Courtesy of Baylor University Athletics.

he connected with Hopkins for a 45-yard gain. In the third quarter, he hit Smith on a 15-yarder; a little later, he found Dupre on a 20-yarder and then tossed to Jones for 23 yards.

But he saved the dazzler for the middle of the fourth quarter. Faking a handoff to fullback Jones, he faded back, took dead aim on the speeding Hopkins, and hit him on the Cal 20. Hopkins carried on to the 1, setting up Baylor's final touchdown. It was a tremendous 61-yard play.

The Baylor attack was one of notable balance. The Bruins rushed for a net of 178 yards and passed for 236 more for a total of 414 yards. And remember, this Cal team was supposed to be heavy on defense. Its key performers were defensive stars of last year's team. Logically enough, the scoring was balanced too. Dupre got one, Coody got one, and Davidson sneaked for two.

Dupre started the first Baylor scoring thrust with a fine run from his own 39 to the Cal 32. Dupre gained 17, then went over the center for 5. Coody plowed straight ahead for 9 to set it up on the 1, and Dupre crashed over. Coody kicked goal.

Baylor's second stringers entered at this point and were almost routed in their first battle. Cal's Talley went wide for 15, Marks whirled wide for 30 more, and Jim Dillon boomed up the middle for another 26.

"Far enough," said Sauer, and back in the game went the Baylor first string. The ball was on the Baylor 9. Talley got 1 at right guard, with James R. Smith stopping him. Talley then was smeared for no gain. Dillon tried right guard, got another yard. On fourth down, Marks was thrown for a yard loss, and Baylor took over on the 8.

After that inspiring stand, the Bruins were eager for a reward, and they churned 92 yards on 14 plays for their second score. Coody got 6 and Jones got 6, then 4, then picked up 4 more. Coody swung wide at end for 8. Jones went up the middle for 5. Crunch. Crunch. Crunch. Just like that.

Francis "Cotton" Davidson (19) and offensive lineman Jim Taylor. Courtesy of Baylor University Athletics.

Finding the short stuff too slow perhaps, Davidson took to the air. His pass was perfect to Hopkins, wide open down the left sideline, and he sped to the 10. Dupre quickly got 7, Coody got 2 more, and Davidson sneaked it over. Coody missed the kick.

Baylor made one more bid before the half ended, driving from its own 41 to Cal's 10. From there, Coody missed a field goal as time ran out.

California received to start the third quarter. Talley returned and fumbled, and Dupre recovered on the Cal 35. Nine plays later, Coody tacked up the third score. Another pass to Charley Smith, this one for 15 yards, was the big gainer.

Later in the half, Coody intercepted a pass on the Baylor 31. Four plays later came that 62-yard dazzler by Davidson and Hopkins that carried to Cal's 1.

Jess Neely, Rice head coach, 1940–66. Courtesy of Rice University Athletics.

Rice All-American Dicky Moegle, who went on to play for the San Francisco 49ers, the Pittsburgh Steelers, and the Dallas Cowboys. Courtesy of Rice University Athletics.

JANUARY 2, 1954

ON SECOND THOUGHT

There must have been at least two morals for the spectators on New Year's Day as Rice walloped Alabama in the annual Cotton Bowl Classic.

Moral No. 1—When Jess Neely has his team's blocking down pat, only a superteam is going to stand much chance against the Owls.

Moral No. 2—Don't automatically give a guy a touchdown just because he's in the clear and the closest pursuer is 20 yards behind. First make sure he's past the enemy's bench.

They'll be talking about Tommy Lewis's unscheduled ambush from the sidelines long after the records of this 1954 game are gathering dust. That little impromptu performance left the big bowl—not to mention Dicky Moegle's head—buzzing like several million colonies of bees had just moved in.

It just shows to what desperate lengths the fancy-stepping Moegle had driven the visitors from the Deep South. And one pity generally overlooked—Lewis wasted one of the prettiest tackles hung on any hustling halfback all season.

Ironically enough, Moegle started his 95-yard scamper from the same end of the field, from almost the same spot, that SMU's Frank Eldom only a few short months

Rice Institute football team, 1953. Courtesy of Rice University Athletics.

ago staggered these same Owls with a 94-yard run. That bit of trickery led to Rice's only loss in the conference race.

Friday was a different story—a new game and a new year. Moegle was doing all the running this time, and not even that tackle from the bench slowed him up for long.

The two boys shook hands on the sidelines right after the incident.

"I just can't believe I did it," said the dazed Lewis.

"Neither can I," replied the equally dazed Moegle.

"GUESS I ACTED ON INSTINCT"

In a later statement given in a secluded sanctuary in the dressing room, Lewis said, "I saw him coming a long ways, and I guess I acted on instinct. I couldn't realize I'd done it when I returned to the bench. It was like a dream." Lewis really shook up Moegle on the tackle, but he was the upset one after it was all over.

"I saw him come off the bench and I thought he had dropped a headgear or something," said Moegle after the game. He had a bruised eye to show for his day's record-breaking performance. "I looked over my shoulder at the guys closing in on me, and then Lewis hit me from the side. It really jarred me. I was dazed."

Both coaches were eager to forget the whole thing. Both said it had no effect at all on the outcome. And they were right. It was the blocking, not the bench-tackling, that spelled Waterloo this time for Alabama.

The incident was sharply similar to the one engineered by a Wake Forest sub against Baylor in Waco in September 1952.

Allen Jones, playing fullback for the green and gold, broke away down the east sidelines and headed for an apparent touchdown. As he passed the Deacon bench, at about the Wake Forest 30, Jones was pulverized by over-zealous Van Seawell. However, Jones had stepped out of bounds several yards back up the field, and as Seawell said later, "I just saved him that long trip to the goal line for nothing." Wake Forest was penalized 15 yards on

Overhead view of the Cotton Bowl as it appeared in the mid-1950s. Courtesy of *Dave Campbell's Texas Football*.

the play for roughing. Baylor went on to win via C. A. Brocato's last-minute field goal.

No rule covers Referee Cliff Shaw's decision to award the Owls a touchdown on such a play. Rules say, in fact, that a touchdown cannot be awarded on a penalty.

Here's what Abb Curtis, chief of Southwest Conference officials, had to say, however: "Shaw had a perfect right to award Rice a touchdown. The rules cover only 'normal' situations, which this certainly was not. It is left to the officials' judgment on situations not specifically covered in the rules. The officials thought Moegle would have scored and so awarded the touchdown."

CAL'S ROY REIGELS NOW HAS COMPANY

The incident brings to mind the oft-told account of the wrong-way run of the University of California's Roy Reigels, which happened in the 1929 Rose Bowl game.

California was meeting Georgia Tech with play in the second period. Neither team had scored. Reigels

Raymond Berry Jr., who saw very few passes thrown in his direction while at SMU during the early 1950s, went on to play for the Baltimore Colts and to coach the New England Patriots in Super Bowl XX. Courtesy of Southern Methodist University Athletics.

took the ball, became confused, ran the wrong way, and finally was tackled 1 foot out from his own goal line by Benny Lom, a teammate. On the next play, Lom punted for California, with Georgia Tech's Maree blocking the kick. A California player managed to touch the ball just before it went out of bounds in the end zone, so Referee Herb Dana ruled it a safety for Tech. The two points later provided the victory margin for the Engineers over California, 8–7.

Now Reigels has company.

OCTOBER 24, 1954

BEARS BOMB AGGIES INTO DEFEAT, 20–7

Confused and almost humiliated for the first 23 minutes of play, the Baylor Bears rallied superbly behind the eye-popping leadership of Billy Hooper, James Ray Smith, and Henry Gremminger to blot out the fighting Texas Aggies, 20–7, before 36,000 homecoming fans at Baylor Stadium Saturday afternoon.

After being chased all over the premises while A&M was rolling up a 7–0 lead in the first quarter, the Bruins awakened to tie the score by halftime, and then in the first 11 minutes of the third quarter, they sewed up the game.

The victory was the Bears' sixth in a row over the maroon and white and their most decisive over the Aggies since 1949.

The Bruins were a spirited, dangerous crew, armed with fast backs and deadly passes. And most pleasing of them all, they finally turned in some bone-rattling defense.

A word about that defense. The most impressive part came early in the fourth quarter, and it thrilled Baylor fans as no offensive effort has this entire season.

The Bruins led at the time, 20–7, with A&M facing a get-started-or-give-up situation. The ball was on the Baylor 16, second and 2.

Quarterback Elwood Kettler, a bold little runner with a lot of heart, ran his favorite option play off to the left, found his hole, and set sail for the goal line. He made it all the way to the 1 before Reuben Saage chilled him.

Even so, that gave the Aggies a first down, and the ball was really on about the 2-foot line. Nobody doubted but that the Aggies would score and perhaps stage another of their typical last-minutes flourishes. Nobody but the Bruins, that is.

The first play gained nothing, as J. R. Smith nailed Kettler hard. The second lost 4, as Allen Jones, Gremminger, and Tony DeGrazier whacked Billy Huddleston

Henry Gremminger. Courtesy of Baylor University Athletics.

A&M coach Bear Bryant (right) talks with Red Grange, the "Galloping Ghost" (left), and broadcaster Lindsey Nelson (center) in the early 1950s. Courtesy of Texas A&M University Athletics.

on a pitchout. On the third try, Kettler tried a fooler, sending his backs one way while he kept the ball and went the other. Gremminger smelled out the play and knifed Kettler down on the 13 before the Aggies could look around. The fourth-down pass try was batted down by Allen Jones at the goal line, and Baylor took over control of the game.

As usual, the Farmers gave it all they had, and for that above-mentioned first quarter, they had much too much for Baylor. Led by Kettler, swift Don Watson, and tough Don Kachtik, the "thin thirty" grabbed a 7–0 lead and licked the Bruins at every turn.

But after getting organized, the Bears acquired poise and punch and proceeded to teach Bear Bryant's hard-nosed youngsters a costly gridiron lesson.

Once started, the teaching came easy. Chief instructor was the chunky Hooper, a cool-eyed lad from Sweetwater who passes more and more like fellow townsman Sammy Baugh.

Billy was the difference in that chips-down struggle. He passed for all three of Baylor's touchdowns, the second game in a row in which he has achieved that feat. He connected on 11 of 13 passes, picking up 126 yards.

Billy, on his first pass, placed one right in Excell Amyett's hands, but Amyett dropped the ball. The next aerial sailed out of bounds as Aggie defenders applied heavy pressure. Then, for the next 11 times in a row, Billy's tosses found their marks. When he retired after 58 minutes of play, his completion streak was still alive, and the Aggies were dead.

Thus Billy was a hero of heroes. But there were others.

Tackle and cocaptain James Ray Smith was a sensation, turning in easily his finest performance of the season. "He made a believer out of me," said one Houston writer. "I didn't think he could play defense before today."

He needed only to have asked the Aggies. A year ago, Jim Smith put on such a tremendous performance against A&M that he was voted the nation's top lineman as a reward. Saturday he had a comparable day. He was in on the first three tackles turned in by the Bruins, and that was just the start.

He turned up everywhere, leading a goal-line stand here, breaking through to dump Kettler for a loss there, falling on a fumble at another spot, and in general playing hob with Bryant's well-laid plans.

Henry Gremminger was Baylor's third ace in the deck, once again leading all Bruins in pass snagging as well as recovering an Aggie fumble and halting any number of Cadet runners.

The start of the game belonged to the Aggies, who racked up the Baylorites in just two plays after a Baylor fumble at the Bear 32. Kettler set it up with a keeper to the 24, then passed beautifully to Billy Huddleston just over the goal line. The ball barely cleared Hooper's waving arm.

Kettler took care of the extra point chores, and the Aggies held a 7–0 lead with a little more than three minutes left in the first quarter.

Both offenses were bogged down for a while, but the Aggies finally found a spark and maneuvered to the Baylor 31, and it began to look as if Baylor's 1954 Bears were about through.

Just as the exes began to frown, the Bruins started their comeback. In two plays, they salted the Aggie surge, with J. R. Smith first tossing Kettler for a yard loss, then Gremminger recovering Easley's fumble on the Baylor 35.

Now Sauer's troops found the range. They became a poised team, deadly both aground and in the air. Significantly enough, a pass from aerial artist Hooper to his favorite battery mate, Gremminger, sent the Bruins in motion. That pass carried to the Baylor 43. The Bears blasted to the Aggie 7, where, facing third and needing 6, Hooper faded and shot a toss to the goal line into the waiting arms of Charley Smith. Later events were to prove that Hooper was just warming up.

Charley Smith kicked goal, and Baylor had the game deadlocked, which is how it remained at the end of the half.

The Aggies took the second-half kickoff, gained one first down, and then fumbled at the Baylor 47, with J. R. Smith grabbing the stray ball.

In 10 plays—4 of them were passes—the Bears struck for the go-ahead touchdown. Facing fourth and 6 from the Aggie 33, Hooper spotted the right answer. He pulled the trigger on a beauty to Charley Smith at the 19, and the Bears gained their vital first down.

Now Holley rambled to the 8 behind superb blocking offered by Pearce, Gremminger, Charley Smith, and J. R. Smith. Two plays gained 5, and then Hooper fired to Holley in the end zone for the score. Charley Smith kicked goal, and the Bears were ahead to stay.

Four plays later, the Bears swung back to the attack as J. R. Smith's raging tackle play bogged down the Aggie offensive. Holley took the resulting Aggie punt and returned 9 yards to the Baylor 43.

In just four plays, Hooper kayoed the Farmers when cool Billy aimed one at Excell Amyett on the Aggie 10. Amyett grabbed this one cleanly, fought off Aggie tackler Huddleston, and lunged into the end zone. Charley Smith missed this extra point try.

A&M coach Bryant called that goal-line stand as a turning point, and Baylor coach George Sauer picked it out as the game's most decisive moment.

BILLY PETE HUDDLESTON

When I became sports editor of the *Waco Tribune-Herald* in 1954, we started the Southwest Conference preseason football press tour that September at Rice, where head football coach Jess Neely was already famous, and then we went to Austin to interview the University of Texas head coach (Ed Price) and some of his players. Then the next day, we were off to the West Texas town of Junction to get the latest word about the Aggies from new Texas A&M coach Bear Bryant. I will never forget that day. We got up early that morning and then drove to Fredericksburg, where we had breakfast at the old Admiral Nimitz Hotel. Then it was on to Junction, where it was very hot and dry.

I knew several players I saw there who had made a name for themselves playing for their high school football teams in Central Texas (Don Watson from Franklin was one), but I never met Gene Stallings or Billy Pete Huddleston. Both of those young student athletes went on to make *quite* a name for themselves—Stallings as a football coach (won an SWC football crown in 1967 as coach of the Aggies and in 1992, as coach of Alabama's Crimson Tide, directed his undefeated team to a national championship by upsetting Miami in the Sugar Bowl) and Billy Pete Huddleston as a petroleum engineer.

It wasn't until many years later that I first met Huddleston, first at a memorial gathering in the backyard of Stanley Weaver, himself a graduate of Texas A&M and my wife's brother. Then a couple of years later, I went to Huddleston's small ranch, which was also home to 150 exotic animals (deer, antelope, etc.) and 150 Brangus cows. The ranch is not far from Stanley Weaver's old home about 5 miles from Navasota, and I was able to interview him for this story.

And it is quite a story. Born in a West Texas oil field camp in Iraan in 1934, Huddleston as a young man became a headline maker for the Iraan football team. Wearing the red and black of the Braves, he was a three-sport athlete, starting every football game for four seasons and winning all-state recognition in football. But he also was all-district in basketball and set a state record in the hurdles while a member of the school's track team.

So as his fame began to spread, the scholarship offers came rushing in—in total, from more than two dozen colleges and universities. But Huddleston had been working in the oil fields since he had been a 12-year-old youngster, and he probably was destined all along for Texas A&M. As he later said, "I felt the most comfortable there. A&M had a lot of small-town country people. I was back in my element."

But the sheer size of the student body amazed him. "The first day of practice was an absolute shock. I never had seen that many people," he said. "We had 133 players [this would have been when he was a freshman, ineligible for SWC varsity play in that era]. I had never seen more than 22 players on the field at any one time. All of them were all-district, all-state, all-something. I had never seen so many big, fast people. It took me awhile to adjust."

But adjust he did. He adjusted so well and his leadership ability became so evident that he was named captain of the 1955 Texas A&M football team, which would have tied TCU for the SWC crown if it had not had to settle for a 7–7 tie playing Arkansas at Fayetteville. And the Aggies did beat TCU that season in Fort Worth, 19–16.

I covered that A&M-TCU game as well as the Baylor-A&M game that season (the Aggies won, 19–7, at Kyle Field), and shortly after that defeat, Baylor coach George Sauer resigned, with his chief assistant coach Sam Boyd taking his place. And then the next season (1956), I covered two of the best and most memorable games I ever covered in my 62 years as a sportswriter—A&M's 7–6 victory over TCU played at Kyle Field (the so-called Hurricane Game) and the following week the 19–13 A&M victory over Baylor in Waco.

But back to Junction for a moment. "The experience at Junction was 10 times harder than spring practice. We went to Junction with 90 to 94 players and came back 10 days later with 34 beat-up players," Huddleston recalls. Or as the A&M sports information director Jones Ramsey in the era liked to say, "We went to Junction in three buses and came back in one."

According to some of the players who were there, about 60 players who quit the team had to walk 10 miles to Junction to escape the verbal abuse of the entire coaching staff, which was as bad as the physical part. According to Huddleston, "For some reason, I totally escaped the verbal, but I was rewarded with eight linemen, two at a time, for a punt return drill. Coach Bryant was the sole coach for two hours. The only comment from Coach was finally, 'Let's go in.'"

"Some people from ESPN later came to interview me about Junction," recalls Huddleston. It had been especially hot and dry that summer in Junction, where the Aggies in their first year under Bryant had worked out in what Huddleston called "a goat pasture." According to Huddleston, the ESPN crew wanted to know if Junction had been the worst experience of his life. "Heavens, no. By no means," he told them. Then what was? "Thermodynamics," he replied.

As Huddleston likes to note, 32 survivors of the Junction experience went on to graduate from A&M and leave an incredible professional record. Among the 32 were 9 engineers, and of those 9, it would be difficult to find one who has established a record that would match that of Billy Pete Huddleston. He graduated in June 1957 with a degree in petroleum engineering, and that degree became a launching pad for a life that has made him one of the best-known petroleum engineers in the country. And one of the most generous when asked to give to worthy causes.

Huddleston coached the A&M freshman football team and went

to most of the varsity coaches meetings. He remembers Coach Bryant's lectures in those meetings as brilliant, but he said Bryant would not tolerate a coach's lack of intensity or logic. "We had many midnight-to-morning meetings that were focused on being prepared," Huddleston said. "I had a good relationship with Coach Bryant even though our personalities were a lot different. He did not pass out a lot of accolades."

But he surely remembers this one: "At my senior year football banquet, Coach Bryant asked me to stand, and he said these words: 'I want my son to grow up like this young man.'" Memorable words, indeed.

But before making the most of his petroleum engineering degree, Huddleston spent a couple of years as a member of a fighter-interceptor squadron for the air force, then he worked for several more years for Marathon Oil before starting his own consulting firm, Huddleston & Co., in 1967.

Then in 1971, he founded Peter Paul Petroleum Co., which now manages interests in more than 2,500 oil and gas properties and 250,000 mineral acres. And Huddleston & Co. now provides petroleum engineering consulting services for more than 500 oil and gas companies, gas transmission companies, banks, and other financial institutions. The firm's database includes more than 100,000 oil and gas properties located in the United States and Canada, and foreign projects include Africa, South and Central America, Australia, China, Indonesia, the North Sea, Russia, and the United Arab Emirates.

An Ivy League endowment fund has been a major partner for more than 30 years.

"Now I've got more than 62 years in the oil business in one form or fashion," Huddleston said. Because of his experiences and reputation in the oil and gas business, Huddleston received an invitation to serve as a visiting professor of petroleum engineering at Texas A&M, and he served in that capacity for 17 years. He believes that at one time, he had taught about 15 percent of all the practicing petroleum engineers in the United States.

Texas A&M has given Huddleston many awards, including TAMU Distinguished Graduate, and he was the second recipient of the TAMU Letterman's Lifetime Achievement Award.

He has retired now, but his two companies, Huddleston & Co. and Peter Paul Petroleum, are still going strong, and Billy Pete, once the unknown kid from Iraan, is still chairman of both companies.

BILLY HUDDLESTON
Courtesy of Cushing Memorial Library and Archives, Texas A&M University

At the time of this writing, he has been married more than 52 years (his wife's name is Flora), or since his fifth year at A&M. But they started out together in the first grade back in Iraan. He calls her "Flos" and notes that she is "supersmart" and does all the financial work for the two companies. "We still work every day," he said not long ago, "and we don't plan on quitting any time soon."

The Huddlestons have eight grandchildren, including two who have become students at Texas A&M. But as I noted earlier, Huddleston is a thoughtful and generous man. "We have had more than 100 scholarships for students, not all at A&M but most of them," he said. "We require each of them to either write us a note or call us at the end of each semester. We've had over a 90 percent success rate. And it's not the money necessarily. It's knowing somebody believes in them and they have support, and that's been very rewarding."

Huddleston is very proud of Texas A&M. He declares that some universities may have more alumni, but none are more loyal to the university than the former students at Texas A&M.

Rice's Dicky Moegle (47) and Kenny Paul (60). Courtesy of Rice University Athletics.

NOVEMBER 29, 1954
ON SECOND THOUGHT

All week it had been obvious that the Baylor Bears were in great danger of being toppled Saturday afternoon. It was nothing you could put your finger on, and yet it was there. Even the Baylor coaches, fretful and nervous, seemed to sense disaster was hovering near.

Before the TCU, Texas, and SMU contests, George Sauer's assistants in particular were an optimistic lot. For instance, line coach Jack Russell confidently predicted they would "win by two touchdowns" when queried before the showdown with the Mustangs in Dallas.

Before the Rice game, he made no such prediction. Instead, he pointedly declined to make a forecast when asked for one. In addition, the entire picture pointed to double trouble for the Bears.

For one thing, they were heavy favorites, a dubious position in this upset-crazy season. They had just put on their finest display of the season the week before in smashing down SMU and thus were in danger of a letdown in performance.

Again, they were playing the Rice Owls, annually the best November team in the conference. Razor sharp on fundamentals, Jess Neely's teams can scrap with the best of them when the chips are on the table, and as far as the Owls were concerned, the chips were all there Saturday.

And then, in addition to all that, the Bruins were facing Dicky Moegle.

There, certainly, is the finest back in the nation. He can do it all. He can beat you in a twinkling with a long run. He can rake the tackles like a fullback. He can snatch passes. He can intercept passes. And he can tackle like Bronco Nagurski.

As far as I am concerned, Dicky Moegle is the finest backfield product this conference has offered since Doak

Baylor wide receiver Del Shofner (center) clowning around with teammates Charley Horton (right) and Jerry Marcontell (left). Courtesy of Baylor University Athletics.

Walker, and in many ways, Moegle is a striking reminder of Walker.

BOTH AT BEST UNDER PRESSURE

Both have, in huge gobs, that indescribable something that functions best when the pressure is highest. They are clutch ballplayers in the finest tradition. Alone, they are worth the price of admissions. Moegle scored two touchdowns Saturday, one on a 91-yarder and another on a 9-yarder. He must have saved at least three others with uncanny defensive play.

First of all, in the second quarter, with Baylor trailing by 7–13, dandy Dicky raced over to knock away at the last instant a touchdown pass to Charley Smith at the Rice 3-yard line.

In the third period, he was the final Owl defender between Allen Jones and the goal line, and he got his man. And then in the final showdown, with swift Del Shofner sprinting desperately for a game-tying touchdown, Moegle raced over and made the tackle on the Owl 6.

Four plays later, on Baylor's final offensive gesture of the ball game, he contributed a mighty hand in helping Gordon Kellogg rub out Shofner on the Rice 3. Moegle's offensive efforts were tremendous, but to my mind, his defensive work was even better.

A second look at the contest indicates that Baylor may have lost the game in the first period, right after the Owls had scored their first touchdown. Shofner took the opening kickoff, returned it to the Baylor 32, was injured, and had to leave the field.

He came back to play great football in the second half, but by now he was operating on a game ankle. Still swift and deadly, he nevertheless had been slowed a vital step or two, and that was just enough for Moegle to haul him onto the Rice 6 late in the fourth period.

Bill Whitmore, Rice's athletic publicist, who understandably is highly impressed with Dicky Moegle, paid perhaps the highest tribute of all to Shofner.

"Well, we're seeing the king and the crown prince today," he said.

Billy Hooper (54) and Bobby Jones (12), a lethal one-two punch at quarterback for Baylor in 1954. Courtesy of Baylor University Athletics.

BIG DIFFERENCE IN FIRST AND LAST

The season actually made a complete cycle for the Bears, but what a difference between the first and the last!

In September, the Bruins opened their season by almost bombing a team from Houston (the University of Houston Cougars) out of the stadium. Billy Hooper and Bob Jones tried long ones, short ones, and middle-sized ones, and everything connected.

In late November, at the climax, the Bruins closed out their season against another team from Houston, and this time, the forward pass (still thrown by Baylor tossers) beat them. Five times did the Owls intercept on Billy Hooper's worst day of all, and that in itself tilted the scales of victory. Last year the Owls also picked off five Baylor aerials. Thus in two years, Rice defenders have intercepted 10 Bruin tosses. That may be a national record of some kind.

The game had another ironical note, the possibility of which was pointed out in this column Saturday morning.

In 1952 Owl safety man Horton Nesrsta came into the final game against Baylor with an excellent chance of winning the national title for punt returns. He got away on a 61-yarder for a touchdown to win his title, and the touchdown beat the Bears. Dicky Moegle came into Saturday's game in the identical situation. He got away on a 91-yarder to win his crown, and that score beat the Bears.

Lightning can strike twice, and with deadly effect.

NOVEMBER 13, 1955

SWINK-LED FROGS STUN LONGHORN HOPES, 47–20

AUSTIN, Tex.—Texas Christian's incredible Jim Swink, a gridiron genius with an abiding scorn for anything short of perfection, put on one of the most magnificent performances in all Southwest Conference history here Saturday afternoon as TCU routed Texas, 47–20, before 55,000 fans.

The rampage of the Purple put Abe Martin's men within sniffing distance of Cotton Bowl riches,

Abe Martin, head coach at TCU, 1953–66, lectures his charges at halftime. Courtesy of Texas Christian University Athletics.

eliminated Texas from championship consideration, and brought the breathtaking Swink into full focus as one of the league's all-time great runners.

He was letter-perfect this afternoon. He was the Four Horsemen, Doak Walker, and Frank Merriwell all rolled into one and supercharged for this significant occasion.

Swink scored four touchdowns on runs of 1, 62, 57, and 34 yards. He carried 15 times and gained 235 yards, returned one punt for 13 yards, brought back two kick-offs for 13 yards, and intercepted a pass.

He blew out all those jinx-producing red candles in colorful Memorial Stadium, and when his job was finished—with 3:35 left to play—he trotted off the field to a tumultuous ovation from a throng both appreciative and convinced. As he neared the sidelines, two brawny, gleeful Froggies came forward to meet him. They hoisted him to their shoulders for the final yards.

Swink scored 26 points in all today in guiding the Frogs to the most decisive whipping ever dished out to a Longhorn 11 by a conference team. His point spree was also an individual high for Memorial Stadium.

Swink now has scored 17 touchdowns and kicked 5 conversions for 107 points. He needs only another 21 to tie the all-time mark set by A&M's immortal Joel Hunt in 1927. No other conference player since 1927 has equaled Swink's point production.

When Swink wasn't running around, through, and between the Longhorns, quarterback Chuck Curtis was having quite a field day himself. Bombardier Chuck, making a powerful bid for all-conference recognition, pulled the trigger on three touchdown passes and used the airways to set up a fourth. The payoff passing plays went 44, 37, and 42 yards, and the fourth toss carried 41 yards and moved the Froggies to the Texas 1, from where Swink scored two plays later.

Although the scoreboard ridicules such a possibility, the Longhorns actually made a game of it for three quarters. They led at one time, 7–6, and trailed by only 20–14 at the end of the third period. At that point, Texas' colors still fluttered gaily, even defiantly, and Longhorn followers dreamed of a second straight 21–20 decision. Then the Frogs exploded with a four-touchdown extravaganza

Jim Swink slips a tackle. Courtesy of Texas Christian University Athletics.

Walter Fondren. Courtesy of University of Texas Athletics.

that took out all the starch and left even wild Bevo feeling tired and weary of it all.

So explosive was the Frog attack that the entire time needed to carve out the seven touchdowns consumed only 10 minutes and 20 seconds. And the first drive, a seven-play, 82-yarder, used up more than 4 of those 10 minutes itself.

The Frog scoring drives went 82, 74, 62, 46, 42, 83, 65, and 34 yards. Thus the Martin men earned all they got, and they got plenty. In all, they picked up 348 yards on the ground and another 175 in the air for a grand total of 523 yards. That total offense figure is the highest ever surrendered by the orange and white.

Swink made the first, third, sixth, and seventh Frog touchdowns. Curtis passed to Ken Wineburg for the second, to Bryan Engram for the fourth, and to O'Day Williams for the fifth.

The Longhorns, who gave their all, were paced by Delano Womack in the backfield and by Johnny Tatum, Gerald Peterson, and Langford Sneed on the line. The Frogs were primed for the versatile Walt Fondren on this balmy, windy afternoon and gave him only 22 yards on eight carries. They also mistreated him on defense, passing over him for one touchdown and running past him for another.

A great Frog line aided and abetted Swink and his backfield mates in all their mischief. Norman Hamilton, in perhaps his finest performance, paced those superb forwards. Hamilton, using fine lateral speed, repeatedly knifed down the Longhorns on their wide efforts. He made Fondren his particular target.

Hugh Pitts, Don Cooper, and Engram also had great days for this greatest Frog victory in history over a Longhorn foe. They collected interest at a fantastic rate for that 35–34 heartbreaker dished out by the Steers in Fort Worth a year ago.

Hugh Pitts (with a young Frogs fan). Courtesy of Texas Christian University Athletics.

Swink and Curtis were the big noisemakers in the backfield, of course, but Vern Hallbeck contributed 44 yards to the attack, Wineburg 42, and Harold Pollard 35. Other than Womack and Fondren, Texas had no runner capable of yardage in double figures.

Stymied early on the ground, the Longhorns tried an all-out aerial attack using the artistry of sophomore Joe Clements. Joe was not at his best today, completing only 7 of 24 passes, and for that he could blame the hard-rushing Frog forwards. In all, Texas tried 29 passes and completed only 8.

It was the climax of a glorious afternoon. Swink made all of his long runs at the north end, with the gusty wind blowing at his back.

"Aw, he's not so good; let's see him do all that going against the wind," one press box jokester said. But not the Longhorns. They saw enough of this thrill-packed afternoon to last them a lifetime.

MAY 13, 1956

FAYETTEVILLE, Ark.—After a struggle that raged on for more than 30 years, West Texas finally hit the jackpot here Saturday as booming Texas Tech was invited to become a member of the Southwest Conference. The welcome mat was put down by unanimous vote of the conference's athletic committee. At the same time, the conference dads completely revoked Texas A&M's two-year probation and opened the way for the NCAA to lift its sentence on the Aggies next August. The conference recommended such action to the NCAA.

The signal for the twin celebrations at Lubbock and College Station came at 10:30 a.m., when the panel completed what one member termed its most harmonious session in years. Actually, both decisions are believed to have been made Friday night, but the official announcement did not come until this morning.

As expected, the language of the approved motion on expansion merely "invites" Texas Tech into the league. No formal date for admittance was set. A committee from the conference and a committee from Tech will work out the many remaining details in the coming months, thus enabling the big Lubbock school to make a gradual entry.

Full-fledged participation in all sports is expected by 1961, when Tech will be able to get a permanent place on all football schedules. Participation in basketball probably will come in two years and in spring sports perhaps by 1957.

Despite that delay, however, the Raiders, for all practical purposes, are "in." The big battle is over, and the Tech representatives preparing for the faculty conferences are jubilant.

E. J. Holub, a standout defensive player for Texas Tech from 1958 to 1960, was inducted into the Kansas City Chiefs Hall of Fame in 1976. Courtesy of Texas Tech University Athletics.

"This means the dawn of a new era for Texas Tech," said athletic director DeWitt Weaver, the university official primarily responsible for directing the long-range push for recognition with undiminished vigor. Dr. J. William Davis, Texas Tech's faculty representative, said, "We're tickled to death." Dr. Davis was the first to hear the good news. The conference's committee called him into the session at 9 o'clock, told him the decision, and then handed him the official statement to read.

While Tech won its bid at last, the University of Houston again failed by a wide margin. A motion to admit Houston died for lack of a second.

Texas Tech's admission will not upset the popular football "round robin." In a bow to the league's smaller schools, the conference committee amended its bylaws to provide that the round-robin schedule in football be required, provided the membership consists of only eight schools. Furthermore, it provided that this eight-school round-robin plan cannot be altered or abolished except by unanimous vote after 30 days' prior notice.

The conference's new member is a school of 7,000 enrollment that has won its Border Conference football title four of the last five years. Tech has been trying to get into the conference since 1927. The Raiders are the first new members in the conference since 1922, when TCU joined the ranks. The addition of the Fort Worth school gave the league a membership of eight at that time. Oklahoma A&M withdrew in May 1925, leaving the conference with the seven members who voted in favor of Tech today.

Only Jones Ramsey, A&M's athletic publicity director, was on hand to receive the good news for the Aggies. Athletic director Paul Bryant had returned to College Station Friday night.

The faculty panel said in its prepared statement that it had received a detailed report from A&M on efforts to correct its recruiting violations. After checking that report, as well as present recruiting practices, the panel said it is convinced that the cleanup has been successful.

"Therefore," the committee said, "the conference hereby terminates the probation of the college as of this date and respectfully recommends to the NCAA that it review its action taken in May 1955, with respect to this matter."

THE GAME THAT BEAR BRYANT COULD NEVER FORGET

Those who saw the October 20, 1956, Texas A&M-TCU game will always consider it a bonus for their memory bank—because the game was unlike any that most members of that overflow crowd had ever seen before. Or since. The violent weather conditions, combined with the game's unusual ebb and flow, made it so.

Indeed, in a special Texas Football poll in 1965, taken to determine which Southwest Conference games were the best over a 20-year period dating back to the end of World War II, this showdown ranked third on the list, right behind the SMU-Notre Dame game of 1949 and the Arkansas-Texas game of 1964.

In short, that '56 Aggie-Frog battle was the best game of the 1950s in the Southwest Conference, featuring coaches, players, teams, and playing conditions that were simply unforgettable.

It was, quite simply, the game Bear Bryant could never forget.

Bear Bryant was as fascinating a person as I have encountered in a career in the sports department that goes back to the late 1940s.

I became sports editor of the Waco Tribune-Herald in December of '53, shortly after the death of my famed predecessor, H. H. "Jinx" Tucker. I had only held that position a few weeks when Texas A&M dismissed Ray George and started looking for a new head football coach. The man they eventually hired was the coach who had been heading up the Kentucky football program: Bear Bryant.

He immediately picked up the pace for Southwest Conference football—in recruiting, in film study, in off-season conditioning work, in a lot of ways.

Mostly because of Bryant and a number of events he was involved in—the 1954 fall camp at Junction, the recruiting rules violations that resulted in 1955 SWC and NCAA sanctions against the A&M program, and such snap-crackle-and-pop games as those against Rice in '55; TCU, Baylor, and Texas in '56; and Arkansas, Rice, and Texas in '57—it was a great time to be young and a sportswriter covering Southwest Conference football.

I was among those who covered the "Hurricane Game" of 1956 and got to witness those incredible developments firsthand. When Baylor played Alabama in September 1979, long after Bryant had turned Alabama into a perennial contender for national titles, I was able to have my last extended interview with him before his death in 1983, and one of the topics we discussed that day was that memorable A&M-TCU game.

That night I found I couldn't keep my eyes off him, even as Alabama was drubbing what turned out to be a fine Baylor team (it went 8–4, including a victory over Clemson in the Peach Bowl).

Several days later I wrote a column for the Waco Tribune-Herald that read, in part, like this:

It was beautiful last Saturday night in Birmingham. The sky was clear, the new moon was out, the stadium was packed for the first 1979 appearance of Bear Bryant's Crimson Tide. The teams came out for the pregame warm-ups, and Bryant walked to midfield and chatted a moment with Grant Teaff.

He didn't appear to study the Baylor players closely as he once studied opposing players. When he was at A&M, he played a Missouri team tutored by rookie coach Frank Broyles. Bryant approached Broyles at midfield during the pregame warm-ups that day and told him, "Frank, I've been looking over your squad. You don't have a single athlete, do you?" Final score: A&M 28, Missouri 0.

But Bryant was much more impressed with the '79 Baylor Bears. "A good solid team, a sound team," he had said in our interview.

Now he was at Legion Field, watching his team warm up, waiting for the game to begin. In such moments, most coaches stroll among their players. Bryant went down to Alabama's end of the field, leaned against a goal post—his houndstooth hat pulled down low over his eyes—and watched silently.

Maybe half a dozen yards away, five or six photographers aimed and clicked, aimed and clicked. That went on and on. He paid them no mind. He stood there at least 10 minutes, talking to no one, scarcely changing expression.

Finally the warm-ups ended and the players returned to their dressing room. Bryant ambled along behind them, his assistants running on ahead. When the Crimson Tide came running out again, all primed for the kickoff, Bryant trailed them again. But his step was much faster now. And when the game began, there was no doubt who was in charge.

> "There's not a substitution made that he doesn't make," one 'Bama assistant said. "We make suggestions, yes, but he makes all the decisions."
>
> One night years ago, at a gathering of newspaper people on the back porch of his A&M home, a few hours after the '56 Aggies defeated Rice and sewed up a share of the first Southwest Conference title the Aggies had won in 15 years, Bryant was in a mellow mood when the regional sports editor of the Associated Press, Harold Ratliff, approached. Ratliff had a laugh that sounded like a rasp grating on sheet metal.
>
> "Bear," said Ratliff, "do you think you're a genius?" Then came that Ratliff laugh.
>
> Bryant smiled and then was serious. "No, Harold," he replied, "but I do think I'm a damned good football coach."
>
> Twenty-three years later, on a gorgeous night in Birmingham, at the age of 66—when his walk has slowed and the shadows have lengthened, when he has moved to within a mere 29 victories of taking the place of Amos Alonzo Stagg as the winningest football coach in history—Paul (Bear) Bryant proved the point still one more time: he was a damned good football coach.
>
> Dave Campbell

To those who were there, the game remains unique, as secure in memory as that first new car. And yet it was 30 years ago this autumn that the dark sky and howling wind and blinding rain turned what already was a classic battle between Aggies and Frogs into an instant entry on the Southwest Conference's list of unforgettable football games.

It became famous almost immediately as the Hurricane Game.

Texas A&M won it, 7–6. TCU fans disputed it. Fans all over the Southwest Conference talked about it for months. Bear Bryant never forgot it.

Almost a quarter of a century later, after he had won 6 national titles and 12 Southeastern Conference crowns at Alabama, Bryant still vividly remembered that October afternoon in 1956 at Kyle Field.

"Usually, when we're at practice and I see that lightning, we stop and go in," he said in that Birmingham interview in 1979. "The other day we had a little lightning while we were out there, and I said to Dee Powell [one of his assistants who played for him in that Hurricane Game], 'Dee, does this remind you of anything?' And Dee smiled and said, 'It sure does.'"

Yes, there was lightning that day at Kyle Field, lightning in the sky and fireworks on the field. But it had started out as just another October Saturday for most Texas cities.

There was nothing on the front page that morning to suggest unforgettable events were in the offing. Actually, the news was rather dull. The race for the White House involving challenger Adlai Stevenson and incumbent Dwight David Eisenhower was nearing its climax, and the top story for most page ones that day had Eisenhower accusing Stevenson of "speaking incredible folly" by saying the military draft is "an incredible waste of manpower and money."

Another page-one story said that Soviet premier Nikita Khrushchev and a trio of top-ranking Soviet army leaders had arrived suddenly and unheralded in Warsaw, apparently to apply the brakes to Poland's headlong advance toward independent communism.

On the lighter side, a high school principal in Lynn, Massachusetts, issued an edict against students "going steady," saying that such actions "lead to sin and forced marriages." And in Chicago, "the most beautiful snake in the world," a blue-eyed white python, was put on special display.

At the movies, *The Search for Bridey Murphy* was getting top billing. Advertisements in the newspaper that day called attention to a barbeque dinner for six priced

Coach Bear Bryant (right) confers with two of his stalwarts, John David Crow (44) and Charlie Krueger (78). Courtesy of Texas A&M University Athletics.

at $1.99. Those hunters looking forward to the chilly mornings that would come with the start of November's deer season could stock up on long-sleeve flannel shirts just $1.38 each.

But in College Station that rather warm, muggy morning, they had time for neither *Bridey Murphy* nor politics nor blue-eyed pythons nor flannel shirt sales. The Texas A&M Aggies and the TCU Horned Frogs were about to clash in what surely would be the Southwest Conference's game of the year.

It was Bear Bryant against Abe Martin. It was hot Heisman Trophy candidate Jim Swink against John David Crow, who would win the Heisman the following season. It was hard-nosed Aggies—confident, controversial, and on NCAA probation—taking on the undefeated, untied, explosive Frogs, who had won the SWC title the previous year, despite losing to the Aggies in Fort Worth.

Now the Frogs wanted revenge. If they got it, they surely would be on their way to another conference championship. Already they had defeated Kansas, 32–0; Arkansas, 41–6; and Alabama, 23–6. Armed virtually with the same team that had posted a 9–1 record the year before, they dared to dream that October morning of national supremacy.

A&M's record was less impressive. The Aggies had blanked Villanova, 19–0; squeezed past LSU, 9–6; and crushed Texas Tech, 40–7. But they had been forced to settle for a 14–14 tie with the Houston Cougars. The Cougars were good, yes; they would go on to win the Missouri Valley Conference title. But they were only 7-2-1 overall. Could an Aggie team that could only tie Houston be able to take the measure of the aroused, onrushing Frogs? The oddsmakers said no. They established TCU as a one- to two-touchdown favorite.

"I thought we would win the game. We thought we had a good team. I remember as we drove down there that day the sun was shining; it was pretty nice," TCU's Swink, now an orthopedic surgeon in Fort Worth, said as he looked back on those events of more than 30 years ago.

Jim Brock, now the executive vice president of the Cotton Bowl, was the sports information director at TCU in 1956. "I remember just before the game started, everything got real calm," he said. "I was down on the field, and I remember I looked over and saw a big black cloud. Somebody said there was a chance we were going to get some rain, but everybody just laughed.

"That was the day Reveille [the Aggies' collie mascot] bit one of our assistant coaches, Walter Roach, when we were out warming up. Somebody said then, 'Boy, this is liable to be a long day.'"

Jones Ramsey, Brock's counterpart at A&M that year (and later the man in charge of publicity for all those great Darrell Royal teams at Texas), remembers the morning of the 1956 game as being "real sunny and fine—somebody said a storm might be brewing, but nobody paid any attention."

They knew, of course, that a storm of a different kind would start as soon as the game began. The Aggies and Frogs were bitter rivals and accurate reflections of the men who coached them.

Martin and Bryant were not so much opponents as opposites. Martin was homespun, folksy, low key—a man who made a lot of his coaching decision by "feel." Bryant was the football scientist who coached hard and recruited harder, who left nothing to chance, who put a premium on "quickness," who brought film study to a high art.

But that day the two coaches shared at least one common thread: their teams came prepared to play that particular game to the hilt.

And 42,000 lucky ticket holders came prepared to yell and scream and watch. The "All Sold Out" sign went up on Aggie ticket windows at noon. By kickoff time, even standing room was scarce.

TCU threatened to draw first blood. The Frogs accepted the opening kickoff and promptly marched to the Aggie 28 before being stopped 12 inches short on a fourth-down play. Swink tried to get the necessary yardage, and Aggie defender Murray Trimble, a feisty guard who only had one arm, wouldn't let him.

On that 43-yard, 12-play drive, TCU quarterback Chuck Curtis completed three passes; it appeared he could pass at will on the Aggies. And the next time the Frogs got the ball, it appeared they could almost move at will. They drove 73 yards in 11 plays; on the 12th play Swink dove into the A&M end zone. But a red flag wiped out the touchdown, and at about that time, the game became of secondary importance to thousands of fans anyway.

Because by then, the storm had struck. It was awesome and terrifying in its fury.

"I can't remember just when the storm hit, but several things I do remember," said Brock. "I remember watching the Kyle Field light standards swaying, rocking back and forth. Those of us in the press box thought they might pop off at any moment. Also, I remember the wind, how it was blowing up one side of the stadium and down the other in a hurricane-like motion, how it just ripped those flags to shreds. Then we got a report from the airport that a lot of planes there had been blown over."

Ramsey remembers the light standards swaying too. "Mainly, I remember that and the rain blowing horizontal," he said. "I remember 150 planes were damaged at Easterwood Airport. Arkansas was playing Texas that night in Austin, so Wilbur Evans [the Texas sports information director] came over to watch our game from the press box. When those light standards started swaying, Wilbur hustled out of there and went back to Austin."

Years later, Swink was to serve with the military forces in Vietnam.

"I went through some terrible weather over there, but nothing like we had that day at Kyle Field," he said.

"You could hardly see. The wind was blowing so hard you could barely breathe. You had to turn your head sideways to get a breath. It was almost impossible to hear. Visibility was almost zero.

"I've always wondered," he said, "why they just didn't stop the game for a few minutes and let the storm blow over."

John David Crow believes he knows why. "Coach Bryant knew we were having enough trouble with Swink in the rain. He sure didn't want him running around out there on a dry field," said Crow.

He continued, "I remember it did rain like hell. But the thing I guess I remember as much as anything—we went out to warm up, and the sun was shining and it was hot. The humidity was terrible. Then we went back in to the meeting room, and Coach Bryant gave us his pregame talk. He told us how we weren't going to let anything distract us—not if a blizzard came through or a hurricane came or anything. I remember standing there sweating and thinking, 'What in the world is he talking about? We're not going to have a blizzard or a hurricane, not on a day like this.'

"Then we went out there and got caught in a hurricane. I thought to myself, 'My God, he knew what he was talking about.'

"We were down on the south end when the storm hit, and it seemed like we were down there forever," Crow said. "You couldn't see much. We were on defense most of the time, but when we had the ball, we weren't going to throw it anyway. Mainly, it was a matter of trying to get the ball from the center to Roddy Osborne [the quarterback]. He carried the ball about half the time."

Indeed, after the Aggies, led by the raging defensive play of linebacker Jack Pardee, had denied Swink and then captured a fumble, Osborne tried to engineer his team out of trouble. He succeeded only in fumbling the ball away himself at the A&M 8-yard line.

The Frogs hammered down to the goal line again, Swink carrying on three of the four plays as the storm

Aggie John David Crow won the Heisman in 1957. Courtesy of Texas A&M University Athletics.

reached its screaming peak. Twice it appeared Swink might have scored. "Yeah, I thought I got across," he says to this day.

But the officials ruled otherwise, stirring a controversy that boiled for weeks.

So it was still a scoreless game when the two teams went to their dressing rooms at intermission.

"I can't remember what Coach Bryant said to us at halftime," said Crow. "I can't remember anything except we were running around trying to find dry jerseys. I wound up putting on No. 84 [he traditionally wore No. 44], I remember that."

(In switching to No. 84, Crow donned the jersey usually worn by William Appelt, and when Crow scored the Aggies' touchdown in the fourth quarter, some writers said the touchdown had been scored by an "Aggie unknown, William Appelt.")

In looking back over the years, Crow is positive of

one aspect of A&M's inspired defensive stand. "I can tell you one thing," he said. "A lot of people claim Swink scored, but he never scored. And I had a great seat; I was right there on the goal line. Coach Bryant told us he figured what had happened was the best thing that could have happened to us.

"And then—it was funny—we went back out for the second half, the skies cleared, the sun came out, and in the fourth quarter, whammo! We got an interception, and it was like wham, wham, wham, and we were in their end zone and won the game."

It wasn't quite that uneventful, however.

The Frogs continued to dominate play in the third quarter, twice moving into position for field goal attempts after driving to the A&M 16- and 23-yard lines. Both attempts missed. As Abe Martin was later to say, "I think I just wasn't destined to win that ball game."

However, following another Osborne fumble at the A&M 29, the Frogs finally hit all the right buttons. They scored in six plays, with Curtis finding end O'Day Williams open for a touchdown pass just before Williams stepped out of the end zone. It was another close call, but that one went to the Frogs.

TCU missed the extra point attempt, but it didn't seem that the miss would matter, because on the third play of the fourth quarter, the Frogs got a huge break. Back to punt on third down. Osborne fumbled the snap and succeeded only in turning the ball over to the Frogs at the A&M 23.

Swink promptly ran to the 17. Although a marked man that day, he was to rush for 82 yards and catch passes for another 17. Some said it was his finest performance of the season. But with the Frogs camped at the A&M 17, Curtis decided to dial another number. He tried to hit a receiver in the end zone, and Don Watson, all 150 pounds of him, was there to intercept for A&M.

And from that point on, Watson and Crow devastated the TCU flanks as the Aggies got stronger and stronger. Crow ran for 21 yards, and Watson swept around the other side for 37 yards to the Frog 20. Crow ran for 2 yards at left tackle, then swung wide again. Watson threw the key block as the big Aggie halfback powered all the way to the TCU 7. A TCU defense that had been anchored by the sizzling play of All-American guard Norman Hamilton was clearly becoming unglued.

Osborne then went to Watson again. Little Don, who the year before had been instrumental in A&M's upset victory in Fort Worth, started to his left, just as he had on his 37-yard spurt. But as desperate Frogs defenders closed in on him, he pulled up and lofted a pretty little pass to an open Crow waiting in the end zone.

At last the Aggies were on the scoreboard. It was a 6–6 game. It stayed that way only a minute. Loyd Taylor, one of the smallest Aggies but consistently big in clutch moments, untied it with a perfect placement. In just six plays and one conversion, the Aggies had won a throbbing 7–6 victory that would send them on their way to their first outright Southwest Conference football championship since 1941.

The Frogs, who never threatened after A&M's touchdown, snapped the ball for 77 of the game's 119 offensive plays. They recovered fumbles on the A&M 8-, 37-, 29-, and 23-yard lines. They were inside the Aggie 30 on seven different occasions. But they still lost.

Later, in the dressing room, Bryant was asked if the game had gone according to plan.

"It went according to prayer," he rumbled in reply. "I don't believe any team ever showed more guts than our team did today. They had their backs to the wall 40 times and still won. They kept battling and battling and wouldn't be denied."

TCU's dressing room was a mixture of rage and tears.

"It was very emotional—people screaming, yelling, throwing things," recalled Brock. "Finally, Swink got up on a chair and talked to everybody and calmed them down. He really showed poise and class.

"You know, that was quite a group. I think of our

seniors, we brought 31 in on scholarships and 29 got their degrees. One quit us and one flunked out."

Because of the poise and class he displayed in that highly charged setting, and for his actions in defusing it, Swink was awarded the national Swede Nelson Sportsmanship Award at the end of the season.

"Movietone News shot that game and later gave me a copy of the film," said Brock. "I still have it somewhere. I know I haven't looked at it in a long time. But you have to see it to believe it—I mean the weather conditions. Just incredible."

Mickey Herskowitz of the *Houston Post* would be the first to agree. Herskowitz was a young sportswriter for the *Post* in 1956, and his primary beat was Texas A&M.

"I went down to the dressing room after the game, and I remember all the women's hats you could see. Expensive hats that had been blown off and ruined by the rain," Herskowitz said. "The hats were floating in little ponds all over the stadium, like toy boats. I can imagine all the hairdos that were ruined that day. I don't think any of us realized at the time what we had survived.

"But oddly enough," he continued, "the thing I guess I remember most about that game is something I didn't hear about until years later, the last time I saw Elmer Smith [one of Bryant's assistants] before he died.

"We got to talking about that game, and Elmer said the phone lines to the A&M coaches' booth in the press box went out as soon as the storm hit. Believe it or not, Bryant told Elmer to go get on a little platform that was down at the end of the stadium, on the scoreboard end, and chart TCU's line splits and let him know what they were.

"So Elmer went down there with a student manager, climbed a ladder they had there, got on the platform, and started doing the charting. He would mark them down on a piece of paper and drop the paper to the student manager—in a sock or something. Then the student manager would run the information to Bryant on the bench.

"The wind was howling, the rain was flooding down, it was almost as dark as night, and Elmer was clinging to a pole that was there to hold up the platform. He was getting drenched, getting almost airsick, and still trying to get information to Bryant.

"Finally the first half ended, and everybody ran to the dressing room, including the student manager. By then the ladder had blown away. And everybody forgot about Elmer. He's up on the platform, clinging to that pole, yelling, 'Help, help, come get me!' And there's nobody there to hear him.

"After about 10 minutes in the dressing room, Bryant turned to ask Elmer something and couldn't find him and then remembered where he was. He sent someone out to rescue him, and by then Elmer could hardly talk."

Ramsey remembers scraps of paper too: "Bear writing down defenses on a scrap of paper, showing them to the defense—of how he wanted them to play against Swink. I'll never forget that sight. TCU scored just the one touchdown, although they were still trying two weeks after the game to get Swink across the goal line.

"Every day they'd write a story in the *Fort Worth Star-Telegram* about how Swink really had scored. Harold Ratliff [then the regional sports editor of the *Associated Press*] would call to get Bear's reaction. Bear just kept saying, 'No comment.'

"Finally, after this had gone on awhile, Bear got mad and said, 'Dammit, Ramsey, tell them this: "If I had known there was going to be all this commotion on the subject, I'd have had us score another touchdown."'

"Then, after a pause, he told me, 'Naw, don't say that. Just tell them, "No comment."'"

Bryant mentioned none of those things when I interviewed him that day in Birmingham in 1979. He did say he had never been in a game like that one, "where the weather was so bad. It was blowing those airplanes away at Easterwood. And we played the entire first half inside

Bryant (in hat and raincoat) on the sidelines with Jack Pardee (32). Courtesy of Texas A&M University Athletics.

our 4-yard line. It was raining and blowing so hard, you couldn't see a thing.

"But," he recalled, smiling at the memory, "when we came out to start the third quarter, the skies were clearing off and the sun was out. I couldn't believe it. Late in the game, TCU tried to pass, and Don Watson intercepted in our end zone. We started on our 20 and ran the same play eight straight times, a run-pass option . . . we scored on the eighth play, and Loyd Taylor kicked the extra point, and we won the game."

Bryant remembered the sequences as if they had just occurred.

"I remember going home with Paul Jr. [his small son] late that afternoon," he continued. "The sky was clear, the sun was shining, the birds were singing. It was beautiful."

And Bryant smiled again at the memory.

Even to the man who eventually broke Alonzo Stagg's record as the winningest college football coach of all time, who enjoyed unparalleled success at Alabama, the Texas A&M-TCU Hurricane Game of October 20, 1956, was one he could never forget.

OCTOBER 28, 1956

BLISTERING AGGIES ROAR BACK IN FINAL QUARTER

Behind by a single point as the final quarter started to unravel, the ruthlessly efficient Texas Aggies threw a 63-yard wet blanket over Baylor's homecoming festivities Saturday night, and the comeback paid off in a 19–13 victory gained before a record-breaking crowd of 50,000.

Big John David Crow, the toughest runner of the night, bolted the final 2 yards to put the Aggies ahead and sent them spinning homeward with visions of the Cotton Bowl dancing in their heads.

They didn't get away without a fight. Six personal fouls were called during the savage showdown, each side drawing three. Two of the Bruins—Charley Dupre and Dugan Pearce—were banished from the bloodletting, but all the Aggies were permitted to stay for the finish.

Paul Bryant's sizzling sharpshooters, as fiery as ever, scored first in this donnybrook, blasting 21 yards in six plays after grabbing off a Baylor pass. Crow pitched a 5-yard pass to end John Tracey for the six-pointer with 9:24 left in the second quarter.

Baylor came back to tie the score shortly before the intermission, driving 67 yards in 11 plays. Larry Hickman, the star of the drive, carried the final 2.

With 4:56 remaining in the third period, the Aggies crunched ahead, completing a 95-yard thrust composed of 12 plays. Jack Pardee, again a mighty man, surged the final 4 after Roddy Osborne had set up the score with a 32-yard pass to "clutch artist" Don Watson.

That left the score reading 12–6, as A&M's Loyd Taylor and Baylor's Junior Beall had trouble finding the extra point range, and set the stage for a rollicking Baylor comeback that hit a happy climax when Bobby Peters jackknifed across from 3 yards out. That scoring march

Baylor football team, 1956. Courtesy of Baylor University Athletics.

went 36 yards in five plays, and when Beall kicked goal this time, moving the Bruins into a 13–12 advantage, the overflow crowd of Baylor partisans went wild.

That was when Crow, flying straight as his namesake, took a personal hand in the proceedings and plunged a knife into Baylor hopes with the 63-yard payoff march. Taylor converted the extra point this time with 9:20 left to play.

Mixed in with all that scoring was a record of muffed opportunities and bitterly waged combat on both sides.

The Aggies, using that crisp, aggressive defense that can do little wrong, dominated most of the first-half play. They had possessions on the Baylor 25, on the 15, and on the 21 before cracking the scoring ice. They had just two big chances in the second half and made them both pay off.

Baylor, spurning the aerial route most of the way, made good on its lone first-half threat but failed on a beauty early in the third period. That one was set up when center Lloyd Hale, on a fourth-down punt situation, snapped the ball over Osborne's head, giving Baylor possession on the Aggie 22. The Bruins worked the ball down to the Cadet 5 before bowing to that inspired defense.

Then with the scoreboard spelling out imminent Baylor defeat, the Bruins stocked up a final drive. That march flickered and produced two first downs before the Bears fumbled and the Aggies took over at their own 33.

Heroes were thick on both sides in this duel to the finish, but first and foremost was that man named Crow. He scored one touchdown, passed for another,

Roddy Osborne (12) was inducted into the Texas A&M Athletic Hall of Fame in 2009. Courtesy of Texas A&M University Athletics.

John David Crow goes around right end, headed upfield against Arkansas. Courtesy of Texas A&M University Athletics.

After graduating from Texas A&M, Charlie Krueger played 16 seasons with the San Francisco 49ers. He was named All-Pro in 1960, 1965, and 1970. Courtesy of Texas A&M University Athletics.

intercepted a Baylor pass, and led all the ball carriers for the night with 76 yards in 14 cracks.

In that final Aggie drive, the one where they had to produce or become just another ball club, Crow launched the effort with a 23-yard burst and finished it with a 2-yarder.

Watson, who beat TCU a week ago, had another heroic night for Bryant. He set up the second Aggie touchdown and grabbed up the fumble that planted the final spike in Baylor's hopes.

Jack Pardee, "too injured to play," played just as everyone figured he would, and played superbly. He got

One of Bear Bryant's "Junction Boys," Jack Pardee became the only head coach to guide teams in college football, the NFL, the USFL, the WFL, and the CFL. Courtesy of Texas A&M University Athletics.

59 yards on 10 carries. Charley Krueger was the mainstay of the Aggie line, which gave up 169 yards to the Bears but very little when the chips were blue.

Bill Glass, moved to left guard and linebacker for this most significant of all Baylor 1956 assignments, again was a mighty warrior, as were Jerry Marcontell, Clyde Letbetter, Dave Lunceford, and Bobby Oliver. On offense, Del Shofner carved out 51 yards to set the pace, while Peters had 47. The most thunderous Baylor runner of the night, however, was Hickman, the talented soph fullback. Larry got 23 yards on just five jolts.

Shofner did some brilliant punting in the first half in helping the Bears escape several Aggie traps. From deep in his own territory, he first kicked 61 yards and then, while standing in his end zone, placed a beauty out of bounds on the Aggie 37.

The game was as intense as any in the young history of Baylor Stadium. Besides the ejection of Baylor players Dupre and Pearce, flags for personal fouls flew all night, eventually helping boost the Bears into the lead.

With the Aggies leading 12–6, the Bears set up shop on the Aggie 36 after a short A&M punt.

From that point, Bobby Jones directed the Bears downfield, with the Aggies lending a mighty hand by contributing 15 yards on—you guessed it—a personal foul. Obviously, the going in the trenches was getting dark and dirty.

The penalty play started with Jones going back to pass and then electing to run. Jones ripped off a solid gain, and the penalty gave the Bears a first down on the 9. In three plays, with Rueben Saage and Bobby Peters carrying, the Bears worked out the touchdown. Peters carried the final 4 yards, jackknifing across in the arms of Pardee; Beall's kick was true; and Baylor was ahead for the first time, 13–12.

Baylor's massed thousands were in an uproar.

The Aggies applied a damper in short order. Taking a kickoff on the 37, they marched right down the field, gouging out huge chunks of territory behind the brutal slants of Crow, Pardee, and Osborne. Several times the Bears had them but couldn't cinch the tackle. Crow started them with a brutal burst to the Baylor 40, and three downs later, Pardee made it a first at the 26.

Pardee's ramble was the key play. As he was hit, he fumbled and the Bears recovered, but the officials ruled that the play had been stopped before the bobble. It was a questionable decision. Osborne, on the next play, ran through half the Baylor team to the 4, and in two tries, Crow carried it over. Taylor's kick this time was good.

Now with 9:20 left, the Bruins made their swan song. They rolled to a pair of first downs, getting to the Aggie 44. Then three more tries surged to the 35. On the big fourth-down effort, Jones tried a handoff, fumbled, and the ever-present Watson recovered.

The Bruins did not get possession again.

NOVEMBER 11, 1956
SHOFNER, BERRY GUIDE BEARS TO 10–7 VICTORY

Del Shofner and Don Berry, much maligned in Baylor's heartbreaking 21–20 defeat at the hands of Texas last season, had a glorious hour of revenge Saturday afternoon at Baylor Stadium as they ran and kicked the Bruins to a 10–7 victory over the hard-fighting Longhorns.

A crowd of 21,000, sitting under cloudless skies, saw Shofner play his most spectacular game of the season. He scored Baylor's touchdown on a 55-yard race down the right sideline in the second quarter, then set up Berry's decisive fourth-quarter field goal with a 46-yard display of ankle magic down that same stripe.

Shofner's second run ended at the Texas 10. Four plays later, Berry made his first appearance of the 1956 season and kicked a three-pointer from the Texas 16 to spell the difference in this ragged but bitterly contested battle between two old rivals.

Last year in Baylor's hour of anguish in Austin, Berry missed the fourth-quarter extra point that would have given the Bruins a tie and in the dying seconds missed a long desperation field goal that would have produced a victory. And Shofner had his moment of disappointment when he permitted Menan Schriewer to grab a touchdown pass away from him on one of the game's decisive plays.

Baylor's long-legged whirlwind of versatility could do no wrong Saturday. Shofner knifed the Longhorns with those two long-distance belts, he knocked down a pass on a spectacular leap in the second quarter, he angled a punt out of bounds on the Longhorn 12 late in the game when Texas was trying for a comeback, and then he drove the final spike into old Bevo's carcass when he intercepted a pass on the Bruin 18 in the final moments.

Until Shofner's interception with 1:42 to play, Baylor banners were beginning to waver. Bruin partisans sat chilled, grim, expecting the worst. They are no strangers to throbbing adversity at the hands of the orange and white. It was on that same Baylor grass four years ago that the Steers squeaked to a 35–33 victory, and twice since then in Austin, they have prevailed by a 21–20 verdict.

So when the Ed Price forces, outplayed most of the way, suddenly cranked up with 3:28 to go and started acquiring real estate in alarming quantities, Baylor hearts started moving into several thousand assorted throats.

With Joe Clements at the throttle, the Steers rolled from their own 25 to the Texas 41, to the 47, and then to the Baylor 38.

Now Clements faded back to pass and shot an arrow all the way to the Baylor goal. End Bob Bryant, tall and sure-fingered, was gliding along inside the Bruin 10 like a messenger of doom. The pass was true, and Bryant, almost at the goal line, reached up to complete Baylor's destruction. But Larry Hickman reached up with him and flicked the ball slightly, just enough to carry it out of reach, and the ball fell to earth harmlessly in the end zone. That flick was the difference between victory and defeat.

Two plays later, the roaming Shofner fielded Clements's shot on the Baylor 18, and that was the ballgame.

Although the Longhorns went down to their fourth straight conference loss and their seventh defeat in eight starts this season, they did not die without a struggle. Ed Price termed this their best performance of the season, and their close followers agreed.

They resisted Baylor's churning ground game fiercely, and except for Shofner's blazing bursts, they succeeded pretty well.

The Baylor touchdown drive covered 75 yards in four plays, with Shofner providing the final 55 on the first play of the second quarter. Junior Beall kicked the extra point.

Berry's big payoff was the climax of a six-play drive of 61 yards, and the field goal went on the board with

14:49 left in the game. After that, Texas could make only the one late threat, which Shofner killed.

In addition to the scoring plays, Baylor lost one touchdown on a penalty, penetrated to the Texas 5 before fumbling into the end zone for a harmless touchback, and failed on other drives to the Texas 31, the 23, and the 21.

Other than their touchdown, the Longhorns produced only one other good threat, moving to the Baylor 20 after recovering a fumble early in the game. Bill Glass, the Bruins' mighty guard, put an end to that bit of mischief by snaring a Clements pass and returning it 29 yards to the Baylor 40.

Texas' heralded aerial game proved to be better for the Bears than for the Longhorns. Shofner caught a Steer pass and so did Glass, Bobby Peters, and Lee Harrington. In all, Texas completed just one more pass (5) than Baylor intercepted (4) in 18 attempts, good for 49 yards. The Bears completed 7 of 13 for 78. Texas got 138 yards on the ground—but very little of it after intermission. The Longhorns managed only 40 total yards and two first downs in the second half.

The oft-criticized Baylor offense powered out 243 yards rushing against the embattled Steers for a total offense figure of 321 yards and looked much better than in last week's TCU contest. There's plenty of room for improvement, but at least the team charged from the huddle and exploded its plays as if it meant business.

Still, it remained for Shofner to provide the spark needed to snap Sam Boyd's edition back to the winning road. The teams were struggling along in an indecisive duel, and Bobby Jones was at the Baylor controls when Shofner first did to the Longhorns what so many of them have done to the Bears down through the years.

The ball was on the Baylor 45. Jones ran a "belly" play to the right and, as Shofner hit the right tackle hole, slammed the ball into his midsection. It appeared the ball hit Shofner's chest and bounced forward, and as he sped past the line of scrimmage, he had it on his fingertips, struggling for control. In another stride he had it, and then he was past the defending halfback, booming away from a startled Joe Clements, and easily outraced them to the end zone.

Fine blocks by Dave Lunceford and Jerry Marcontell opened the hole, and another downfield gain by Earl Wayne Miller made things secure.

The 46-yard scamper that set up the winning field goal was a similar play, only this one went a little wider to the right. Shofner ran out of running room at about the 15 and managed to cut back and get another 5 yards before Chris Shaw nailed him.

In addition to those scorchers, Shofner had another run of 14 yards, completed a pass to Peters for 7 more, and took a screen pass 26 yards to the Texas 31 as the clock ran out in the first half.

At the finish, he had run for 125 yards on six carries and caught three passes for 48 more. Bounding Larry Hartman added another 58 yards overland on 16 attempts.

Jimmy Welch paced Texas with 65 yards on 14 carries, but the Bears were prepared for the tricky Walter Fondren, limiting the Longhorns' leading rusher to 25 yards on 11 tries.

Defensively, Garland Kennon was Texas' best by far, with a hand in 14 tackles. Ends Shaw and Danny Myers also had their moments, with Myers making a crucial stop on Hickman to end a Baylor drive at the Texas 21.

Glass had another fine day for the Bruins but had to share honors with the fiery Harrington, who played almost the entire game and had a hand in 15 tackles in addition to his interception. Marcontell also had 15 stops, Glass 14 (plus an interception), and Charles Horton 12.

Horton also had another terrific block, this time almost knocking Clements senseless. It was a near duplicate of the blockbuster he unloaded last week on TCU's star lineman Norman Hamilton.

Sam Boyd employed three quarterbacks—Bobby Jones, Buddy Humphrey, and Carroll Overton—and all three showed improvement over their TCU performances. Jones was in control on both of Baylor's scoring drives. Humphrey played almost as much and showed promise. Overton was used less but did have one brief moment of glory, running 17 yards for a touchdown only to lose it on a holding penalty.

The victory left Baylor with a 2–2 conference mark and a nonconference date with Nebraska ahead before resuming the league wars against SMU in Dallas.

JANUARY 1, 1957

BAYLOR UPSETS TENNESSEE 13–7, THRILLING 82,000 FANS IN SUGAR BOWL

NEW ORLEANS, La.—Sam Boyd's Baylor Bears, sublime in the greatest test in history, opened a glorious new year with a 60-minute thunderclap of furious football here Tuesday, smashing down hitherto invincible Tennessee, 13–7, before 82,000 amazed fans in the 23rd annual Sugar Bowl Classic.

Already it is a glorious new year, and after this overwhelming display of "desire" football, who is to say that a glorious new football era has not dawned for the long down-trodden Bears as well?

In blasting out their first major bowl victory, the Bears tore the heart from Bowden Wyatt's vaunted Volunteers. They took all that the power-conscious Tennesseans could dish out, then threw the book at them.

They flattened them—they did it convincingly and they did it the hard way by coming from behind in the fateful fourth quarter when the scoreboard flashed a 6–7 count against them.

Then with all the chips on the table, when the two teams were peering into each other's hearts in a severe contest of courage and dedication, it was unbeaten Tennessee, the nation's No. 2 team, that went down in unconditional surrender.

The final quarter started with the Bears marching into Volunteer country. They ripped to the Tennessee 25, but a penalty hurled them back 15 yards. Del Shofner had to punt. He got off a low boomer that carried to All-American Johnny Majors down on the Tennessee 5.

Majors snared the ball, tucked it away, and whipped out to the 15. There he was hit. No, he wasn't hit; he was pulverized. Bobby Jack Oliver, Dave Lunceford, and Clyde Letbetter smeared him . . . and the ball bounced free.

Reuben Saage fell on it for Baylor.

From there, in six quick plays, the Bruins drove for the decisive touchdown, with sophomore quarterback Buddy Humphrey sneaking across the goal line from the 1-foot line.

Don Berry kicked goal. Baylor's delighted partisans let out a mighty roar and then braced themselves for Tennessee's worst.

It was not long in coming. And it also was not long in fizzling out. The enemy got as far as the Baylor 32. Then as an aroused wrecking machine named Clyde Letbetter put on a superhuman show, the Bears proved to each and every one of these breathless guests exactly who was going to be boss on this day of days.

They put the Volunteers into steady retreat, took away the ball, and then deliberately dallied away the final seconds as their wildly jubilant followers chorused out a crashing roar of victory.

Don't let that fumble recovery mislead you. It was the big play, but it was a break the Bears made for themselves, just as they performed most of the other deeds of valor on this overcast, sometimes rainy afternoon.

The Bears richly deserved to win.

They scored first, booming 80 yards in eight plays for six points and picking up the final 12 on a pass from Bobby Jones to Jerry Marcontell. Del Shofner, voted the game's outstanding player, set the touchdown up with a brilliant 54-yard run to the Tennessee 26.

In addition, in that first half, they bulled to the Tennessee 4 and missed a field goal, then drove to the Volunteer 39 and later to the 34.

And in that first 30 minutes, they refused to permit the Vols inside their 30.

After surviving a Tennessee flurry in the third quarter, which produced the one touchdown and then came back with a drive to the Baylor 32, the Bears monopolized all the rest of the action. They even gave their followers mass heart attacks late in the game by trying a futile fourth-down play on the Vols' 48. The try, sneaked by Carroll Overton, failed to gain the necessary 12 inches, and the Bears had to give up the ball. Fortunately, Letbetter saved the day.

In the final quarter, they ran 22 plays to Tennessee's desperate 14, intercepted two passes, and left Wyatt's forces a dead-tired, defeated foe.

All in all, the Bears rolled back that famed Tennessee line for 275 yards while giving up only 146. They had a 13–10 advantage on first downs, the edge in passing, and decisive superiority in pass interceptions (four to zero) and fumbles recovered (one to zero).

You could say the Bruins beat the Vols at their own game. They got the fumble that won the game, and those four pass interceptions made significant victory contributions.

Del Shofner made the biggest of those interceptions—a remarkable grab in the end zone—taking the ball away from Tennessee's All-American end Buddy Cruze to wipe out a late first-half threat.

Shofner also tackled like a demon and paced all ball carriers with 88 yards in 14 carries in winning the outstanding player award.

Even so, Del had terrific competition. In those final minutes, when the Vols had to be stopped or else, it was a raging Letbetter who put a tip of steel into that good old Baylor line.

Crashing from his middle guard position, he rushed the Volunteer passers unmercifully, threw them off

Baylor guard Bill Glass was an All-American in 1956. He went in the first round of the 1957 NFL draft, playing for Detroit and Cleveland. Courtesy of Baylor University Athletics.

balance, hounded them and plagued them and made them throw into Baylor hands.

In Tennessee's last big bid, when the Vols had marched to the Baylor 32 and marked up a first down, Letbetter played the decisive role. First he tossed Johnny Majors's substitute, Bobby Gordan, for a 5-yard loss. Then on third down, he broke through and mauled a Tennessee blocker and blasted at Gordan. Paul Dickson came in to seal the tackle on the Tennessee 47, and that, for all practical purposes, won the ball game and sent Baylor's roaring thousands waltzing in triumph back to Bourbon Street, walking all the way over the bodies of dazed Tennesseans who still can't believe what unfolded in front of their eyes.

LONG LIST OF HEROES

In addition to Shofner and Letbetter, the Bruins also got sparkling play from Bill Glass, Bobby Jack Oliver, Dugan Pearce, Bobby Peters, Reuben Saage, Bobby Jones, and Lee Harington. And that list is just a starter. They were all magnificent in a tremendous team effort.

Peters, who started the Bears off on the right foot by returning the opening kickoff all the way to the Tennessee 45, gained 60 yards in eight tries for the afternoon to rank next to Shofner. Reuben Saage had 39, and Junior Beall had 18.

Majors, a dangerous operative indeed for Vols, had 51 yards on 15 carries, and his fullback, Tommy Bronson, had 56 on 8. Gordan had 40 on 9.

Majors could complete only one of his tosses in seven tries, however, and had two of them intercepted, as the Bears showed they had no respect for reputations. And his fumble ultimately beat them.

In the line, Tennessee's John Gordy, Bubba Howe, Roger Urbano, and Bill Johnson were outstanding. But the main heroes, without question, wore green and gold on this brilliant day for Baylor.

Here's how the Bears went about accomplishing their cherished upset: Tennessee won the toss and elected to defend the south goal, from where a fairly steady breeze was blowing. The Bears decided to receive.

Burklow pumped the kickoff to Peters, and Bobby, running behind fine interference, bounded up the middle to about the 35, then cut to the right sideline and ran to the Tennessee 45 before Majors cut him down. It was a 51-yard run and put the stands in an uproar.

Shofner and Dupre gouged out a first down to the 34, then Jones went back to pass and instead ran 9 yards to the 25. That was a signal for Peters, riding behind Charley Horton's great block, to dash all the way to the Tennessee 9 before Majors made another touchdown-saving tackle.

Now the Volunteers toughened. Shofner could get only a yard at left tackle. Peters churned to the 5. Bobby Jones tried to sneak and was hammered down at the 4. Then as the Bears deliberated over their play, time ran out on them, and they were penalized 5 yards for delaying the game. So from the 9-yard line, Don Berry tried a field goal, and it sailed wide to the left.

VOLS QUICK KICK

Tennessee took over on its 20, ran one play, and Majors quick-kicked. The ball took a reverse bounce, and the Bears got the ball on their 40.

The Vols stopped Boyd's fired-up forces this time, and Shofner punted to Majors at the 13. The Volunteer ace returned to the 31, and from there, Wyatt's men worked up their first threat. Majors got one first down at the 44, then Bronson broke away on a fullback trap play and romped to the Baylor 34. Junior Beall stopped all that mischief making, however, by intercepting a wobbly Majors pass, and the Bears took over on their 21.

By now, black clouds were overhead and rain seemed inevitable. The Bears came ripping back, rolling for two first downs behind the running of Saage, Beall, and Buddy Humphrey. Then Saage broke away on an 11-yarder to the Tennessee 40, and the Bears appeared on their way once more.

The drive bogged down, however: a pass failed at the Vol 10, and Shofner kicked over the goal, just missing coffin corner.

TRAYLOR AT HELM

Tennessee drove for one first down but then had to kick, and the Bears started anew on their own 32. This time Doyle Traylor took over the controls and on the first play sent Bobby Peters scampering away on a 30-yard burst to the Tennessee 38. Three jabs gained only 4 yards, however, and on fourth down, a Traylor pass to Shofner was in Del's arms and then out again.

Tennessee, resorting to the quick kick again, booted the ball over the goal, and the Bears took over this time on their 20. On the first play, Shofner got free around right end and ran 54 yards to the Tennessee 26.

That was the big one because it ignited the Bruins into a payoff drive this time. With Bob Jones at the wheel, the Bears flashed behind Hickman for one first down to the 14. Then Hickman gouged to the 12. The next two passes failed, and it appeared still another good chance was going to fade away. But on the big fourth down, Jones took his time and hit Marcontell on the 5, and Jerry whipped into the end zone.

Don Berry's kick was wide. The score came with 8:31 left in the second quarter.

As Glass boomed his kickoff into the Tennessee end zone, rain started peppering down. The Vols put the ball in play on their own 20 and drove for a first down on a 15-yard run by Gordon to the 35. The Bears tightened and forced a punt, however, and set up camp on their own 31. Four plays later, Shofner punted to Tennessee's 35.

SHOFNER MAKES SAVE

From that point, the Vols launched a bruising drive, flashing to the Baylor 35 in three plays. Another gained to the 30. Then Gordon faded, faked a run, and aimed a bullet into the end zone. Buddy Cruze was waiting . . . but so was Shofner, and Del came down with the saving grab as the final first-half seconds ticked away.

It was a half that belonged entirely to Baylor.

The game took on a different tone in the third period. Peters fumbled the kickoff and was downed on the 13, and Baylor did not get out of the hole until Tennessee had scored.

The Vols got the ball on their 46 but moved immediately to the Baylor 39 on a roughness penalty. Majors got this touchdown in 10 plays, although he had to overcome one 15-yard penalty on the way. Most of the yardage came on drives inside the Baylor ends.

Even so, the Bears died hard—tremendously hard. The Vols had set up a first down on the 3. Bronson tried for a touchdown and was knocked down at the 2. Majors tried at right tackle, and Saage and Shofner flattened him at the 2. Then, running the other way, Johnny managed to pull away from Harrington at the 5 and squirmed into the end zone. Harrington was left holding a handful of Johnny's tear-away jersey.

Sam Burklow kicked the big extra point with 7:06 left to go in the third period, and Tennessee's massed thousands immediately began setting up a clamor for a rout.

For a moment it appeared they might get one.

The Bears received and had to punt, and Tennessee got the ball on the Baylor 42. A score at this point might have won the game.

The Bears were having none of that, however.

They stopped Bronson at the 38, then knocked down a long Majors pass at the 5. An offsides penalty moved Tennessee back to the 43. Now came a rough play, with Majors fading to throw and being swarmed by the Bears. In all the savage wrestling, blows were exchanged on both sides, and Larry Hickman was banished from the game. Both sides were ruled guilty of violations, and no penalties were stepped off. Tennessee's Bruce Brunham was carried off the field as the crowd booed.

When order was restored, Tennessee punted into the Bruins' end zone, and from that point on, it was Baylor's show.

The Bears, working Humphrey's smooth calls, carved out three first downs to the Tennessee 34 as Dupre, Beall, Fisher, and Buddy himself contributed to the big gains.

On the first play of the fourth quarter, Saage ripped through for 15 yards to the 34. Now a penalty stalled the machinery, and when Traylor was swarmed under at the 48, the Bears had to punt.

And that was the big one.

The rest you know: How Letbetter, Oliver, and Lunceford came tearing down to chill Majors and made him fumble; how Saage made the big recovery; and how the Bears then scored in six plays, with Humphrey taking it over and Berry getting the extra point. And then how Letbetter smeared the enemy with his relentless rushes and how Bob Jones and Beall came up with two interceptions in the final moments to make this most precious of all Baylor victories complete.

The victory was Baylor's first major bowl decision after defeats in the Orange and Gator. And it kept clean the record of Southwest Conference representatives in this rich and colorful bowl. Five times the conference's team has come marching into the bowl, and five times it has gone away victorious.

But always before the Southwest team was given the edge. This time, the Bears were given little chance by the experts. And none at all by scornful Tennesseans. Thus this becomes the brightest page of them all.

Particularly so for Baylor, because those Bears finally won that "big one" that has so frequently eluded them in the past.

ON SECOND THOUGHT
JANUARY 3, 1957

NEW ORLEANS, La.—Walter Stewart, the wit and famed sports observer from Memphis, pinpointed the 1956 Baylor Bears in a postgame talk with Sam Boyd.

"Sam, I saw your team play Arkansas in October," he said. "The only resemblance between that team and the one that beat Tennessee today was the green jersey."

The Bears, indeed, came a long way in 1956, from a shaky one-point victory over California in September to the sweetest of all victories, a decisive conquest of unbeaten, highly ranked Tennessee in the Sugar Bowl.

And the seniors also came a long way, from national embarrassment suffered while taking a strapping in the Gator Bowl as sophomores two years ago to the unchallenged heroes of New Orleans on New Year's Day in 1957.

Because this was the grand finale for those seniors, a review of their contributions in the Tuesday classic is appropriate.

First, of course, there's Del Shofner, an incomparable back who proved to 80,000 fans his colors are of the same All-America hue as those of Johnny Majors. Voted the game's most outstanding player, he had Canadian pro coach Jim Trimble drooling in the press box before the game was five minutes old.

Against Tennessee, Shofner set up Baylor's first touchdown with a 54-yard scamper, saved another score with an end-zone interception, punted well under pressure, tackled fiercely, helped knock down another pass, and led all ground gainers for the day with 88 yards on 14 carries.

Shofner played a mighty part in getting the winning touchdown, by the way. With the ball on the Vol 15, and with Tennessee's defenders drawn in close for a make-or-break battle, Shofner plunged straight ahead into the trenches three times and came back with a first down on the Vol 5. That was superb clutch running against some of the best chips-down defenders in the business.

Along with Shofner in the backfield, you'll want to remember the names of Charley Dupre, Reuben Saage, and Bobby Jones. Those three seniors had themselves a day. Dupre was his usual rugged self on defense and got 13 yards on five carries offensively. Saage did even better, blasting out 39 yards on seven cracks. And he applied two of the game's most vicious tackles.

When Tennessee was trying to score in the third period from the Baylor 3, Majors swung wide at right end. The Baylor end rolled up the interference and left Johnny open game for Saage and Shofner. Reuben nearly sliced the Volunteer ace in half in pinning him on the 2. Later, he crashed head on into tailback Bobby Gordon on the Baylor 42 when the Vols were trying for a comeback, and Gordon dropped like a stone.

Jones had one of the best days of his career. The sometimes maligned Bruin signal caller passed for one touchdown, intercepted a pass, ran his team smoothly, and took full advantage of the Vols' defensive weaknesses. One of his best calls came in the second quarter when the Vols had pushed the Bruins back to their own 10.

"Tennessee had been pinching heavily, really guarding the middle on first down when they had us backed up deep in our territory, so I decided to try to hit them with a quick wide one," Bobby said. So he sent Shofner off around right end on first down, Larry

Sam Boyd, Baylor head coach, 1956–58. Courtesy of Baylor University Athletics.

Ruben Saage. Courtesy of Baylor University Athletics.

Hickman threw a key block, and Del bounded 54 yards to set up the first score.

In the line, seniors Bill Glass, Dugan Pearce, Dave Lunceford, and Tony DeGrazier also had great days.

At a press dinner after the game, some sportswriters were comparing the abilities of Glass and Rice's former All-American Weldon Humble. "Humble was better," said one. "He was faster, more aggressive, and could do more things."

"Well, I didn't see Humble play," said Minneapolis's Charley Johnson, one of the nation's most renowned writers. "But I would have to have a lot of proof to believe he was better than Glass. That kid's tremendous."

Pearce backed up Bill ably against Tennessee as the two divided the left guard and linebacking duties. Injured painfully midway through the third period, he came back to make tackles all over the field.

Lunceford, dubbed "too slow" to help much against Tennessee by one national publication, laughed at such a prediction and finished out his Baylor career on a glorious note. He was one of the barriers in the middle, which Bowden Wyatt claims was "tougher than we expected," and Lunceford was in on that big tackle of Majors that resulted in the fumble and subsequent Baylor touchdown.

DeGrazier, who was injured much of the season, won Boyd's praise for his strong defensive play. "You might not have noticed what Tony was doing," he said. "His job was to crash in there and help take away that interference so someone else could take a crack at the ball carrier. He did a great job."

Those were the big names in the senior cast that helped bring Baylor its finest football hour.

JANUARY 1, 1957

CURTIS, FROGS SHAKE COTTON BOWL JINX, NUDGE SYRACUSE, BROWN, 28–27

EARL GOLDING

DALLAS, Tex.—The Texas Christian Horned Frogs finally shattered their Cotton Bowl jinx today, and the guy who had the biggest hand in it had been living for this game for exactly one year.

Chuck Curtis, the gangling quarterback who was hurt on the very first play of the 1956 Cotton Bowl, went nearly all the way on this sunny New Year's Day, and the Froggies rode his sensational passing to a spine-tingling 28–27 triumph over a sound Syracuse power that rubbed out a lot of cracks about the inferior brand of football they play in the East.

A stand-up crowd of 68,000—about 7,000 below capacity—left this giant stadium thoroughly convinced that Syracuse belonged with the elite ranking of the country and that they'd seen one of the greatest backs in the land almost pull it out for the Orangemen. Mighty Jim Brown, the tremendous 218-pound Negro All-American halfback, came within a blocked conversion attempt of giving the visiting New Yorkers a tie. It was almost a single-handed offensive show for Brown, who scored 21 points, raced and smashed for 132 yards, and never gave the partisan Texas crowd a relaxed moment.

The margin of victory was wrapped up in four perfect conversions by TCU's Harold Pollard and a blocked conversion attempt after the third Syracuse touchdown by Froggie reserve end Chico Mendoza.

The triumph was TCU's first in four Cotton Bowl appearances and was a personal victory for Curtis, the string-bean senior quarterback whose career had been full and had its very good and sometimes-not-so-good days. In last year's Cotton Bowl, he was injured on the first play, and Mississippi went on to win by one point. Curtis made a vow then that he'd be back this year and play it to the hilt.

He got that chance, although the Froggies finished second to Southwest Conference champion Texas A&M, which was barred from bowl participation by an NCAA ruling. And Chuck made good on that vow. He passed for the first two TCU touchdowns and set up the fourth and at times faked beautifully to help send backs Jim Swink, Buddy Dike, Ken Wineburg, and Jimmy Shofner tearing for needed yardage. In all, Curtis completed 12 of 15 passes for 174 yards.

The awesome Brown was voted the classic's outstanding back by covering sportswriters, with TCU tackle Norman Hamilton named the outstanding lineman. Brown received 25½ votes in the poll, while Curtis was second with 15½.

Swink, the 1951 Frog All-American who didn't make it this trip, was TCU's best runner, along with the hard-hitting Dike, and scored one touchdown. It was the 35th of his three-year varsity career, tying the Southwest Conference record set by SMU's Doak Walker. There was never any doubt, however, that Curtis was the big man in the Froggie machine on this day. With TCU out in front by two touchdowns in the second period, Coach Abe Martin lifted Curtis and sent in reserve Dick Finney, and the Purple stumbled and fumbled away the lead. The teams left the field at the intermission tied 14–14.

Curtis was back the saddle to start the second half and sparked TCU to a 28–14 lead early in the fourth period. Then Syracuse punched over two last-quarter tallies to wind up the rush, but Mendoza's block on that third conversion try by Brown proved to be the difference.

Curtis passed to end John Nikkel for a 6-yard touchdown in the first period, hit Shofner for a 10-yard tally in the second, and ran 8 yards on a rollout for the third. Swink went over from 3 yards out to the get the fourth.

Jim Swink (23) snags a reception for TCU in the 1957 Cotton Bowl as Syracuse's mighty Jim Brown (44) looms near. Courtesy of Texas Christian University Athletics.

Brown got the first three orange touchdowns on runs of 2, 4, and 1 yards, with the fourth coming on a 28-yard pass from quarterback Charles Zimmerman to halfback James Ridlon.

Hamilton was again rocklike in the line for the Froggies, but end O'Day Williams, having one of his very best days, was a close second in effectiveness. Many thought the day's best lineman, however, was Syracuse end Richard Lasse, a defensive terror all afternoon. Tackle Jerome Cashman and guard Edward Bailey were also line stars for the eastern champions. TCU got strong play up front from Mendoza and center Joe Williams.

TCU hammered 69 yards to get its first touchdown, with the payoff coming on the 6-yard pass from Curtis to Nikkel, who was all alone in an orange secondary that leaked badly against passes throughout the game. Early in the second period, the Froggies pushed it to 14–0, with Curtis finding Shofner for a 10-yard marker and Pollard again converting.

Then it was Syracuse's turn. Brown ran the following kickoff back 30 yards, then personally accounted for 58 yards of the following 70-yard drive. He climaxed it from the 2 and made good on the first of his conversions.

Shortly before the half ended, Brown again plowed over—this time from the 4 to wind up a 21-yard drive that had been launched after the Orange recovered a Finney fumble.

TCU came back to again take command in the third quarter, driving 51 yards for the third Frog touchdown. Curtis, on a keeper, went over from 8 yards out, and Pollard kicked true to make it 21–14. Early in the fourth, the Christians drove 69 yards, with Swink scoring from the 3 and Pollard making it 28–14.

But back came the New Yorkers. Brown plowed over for one touchdown, and with 1:16 left, Zimmerman hit Ridlon for the fourth. But Mendoza's all-important block of the third conversion try by Brown was good enough to rub out the Syracuse threat.

OCTOBER 20, 1957

OUTFOUGHT AGGIES SUBDUE PESKY FROGS 7–0

FORT WORTH, Tex.—Texas A&M's goal-line defense remained as steadfast and true as Reveille here this sun-splashed afternoon, enabling the unbeaten Aggies to take home an impressive 7–0 victory over a Texas Christian team that treated Aggie reputations with utter scorn.

A shocked, often gleeful throng of 46,000 saw the proud Purple, still smoldering over the Aggies' tainted victory last year, humiliate Paul Bryant's defending champions from 15-yard line to 15-yard line.

The losers were within leapfrog distance at the Aggie goal four times—at the 5-, 10-, 6-, and 4-yard lines. They outgained the Aggies 276 yards to 122. They out-first-downed them 17 to 7. Through the midportion of the game, for 40 minutes and 16 seconds, the ready and capable Frogs held the Maroon without a single first down.

But still they lost by seven points and in so doing toppled out of serious contention for the 1957 conference crown. They previously had lost to Arkansas.

For the Aggies, it was a shaky first step toward the throne room they occupied so spectacularly a year ago. If this afternoon's work is any indication, trouble may be coming their way frequently in huge packages for the rest of the season.

A victory was what the Aggies came for here today, however, and a victory is what they got. They got it because of that punishing defense and because the Frogs gave them two big early chances.

TCU fumbled on the opening play of the game, and the Aggies got the ball on the Frog 32. They fumbled it back six plays later at the Purple 10. The Frogs then fumbled right back at the 15, and from there the opportunistic champions scored in three plays.

Tackle Kenny Beck, a mighty man for the Maroon, made the big recovery, and dangerous Roddy Osborne passed for the score, hitting a wide-open Bobby Marks in the end zone on a 10-yard pass.

On the pass, Osborne rolled out to his right, ran into deep trouble in the person of Frog Ken Miller, reversed his field, and pitched. Marks was as uncovered as Candy Barr.

Bobby Conrad kicked the goal, and it looked like an Aggie runaway. The score had come in 5 minutes and 20 seconds of play.

From that point on, the nation's No. 3 team did not crack the Frog 40 until less than four minutes remained in the game. As time ran out and the Frogs unwound, the Aggies put on a crunching march that carried to the TCU 6 at the final gun. The story of this game, however, is what happened from the time the Cadets scored until they launched their late clock-killing drive. It is a story of a TCU team that used power, pure and simple, to roll up the yardage and set up the threats.

The Frogs controlled the ball like Baylor did against Arkansas, and ironically, the scoreboard results were the same. Abe Martin's souped-up soldiers ran up the middle on the Aggies in a way few people believed possible.

The battering rams were carried by soph Marvin Lasater and senior Jim Shofner and another senior named Buddy Dike, who was all over the place all day. Dike gained 73 yards on 24 carries, Lasater 56 on 14, and Shofner 48 on 14, and not a gain was made the easy way. The story of the game is also the clutch defensive work of mean John Crow and his brutal Aggie associates, who literally go for the throat.

Crow, the Aggie bull who cherishes the rank of an All-American, was no better than several of the Frogs on offense, but on defense, he was true blue. He personally saved the Aggies three times, making a big fourth-down stop on the A&M 6, intercepting a long Frog pass on

In the 1950s and early 1960s, players commonly went both ways. John David Crow (44), a Heisman-winning running back, was also a mainstay of the Aggie defense, as shown here by his help in stopping an Arkansas ball carrier. Courtesy of Texas A&M University Athletics.

the Aggie 8, and recovering a tide-turning Dick Finney fumble on the Cadet 6.

The Aggies would have been in trouble without Crow. They also would have been embarrassed without fullback Richard Gay, a linebacker who is all shoulders and a yard wide. Gay hits like a two-ton truck. He is as destructive as the man he replaced—All-American Jack Pardee.

He made more tackles than anybody on the field today, 19, and when the Frogs were down snarling at the Aggie end zone, it was always that flaming No. 30 they couldn't combat. Crow and Gay had thunderous help from Beck, Bobby Marks, John Tracey, and Charley Krueger.

TCU's Dike put up a worthy defensive challenge to Gay, getting in on 14 tackles himself. Defensively, it was a battle between fullbacks.

The Aggies' top runners were Crow, with 40 yards on 12 carries, and Gay, with 25 on 9. The Cadets were on defense too much to have many offensive standouts. Osborne, the quarterback who loves to run that ball, wound up with minus 2 yards, one of the worst days of his career as a runner.

The fierce battle was fought primarily between the starting forces of both teams. Abe Martin's starters played almost 45 minutes, and Bryant had his proven 11 in there when the going got tough and the game was to be won or lost.

It was an exceptionally clean game. The Aggies were penalized 10 yards, the Frogs 15. The Aggies fumbled seven times and grabbed five of them back. The Frogs bobbled on six occasions, and three of them were lost for keeps.

Two of the three probably decided the game, because one set up the Aggie touchdown and another stopped the Frogs when they had ripped to the Aggie four.

Owl quarterback King Hill (26) and receiver Buddy Dial (84) combined for many memorable aerial gains. Courtesy of Rice University Athletics.

OCTOBER 22, 1957

ON SECOND THOUGHT

When quizzed in September about the chances of the 1957 Texas Aggie team having an improved passing attack, Paul Bryant entered a mild protest. "Nobody thought we had much of a passing attack last year but me," he said. "But in answer to your question, we'll be able to pass."

A&M's passing this year fits neatly into the 1956 pattern. It might not excite the purists who like to see the Sam Baughs at work, but it pleases Bryant. It produces results, and those results are often spelled out loud and clear on the scoreboard.

In the weekend football doubleheader involving the Aggies against the Frogs and the Owls against the Mustangs, passes decided both games. Rice did it the conventional way, with King Hill dropping straight back from a T formation and throwing beautifully to expert receiver Buddy Dial. That was passing in the old SWC pattern—in a way aerialists could appreciate. It was passing at its best.

A&M's passing was different. It was more like . . . well, more like the Aggie pass. And yet the results were comparable.

Hill's shots to Dial went 55 yards for a touchdown and 40 yards to set up another. Those were the decisive strokes in the 27–21 game. And yet it is not the complete story. Rice's Frank Ryan tried a fourth-down pass from the Mustang 8; he missed his target in the flat, and swift Charley Jackson was able to intercept and return 100 yards for a Pony score. SMU was a pretty forlorn club until that happened.

In Fort Worth, the Aggies tried just five passes, completed four of them, and had none intercepted. One of the four completions provided the six points that won the ballgame. Roddy Osborne pitched it, and Bobby Marks caught it 10 yards away in the end zone.

The Osborne pass didn't compare with Hill's in beauty, and yet the scoreboard influence was the same. The whole thing points back to Bryant's cardinal rules on passing. He outlined them this fall on Aggieland "press day."

A&M pass plays are predominantly run-pass options rather than the drop-back variety. On the option, Bryant has three rules: (1) if the passer can run with the ball and make as much as 4 yards, Bryant wants him to run, even if the receiver is as wide open as a barn door—"Run down there and hand him the ball" is the way Bear would put it—(2) if the passer can't make 4 yards, and if the receiver is completely uncovered, then the pass should be thrown; and (3) if there is any question whatsoever about the receiver being open, the passer should run, even if he loses yardage.

The overarching rule, of course, is to use the pass sparingly. The Aggies still are a basic split-T team, which means they prefer the run over the aerial. They follow the axiom that when you put the ball in the air, you share possession. Because they put such pressure on the defense with their runs, the few passes they throw profit greatly from the surprise factor.

This year, the Aggies have attempted 37 tosses and completed 20 for a .541 accuracy mark. Four of them have gone for touchdowns and only two have been intercepted.

The final toss they completed against TCU Saturday is typical of their entire aerial attack. Roddy Osborne started off on a run to his left as Bobby Conrad drifted downfield. TCU defenders came up to seal off the run, leaving Conrad open. Osborne's pass was gosh-awful in its execution—it went through the air like a dying quail—but it was on target, and Conrad was wide open, and the net result was a 13-yard gain.

Rice's Hill and Ryan, an electrifying combination and a pleasure to watch, would have done it smoother and neater. They would have had a hard time improving on the end product.

OCTOBER 27, 1957

AGGIES, CROW LOWER BRUTAL AXE

COLLEGE STATION, Tex.—The Texas Aggies struck early and late and played bullet-proof defense in between here Saturday to subdue aroused Baylor, 14–0, and blot the Bears from the conference race.

A sellout crowd of 42,000, watching in Kyle Field's autumn crispness, saw Paul Bryant's defending champions come up with every big play they needed to capture the prize, which the September forecasters said would be the "big one" in this 1957 chase.

The Aggie victory march was played in the drumbeat of John Crow's flying feet. The most demanding runner on the field, the Aggies' great left halfback scored the Cadets' second touchdown with an artistic 8-yard burst and set up the first one with a 16-yard spurt to the Baylor 3.

Roddy Osborne put the touchdown on the record book from the Baylor 1-yard line three plays later.

The first Aggie score came in the first 6 minutes of play, the first time Bryant's men got the ball. They moved 54 yards in 10 plays, and Crow made 33 of them. The second touchdown went on the scoreboard with 6:40 left to play in the game and came as the climax of a seven-play, 42-yard drive against a Baylor team that had fought gamely and well and that now was spent.

Little Loyd Taylor kicked the first extra point, Bobby Conrad the second. The conversions kept the Aggie record clean. They haven't missed a one this year.

They haven't missed a chance to win a game either, and so this morning they are riding along with their victory string still intact, and their chances of maintaining conference supremacy are as strong as the Aggie corps' cheering throats.

The latest one came hard, however, because the Bruins came to play. They were ragged and overanxious and

Charley Horton. Courtesy of Baylor University Athletics.

John David Crow with his Heisman Trophy. Courtesy of Texas A&M University Athletics.

Clyde Letbetter. Courtesy of Baylor University Athletics.

sometimes a little inept, but the 60-minute effort was heartwarming.

In addition to getting their 14 points, the Aggies missed another touchdown (after actually scoring it) when an ineligible receiver downfield rubbed out a 10-yard Osborne scoring pass to Don McClelland. Penalized back to the Baylor 25, Charley Milstead tried a field goal, and Charley Horton—a strong Baylor hero until injured—partially blocked it.

The two touchdown marches and the futile field goal try represented A&M's best offensive efforts until Richard Gay intercepted Buddy Humphrey's last-ditch pass in the final minute and returned 22 yards to the Baylor 8. The great Crow drove to the Bruin 3 as the game ended.

Final first downs favored the Cadets, 16 to 11, and they also won the war on the ground, 228 to 121, and in the air, 60 to 53. Poised and polished, they always seemed to be in control of the combat. Crow was the game's leading runner with 78 yards on 19 carries. Osborne had 36 on 7, Taylor 41 on 9, Gay 33 on 7, and Conrad 24 on 5. Those were the five big Aggies on offense, and of the five, Crow was king without dispute.

Baylor's top runner was Hickman with 39 yards on 13 carries. Bobby Peters got 26 on 5, and Carroll Overton got 23 on 3. It was a hard day on Baylor ball carriers. Humphrey got 30 yards on three completions and Traylor 23 on four.

Defensively, the Aggies got great play from Krueger, Ken Beck, Marks, Crow, and Gay.

They were no better, however, than Baylor's Bobby Jack Oliver, Earl Miller, Charley Horton, and Clyde Letbetter. Letbetter came in after Horton was injured and at one point almost devoured the Aggies by himself.

The Maroon managed to score only the second shutout in the Bruins' last 76 games. It usually takes some defense to blank the Bears, but then that's how the Aggies are moving back toward the conference throne room—on defense.

NOVEMBER 10, 1957

ON SECOND THOUGHT

Popular opinion these days holds that big football staffs are necessary for big scoreboard returns, but Texas Christian begs to differ. The Frogs have the smallest coaching staff in the conference. Over the last two seasons, they have one of the best won-loss records.

All that might be dismissed as luck of the draw or the net result of an exceptional crop of recruits except for two additional points:

1. The Frogs this year rank with Texas as the pleasant surprise of the league. Generally picked in the lower echelons in September and consigned to the cellar itself by a number of forecasters, the Frogs at midseason are over the .500 mark in season play and are still thinking in terms of bowls.
2. No team in the conference has more reason to look forward to that elusive "next year" with more confidence than the Frogs. The Purple has got 'em on the varsity, and it's got more of 'em on the way.

You have to count it all as a testimonial to the sometimes overlooked talents of Abe Martin. In his own flavorful way, philosopher Abe can really get things done.

His best time for getting them done is early in the morning. Abe is a firm believer in the "early to rise" school.

"Abe is never at work later than six in the morning," the Frogs' ace drumbeater, Jim Brock, notes. "He'll come down long before the other coaches get here, look at the movies by himself, make his plans, figure out what he wants the team to work on that day. Abe says that's when he gets all his work done."

When you say Abe is down "before the other coaches," you are speaking of his three assistants. They are line coach Allie White, backfield coach Walter Roach, and freshman coach Fred Taylor. The likeable Buster Brannon adds his talent early in the season before basketball steals him away.

Basically, it is a four-man staff. By contrast, the Texas Aggies have a nine-man coaching lineup, Texas eight, Arkansas seven, SMU eight, Rice eight, Texas Tech seven, and Baylor six. (And in addition, the Bruins have full-time scouting help from Bill Henderson and Jim Crow.)

At first glance, it would appear the Frogs are hopelessly outmanned on such vital fronts as recruiting. Yet

Abe Martin on the sidelines, talking with his quarterback, Sonny Gibbs. Courtesy of Texas Christian University Athletics.

they do one of the league's better jobs. How do they manage it?

"We split the state into four sections," Brock reports. "Allie takes West Texas, Walter East Texas, Fred Taylor Center and South Texas. Then they all help on North Texas, but that's Abe primarily."

For on-the-field coaching, White handles both the offensive and the defensive tutoring of the line, and Roach handles the backfield. Martin oversees it all, of course, but works constantly with the offense. Taylor works with the ends until the frosh report in mid-September.

That is the setup that must compete with schools that have separate coaches for the guards, the tackles, the centers, and on down the line. Or, at the very least, the rivals all have separate coaches for the offensive line, the defensive line, the offensive backfield, and the defensive backfield.

Doesn't all that constitute a major handicap to the Frogs?

Abe was asked that question the other day. His reply: "Well, you see, I don't have to spend all my time coaching the coaches." He meant that his assistants are all veterans with much experience and that the operation is a model of harmony. And those in the know report that is true.

Despite the 1956 graduation of such superstars as Jim Swink and Norman Hamilton and the loss of practically the entire group that carried the Purple to two Cotton Bowls, Abe has come up this year with a team capable of upsetting Big 10 leader Ohio State and playing top-rated Texas A&M off its feet.

All that with a 70-man squad, which includes just 10 seniors.

The scarcity of seniors points up the idea that the Frogs are going to be tough for several years to come. The sophs this year—such boys as Marvin Lasater, Jack Spikes, William Roach, Ramon Armstrong, Don Floyd—are among the best in the league.

Don Meredith, future Dallas Cowboy great, won All-America honors at SMU in 1958 and 1959. Courtesy of Southern Methodist University Athletics.

Joining those sophs next year will be graduates of a 1957 Wog team that Taylor compares favorably to the great Swink-Hamilton crew of '53—only these boys have more size. This is the biggest Wog team of them all. The line averages 219. It includes such strong men as tackles Clarence Young (215) and Robert Lilly (230).

"They could move in right now and be No. 1 on the varsity," bubbles the optimistic Fort Worth writer Dan Jenkins. In the backfield, Abe thinks he has six boys of great varsity potential, including the fabulous hare Harry Moreland.

The way some see it, the Frogs may have unexpected trouble next year because of the graduation of three outstanding defensive backs—Jim Shofner, Buddy Dike, and Dick Finney.

But White counters, "We could be so good, we'll just scare them all to death."

Exaggeration or not, it's quite a tribute to the smallest coaching staff in the Southwest Conference.

NOVEMBER 16, 1958

FROGS RIDE STEERS TOWARD COTTON BOWL: TCU WHIPS TEXAS, 22–8, LEADS SWC

FORT WORTH, Tex.—Brawny Texas Christian spent the first half day-dreaming about the Cotton Bowl and the last half playing like it belonged there in stampeding past game but outclassed Texas 22–8 here Saturday.

A properly impressed Cowtown audience of 39,000 saw Abe Martin's rollicking crew seize undisputed possession of first place in the Southwest Conference race with a rousing 30-minute show of football might.

That show quickly wiped out an 8–0 lead Texas had staked out in the first half, and then it all but swept the Longhorn Orange out of the stadium. A Darrell Royal team that had been in full control of the regionally televised contest for two quarters found itself unable to get off its own grass in the last two.

The Frogs not only held their quests to just two puny first downs (and one of those came on a 15-yard penalty); they chocked them off with a minus 4 yards rushing and passing for the second half. In those final moments of truth, the Longhorns could do no more than the Texas team that was routed, 46–0, here two years ago.

DOORWAY OPEN

TCU used that sweeping victory in 1956 as the springboard to a New Year's Day date in Dallas, and with the

Saturday failures of both Rice and Southern Methodist, the way now appears open for history to repeat.

Quarterback Hunter Enis, who dotes on the touchdown pass, ran for the first TCU score and passed 11 yards to end Jimmy Gilmore for the second in breaking the game wide open.

Then Marvin Lasater put seven points of insurance on the scoreboard with a 41-yard touchdown pass to Marshall Harris midway through the final quarter.

TCU drove 68 yards in 12 plays for the first score, Enis diving over from the 1 at the 5:34 mark of the third period. The often underrated Frog signal caller then passed to driving Jack Spikes in the end zone for the two-point conversion that tied the score.

Center Dale Walker set up the tie breaker by intercepting a Texas pass and returning 13 yards to the Longhorn 23. Enis put the TCU Purple ahead in just three plays, the payoff being the pass to Gilmore 3 minutes deep in the final quarter.

THREE PLAYS

The final scoring spurt needed just three plays too. It went 52 yards; Harris got in behind Bobby Lackey and Bobby Matocha and made a nifty catch of Lasater's pass to put the Longhorns down for the count.

GET SAFETY

The Longhorns got the equivalent of a two-point conversion a little later, however, when TCU's Gilmore, back to punt in his own end zone, dropped the snap and was tackled for a safety.

Another fullback, Texas' Dowdle, challenged Spikes for ground, gaining honors with 51 yards on 13 carries.

Don Floyd. Courtesy of Texas Christian University Athletics.

Lasater had 33 yards for TCU, Larry Dawson 35, Merlin Priddy 31, Billy Gault 26, and Harry Moreland 22—and almost all that yardage came in the late flash-flood of TCU power.

Playing catch-up ball, Texas didn't have a chance. The best the Longhorns could do was reach the 41. But by now, TCU's Floyd, Headrick, Robert Lilly, Walker, Gilmore, and Peebles were in full cry defensively, and Texas couldn't match them.

NOVEMBER 30, 1958

OWLS FINALLY RUB OUT PISTOL PACKIN' BEARS: HUMPHREY HANGS UP 387 YARDS

The alert Rice Owls hawked both the ball and the breaks in the big moments at Baylor Stadium Saturday to shoot down the thrill-a-minute Bears in an offensive extravaganza, but not before magnificent Buddy Humphrey had established himself as the all-time top gun in Southwest Conference history.

The scoreboard belonged to the Owls, 33–21, but the afternoon belonged to the mighty Humphrey—both the good and the bad parts of it.

The tall, cool-eyed Kilgore slinger, putting on one last great show for the home folks, shattered the all-time conference passing marks both for a single game and for a season before finally surrendering to the unsympathetic clock.

And fittingly, he won himself a national passing championship in the process.

Humphrey hurled 37 times, completed 22, and saw at least 4 others dropped. The completions were good for a whopping 387 yards and two touchdowns.

The yardage gained represents a new league record for a single afternoon of play, and Buddy's final total of 112 completions for the season also wipes out all existing SWC marks.

The old single-game yardage record was 336 yards, established by Fred Benners against Notre Dame in 1951. The old season mark was 110 completions shared by Davey O'Brien, Adrian Burk, and Benners.

The 112 completions also left Buddy high and dry as the top passer for the 1958 collegiate season.

But at the finish, all that marvelous sharpshooting just added up to another near miss for the luckless, courageous, never-quit Bears, and the main reason was a boy named Billy Bucek.

Bucek intercepted three of the four Humphrey shots that strayed off target. One of them prevented a Baylor touchdown, and the other two, returned for a total of 81 yards, set up Rice scores.

Big tackle Gene Miller, a senior returning to the starting lineup for his last game, hawked two Baylor fumbles deep in Bruin territory, and those also were turned into Owl touchdowns.

The crowd of 20,000, getting its money's worth on almost every play, saw the Owls cash in on five of their six big chances. The Bruins were inside the Owl 20 on seven different occasions but could punch across only three times.

BAYLOR GETS 571 YARDS

As additional evidence of the kind of day it was, Baylor gained an unbelievable 574 yards against Rice defenses yet lost by two touchdowns.

The Owls got only 328 yards, but those interceptions and fumble recoveries more than balanced the books.

Halfback Pat Bailey got the first touchdown on a 3-yard dive, sophomore quarterback Alvin Hartman got the second and third on passes of 6 yards to Bill Simmons and Buddy Dial, fullback Hart Peebles added the fourth with a plunge from the 1, and Hartman wrapped it up with another dive from the 1.

In scoring one touchdown and throwing for two more, Martman joined Bucek, Miller, and Dial as high and mighty Owls here Saturday.

POINTS THE HARD WAY

Baylor had to get all its points the hard way, although a Humphrey-to-Austin Gonsoulin combination made them seem easy.

The Bears went 80, 82, and 84 yards, and the super aerial combination was in sharp working order, paying big dividends on all three.

Buddy Humphrey. Courtesy of Baylor University Athletics.

Then when Rice had climbed into a 26–15 lead, Humphrey hit Gonsoulin on a 50-yard gain that set up the final score, and Larry Hickman got the touchdown. Though the march needed only two plays, the last one required 9 yards.

Almost lost in the aerial fireworks was another standout afternoon of line-blasting by a veteran member of the Baylor infantry—Larry Hickman.

The most powerful battering ram Baylor ever had closed out a memorable career by blasting for 87 yards in 17 carries—good enough for the conference ground-gaining championship. Hickman last week had set a new three-year rushing record for Baylor. He finished with 670 yards this year (which also is a new single-season Bruin mark) and a career total of 1,713 yards—almost a mile of football real estate.

NOVEMBER 27, 1958

RENE RAMIREZ RIDES AGAIN AS TEXAS SPLATTERS AGGIES

AL WARD

AUSTIN, Tex.—Workmanlike Texas started reassembling the scattered traditions here Thursday afternoon.

The blood-hunting Longhorns, with Rene Ramirez riding again, knocked out Texas A&M, 27–0, in this storied rivalry, posting the series' first shutout since 1950.

It was all done in Memorial Stadium, which two years ago saw its apparently deathless hex on Aggie victories relinquished before 52,000 shivering customers on a miserably cold and wet Thanksgiving Day.

Instances in the conduct of the game might indicate it could have been close, but this is questionable. The Aggies five times hammered inside the Texas 20, there to trip against an elastic Longhorn defense that yielded with the midfield charge, then hit its maximum stretch short of the goal and snapped back sharply.

LONGHORNS PROVE SUPERIOR

This clutch toughness was a big particle in the usual inspired Texas effort, an effort matched briefly by the

Aggies, then submerged under the Longhorns' superior firepower.

Texas did it up without adornments, without any frills—just basic football dipped in the hot turkey-day emotions.

It assured the Longhorns a possible tie for second in the SWC race with a 3–3 league record; it completed a 7–3 season, best for a Texas team since 1952, and goes into the alumni book as a "fine season," what with the early triumph over Oklahoma.

Rene Ramirez, the redoubtable Latin halfback who was playing his first full-time game since the Arkansas contest, ran for two touchdowns and caught a pass for a third as Texas bounded to a 21–0 halftime lead, scored again early in the third period, then turned the game over to the reserves and to the record book.

A shoulder-thudding Texas defense, on the other hand, turned to hardened concrete inside the Longhorn 20, holding off Milstead-paced charges to the Longhorn 1-, the 2-, the 12-, the 16-, and the 18-yard lines.

A major part of the afternoon, in fact, was burned up with the Aggies searching fruitlessly for touchdown keys deep in Texas territory, moved there chiefly by the passing heroics of tailback Charley Milstead, who absorbed tremendous punishment in playing out a long, cold afternoon as his team's lone offensive hope.

The Aggies decided early that they couldn't move through the thorny Texas line thickets, which absorbed ground thrusts like a thirsty blotter, and turned wholly to Milstead's passing.

WORKS OFF SPREAD FORMATION

The tall blond junior worked off what amounted to a spread formation much of the time, and when Texas rushers weren't hammering him to the ground, his properly aimed tosses were coming off his slick fingers without their usual accuracy.

Game-time temperature was 41 degrees, and to this the elements added a fairly brisk wind and a steady drizzle of rain. Footing held up rather firm through the nationally televised show, but the ball was too slick for a great passing performance.

Milstead nevertheless hit on 14 of 33 tosses for 191 yards, but other serves slipped out of reach or were dropped, and three were intercepted.

While it lasted, the aerial emphasis put six new records into the all-time Aggie book: Milstead's one-season total offense (1,332), Milstead's total passing yardage in one season (1,135), Milstead's total plays in one game (46), and three receiving records for senior end John Tracey—most career catches (47), most catches one season (37), and most career yards as a receiver (466).

Texas acted like it didn't need the forward pass and usually didn't. The first two touchdown drives of 28 and 65 yards were straight accomplishments, and for the entire game, Texas threw seven times and hit on four.

Behind what was probably Texas' best line blocking of the year, backs Ramirez, George Blanch, Clair Branch, and Mike Dowdle bowled for gains that ate up most of Texas' 212-yard rushing total. Ramirez and Branch tied for high-man honors with 49 yards each, and Luther Hall led the Aggies with 47.

RAMIREZ IN KILLER ROLE

Ramirez, dogged through most of October and November with injuries, was in his familiar killer role again. He scored the first touchdown on a 5-yard slash at right tackle, let Mike Dowdle have 1-yard honors on the second, sailed around left end for 5 yards and third touchdown, and took a 14-yard pass from Bobby Lackey for the final points.

The Aggies ended the game with 39 yards net rushing, much of the minus total credited to Milstead when he was downed looking for receivers, and the Longhorn line bristled with heroes.

None stood higher than string-thin guard Bob Harwerth, who dogged the Aggie rushing game and contacted almost as many Milstead passes as Tracey, knocking down three and intercepting one. Other

Rene Ramirez joined the University of Texas Men's Athletics Hall of Honor in 2013. Courtesy of University of Texas Athletics.

Longhorn line stars were end Richard Schulte, center Jerry Muennink, and guard J. B. Padgett.

For the Aggies, guard Allen Goehring and end Tracey were key defenders.

AGGIES GET FIRST BREAK

The elements of fate at first appeared to favor the Aggies when Texas' Bob Bryant picked up the opening kickoff, was hit and fumbled, and Aggie Joe Munson recovered on the Longhorn 42. But the Longhorns held on their 18, and Lackey punted 53 yards to the Aggie 26.

On the first play from here, Hall was hit by Stolhandske and fumbled, with Blanch recovering on the 28. Texas scored in six plays, with Ramirez's 14-yard jaunt to the Aggie 5 the big play. On third down from the 2, Ramirez rode blocks by Doke and Stolhandske for the points, and Lackey kicked goal with 7:30 left.

The Aggies hammered back with the kickoff, again relying on Milstead's passes, marching form their own 37 to a first on the Texas 6. Two plays gained 1 yard, then Milstead hammered to the 1-foot line. On fourth down, Hall was nailed on the 1 by Muennink, and Cooper punted 52 yards out of danger.

TEXAS SCORES AGAIN

On the first play from here, Blanch intercepted Milstead's pass, and the Steers were on the move again. A clipping penalty moved the ball to the Texas 35, but from here, Texas moved 65 yards in 13 plays for another score.

Mike Dowdle's bulling across the middle furnished 38 yards on eight carries, and he rode the blocking Parkhurst and Padgett to score from the Aggie 1. Lackey kicked goal, and it was 14–0 with 10:15 left in the second period.

Late in the same quarter, the Steers saddled up for their third score, this one covering 38 yards in eight plays. Ramirez, with Cooper throwing the key block, swept around left end from 5 yards out, and Shillingburg's kick made it 21–0 at the half.

SHORT AGGIE PUNT

After the halftime break, Texas grabbed a short Milstead punt and wheeled 38 yards in seven plays for the Longhorns' fourth touchdown.

Tackle Tillman O'Brien put a big rush on Milstead, almost blocking a high punt that sailed only 15 yards to the Aggie 38. Branch carried three times to the 25, and Ramirez bounded to the 21.

Larkey then warmed up a cold passing arm with a toss to Blanch on the 14, then came back with the killer. He slid to his right as if on the option play, was hit, and flipped quickly to Ramirez on the 7. Ramirez was hit by Milstead on the 4 but held his feet and fell across the goal. Lackey's kick was not good, and Texas led 27–0 with 9:36 left in the third period.

Milstead's passes and a 25-yard pass interference penalty then combined to give the Aggies another good threat that reached second down on the Texas 2. Here it died on a fumble, an incompletion, and on fourth down, Ramirez's interception of a Milstead pass in the end zone.

Reserves clogged the field in the fading minutes, during which Milstead's passes paced another threat down to the Texas 12, where a penalty set it back.

This was the game's, and the Aggies', final gasp.

OCTOBER 10, 1959
STEERS FIGHT BACK, GET 19–12 VICTORY

DALLAS, Tex.—Invaders from Oklahoma Indian territory applied the acid test to Texas' spotless football record here Saturday and found it above reproach.

As a sun-drenched Cotton Bowl crowd of 76,000 roared to the action, the nation's fourth-ranking team, its end zone stained for the first time this year by two quick Sooner touchdowns, came off the floor gallantly and knocked once invincible Oklahoma into a 19–12 defeat.

The Sooners had no excuses. This was a classic comeback achieved in a classic football rivalry by a team that today had the classic tools of greatness. For Texas, this was a second straight golden hour over a team that once plundered it with shocking ease. For Darrell Royal, this was new proof positive that pupils sometimes can teach the masters. Twice now Bud Wilkinson has found Royal-coached teams as hard on the stomach as the Sooners' infamous meal in Chicago two weeks ago. That's when 12 Sooners fell ill from food poisoning and OU fell, 45–13, at Northwestern.

And for the Southwest Conference, this was a warning, pure and simple. The Longhorns are not coming, they are here . . . wonderfully quick, magnificently armed, alert and deadly. With their record of four straight victories, the Longhorns now are the team to beat.

For the first quarter Saturday, Oklahoma appeared to be the team to do just that.

Paced by a raging fullback named Prentice Gautt, the Sooners swarmed 32 yards in three plays for their first touchdown, and the next time they got the ball, they boomed 59 yards in seven plays for six more points.

With two minutes still left in the first quarter, smoke signals filled the Cotton Bowl air, all beamed back to Norman. They told the natives to relax, that Sooner supremacy in this blood duel had been reestablished, that the Texans were in full retreat.

Then the reeling Longhorns, reacting like champions, started to prove themselves.

With Rene Ramirez in the saddle, accounting for 51 yards with his runs, his passes, and his catches, the men from Forty Acres drove 73 yards in 14 plays for the score.

And then, as the clock foreclosed rapidly on the second-quarter action, rabbit James Saxton spurred the Longhorns magnificently for 61 yards in nine plays for the go-ahead points.

Mike Dowdle, diving over from the 1-yard line, planted the Texas victory stake in the Sooner end zone with 10 seconds left in the half to give the Longhorns the lead.

Although they tried and tried and threatened and threatened, the Sooners never could get that stake removed, and finally in the last two minutes, with Texas now ahead by 19–12 and Oklahoma desperately marching at the Longhorn 31, sophomore Mike Cotten raced in to field a Sooner overthrow and put the game away for good.

Given possession at their own 8, the Longhorns

Rene Ramirez scores for Texas. Courtesy of University of Texas Athletics.

simply let Bobby Lackey run out the clock with plunges into the aching Sooner midsection.

So it was Ramirez and Saxton and Cotten and Jack Collins and a list of other Longhorn heroes as long as your arm who finally slew the Oklahoma dragon for the second straight year. Texas has not known such prosperity in this series in a decade.

Ramirez and Saxton and Cotten you know about. Collins's contribution was the clincher—a 61-yard run with a Cotten pass that was made possible by rolling thunder in the form of blocker Larry Cooper.

That touchdown went on the scoreboard at the 8:38 mark of the final quarter. It wound up a 63-yard drive that used just three plays, and it left still-quarrelsome Oklahoma in a situation where a field goal no longer would win the game.

Cooper the blocker earlier had been Cooper the catcher, snagging an 11-yard pass from the rampaging Ramirez to wind up Texas' first touchdown drive. Lackey kicked the extra point after that touchdown—or rather, he kicked the ball and it bounced off a broad Sooner back and through the uprights. The score came with 4:03 left in the second quarter.

That left Texas in a 13–12 advantage at halftime, the comeback wiping out Oklahoma's earlier advantages secured on a 23-yard touchdown pass from Bob Cornell to Jackie Holt and a 37-yard sideline run by Dick Carpenter. Carpenter's dash, made down the extreme eastern edge of the playing field, came with 2:21 left before halftime. As he fled down the sideline, Bud Wilkinson fled almost as fast, clapping and cheering him on.

Never again did the Sooners get to yell quite so loudly. Storm clouds were gathering on the opposite side of the field, and when they finally broke, Oklahoma was caught up in a Texas-size tornado.

James Saxton. Courtesy of University of Texas Athletics.

Jack Collins. Courtesy of University of Texas Athletics.

The figures help tell the dimension of the Texas comeback. After falling behind by 12 points and failing to get a first down for the entire first quarter, Texas came back to get a 7-point victory and a 313 to 307 edge in total offense.

Much of the Oklahoma yardage (135 yards) came from Gautt's punishing runs, and all afternoon it seemed he was about to get away. But he never did.

For that matter, for much of the second half it seemed that Oklahoma was about to get away, but in the big moments either the Sooners miscued or Texas stopped them.

In the first half, both teams converted their best chances into touchdowns. In the second half, while Texas was getting six points out of its only sashay into Sooner country, Oklahoma was muffing chances that carried to the Texas 9, the 36, the 35, and the 31. Fumbles by Bennett Watts and Ronnie Hartline killed the first two, and interceptions by George Blanch at the 19 and Cotten at the 8 killed the others.

Texas made few errors. The Longhorns fumbled just once, were penalized only twice, and gave up the ball only once on an interception.

Oklahoma lost two fumbles and two interceptions, and those errors probably were the difference between victory and defeat. You don't give this Texas team much and beat it.

Credit the Sooners, though, because they almost won in spite of themselves. In fact, they appeared to be in fine shape when they set up shop at the Texas 36 midway through the final quarter. But Oklahoma fumbled on the first play, and Clair Branch got the big bobble for the Longhorns.

From there, lightning struck. Cotten pitched to Collins on the third play, and Collins, racing behind Cooper's great block, went down the sideline untouched.

Texas tried for a two-point conversion and got it, but a penalty rubbed out the play. Forced to try for a one-point conversion from 17 yards out, Lackey saw his kick sail wide.

It didn't matter.

Oklahoma came roaring back to the Texas 35 behind quarterback Bobby Boyd and Gautt, but Blanch stopped them with an interception at the 19.

And then in the game's last great moment of truth, after Boyd had directed the Sooners to the Texas 30, the Oklahoma field general fired too tall for Carpenter down the middle, and Cotten came scrambling in to intercept.

A minute and 40 seconds showed on the clock. The Sooners were stone-cold dead.

OCTOBER 25, 1959

BEARS END AGGIE STREAK WITH 13–0 VICTORY: PLY LEADS REVENGE WIN FOR BRUINS

COLLEGE STATION, Tex.—In a game of red flags and red faces that left football perfectionists weeping in despair, the Baylor Bears dropped the Texas Aggies, 13–0, here Saturday and wiped out an Aggie run of supremacy that had extended through four years.

Seldom has a Southwest Conference game produced more ragged play. Officials sent the penalty flag flying 23 times and stepped off 185 yards, and in addition, there were six fumbles, two pass interceptions, and an incredible boner by the officials, who misplaced 5 yards while the teams were changing sides for the fourth quarter.

The official who put the ball down wrong, thus making Baylor travel an extra 5 yards for its second touchdown, was Napper Davis, central figure in the SMU-Rice dispute last week. But Napper shouldn't be faulted too strongly. In a game such as this, no one remained blameless long.

However, at the final gun the Bears had what they came for, and they had it with room to spare, adding up to an escape from the conference cellar and Baylor's first conference victory in 13 months.

Bobby Ply, playing his best game yet, turned runner as well as passer and engineer in sparking the Bears to their touchdowns. The first one came in the second quarter, Ply hurling the final 15 yards to Sonny Davis to climax a drive that carried 65 yards in 12 plays. Because of the red flags that fell from time to time, plus a fumble that lost 7 yards, the Bears actually had to gain 87 yards. Ply's running and passing gained 81 of it.

After a scoreless third quarter, the Bears finally crashed through for their final six points early in the final period. Fullback Jim Evans carried the last 2 yards on a drive that went 41 yards in six plays, although Napper's boner really made the Bears go 46 yards.

Ply passed for the first 26 yards and then Bull ran 12 yards to the Aggie 4-yard line to set the stage for Evans's scoring plunge.

After going ahead by 13 points with a little more than 13 minutes remaining, the Bears came back to spring speedster Tommy Minter loose on a 57-yard touchdown scamper that was wiped out by a clipping penalty.

Rebuffed on that surge, the Bears didn't get in position for any more offensive fireworks until the final seconds, and by then, John Bridgers had the reserves in, mopping up.

The Aggies crowded most of their big moments into the first quarter. They drove once to the Baylor 24 before a fumble stopped them. Later they stormed to the Baylor 3 before a crushing high-low tackle by Dean Blair and Al Witcher on fullback Gordon LeBoeuf knocked the ball loose on the Baylor 5.

Albert Witcher. Courtesy of Baylor University Athletics.

Then at the start of the third quarter, they took the kickoff and moved from their own 27 to the Baylor 17.

From there, on fourth down, Charley Milstead passed into the right flat, and Evans was there to intercept and return 23 yards to the Baylor 29. For the Aggies, that was the ball game.

The dangerous Milstead was hurt on the play, and when he was helped off the field with 8:30 still showing on the clock in the third quarter, the Aggies were through. They never did get into Baylor territory again until their final possession, when the Bears punted short into the brisk north breeze.

While the Bears had their offensive troubles, the defense seldom faltered. Paced by Everett Frazier, Royce West, Buddy Dansby, Sonny Davis, Gerry Moore, and Buck McLeod in the line and by Austin Gonsoulin, Ply, and Ronnie Bull in the secondary, the Bears came up with the defensive stops that made the difference. It was their first shutout over an Aggie team in 10 years.

Even before reinjuring his knee, Milstead had found Baylor's aerial picket line tough. He completed only 4 of 10 throws for 49 yards.

Meanwhile, Ply was pacing all Baylor rushers with 46 yards on seven carries and completing 9 of 13 passes for 107 yards and one touchdown.

Bull found the Aggies laying for him and gained only 20 yards on 7 carries. Evans got 21 on 10 and Billy Pavliska 16 on 6.

LeBouef gained 46 yards on 13 carries for A&M, and Powell Berry added 39 on 12.

Statistically, the Aggies led in first downs, 13 to 12, and in rushing, 137 to 128. Baylor won the aerial war, 107 to 49, and prevailed in total offense, 235 to 186. And they also were well ahead in penalties, drawing 120 yards for 16 infractions.

The game featured a fine punting display by Berry, who got off kicks of 58 and 76 yards.

But it didn't matter. The Bears had their victory, and they still had life in the conference race. And no amount of movie reviewing could change that.

NOVEMBER 8, 1959

BEARS MISS HISTORIC UPSET BY ONE POINT

AUSTIN, Tex.—Baylor's gallant young Bears had a date with history Saturday afternoon and played their hearts out trying to keep it. They failed by a single point.

Scorning the odds and the reputations facing them across the battle line, the 17-point underdogs played with reckless fury and flaming determination, gave the nation's third-ranked Texas Longhorns every bit as good as they got, led the undefeated Steers by five points until less than five minutes remained to play, and then had to surrender in the game's last great moment of truth, 13–12.

Even after Texas had gone ahead with 4:57 to play, the Bears died hard and oh so slowly. They took a Longhorn kickoff and drove brilliantly from their own 35 to the Texas 27 before, on fourth down, a desperation field goal attempt fell far short.

The Longhorns, content by then to win by any margin, ran out the clock on fourth down from their own 15-yard line.

Thus did Texas, a fighting team with great clutch qualities, advance one more tortuous step toward a perfect season and perhaps a national championship. And thus did the Longhorns manage to escape, by the barest of margins, the same type of Baylor ambush that felled another great Texas team 18 years ago today.

Seldom has a Baylor team played better. Never has one played with more verve and heart. And yet the Longhorns were still ahead at the finish, thanks in large part to Bobby Lackey's perfect toe, to a fumble recovery by end Larry Cooper, and to two great fourth-down runs for first-down yardage by shining sophomore Jack Collins.

With the reeling orange behind, 7–12, in the telltale moments of the final quarter, and with Baylor driving out of trouble after stopping Texas on the Bruin 14, Cooper fell on a Jim Evans fumble at the Baylor 39 after the fullback had run savagely for 14 yards.

Until that moment, Texas was a beaten team. Given a reprieve it didn't expect, the Longhorns cranked up and drove in for the victory this time, grinding the distance in 10 plays against the fiercely resisting Bears.

On the fifth play of the drive, Collins ran for 5 yards when the Longhorns had to have 4 to stay alive. And then four plays later, with the ball on the 11, Collins swept end to the 3-yard line when anything less than a 6-yard gain would have given Baylor the ball.

From that point, fullback Clair Branch punched into the end zone, giving the Longhorns their eighth straight victory of the year. Baylor came back hard under the direction of Ronnie Stanley, who was brilliant today, but the Longhorns had one more great defensive effort left and dropped Stanley on third down for a loss of 8 yards back to the Longhorn 35.

So on fourth down, from the 40, Larry Corley tried the long-shot field goal that didn't come close. When the ball came down short, the Bears did too.

It was a tremendous game, overflowing with thrills, key plays, and magnificent deeds done above and beyond the call of duty. The crowd of 40,000, set into full-throated cry by a 38-yard Baylor gain on the opening play, never got a chance to rest its voice again.

Texas wound up moving 19 and 39 yards for its touchdowns. It failed on drives that carried to the Bruin 7, the 26, the 8, and the 14.

Baylor had to drive 74 and 80 yards for its points. In addition, it failed on bids that got to the Texas 24- and 23-yard lines.

The Longhorns did their damage with a crackling ground game that chewed hard on Baylor's flanks. With Collins leading the way, the Texas infantry gained 253 yards, although those who saw Everett Frazier, Bill Hicks, and Herby Adkins in action will wonder how.

Frazier, hard-nosed all the way, smashed down 14 Longhorn plays, and the driving Hicks stopped 12. Adkins, who was knocked senseless in the first quarter, didn't remember a thing at the finish. But he got in on 10 tackles. A hard knock also failed to faze Stanley, who got a four-stitch gash sewed up at halftime and came back to play like a future All-American. On defense, he got in on eight tackles, as did the great Ronnie Bull.

Those were the big defensive heroes in a game that was overset in heroes all the way.

Although Collins got the clutch yardage while running behind Cotten's great blocking, Branch led all rushers with 74 yards on 17 carries. Collins got 58 on 16, Mike Dowdle gained 46, Bobby Gurwitz 31, and Rene Ramirez 19.

Evans paced the Bruin ground game with 53 yards, Stanley got 34, and Bull 31.

The vicious Longhorn line, paced by Jerry Muennink, Monte Lee, David Kristynik, and Cooper, held the Bears to 106 yards on the ground.

In all, the Bears completed 15 of 27 passes for 153 yards and finished with 259 yards in total offense.

Monte Lee. Courtesy of University of Texas Athletics.

Texas, held to 27 yards in the air, got 280 yards total. Baylor earned 16 first downs to Texas' 15.

So it was all as close as the score indicates, and Lackey's toe was there to push the Longhorns ahead at the finish.

NOVEMBER 14, 1959

TCU FLOORS UNBEATEN LONGHORNS, 14–9

AUSTIN, Tex.—Behind by nine points on a day as cold as the cranberry business, Texas Christians' heavy-handed giants drove Texas into the ropes with a hot third quarter and then used one brilliant 56-yard scoring run by little Harry Moreland to yank the Longhorns out of the clouds, out of the ball game, out of the ranks of the unbeaten and untied, and out of all reach of a national championship.

The final score was 14–9, and the team that deserved to win did win. In blasting their way into a share of the conference lead, the defending champion Frogs held Texas to one first down and 21 yards in the game's final 30 minutes.

Moreland's lethal burst, which chilled the Longhorn partisans even more than the bitter 31-degree north wind, came with slightly less than eight minutes left in the game.

Faced up then to the cold facts of life, the nation's No. 2 team tried twice to salvage victory, record, and reputation, and couldn't even get out of its own end of the field.

The Frogs finished the game on the Texas 14-yard line.

In an ironical development, however, the winners lost and the losers won in one respect. In Dallas, 30 minutes after the Frogs had hammered Texas back to earth, Arkansas flattened Southern Methodist and drove into a triple-tie for the conference lead.

Since the Razorbacks are home free with a 5–1 lead and thus can do no worse than tie for the title, and since they beat TCU in an early season meeting, the Frogs were knocked out of the Cotton Bowl picture even as they won their biggest game of the season.

TCU now has a 3–1 record with Rice and SMU still to be faced. Texas has a 4–1 mark with the Texas Aggies still to be heard from. If both the Frogs and the Longhorns win the remainder of their games, the conference championship pie will be split three ways.

In such instances, a conference rule provides that the team that has gone the longest without a Cotton Bowl trip shall get the bid. That team would be Texas.

If the Longhorns should stumble against the Aggies, Arkansas would get the bid. But having lost to Arkansas, TCU cannot return to the New Year's Day extravaganza it has dominated the last four years.

If that prospect bothered Abe Martin's veteran troops, they didn't show it. They let the Longhorns out of their own territory only twice, and they dominated proceedings except for one four-minute stretch during which the losers scored all their points.

David Kristynik, a fireball guard, sent the Longhorns two points ahead with 16 seconds left in the first quarter when he blocked Larry Terrell's kick and the ball bounced out of the TCU end zone for a safety.

The Longhorns then took TCU's free kick and returned the ball to the Frog 45.

From there, with James Saxton directing and Mike Dowdle ramming with the ball on the last five plays, they punched for a touchdown in eight plays.

Dowdle blasted the last 2 yards, and Bobby Lackey kicked the extra point. The clock showed 11:40 remaining to play in the half, and it looked like the Longhorns' day.

But looks were deceiving. Frog muscle—and there are gobs of it—had yet to take its toll.

And Moreland had yet to run.

Fort Worth's favorite son, a 168-pounder who is as dangerous as a switchblade knife, blinked the touchdown button just after the Longhorns had thrown back one TCU thrust. Darrell Royal's hard-pressed troops, by now facing the icy, fourth-quarter wind, still led by a 9–7 margin.

The Longhorns stopped the Frogs and gained possession on their own 20, and four plays later, Jack Collins punted to TCU's 40-yard line.

Marshall Harris squirmed to the 44 on the first play and then Donald George called Moreland's number.

The scatback crossed over from left half and darted inside right end as Jack Spikes blocked out the defensive end and Paul Peebles and Harris pushed aside the tackle. The hole was there and Moreland found it, escorted by Roy Lee Rambo.

Longhorns snapped at his heels, and Moreland couldn't find room until Mike Cotton challenged him at about the Texas 45. Cotton got an arm on Moreland and jarred him, then fell off.

Hairbreadth Harry stumbled, regained his balance, darted off to the left, and turned on his famed sprinter's speed.

Rene Ramirez came over, trying to head him off, but Jimmy Gilmore came out of nowhere to screen Ramirez out of the play, and Moreland romped jubilantly into the end zone with the touchdown that killed the Longhorns and their eight-game winning streak.

Moreland made it look so easy that for a second, the 43,000 paying guests just looked on in wonder, watching Harry run, and then as he hit the end zone and leaped high in ecstasy, the TCU patriots made their presence known.

Here was a team that was left for dead in early October suddenly grown back to full size, playing as September headlines had insisted they would play all along.

Moreland's electrifying dash over a turf still marked by sleet was the difference on the scoreboard.

But the play that really brought TCU back to life and changed the course of the game came early in the third quarter. TCU had taken the second-half kickoff and had been stopped. Gilmore punted dead at Texas' 29-yard line, and the Longhorns, the wind at their backs, were ready to move.

But on the play, tackle Dick Jones roughed the kicker, the ball was brought back, and Texas penalized 15 yards.

Given a new chance at midfield, TCU drove to the Longhorn 18 as battering Jack Spikes pounded away like the All-American fullback he is. But then Marshall Harris fumbled when hit hard by Mike Dowdle, and Cotton recovered on the Texas 13.

The aroused Frogs stopped the Longhorns cold and forced a punt, and Harris returned the kick 8 yards to the Texas 48. From there, in seven plays, Larry Dawson hurried the Frogs to the payoff.

First he threw 13 yards to Paul Peebles, then handed to Marvin Lasater, and the Frog veteran ran 11 yards. Spikes hammered into the middle but was stopped and sent a lateral back to Dawson, and the Frog signal caller ran on to the 20. Spikes punched to the 18.

Now came the crusher. Dawson sent Spikes into the middle, then faked a jump pass. As the Longhorns closed in, he stepped back and threw to Harris, wide open in the right flat. Bart Shirley finally tackled the flying Frog on the 5.

It took two plays from there, Spikes driving to the 4 and then Lasater, running the same pattern that Moreland was later to break free on, whirling over for the touchdown.

R. E. Dodson kicked the extra point, and the Frogs were back in the game. Dodson also added the extra point after Moreland had won the game. The Frog with the gold toe now has kicked 13 in a row this year.

They had ample defensive opportunities of course; TCU controlled the ball, running 70 plays to Texas' 46. The Frogs' magnificent defenders, paced by Arvie Martin and giant Robert Lilly, gave ground grudgingly and sometimes not at all. Martin was in on 13 tackles, Lilly on 11, and the great Frog tackle Lilly also recovered a Texas fumble.

Other than its scoring drive, Texas' best effort was a brief push that carried to the Frog 11. It came just ahead of the Longhorns' nine-point outburst.

TCU, winning the toss, had kicked off, stopped Texas, and then driven behind the magnificent Spikes for 36 yards in 10 plays to the Texas 29 before missing a long field goal.

The Longhorns kicked back only 14 yards into the wind, and TCU was in good position at its own 46 when first a holding penalty and then a 10-yard loss on an attempted pass reversed early proceedings. Donald George punted, and Bart Shirley returned 11 yards to the Frog 44.

In three plays the Longhorns wound up losing a yard, but Shirley punted 38 yards dead at the TCU 7, and the Frogs didn't get out of the hole until they had surrendered nine points.

First the dangerous Moreland rammed at left guard and fumbled, and Milton Ham recovered to barely stave off disaster at the 8. George pushed to the 10, then went back to punt. Krystinik bombed through and blocked the ball solidly. It ricocheted out of the end zone and bounded on back 20 more yards.

That gave Texas two points and the eight-play, 45-yard march, with TCU's return kick giving them seven more. A double reverse that Ramirez carried for 12 yards started things, and a James Saxton scatter run for another 12 gave it momentum.

Saxton's run carried to the TCU 18, and then Dowdle took over. He plowed to the 11, to the 8, the 3, the 2, and finally into the end zone.

In the last half, as Texas was held to 7 yards rushing and 14 passing. While TCU was getting 196 yards and 14 points, the Longhorns got out only as far as their own 46-yard line.

Final statistics gave TCU 17 first downs and Texas 6, TCU 233 yards rushing and Texas 97, and the Frogs 263 yards in total offense and Texas 123.

Moreland, the boy who turned back the pages on Texas to another November and another biting Frog victory 18 years ago, led all the rushers with 73 yards in 6 carries. Spikes, never thrown for a loss, gained 71 on 19 tries. Harris got 48 yards on 9 bites into Longhorn trenches.

Dowdle got 32 yards on 11 tries for Texas, and Rene Ramirez got 29 yards on 6.

Jack Collins, a many-splendored hero for Texas all season, was held to 3 yards on 8 carries. It was no day for Collins, for Texas, or for the most ambitious Longhorn bid for a perfect season in 39 years. But when the opposition has a Moreland, a Spikes, and a blue-steel line, perfect seasons are hard to come by.

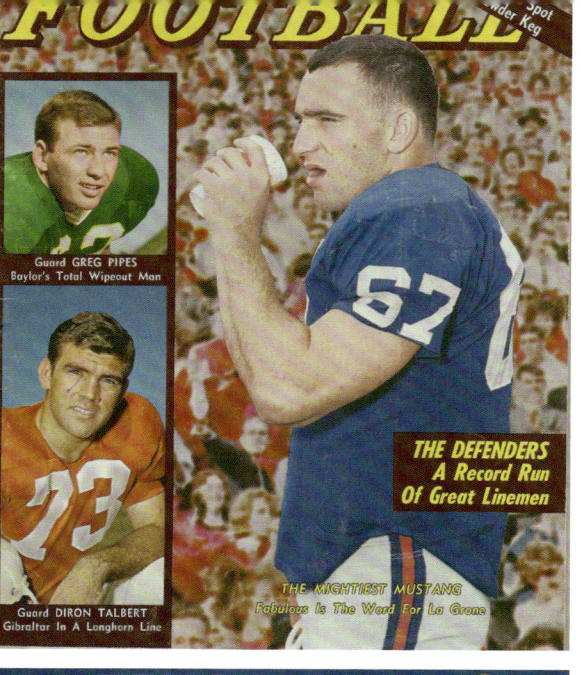
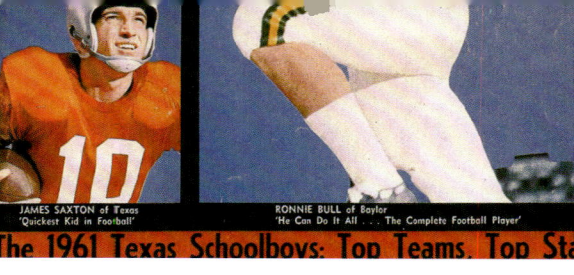

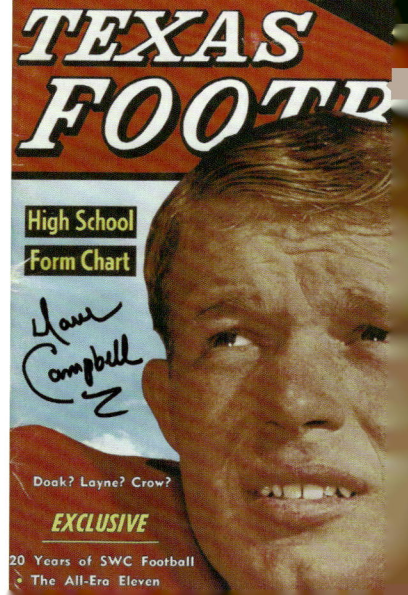

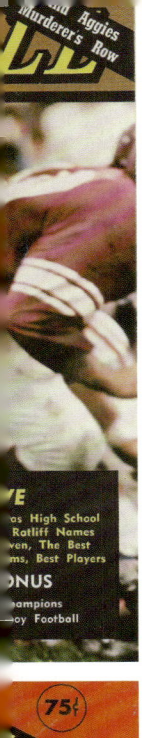

2
A ROYAL ARRIVAL, A JUNCTION BOY MAKES GOOD, AND THE "BIG SHOOTOUT" IN ARKANSAS
1960–1969

In 1953, when I started covering those early games, it was still seven years until I would start *Texas Football* magazine with the help of Hollis Biddle, Jim Montgomery, and Al Ward. Starting in 1960, we pasted up those early issues on my kitchen table.

For the cover photo of our first magazine, we selected Jack Collins, the great running back for the University of Texas. You can see his features really well because in those days, the helmets often didn't have face masks. That improvement in player equipment and safety was invented in 1955, but it wouldn't show up on our cover until the 1967 issue, which pictured Texas A&M's Mo Moorman, an outstanding offensive lineman who went on to play for the Kansas City Chiefs.

65

Courtesy of the *Waco Tribune-Herald*.

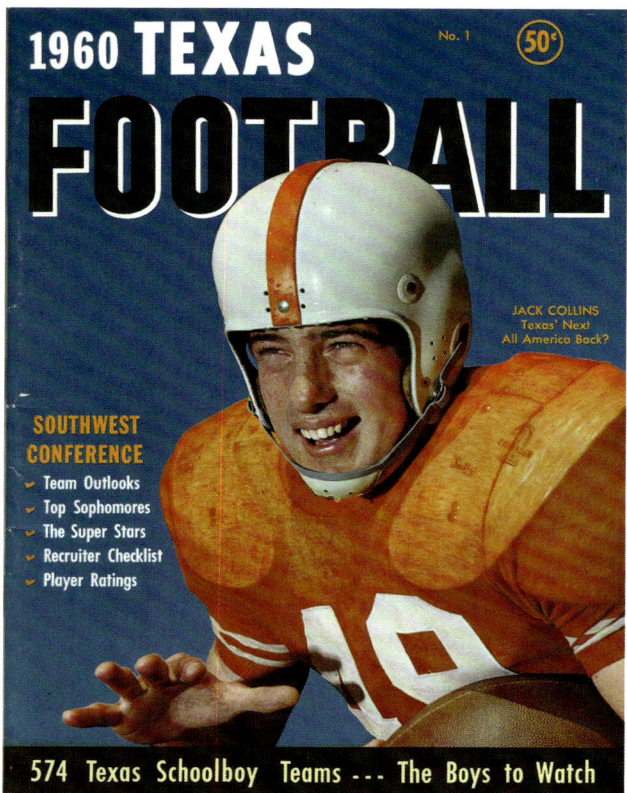

Courtesy of *Dave Campbell's Texas Football*.

NOVEMBER 13, 1960

PETTY'S TOE KNOCKS TCU FROM RACE

FORT WORTH, Tex.—Texas and TCU, two desperate characters in the Southwest Conference football race, fought in a manner fully befitting their predicaments here Saturday and produced the first 3–2 decision in league history. Texas, the team that got the three points, was saved by the bell at the finish.

A windswept TCU homecoming crowd of 40,000 saw the Longhorns' sure-toed Dan Petty make the 25-yard field goal that kicked the brawny old Frogs out of contention for 1960 championship honors.

Just as important to the harried, laboring orange, however, was the final sweep of the second hand on the scoreboard clock, which foreclosed on the Frogs just as they completed a long pass to the Texas 14-yard line. One more play might have given the Frogs the field goal they needed to win and keep their title hopes alive. In such a game as this, no one would have bet they couldn't have made it.

Petty's field goal, his fifth in the last seven games without a miss, was just enough to deliver the Longhorns from the safety that went on the scoreboard when jitterbug James Saxton was tackled in his own end zone.

Petty kicked his three-pointer from the TCU 15-yard line with 3:53 left in the first quarter. Saxton went crashing to earth on the two-point play with 8:24 to go in the game. TCU end Milton Ham made the tackle as Saxton tried to run a double reverse.

Sandwiched between those two plays, and after, was a bitter battle for survival that saw Texas clearly win the first half but almost fumble away the game and its breath of life in the championship hunt in the final minutes.

James Saxton. Courtesy of University of Texas Athletics.

Future Dallas Cowboy stalwart Bob Lilly brought All-America honors to TCU in 1960. Courtesy of Texas Christian University Athletics.

The Longhorns bobbled twice in the last five minutes, and towering Guy Gibbs, TCU's man-mountain quarterback who was just another good sophomore here today, almost made the visitors pay for it. The clock showed 1:54 to go when the explosive Saxton (my, how that name keeps turning up in the big plays on Saturday!) let the ball get away for the last time. Dale Glasscock recovered on the TCU 25.

Gibbs passed once and missed, then tossed to Ham, and the Frogs' star receiver dropped the ball at the TCU 43. R. E. Dodson got only 2 yards on a draw play, and TCU was down to its last gasp. On fourth down, Gibbs threw a screen pass to Max Pierce, and the fullback wiggled to the 35, getting the first down by inches.

Gibbs threw again, and Saxton bounded forward for the apparent clinching interception, but offsetting personal fouls wiped out the play. Gibbs then found Billy Gault at the TCU 45 and hit Ham for 7 at the Texas 48. The Frogs were moving, but the clock was moving faster. Fewer than 30 seconds remained.

A long pass missed badly, but the ball hit the ground with one second left, stopping the clock. And the Frogs drew a penalty on the play.

On the final snap, Gibbs faded, shook off the rushers, and threw deep. Gault and four Longhorns went up for the ball at the Texas 14. Somehow, Gault came down with the ball, but the Longhorns came down with Gault. They stood there with him, surrounding him, propping him up and holding him, letting him go no farther than Custer went at the Little Big Horn.

And in stopping him, they stopped the Frogs for good.

Thus the Longhorns finally broke a Fort Worth jinx

that dated to 1954, when Texas also won by a single point, 35–34.

The raging Lilly, who stuck a big paw in everything he could reach (and he reached plenty), did the most to foil the best-laid Longhorn plans. Playing his best game of the season, he made nine solo tackles, had a hand in eight others, recovered two fumbles, and blocked a punt.

When the Longhorns were threatening at the TCU 11, it was Lilly who reached across and held Mike Cotten short of a first down, forcing the field goal bid. And early in the second quarter, with Texas at the TCU 18, it was Lilly who crashed in to start fullback John Cook spinning toward a 4-yard loss.

Lilly got strong help from fellow tackles Bobby Plummer and Ted Crenwelge, as coach Abe Martin managed to work all three into his first-team defensive line. Martin did it by using Crenwelge instead of a defensive fullback. Lynn Morrison and Milton Ham also came up with strong defensive efforts for TCU.

Texas' stand was sparked by Lee, Jim Moffett, Tommy Lucas, and Marvin Kubin in the line and by Cotten and Pat Culpepper in the backfield.

NOVEMBER 21, 1961
ON SECOND THOUGHT

History surely will mark down this season's TCU 11 as the most unpredictable of football teams. The Frogs lack great talent, but when properly aroused, they play like champions. They proved that against Kansas, against Ohio State, and again last Saturday when they beat the nation's No. 1 college team in its own back pasture.

Those have been the sublime moments. Yet at other times, the Frogs have looked like two cents. They failed to get inside Texas Tech's 40-yard line all night, they fumbled and bumbled around against Baylor, and they were badly cuffed by Arkansas.

"I'm the publicity man and should be as close to the team as anyone," declared Jim Brock Saturday night when a few witnesses of that 6–0 Memorial Stadium struggle had gathered to review the details with Texas coach Darrell Royal.

"Every week," Brock said, "I participate in a score-guessing contest that they have there in Fort Worth. I'm on the panel that's supposed to pick the winners. I've been wrong eight straight weeks on TCU. You can look it up."

Brock was not the only one wrong on the Frogs last week. A number of people thought they might make a good game of it against Texas; few thought they could win. They didn't have the speed or defense, everyone agreed.

Abe Martin had done his best to get the team ready. Indeed, it is the feeling here that Abe had been pointing his Frogs toward Texas for three weeks. By midweek he could sense that the Frogs would make a massive effort. "It can be done in '61" was the battle cry on campus, and before the game, Abe reminded his pupils, "It's downright disgraceful for a TCU team to be an underdog by 22½ points. I don't care if they are No. 1."

But when Abe was encountered an hour before kickoff, resting with two assistants at the south end of the playing field, he said he had no great hopes. And he meant it.

He said his team would have to get five Texas fumbles to have a chance, and when a Houston writer reminded him that Jess Neely had said three weeks earlier that Texas wouldn't lose a game, Abe replied, "I've said that all along."

The Frogs went out to warm up, and they weren't impressive. They didn't look as big as in the past, and much of the time they seemed disinterested—"Kind of disorganized, just standing around looking at Texas," said one Austin observer.

When that statement was brought up after the game, Royal glumly observed, "Well, they go about things a little different than we do . . . like winning."

But a victory didn't seem to be in the cards for TCU in the early moments. Sonny Gibbs tried a long pass on the first play and Texas intercepted, and a press box witness said, "Abe's going for broke all the way, isn't he?" Maybe that should have been a tip-off. But the real one was yet to come.

On the first Texas play, scatter-legged James Saxton broke wide at right end and romped 16 yards, and three plays later he went into the right flat, caught a pass from Mike Cotten, and almost went all the way. He broke two tackles and fled down the sideline before encountering halfback Donny Smith, the last man who had a chance to get him, at the TCU 18. He cut back as only Saxton can, but somehow Smith tripped him up.

"That guy made a heckuva play," Royal said later. "You put a man in that position against Saxton, and he's got a real job. That was a real big play."

It became apparent just how big a play it was as the game wore on, because in trying to get up, Saxton ran head-on into tackle Bobby Plummer's thigh. He went to the ground, knocked senseless.

Texas had 11 offensive possessions, and Saxton was on the field at least part of the time for 9 of them. But he really wasn't the Saxton of old. He ran well and almost squirted free a couple times, but he wasn't quite up to it.

During film review, Royal picked out Plummer as perhaps the Frogs' top defender. "He played a magnificent game, he and the tackles and linebackers," Royal said. But Plummer's big contribution, as freakish and unavoidable as it was, was his collision with Saxton. For with Saxton partially subdued and fullback Ray Poage out of the game entirely, the Longhorns were in trouble offensively.

That is Point 1 for those interested in the anatomy of an upset. The other points were provided by TCU.

To be sure, Texas made some mistakes. After viewing the film, Royal said the team simply broke down on its goal-line execution. But certainly TCU deserves full credit for helping that execution break down. The Frogs got the victory and deserved it, and they got it with (1) defense, (2) a perfectly executed trick play, and (3) effort.

Martin said before the game that it would require "150 percent effort to win." As guard Bill Phillips put it, the Frogs gave him 170.

Martin gave this example of what effort can do. In the third quarter, Saxton swung wide and appeared to be headed for a good gain, but reserve fullback Lloyd Mynatt nailed him with a fine open-field tackle.

"Mynatt hadn't made a play like that all year," Martin said. "He ain't that fast to catch Saxton. But he got him. . . . The kids just outdid themselves. They outhit 'em, outfought 'em. That's all."

DECEMBER 3, 1961

OWLS STEP OVER BEARS INTO BLUEBONNET: BLUME TRIGGERS VICTORY ASSAULT, 26–14, LITTLE SENIOR COPS SWC SCORING TITLE

WACO, Tex.—Quick and nimble Les (Butch) Blume was in full bloom here Saturday, and that was all Rice needed to defeat Baylor, 26–14, and nail down an invitation to the Bluebonnet Bowl.

Butch, playing a hot hand in his final regular-season game as an Owl, put 20 points on the scoreboard with his running and kicking—more than enough to give him the Southwest Conference scoring championship.

He needed only three points to wrap up that title and got them in less than a quarter, kicking a 27-yard field goal with 2:06 left in the period. The kick gave the Owls (7–3) a lead they never lost en route to their fifth SWC win of the season and exacted full revenge for that last-minute heartbreak the Bears pinned on them a year ago in Waco.

Baylor won that 1960 game with a fast finish. The Owls, with memories as long as elephants, made sure they finished fast and first this time as 30,000 witnesses watched.

The moment of truth for Jess Neely's team came with 4:27 left in the third quarter, after Baylor had narrowed Rice's margin to 16–14 by driving 57 yards in four plays.

The Owls answered with a 61-yard scoring drive of their own that consumed 13 plays and pushed their advantage to 23–14.

Then after fighting off three Baylor thrusts that struck into Rice territory, the Owls late in the game drove 35 yards in four plays to the Baylor 16 and called upon Blume for the last time.

Blume's 33-yard field goal attempt sailed high enough but seemed to drift a trifle wide. Then it hit the goal post and bounced right—right through—and the Owls had 26 points.

For the afternoon, Blume had the two field goals, touchdown runs of 50 and 4 yards, and two successful point-afters in three attempts.

The two field goals made him Rice's all-time champion for a single season in that department, with six, and he led all rushers with 72 yards on 10 carries.

The Bluebonnet Bowl selection committee, properly impressed, hurried an invitation for Neely and his Owls to meet Kansas in the December 16 Houston bowl game, and the Owls just as quickly accepted.

Gotham Bowl representative Bill Stein, watching the Baylor team that will meet Utah State in New York's Polo Grounds next Saturday, was naturally disappointed but not chagrined.

He liked what he saw of a Baylor offense that produced 264 yards and two touchdowns, plus a full-blown scoring threat that died with an interception after pushing to the Owls' 19-yard line.

Owl tackle Robert Johnston's climactic contribution came late in the game, when Jerry Candler broke away at left guard and ran 29 yards to the Baylor 22, setting up Blume's final field goal. Candler found his running room down the east sideline. Ronnie Bull, winding up a great career at Baylor, awaited him at the 25. Johnston came rushing up and plowed into Bull, and all three—blocker, defender, and runner—went down. Bull and Johnston also went out of the game, both bruised on the play.

Trull and Bull were Baylor's leading rushers, gaining 29 and 19 yards, respectively. But thanks to yardage lost on passing attempts, the Bears wound up with a net of only 25 yards rushing. Defensively the Bears got strong contributions from Butch Maples, Ken Hays, Buddy White, Herby Adkins, and Sonny Whorton. Maples and White were in on eight tackles, Adkins on seven.

Rice Owls bound for the Bluebonnet Bowl in 1961. Courtesy of Rice University Athletics.

All-Southwest Conference lineman Robert Johnston won a Rhodes Scholarship in 1961. Courtesy of Rice University Athletics.

Ronnie Bull, a standout at Baylor, went on to play for the Chicago Bears and the Philadelphia Eagles. Courtesy of Baylor University Athletics.

DECEMBER 10, 1961

BRUIN SLINGSHOTS PRODUCE 24–9 VICTORY OVER UTAH STATE GOLIATHS IN GOTHAM BOWL: RONNIE BULL NAMED MOST VALUABLE BACK

NEW YORK, N.Y.—Baylor cut the Men from the Mountain down to size here Saturday, capitalizing on fumble recoveries and its own smooth aerial game to upset 10th-ranked Utah State, 24–9, before a thoroughly chilled gathering of 15,123 fans in the first annual Gotham Bowl game.

Although the temperature read 36 degrees at kickoff, the Bears quickly warmed to their tasks, while the Aggies never really did.

The Bears grabbed the first of the five fumbles that Utah Staters were to lose and charged 45 yards in four plays for a touchdown the first time they got the ball.

Ronnie Bull, who had a big afternoon before the sparse Polo Grounds audience and was voted the game's most outstanding player, broke between left guard and tackle on a neatly executed trap play and ran the last 15 yards for the score.

Carl Choate kicked a 22-yard field goal before halftime, giving the Bears a 10–0 lead. Then after surrendering a field goal to the monsters from Logan, they wrapped up the game in the final 30 minutes with scoring drives of 21 and 83 yards.

Sophomore Don Trull, the best quarterback on the field, directed the Bears to two of their three touchdowns and scored the second one on a sneak of 2 yards. He also passed beautifully to Ted Plumb for the final score, the play covering 38 yards.

Choate was in his usual groove on the conversion attempts, running his streak of perfection to 26 for the season.

However, he missed a field goal early in the contest, a real rarity for him. But the fault was not all the kicker's. He was badly rushed, and the holder barely had time to get the ball to the ground before the big Utah Staters were upon him.

Utah State grabbed a Baylor fumble on the Bruin 48 early in the second half and in eight plays drove to the 19, where the Baylor defense stalled operations. So Jim Turner kicked a 36-yard field goal, putting the U-Aggies on the scoreboard for the first time.

Late in the game, when Ronnie Stanley tried a reckless pass from deep in his own territory, Bob Novotny intercepted and returned to the Baylor 16, and U-State scored from there in three plays. Bill Munson ran the last 4 yards, but a two-point conversion play was stopped a few feet short of success.

Stanley's ill-fated pass attempt ended in real disaster for the Bruin senior. Moving in to make the tackle on the interceptor, he suffered a double fracture of the right leg and was carried off the battle scene in an ambulance.

The victory actually was accomplished much easier than even the score indicates. The Baylor defense, which was supposed to be overpowered by Utah State's great power game, never let John Railston's undefeated legions inside the Baylor 35-yard line in the first half while the Bears were building up their 10–0 lead and in the second half held the visitors well in check except for three threats.

Meanwhile, the Bears, no doubt plagued by frostbitten fingers, missed several golden chances. They drove to the Utah State 6 before falling back late in the first quarter and to the 23 late in the game before being tossed back again.

The Bears also had one beautiful scoring pass, Bobby Ply to James Ingram for 45 yards, rubbed out because of a penalty and once dropped a touchdown pass.

Very likely the team also lost a touchdown on a freak fumble on the last play of the first half. Ronnie Bull caught a screen pass from Trull after a fake field goal. He was hit hard twice after running about 5 yards. But he managed to keep his feet, maneuvered into the open, cut to his left, and appeared long gone. But running in the clear, with no Utah Staters near him, he somehow lost possession of the ball at about the Aggie 20 and had to scramble to recover.

As you can see, it was ragged at times, and the muffed opportunities were many, but the performance overall was a highly gratifying one for the Bears, who went into the game carrying a 5–5 record and were generally scorned by all the handicappers.

They came out of the contest having scored more points than anyone this season on Utah State, which boasted the nation's second-ranking defense. And at the same time, they held the nation's highest-scoring team to its lowest total in 11 games.

The Bears held Utah State to 10 first downs, 153 yards rushing, and just 41 yards passing. The Aggies could complete but 3 of 14 passes, or the same number they also completed to Baylor defenders. Bill Hicks, Ronnie Goodwin, and guard Robert Mankin picked off the enemy passes, and Tommy Minter, Don Adams, Mankin, Stanley, and Bob Lane made the fumble recoveries that made it a big day for the Bears in their first appearance before a New York crowd.

Although Utah State's big tandem tackle combination of Merlin Olsen and Clark Miller often stopped Baylor footmen in their tracks, the Bears managed 113 rushing and 153 yards passing and 14 first downs. All that added up to Baylor's third bowl victory in history and Utah State's fourth straight postseason defeat.

Bull easily paced all the rushers, getting 61 yards on 13 carries. Quarterback Mel Montalbo emerged as the Aggies' leading ball carrier, getting 35 yards on 4 carries. Tom Larscheid, pride of the Utah State backfield and one of the nation's ranking scorers and rushers, could

Bobbie Ply quarterbacked for Baylor but switched to defensive back during his six seasons in the American Football League. Courtesy of Baylor University Athletics.

get but 25 yards on 11 tries as the Bears swarmed him under consistently.

Leaders in that surprisingly stout Baylor defensive performance were Hicks, Lane, Mankin, Herby Adkins, John Frongillo, Robert Burk, Ronnie Rogers, and Pete Nicklas.

Utah State had to play without one of its highly regarded tackles, Clyde Brock, who was kept out of the game upon the advice of the NCAA. Brock allegedly signed a pro contract with the Chicago Bears several days ago, making him ineligible for all NCAA competition.

Playing on the grounds where the New York

professional Titans play their home games, the Bears got the game's first big break and parlayed it into seven points.

Utah State won the toss after the television introductions, ran four plays, and fumbled. Ron Prince rammed into the line, was smashed hard by Hicks, and bobbled the ball forward, and Minter recovered on the U-State 45.

Ply wasted no time. He pitched out to Minter on the first play, and that speedster darted around right end nicely for 14 yards. Bull tried to go wide at the other side, but the Aggies tossed him back to the 35. On third down Plumb went deep for a pass, and Utah State's Jim Smith knocked him flat before the ball arrived. Pass interference was called at the Aggies' 15.

From there it was just one lovely trap play, Bull breaking away and running across standing up. Choate's kick made it 7–0 with fewer than four minutes played.

The Aggies fumbled the next kickoff but managed to recover by scrambling. However, they quickly had to punt when confronted with the aggressive Baylor defense, and after getting a first down on their next possession, they committed their second costly fumble. Bill Mattson bobbled, and Don Adams recovered on the Utah State 43.

Now Don Trull faked beautifully and passed 12 yards to Herb Harlan, then sent Bull on a double reverse around left end to the 9. It was a 14-yard run that almost went all the way. Trull sneaked to the 6 but then slipped down back on the 11 trying to roll out and pass, and on the fourth down, Choate went in and tried an unsuccessful field goal from the 24.

After a punt exchange, the Bears began from their own 37 and started moving again. Bull got away well on a draw play, survived two stiff challenges, and ran 13 yards to the Aggie 41. But then the Bears bogged down, and Corely punted high and well to the Utah State 3. Larscheid tried to field the ball and fumbled, and Lane recovered on the 5.

It was a wonderful opportunity, but the Utah Staters made the Bears earn everything they got, and all that they got was three points. Three plays gained not an inch, so on fourth down, Choate kicked high and true for his sixth field goal of the season, a new Baylor record in that department.

Late in the half, the Bears got another chance when Mankin alertly intercepted and returned 27 yards to the Aggie 41. On the first play, the Bears pulled what John Bridgers calls the "alumni play," a double handoff with a pitch back to Trull, and the passer threw long to Minter at about the U-State 15, but Tommy dropped it.

On fourth down, needing a yard, and with only 10 seconds showing on the clock, Choate went in apparently for a field goal effort. But instead, Trull straightened and passed to Bull, and that Bruin wonder boy got away from at least four tacklers and was going full blast at the 20 when he fumbled without being touched.

He trotted sheepishly off the field along with his mates for intermission while a drill team and the New York Sanitation Department band took over proceedings. The way the teams had been playing in sports, the presence of the bandsmen was appropriate.

Four plays deep into the second half, Whorton fumbled when knocked cold by guard Jim Smith. While the Bruin fullback was carried off the field, Utah State took over on the Baylor 48 and drove well in eight plays to the Baylor 19. Mattson's 9-yard run was the big one. But three plays gained only 2 yards, so on fourth down, Turner toed his field goal from the 26.

The Bears returned the kickoff to the 35. Ply passed quickly to Lane, who made a great catch at the Utah State 45. Then he rolled out, faked a short throw, and then threw deep to Ingram, who was well behind all defenders. It was an easy touchdown, but it didn't count because the Bears were offside at the start.

However, the setback was a temporary one. After Corley's punt had died on the enemy 15, the Aggies ran three plays and fumbled. Roger Leonard gave up the ball to Mankin on the 21. From there Baylor scored in five plays. Adams ran well to the 12, Bull to the 7, Kelly Roberts to the 2, and Trull sneaked across. The clock showed 1:25 to go in the third quarter.

Utah State's answer to that was a bruising march, its best of the day. Six plays moved the ball to the Baylor 24, but the seventh one was fatal. Prince fumbled when smacked hard by Adkins, and Stanley recovered on the 17.

Trull pushed the right buttons in short order from there. He passed to Bull to the 27, to Plumb to the 41, then to Bull on a screen pass that carried beautifully to the Utah State 40.

Bull swung wide for 2, then Trull faked and threw deep to Plumb, who caught the ball at the 8-yard line and stepped into the end zone.

Choate's kick, perfect for the 26th straight time, made it 24–3 with 9:50 left to go, and even Utah State recognized the inevitable.

But the Aggies managed to crowd onto the scoreboard in the remaining minutes. When Stanley's pass was intercepted by Novotny, Utah State had its best chance of the game at the Baylor 16. Montalbo rolled out and ran to the 5 on the first play, and Bull Munson drove across from the 2-yard line two plays later.

In the last frantic minutes, Utah State tried unsuccessfully to explore the air lanes. Hicks intercepted one pass and returned to the Utah State 38, and on the game's final play, Ronnie Goodwin went up and took away a throw from a receiver at the Aggie 49.

For the Bears it was a smashing climax to a big trip. They quickly scattered to the crowded sidewalks of New York to celebrate before flying home Sunday afternoon.

JANUARY 1, 1962

INSPIRED LONGHORNS SURPRISE MISSISSIPPI IN COTTON BOWL: UT INTERCEPTIONS DUMP REBELS, 12–7

DALLAS, Tex.—The quick and eager Texas Longhorns, rising majestically to the occasion, welcomed in a bright and shiny new year with touchdowns and pass interceptions Monday and packaged them all into a joyous Cotton Bowl surprise, a 12–7 victory over Ole Miss.

A gay holiday crowd of 75,504, all the big concrete structure will hold, saw Texas uphold its own vast reputation and that of the Southwest Conference in a rousing, exciting battle that left the audience limp at the finish.

Playing in perfect football weather, crisp and crystal clear, the Longhorns jumped to a two-touchdown lead in the first 30 minutes, then brought their defensive muscle into play, fighting off the desperate closing efforts of the mighty men from delta country.

Texas came into this 26th annual classic a three-and-a-half-point underdog, and when the teams lined up for the opening kickoff, the odds looked all too true.

Ole Miss was the bigger team by 17 pounds per man. And as it developed, the Rebels were all they were supposed to be from tackle to tackle, and they were supposed to be mighty good. At first glance, this looked like a battle of men against boys. Yet the boys won, and there was nothing freakish or tainted about their victory. They carried the fight to the enemy, played smart and alert football, and kept turning the pressure on. Surprisingly, it was Ole Miss that cracked.

Texas did it mainly by intercepting five (that's right, five) passes, by cashing in on most of its own big chances, and finally by stopping Johnny Vaught's heavyweights in the game's last great moment of truth.

Bob Moses. Courtesy of University of Texas Athletics.

That came in the fourth quarter with just a bit over six minutes to play. Ole Miss, trailing by only five, had moved in four plays from its own 45 to the Texas 31.

On first down, the tricky Rebel sharpshooter Glynn Griffing passed for 6 yards to Louis Guy, although he was almost rushed off his feet before he could get the ball away. Then the junior quarterback rolled left and ran to the Longhorn 23, still 2 yards short of a first down. Griffing then tried to cross up Texas by throwing deep. But Longhorn defender Duke Carlisle hit receiver Woody Dabbs so hard at the 10-yard line that he couldn't hold the pass.

So it was fourth down with the game hanging in the balance. Griffing took the snap and sprinted right, hoping either to throw or skirt the Longhorn flank for the first down.

But suddenly there was no open country there, just Longhorns. George Brucks and Bob Moses crashed in upon him, spilling him before he could throw, and Texas took over on its own 24. Ole Miss never got out of its own territory again.

It was the final big play in an afternoon of big plays leading to Texas' first bowl victory in nine years—and Ole Miss's first bowl defeat since 1955. The Rebels had won five straight postseason adventures since losing that '55 test to Navy in New Orleans, and one of those victories was a 39–7 rout of Texas in the 1958 Sugar Bowl.

Texas moved 34 yards in seven plays late in the opening quarter for its first touchdown and 72 yards in nine plays for its final score in the second period.

Slick James Saxton, who bedeviled the Rebels all afternoon but never quite got away, scored the first one, nudging the ball across the Ole Miss goal from less than a foot away.

A hero of equal stature, Jack Collins, snared Mike Cotten's pass and fled 24 yards with it to cap the second drive. Collins cut across the middle and took the toss, got a clearing block by soph end Charles Talbert, and escaped down the sidelines for six points.

One of those Ole Miss giants, raging tackle Jimmy Dunaway, blocked Eldon Moritz's conversion attempt after the first score, and Collins was stopped a yard short on a two-point try after the second.

Disorganized and discouraged offensively after giving up five interceptions, Ole Miss finally got its house in order and bombed 86 yards in eight plays for its touchdown, which came with 3:35 remaining in the third quarter.

Wes Sullivan kicked the extra point to make it 12–7 and Ole Miss's game to win if they could maintain their momentum. They couldn't, although in the closing moments, Griffing gave Longhorn partisans a bigger headache than the refreshments they'd consumed in ringing in the new year.

Griffing completed 12 of 29 passes for 163 yards and rushed for another 45 while outshining his more heralded running mate, Doug Elmore. But both of them had to bow to Texas' gritty old pro, Iron Mike Cotten, who directed the Longhorns every step of the way offensively and was voted the game's outstanding back. Longhorn end Bob Moses, the hero of that last big stand

Ray Poage tries to elude a tackler. Courtesy of University of Texas Athletics.

and a lot of others, was voted the game's outstanding lineman.

Appropriately, Texas' first touchdown drive was ignited by an interception, the second of four the Rebels threw in the first half. But it was the last of those four that probably hurt most of all. It came just after Texas had scored to go up 12–0 and after Griffing had spurred the Rebels 70 yards in five plays to the Longhorn 7-yard line.

With 55 seconds left in the half, Griffing tried for a quick strike, but his pass was tipped off course by Johnny Treadwell and grabbed by an alert Jerry Cook at the Texas 2.

Mark down Cook as another blue-ribbon Longhorn hero. That one glorious bit of goaltending would have qualified him, but he also intercepted two other Ole Miss throws.

Just about everything happened to the Rebels in that first half, and almost all of it was bad. They fumbled on their own 29 on the second play of the game, surrendered four interceptions, committed three costly penalties, and dropped an important pass.

That sounds like they were ragged in their execution, and they were, but as they were quick to note when the combat had ended, the fiery-eyed Longhorn aggressiveness had a lot to do with it.

Texas stopped Ole Miss's running game cold, except for a few sprint-out run-pass options, and managed to put good pressure on the passer. The Longhorns got an added break when the Rebels' starting fullback, Buck Randall, suffered a concussion in the second quarter.

That left Vaught without his top two fullbacks (All-American Billy Ray Adams was hurt in an auto wreck several weeks ago and did not make the Cotton Bowl trip), and he was unable to replace them adequately. Ole Miss wound up gaining 127 yards rushing and 192 passing.

Other than their two touchdowns, the Longhorns produced three other threats, reaching the Rebel 8-, 26-, and 30-yard lines before giving up the ball. A pass

Eddie Padgett (74) and Pat Culpepper (31) close in on an opposing quarterback. Courtesy of University of Texas Athletics.

interception, one of three by Ole Miss, snuffed out the Longhorns' only second-half threat at the 8.

Ole Miss had drives that reached the Texas 7, 23, and 36 (twice) without producing points.

Texas gained most of its yardage outside the Rebel flanks, mostly by using the powerful runs of swift fullback Ray Poage or the artful scampers of Saxton, who was set often as a receiver in the flat.

Poage led Texas in rushing with 54 yards, while Cotten ran for 43 (reduced to 25 by losses on pass plays) and Saxton 22.

Cotten completed 6 of 13 passes for 90 yards despite going 0-for-6 in the second half.

The Longhorns found out early that the Rebel defense was tough. Ed Padgett covered a fumble on the second play of the game at the Ole Miss 26, but Texas lost 7 yards in three plays, and Moritz's field goal try was partially blocked.

The Longhorns failed to cash in when Cook ended the Rebels' next drive with the first of his three interceptions, but they soon got another chance when Tommy Ford intercepted Griffing at the Ole Miss 34 and finally made the Rebels pay. Pat Culpepper circled right end with a Cotten pitchout for 12 yards, and Poage, going the other way, dashed for 11. Poage came right back on the same play for 6 more yards to the 5, and then David Russell got away on a reverse and almost scored before Elmore knocked him out of bounds a foot short of the goal. Cotten was stymied on a sneak but handed to Saxton on the next play for the opening score.

Texas got another big chance a moment later when Culpepper intercepted Griffing at the Ole Miss 41. But Collins fumbled on a hard hit by Richard Ross, and the Rebels' Jerry Brown recovered at the 32.

Texas' second touchdown thrust was touched off by Cotten's swing passes to Saxton, leading to a first down at the Longhorn 39. Then Cotten faked a pitchout, circled right end, cut back, and scampered down to the Ole Miss 36. Another swing pass, this one to Ford, gained 12, and two plays later, Cotten hit the jackpot, finding Collins crossing for the 25-yard touchdown and a 12–0 lead.

OCTOBER 14, 1962

TEXAS EDGES OKIES: FUMBLES PAVE WAY TO LONGHORN WIN

JIM MONTGOMERY

DALLAS, Tex.—Hectic, heart-wrecking football returned to the storied Texas-Oklahoma series Saturday in an overcrowded Cotton Bowl with the boot-tough Longhorn defense defeating the Sooners, 9–6.

It was a nerve shredder for 60 minutes and found the luckless underdog Okies carrying the warfare to their vaunted enemies, smothering the Steer attack and precipitating an 80-man mob brawl in the closing seconds.

It was also far removed from the lopsided Longhorn victories of the past two years.

Texas' winning touchdown came via a freakish second-period play in which a fumbled Oklahoma pitchout bounced into the Sooner end zone, where senior center Perry McWilliams covered it for six points.

Prior to that, the suicidally inclined Sooners had assisted Texas to a field goal by Tony Crosby through another fumble to leave a taint on every point scored by the Longhorns, ranked first nationally before the game.

All the scoring came in the second quarter, Oklahoma notching its touchdown through a sophomore passing combination that sucked in 73 yards in two win-quick strikes. The last one was for 34 yards, Ronald Fletcher throwing in the end zone to Lance Rentzel.

That left it 9–6 at halftime, and the rest of the action consisted mostly of Oklahoma sniping at the Texas goal, helped somewhat by the briar-patch Steer defense.

The Oklahomans, a dedicated team this day in the steamy Fair Park saucer, twice forged into Texas territory in the second half—both times in the third quarter.

One thrust, aided mightily by a 15-yard fine against the Steers, reached a first-down situation on the Texas 27. The Steers, led by fantastic linebacker Pat Culpepper, took over on downs at their 18.

The second push ended when Texas, this time ramrodded by Tommy Ford and Johnny Treadwell, held and forced a punt from the Longhorn 38 late in the third period.

From that point until game's end, a span of more than 26 playing minutes, the Okies were unable to gouge so much as a first down from the brutal Steer defenders and amassed a grand net-total offense of exactly 6 yards as the Orange sandbagged everything that hinted of a Sooner attack.

And in the last pulse-pounding moment of truth, the Texas defense that had stayed in stodgy low gear all day cranked up and drove 38 yards from the Longhorn 38 to the Sooner 34—consuming the last three minutes and 40 seconds on the clock and dooming the valiant Sooners to their fifth straight defeat against Darrell Royal's troops.

It was a vicious, punishing battle down there on the bright-green Cotton Bowl floor, and the bitter feelings spouted into gang warfare at the end.

When order was restored, officials ruled a personal foul on both teams, Texas ran one more play, and the day was done.

And every walking coronary case who filed out of the stadium had to go away in awe of the ferocious Texas defense. Barring that single two-play lapse that permitted Oklahoma's touchdown, the Longhorns were impervious.

The Sooners got across midfield unassisted only three times—once on the scoring march and those two third-period efforts that Texas belted down, with damage only to onlookers' nerves.

More important, the Longhorn stoppers actually scored Texas' only touchdown—McWilliams's fumble recovery—and set up the field goal by grabbing another Sooner bobble at the Oklahoma 27.

Tommy Ford (24), off to the races against SML. Courtesy of University of Texas Athletics.

Johnny Treadwell. Courtesy of University of Texas Athletics.

So if the points came easily to Texas, the Longhorns in reality paid for them later with that marvelous defending Sooner fullback Joe Don Looney—ironically a Texas student two years ago—who was the only man who could gain through it.

Looney got 81 yards on 19 carries, top figures for the game. The Steers, in a way, got back 47 of those yards by throwing Oklahoma backs for losses.

Ray Poage was the leading runner for Texas, but the Sooners above all else were keyed to stop the *Saturday Evening Post* cover boy and did so. Poage wound up with 66 yards on 18 tries.

Ford got that last Longhorn victory-cinching drive under way with an 18-yard burst out to the 43, and he bucked for 4 yards on a big third and 2 play a moment later to keep the Steers rolling. Ford garnered 55 yards in 11 tries.

In the superlative Texas defense, recognition must begin with the raging Culpepper—who bagged nine unassisted tackles—and continue on through Treadwell, Tommy Lucas, Ken Ferguson, David and Perry McWilliams, George Brucks, Staley Faulkner, and Ford again, who twice blasted Sooner pass receivers loose from priceless footballs.

OCTOBER 28, 1962

AGGIES' LATE FIELD GOALS SPOIL BAYLOR'S HOMECOMING, 6-3: CLARK'S TOE KILLS BEAR TITLE HOPES

The Texas Aggies waited until the last 36 seconds at Baylor Stadium Saturday night and then kicked and shocked the dismayed Bruins through a trapdoor into football's never, never land.

Big Mike Clark, an obscure tight end who enters the game only when field goals are wanted, entered twice in the fourth quarter and kicked the Bears into a 6–3 defeat as an audience of 35,000 watched with highly mixed emotions.

The A&M Cadets loved it. But Baylor's old grads, back for a homecoming that had been exciting and enjoyable for three quarters, could hardly believe their eyes.

Always, it seemed, the Bears were about to zoom off on a runaway victory. Yet in the clutch moments, the Aggies held them, and then in a frantic, driving finish, they beat them.

Clark pumped his first field goal onto the scoreboard with 4:52 remaining in the game, matching a 23-yard three-pointer Carl Choate had kicked for Baylor the first time the Bears got their hands on the ball.

Then after the Bears had twice grappled for a breakthrough and missed, the Cadets struck once more. They flashed 44 yards on just one play—a Jim Keller pass to George Hargett—and three plays later, from the Bruin 32, Clark swung his foot again.

Clark's kicks were the decisive plays, but two passes unlocked the door. The first went from Keller to Ken Kipp and gained 17 yards to the Baylor 18. The second one, of course, was the 44-yarder to Hargett.

Those were the only passes the Aggies completed all night.

Baylor completed 14 passes for 158 yards, and in general, the Bruin attack made the Aggie offense appear plodding in comparison—except where it counted most.

Only on two pass plays, and one pass interference penalty that netted 30 yards, did the Aggies manage a long gain as the Bears played their best defensive game of the season. But the Aggies, it developed, had their kicks coming, and they made the most of them and sent the Bears tumbling to their second conference defeat in three games.

The Bears did everything but move across the Aggie goal line in the first half, and although the Cadets managed one menacing drive themselves, it was a half that clearly belonged to the swifter, better-armed Bruins.

Trull stoked up the Baylor offense for the first time from the Bruin 37. On the drive's second play, Trull faded quickly and fired to Goodwin in the left flat. The Baylor halfback reached slightly behind him, snared the ball at about neck high, and started running. Five yards downfield he cut to his right and picked up a convoy of blockers as he sprinted to the east sideline, and then he was in the clear.

He outmaneuvered a couple of Aggies who cut across trying to head him off, but Keller finally got him at the Aggie 14. It was a 44-yard gain. Now the yardage came tough and in small chunks. Dalton Hoffman got 4 and Don Adams 3, and Hoffman on third down got only a yard as the mass met him at left guard. So on fourth down, Choate took aim from the Aggie 13 and sent the field goal soaring through the goal posts. The clock showed 8:49 in the first quarter.

The Aggies counterpunched all the way to the Bruin 17 when they got possession, but at the 17, on first down, A&M quarterback Jim Willenborg tried a pitchout to Jim Linnstaedter. The Bears were waiting for it. A couple of them piled into the Aggie halfback; he fumbled back on the 21, and Butch Maples recovered.

Don Trull, Baylor quarterback. Courtesy of Baylor University Athletics.

From that point, the game settled into a pattern, with the Bears frequently marching deep into Cadet territory and the Aggie offense not doing much of anything. But although the Bears dominated play, they did not dominate the scoreboard, which remained 3–0 well into the second half.

Late in the third period, the Bears maneuvered deep into Aggieland one more time, this time earning a first down at the A&M 29. At this point, it seemed only a matter of time. The Bears, battering continually at the door, appeared certain to break through sooner or later.

But now Aggies started playing that defense well. They tossed Elkins for a 2-yard loss. Trull fired to Elkins for 7, but his third-down aerial fell incomplete. On fourth down, with 6 yards needed, Choate tried for three points of insurance. His kick veered low and to the left.

The Cadets growled back, painstakingly grinding out two first downs with their power game, but the Bears stopped them at the Aggie 44, and Keller punted. Elkins bobbled the kick briefly and then was snowed under at the Baylor 8.

Right there, it seemed, the tide turned.

The Bears—or rather, the many-splendored Goodwin—tugged out one first down to the 18, but a

Ronnie Goodwin. Courtesy of Baylor University Athletics.

passing flurry failed, and the Aggies got the ball at the Cadet 47.

Now they struck. Not like a gusher. More like a steady rain. Power, power, power for 9 yards, and on fourth down, needing 1, Willenborg swept the end for a first down to the Baylor 41.

Two more surges into the line gained 6, and then came a backbreaker. Keller fired to Ken Kipp. The receiver juggled the ball a moment, then captured it and stumbled to the 18—a 17-yard gain. The Aggie Corps now burst into full cry, and Willenborg sent them an octave higher with a sweep around the end to the 10. Mike Kohlman powered to the 6 for a first down.

At that point, aided by a 5-yard penalty, the Bears held them. On fourth down, Willenborg knelt at the Baylor 18, and Clark coolly tied the score.

Hank Foldberg coached the Aggies from 1962 to 1964. Courtesy of Texas A&M University Athletics.

Almost five minutes remained—easily enough time if the Bears could click. In fact, the Bears gained two possessions but punted away both times, the final one to the Aggie 41 with 1:09 left in the game.

That was enough time. On second down, Hargett sneaked free down the right side and Keller hit him, and he fled to the Baylor 15. For the reeling Bears, it was like a blow to the kidney.

Keller fired to Hargett again, and he made a diving catch—just inches out of the end zone.

It was a last-minute reprieve, and the Bears tried to make the most of it. First the Aggies drew a 5-yard penalty for taking too much time, and then Ronnie Rogers and James Moore tossed Keller back on the 25.

Third down and 36 seconds left. Aggie coach Hank Foldberg took no more chances. Johnny Erickson and Mike Clark came in, Erickson took the snap at the Baylor 32 and put down the ball, Clark swung his foot, and the ball soared high and long and true—and it was 6–3.

NOVEMBER 18, 1962

TEXAS DEFENSE STRANGLES FROGGIES, 14–0: LONGHORNS EYE UNBEATEN YEAR

FORT WORTH, Tex.—Heavy-handed Texas coldly and deliberately seized TCU around the windpipe here this chill and somber Saturday and squeezed and squeezed and squeezed. After 60 minutes of that, unbeaten Texas had 14 points, and the stone-cold dead Frogs had none.

It wasn't pretty and it wasn't quick and it wasn't a textbook example of wildly exciting spectator football, but it was as decisive as all get out. And it put Texas within one more gulp of an uncontested Southwest Conference championship, a trip to the Cotton Bowl and its first undefeated season since 1923.

All that should fall into place neatly this coming Thursday afternoon when the Longhorns turn their demon defenders loose on toothless Texas A&M.

An overcoat crowd of 42,393 saw the Longhorns twice use key penalty yardage to push across third- and fourth-down touchdowns against the fiercely resisting Frogs, who spent a lifetime on defense Saturday. The Longhorns, after being repulsed four times inside the Frog 20-yard line in the first half, drove 46 yards in 10 plays and 53 yards in 13 plays on successive possessions for the points that spelled the difference.

Leggy fullback Ray Poage scored both touchdowns, the first on a 1-yard squirt after a 19-yard pass interference call had put the Longhorns in business on the TCU

3 and the second on an 8-yard gallop after the Frogs had drawn an 8-yard penalty to their own 8-yard line for a personal foul.

The pass interference call, Abe Martin later said, was the turning point.

The Frogs weren't about to score themselves. Facing a wrathful Longhorn team still doing a slow burn over 1961's shames and wrongs at the hands of another TCU team, the Frogs were out of their own end of the field only once, and then only briefly.

That lone chance came on the game's first play, when hard-running Jerry Cook, who later ran well on both of Texas' touchdown drives, fumbled when hit hard by tackle Rudy Matthews at the Texas 33. Tommy Crutcher recovered, and the Frogs for a moment had visions of another tasty feast at the expense of orange and white.

Quarterback Sonny Gibbs used his runners to twice test the Longhorn trench and gained 6 yards. On third down, tall Sonny flipped a pass that should have been caught at the Texas 20, but Marvin Chipman dropped it. On fourth down, kicking specialist Marvin Macicek tried a field goal from the 33 that flew wide. No one dreamed it at the time, but the Frogs, offensively, were through right then and there.

Only once during the remainder of the game did they manage to push out as far as their own 40-yard line, and when that happened, the crushing Longhorn defense promptly chased the Frogs back into their own corner again.

TCU managed to get one first down in each of the first three quarters. Only one in each. In the final period, as the awful truth became apparent even to the old TCU grads back for homecoming, the Frogs gouged out four meaningless first downs, and by that time, Texas had a lot of fresh meat on the field.

As you can see, the teams could have played until Cotton Bowl weekend and TCU couldn't have scored. Blame most of it on that raging Longhorn defense, led by Pat Culpepper and Johnny Treadwell and Scott

Scott Appleton. Courtesy of University of Texas Athletics.

Appleton, and the rest on sloppy Frog execution and TCU's impossible field position.

The Frogs had the ball for 14 possessions. On 13 of them, they started their maneuvers from their own 1-, 3-, 6-, 9-, 10-, 13-, 16-, 19-, 20-, 20-, 20-, 22-, and 27-yard lines. The other possession, of course, was that fumble recovery on the Texas 33.

While TCU had miserable field position all afternoon, Texas had opportunity after opportunity to throw it all at the Frogs. The Frogs soaked up most of the blows and came back for more. Texas started drives from these advantageous points: the Texas 47, midfield, and the TCU 19-, 23-, 24-, 29-, 35-, 41-, 46-, and 47-yard lines. In other words, the Longhorns gained possession nine times at midfield or in TCU country as their defense kept the clamps on tight and their safety men repeatedly counterpunched well on long Frog punts.

But only twice could they score, and it took those penalty plays to unlock the door. On other occasions, the Longhorns pushed to the Frog 1-, 5-, 6-, 15-, and 19-yard lines before bogging down.

Robert Mangum played a tremendous game for TCU at linebacker. The closer Texas came to the TCU goal line, the more resolute the junior became, and when the Longhorns got to the goal line itself, he became TCU's bulletproof vest. To score, Texas had to send Poage to the side away from Mangum. On both of the Longhorns' scoring thrusts, it appeared that the Frogs had them stopped before the red danger light came on.

Although both coaches had fretted about injuries before the game, TCU was able to use both of Gibbs's favorite targets, Tommy Magoffin and Ben Nix, and Royal had Ernie Koy in the lineup for punting chores. Koy punted three times, and his kicks died or were killed at the TCU 10, 16-, and 6-yard lines.

Always, you see, the Frogs were in a hole, and the hole finally became a grave. Texas, remembering 1961, planned it that way.

In late winter and early spring of 1963, when those of us at Texas Football *were beginning to ponder what special features we would include in the big summer issue that year, Darrel Royal was already widely recognized as one of the SWC's "young Turks" (a terminology used by the late and famed Ken Tips). But his Longhorns had only won a single undisputed conference crown (1962) after getting pieces of the title in 1959 and '61.*

Even so, his personality, his original and colorful way of saying things, his rock-solid approach to the game, and the kind of program he had built at Texas in the six years he had been there marked him as a man sure to cast a long shadow in the SWC for years to come.

More and more in those days, most football roads led to Austin, to the camp of the coach often described by Austin American-Statesman *sports editor Lou Maysel as a man favored by "a lucky star."*

So the time was appropriate for Texas Football *to go backstage and answer for its readers the questions, What makes Royal run? What drives him?*

As it turned out, Al Ward's report was more appropriate than we could have imagined. Because a few weeks after that 1963 edition appeared, the Longhorns began the two-a-day workouts that would lead them to the summit of major college football.

That 1963 team became the first of Royal's UT collections to win the national championship. They would miss by the slim margin of an incomplete pass on a two-point conversion attempt against Arkansas of repeating their perfect season the following year.

Then starting in 1968, they began a reign that is still unique in SWC history.

By the time the Longhorns in 1973 had won their fifth undisputed SWC crown in a row—a march of success that included one national championship and a share of another, plus the share of still another conference title—observers were no longer asking themselves what made Royal run.

They just knew his drive and way of doing things had brought results the likes of which the conference had never seen before. But Ward's incisive report already had laid it out for them years earlier.

Years after serving in Harry Truman's administration as Secretary of State when all those post–World War II programs that led to the recovery and salvation of Western Europe were put into place, Dean Acheson wrote a book entitled Present at the Creation. *If Al Ward should ever want to write a similar book concerning* Texas Football, *he certainly would be qualified, because he was present at that particular creation.*

In the beginning, there were just four of us who had anything to do with the editorial product of Texas Football: *Al Ward, Jim Montgomery, Hollis Biddle, and myself. And certainly Ward was a key figure in the writing, the planning, and the headache solving.*

In that 1960 magazine, he personally wrote the stories having to do with Texas, SMU, TCU, and Texas Tech, and he also wrote the feature on Ronnie Bull in the Baylor section.

Shortly after production on the 1960 issue began, he left the sports staff of the Waco Tribune-Herald *to become public relations director of* the American Football League, which had just been launched by Lamar Hunt, Bud Adams, and their associates. But he continued to make massive contributions to the football magazine. One of the most notable ones concerned the motivations of Darrell Royal, of what made him run.

Later, Ward would leave the AFL to become information director of the Southwest Conference, then PR man for the Dallas Cowboys, general manager of the New York Jets, and finally assistant to the president of the NFL's American Football Conference, with offices in New York.

But even in the Big Apple, Ward never lost his abiding interest in Texas football and the SWC. Annually, I would get a call from him shortly after recruiting season had ended, wanting to know which schools had signed the good ones.

Most critics agreed that Texas Football emphasized quality from the start. Certainly Al Ward and his award-winning pen helped make that quality possible.

Dave Campbell

WHAT MAKES ROYAL RUN
AL WARD

"We had a place on the end of Hollis, a little house with a milk cow and chickens and a garden," Darrell Royal was saying. "It was right by Highway 62, and I used to stand in the front yard watching the cars and trucks go by with people jammed in and water jugs banging the sides. They were all heading the same way—west. I must have been 13 or 14 then."

Nights following the days, 13- or 14-year-old Darrell Royal of Hollis slept with a wet washrag over his face to filter the dust. These were the Dust Bowl days in Oklahoma, and the state was being stripped of its riches—strong west winds rifling the once fertile farmlands away, and the land's people bucking those same winds in a mass jalopy migration to California.

There were six children in the Royal family, and Darrell was the youngest of four sons. His father scratched out a living as a night watchman and by driving a gas truck for a farmer's co-op.

One day, just before Darrell's sophomore year at Hollis High, he joined his family in the move west and worked in the fruit fields.

Oklahoma and its virtually homeless people survived the dust and the Depression, but out of the experience came an entire state with an inferiority complex. The snide term "Okie!" became a national identification that scorched sensitive skin then and itches even now.

Even the young were touched. More than 25 years later, Darrell Royal remembered it all in a voice almost soft enough to hide the hurt.

"There's something pretty unjust about things when a whole group of people are made to feel inferior when all they're after is enough honest work to live on."

Darrell Royal is 39 years old today (in 1963) and is at the summit of an uncertain, unsentimental craft. If you inspect his rise and are exposed to the intense personality behind it, you cannot avoid wondering how much of his drive springs from those dusty days by Highway 62 and points west.

He is, first, a man of such hot pride that success is self-demanding inside him.

"I remember they used to hand out those 'commodity clothes,' blue overalls and shirts. Lots of families wore them, and I was always afraid that we would have to. Dad worked hard for his ten cents an hour, but I like to remember we bought our own clothes."

Royal at 39 still has a boyish attachment for any tangible that represents a personal accomplishment. He tells of an orange blanket the Texas "T Association" gave him.

"It was for an honorary membership, and they don't give many of those. It was an awful nice thing they did, and I tried to tell them what it meant.

"It means as much to me as the little football letter, a blocked white 'H,' I got in junior high. I took it everywhere. I'd get it all dirty, then go home and rub oatmeal on it to bring back the white. To me, it was never a little thing; it was pure gold."

If Royal now delights in the mementos and acclaim that surround him, he is also bothered by them.

"There's a lot of hero worship in football. I'd like to squash it down to an even level—not too much praise when we win and not so much

Coach Royal celebrates with his players. Courtesy of University of Texas Athletics.

criticism when we don't. We're not going to be up there forever, and I'd like to be thought of the same way at both levels."

There is also a high sensitivity in Royal, though he has learned to control most of it.

"When we were at Washington," an assistant remembers, "there was a clever columnist who liked to dig people. During the season, I never had to read him; I just checked to see how purple Darrell was each morning."

Royal once read every letter addressed to him, but some of the crank pieces so distressed him that the office now screens all mail.

This also saves time, for Royal frequently splits his days in seconds. He likes to arrive at an airport five minutes before flight time, seldom plays with a meal longer than 15 minutes, and his idea of perfect relaxation is 45 holes of golf followed by a marathon round of chess.

"He flips pages of a book," says a friend, "like there's a stopwatch on him."

In all things, the same competitive blood that made Royal an All-American quarterback at 155 pounds at Oklahoma is working full-spray. When any element of competition is at hand, he surrounds himself with enemies, possibly to warm his winning instincts.

"Darrell could love you like a brother," says an assistant, "but if your team plays us, he just loves you 51 weeks. The other seven days, I think he almost hates you. He calls it putting on a 'game face,' and it's a serious thing."

With their leader vibrating from every pore against the week's enemy, the players sense the feeling and take it up. And it is in the area of discipline and morale where Royal truly excels.

Discipline was installed in a sudden test that game a few weeks after Royal arrived in Texas. The squad of '57 was drastically shy of proven players, and the new coach was informed by telephone one afternoon that one of the key returnees was talking about quitting school. There was desperation in the assistant's voice as he asked, "What shall I tell him?"

"Tell him good-bye," snapped Royal, hanging up.

"Coach Royal has one set of rules," says Scott Appleton. "They're the same for a No. 1 fullback or a No. 6 guard, and they don't bend." Royal also rewards effort by any player; therefore, he gets it from most.

"A boy shows how much he wants to play in the spring, when it's tough, and during the two-a-days, when it's hot and tough. I don't count on the boy who waits till October, when it's cool and fun, then decides he wants to play. Maybe he's better than three guys ahead of him, but I know those three won't change their minds in the fourth quarter."

His approach to morale is strongly personal. He gets close to his captains and seniors, stays on top of the "feel" of his squad, and throws the door open to all players.

"Most everybody here," says a '63 senior, "has gone to him with personal problems."

"Morale is one of the biggest jobs a coach has, morale on his staff and his squad.

"I'll sacrifice a whole day of practice, and the execution that we'll lose, for the sake of morale."

Perhaps Royal's success with players comes from his obvious warmth for them. Walking out of the gym one day with a visitor, he stopped suddenly and pointed to a group of students across the campus.

"Some of our freshmen," he explained, smiling. "You can tell 'em, can't you? When they're walking with a group? You sure can." There was a proud excitement in his voice.

Says graduated guard Marvin Kubin, "When he talked to us before a game, he was like a man who was going to play himself. He's so sincere about what has to be done. I heard him three years and believed him."

"You can't kid a kid. If you're not honest with your players, you're kidding yourself."

Royal at 39 is still referred to as "Texas' boyish young coach." Perhaps his rapport with his players keeps him boyish and enhances his morale approach.

"A lot of coaches feel that a boy doesn't have to like you as long as he respects you. But if I had all the rest—respect, discipline, all that—and a boy left this school without a personal feeling for me, it would be an empty profession."

When Royal asks young men to give themselves to a football cause, it may be that the message penetrates because the speaker believes more strongly in the game than the average coach.

"When I enrolled at Oklahoma in 1946, I drove to Norman in a rented club coupe with a baby daughter and a young wife. Everything we owned was in that car, and there was lots of room left. Yes, I have a feeling about college football."

These are some of the feelings and thoughts and events that made Darrel Royal run. And win.

OCTOBER 12, 1963

BREATHLESS MUSTANG FINISH STUNS FOURTH-RATED NAVY, 32–28

DALLAS, Tex.—In a wild-eyed, throbbing thriller that left 37,000 fans limp, inspired Southern Methodist rushed from behind with some unbelievable offensive fireworks and blew down highly favored, unbeaten Navy, 32–28, in the Cotton Bowl Friday night.

It was a script no movie writer would dare submit, so bizarre were the back-and-forth, up-and-down surprises in the plot.

Finally ahead once more by four points with two minutes and five seconds to go, the Mustangs had to withstand one last Navy surge, engineered by a Houdini named Roger Staubach. The great Middie field general squeezed every ounce of drama out of the occasion, moving Navy from its own 40 to the SMU 8-yard line as time ran out.

The game's last two plays saw Staubach fire into the SMU end zone and battling Mustangs knock down the touchdown threats.

It was a game that defies description, a flashback to the old Doak Walker glory days, and in such a setting, before a howling mob that seldom sat, the Mustangs may have discovered a reasonable facsimile of the great Doaker—sophomore halfback John Roderick.

When all seemed lost, the jet-swift Roderick brought

the Mustangs back, and now it is a case of where they will stop. They didn't have enough defense tonight—but oh, that offense. And oh, that Roderick.

He is a recruit from the SMU track team and he has run a 9.4 100-yard dash, and he doesn't lose much of that in a football uniform. Navy couldn't catch him—couldn't even come close.

He scored two touchdowns and had a decisive hand in every SMU scoring drive while carrying the ball 11 times for a whopping 146 yards. And that was against the team that came into the game with the nation's third-best defense.

The moral of that story, of course, is that you can't stop what you can't catch.

At the finish, Navy had a blistering 462 yards in total offense and 24 first downs; SMU a more modest 290 yards and 11 first downs. But the Mustangs had 'em on points.

Darrell Royal, who will turn his Longhorns loose against top-ranked Oklahoma here Saturday, was among the witnesses, and he must have blanched at the liberty taken with the defenses on both sides.

Yet oddly enough, both teams came up with several outstanding defensive plays. But not many. It was an offensive show that not even the Lions and Cowboys are going to top here Sunday.

It finally boiled down to a contest between Staubach and Roderick, and while Staubach was unbelievable, Roderick beat him with his sheer blinding speed. Most of his runs came on quick pitchouts or delayed split-T options. The maneuvers usually sent him into a scattered field around the end, and that was all he asked.

However, Staubach caused more nervous breakdowns. Always he was getting trapped for huge yardage and always he was getting away as tortured Mustangs groaned in dismay. Before the final gun had sounded, he had rushed for 107 yards and passed for 128 and had almost driven coach Hayden Fry out of his mind.

The man is a marvel who has to be seen to be believed.

Hayden Fry coached the SMU Mustangs from 1962 to 1972. Courtesy of Southern Methodist University Athletics.

Oddly enough, the Mustangs trapped him and tossed him for a 13-yard loss on the game's first play. It decidedly was not a trend.

Navy, favored by two touchdowns, looked as if it might score a runaway, driving 80 yards for a field goal, then going 37 yards for a touchdown and a 10–0 lead with 2:49 remaining in the first quarter.

It was after the Middies had jumped into their 10–0 lead that SMU first flashed its blitzkrieg potential. Starting on the Pony 47, the Mustangs went 53 yards in four plays, Roderick igniting things with a 26-yard burst around the end. Mac White scored the touchdown on a heady 22-yard run that started as a pass and turned into a scamper up the middle.

Navy's answer: a 69-yard scorched-earth policy that saw Pat Donnelly break away at left tackle and romp 50 yards on the drive's first play. Sai got the score four plays later by diving over a piled-up mass at the 1-yard line. For variety, Staubach ran for the extra points.

Late in the half, the Mustangs gained possession at the Navy 29. The Ponies advanced to the 3 as the clock wound down, and finally, with five seconds left and the fans shouting "Hurry, hurry!" Thomas threw perfectly to Hillary for the score. The two-point conversion attempt failed.

That had seemed like a full 30 minutes of spectaculars, but as it developed, the audience hadn't seen anything yet.

Staubach set off a series of torpedoes midway through the third that quickly took Navy from its own 41 to the Mustang end zone. Staubach applied the finishing touches, firing to Markoff at the 17 and then to clever Ed Merino for the touchdown. Marlin's kick made it 25–13.

SMU retaliated in a way that took Navy's breath away. Roderick swung wide and ran 22 yards, then fumbled, and his buddy White recovered. White ran for 8 yards to the Navy 45, then faked the same play again and instead fed the ball to Roderick, and there he went—around left end, then angling across the middle and down the east sideline behind good blocking.

What a zip code that kid has!

A pass for two points failed, leaving the Mustangs trailing by six. But when Staubach, badly rushed by Ron Merrit, passed short into the left flat, Dave Corder intercepted and returned to the Navy 40, and the Mustangs were on their way.

Roderick did it again, turning a fourth-and-12 play into a 19-yard gain to the Navy 24. Then the harried Midshipmen piled on, the red flags flew, and the ball moved on to the Navy 13. Roderick carried to the 3, then punched over from the 2. Richey kicked the extra point that put the Ponies ahead for the first time, 26–25.

Navy had 19 minutes to come back—time enough for two or three comebacks, the way these two teams were going.

First, the Mustangs stopped the Middies, then they all but handed them the game, with Don Campbell fumbling when hit hard by Navy's great tackle Jim Freeman at the SMU 21. Four plays later, Marlin kicked a 20-yard field goal to put his team back ahead.

So—could SMU come back one last time? Boy, could they! On the first play, Thomas passed to Gannon for 24 yards to the Navy 46. Roderick took a pitchout and raced around end to the 23, moving like a streak. Then Thomas faded again, encountered great pressure, and threw a "waste pass." But Navy defender Ed Orr interfered flagrantly with Hillary, and the red flag fell at the Navy 1. Gannon drove in for the score, and there was pandemonium in the house.

Now it was a question of whether the Mustangs could hold them. They just did make it. On a big fourth-down play, Staubach got away and ran 16 yards to the Pony 43, then passed to the 25. A 15-yard penalty sent him all the way back to the 40, but he passed to Orr at the 28, then ran to the 13. A personal foul gave Navy one last chance at the Mustang 8.

But the final gun caught the Middies there firing blanks into the end zone. It was about time.

OCTOBER 22, 1963
ON SECOND THOUGHT

In Lubbock Saturday, it was "Beat Baylor Day," so proclaimed by the mayor of the town. And for 58 minutes Saturday night at rain-spattered Jones Stadium, it was just that.

But then the Bears came back, sensationally, and Monday morning, appearing before Baylor Bear Club members, John Bridgers was ready to proclaim another day—Don Trull Day.

It's getting to be a habit.

Every time the Bears have gone out to face an enemy this season, it's Don Trull Day. And when the postmortems are added up Monday, it's Don Trull Day again.

Saturday night against Tech, the Baylor bomber passed for 262 yards, hitting 19 of 32 passes. At least seven other shots, Bridgers declared, were dropped. If the catchers had been sure-fingered, Trull would have gone 26 for 32—"A pretty good percentage," the Baylor coach noted.

But he was ready to settle for the percentage Trull delivered, since it was the winning percentage, compiled

Tech's All-Southwest Conference quarterback, Tom Wilson (13), releases a pass. Courtesy of Texas Tech University Athletics.

for the most part under great pressure and under adverse weather conditions. "It had rained all day, and they don't have a field cover," Bridgers said. "The footing was good, but Trull complained about the ball being wet."

("What did the rain look like?" one Bear Club member, obviously a man with watering problems, asked enviously.)

ONE OF THE GREATEST EVER

Rain and all, the toothy aerial artist from Oklahoma City won the Bears another football game, and Bridgers Monday was ready to shout his own personal verdict from the rooftops: "This is the fourth straight week Trull has been great. He's proved he's one of the greatest college quarterbacks ever to play the game. I've never seen a quarterback have four games in a row as he's had."

After those four games, Trull now is running so far ahead of his record-breaking pace of 1962 that he's threatening to rewrite the NCAA's record book, to say nothing of the Southwest Conference and Baylor all-time marks.

"Don Trull Shoots for the Moon," read the heading on the weekly statistical release from the conference

Dave Parks, an All-American at Tech in 1963, was drafted at No. 1 in 1964 by the San Francisco 49ers. Courtesy of Texas Tech University Athletics.

Donny Anderson (44), future great for Green Bay and St. Louis, catching a pass for Tech. Courtesy of Texas Tech University Athletics.

office in Dallas Monday, and that was appropriate. While the Bears' one-man gang shoots for the moon, Baylor shoots for the equivalent. You know—"Our goal is the Cotton Bowl."

If this be the road to the Cotton Bowl, by necessity this year it led through Lubbock, and with six minutes to go Saturday night, the Bears were in a chughole. Texas Tech had a 17–9 lead, and momentum was on the side of the Red Raiders.

In such a situation, Bridgers knew where to find his meal ticket. He summoned the remarkable Trull to his side and told him, "Don, we'll have to go to our two-minute offense right now."

"You mean throw on every down, Coach?"

"Yes," Bridgers replied. "Unless it's third and 1."

SIMPLIFYING THE ISSUE

"So from then on," he continued for Bear Club members Monday, "Don didn't miss a pass. I guess," he said and chortled, "there wasn't anything to confuse the issue."

"On the first touchdown pass to James Ingram, Don's primary target was Lawrence Elkins, but he was covered. Our protection was good, and Don was able to hold on to the ball quite a while before throwing. Then the Tech defensive man covering Ingram gambled and lost. He dove for the ball and missed. Ingram got a clearing block from Dalton Hoffman on [Donny] Anderson and scored.

"We had a mix-up then on our pass for two points. We're going to have to work on that two-point play.

"On our last touchdown drive, Don hit five straight. I never saw a more perfect pass thrown than the one to Ingram for the winning touchdown. Ingram caught the ball and scored and then threw the ball about 50 feet in the air and jumped about 10 feet in the air himself. I jumped a few feet myself."

While the Baylor untouchable finds ways each week to rise to new heights, those who see him, and face him, are rapidly running out of adjectives.

Listen as the experts speak:

"He's all you want in a quarterback . . . all you want," said Houston coach Bill Yeoman.

"Because of Trull," said Frank Broyles of Arkansas, "Baylor is running more offense and doing it better than any team in the country."

Said Oregon State's Tommy Prothro, "We had practiced against the weaknesses shown by Baylor, but Trull kept changing things. . . . His check-off passes were terrific."

"Just fantastic," said Darrell Royal after watching Trull against Arkansas.

"He's the finest quarterback in the country. He does the best job in college football when it comes to tearing down your pass defense," said the latest coach to be burned, Texas Tech's J. T. King.

They haven't come right out and said yet that Don Trull is football's unstoppable man. That probably will come shortly.

NOVEMBER 10, 1963

TOP-RANKED LONGHORNS SPLATTER BAYLOR'S COTTON BOWL HOPES, 7–0

AUSTIN, Tex.—With 29 seconds remaining in the season's greatest showdown in the Southwest Conference, Baylor's incredible triggerman Don Trull faded from the Texas 19-yard line and threw deep—and 65,000 hearts stood still.

Swift Lawrence Elkins, the greatest receiver in the whole wide world, flashed into the Texas end zone, his rendezvous with the touchdown pass and immortality only a tick away.

The pass was there and Elkins was there—but so at the last possible instant was the Longhorns' Duke Carlisle. Carlisle, diving desperately, caught the pass, smote the Bears, and saved the long, hard afternoon for the Longhorns, enabling them to escape with a sweet 7–0 victory, their winning streak and their place at the very front of the nation's football parade intact.

Texas got all the points it needed by driving 45 yards in 10 plays in the third quarter. Spare fullback Tommy Stockton drove the final yard for the score after that thunderous little man, Tommy Ford, had set up a touchdown with a charge off-tackle to the Baylor 1-yard line.

Tony Crosby trotted out, his kicking foot covered only by a sock as usual, and kicked the extra point, the 23rd straight time he has done that this year. He has yet to miss.

Nobody in throbbing, sold-out Memorial Stadium thought those seven points would hold up. It seemed only a matter of time until Trull and Elkins would rearrange the scoreboard to suit themselves—and to suit all those green socks from Waco.

They fired and fired. They revamped the record book. They gave the top-ranked Longhorns and all their thousands of patrons a maddening case of heart palpitations. But never did they quite break through.

So at the finish, the Longhorns had their sixth straight victory over Baylor, and the Bears had been blanked for the first time in the hair-raising old series since 1949, and who would have thought it?

Of all the predictions made about this game of games, probably nobody settled on a 7–0 score. Certainly no one thought the Longhorns could win with a single touchdown. But at the finish, it was simply a new and nerve-wrecking chapter in an old story—too much Longhorn defense when the chips were down.

TOO MUCH CARLISLE

And if you want to settle it to one man, too much Carlisle.

Carlisle made the interception that saved the bacon, and he directed the Longhorns to their touchdown, and he ran well and even passed well in several clutch situations.

But don't narrow the field to just Carlisle. Don't

Lawrence Elkins, Baylor's great wide receiver, later played for the Houston Oilers. He was inducted into the Texas Sports Hall of Fame in 2010. Courtesy of Texas Sports Hall of Fame.

overlook the Longhorn dagger, Tommy Ford, and their Gibraltar on defense, the raging Scott Appleton.

Twenty-seven times . . . that's right, a whopping 27 times . . . Ford drove into the fiercely resisting Baylor defense, extracting 101 yards and doing the most to enable the Longhorns to play their favorite game—ball control.

So well did Texas play keep-away from Baylor that the Bears ran only six plays from scrimmage in the second quarter and only six more in the third quarter. Not once during that 30-minute span did the Bears get a first down, so well did Carlisle and Ford do their work offensively, and so well did Appleton and his fired-up mates perform when they were called upon to speak for the defense.

But in the game's other 30 minutes—the first quarter and the last—Trull and Elkins and the Bears argued their case extremely well. At the finish, nobody in the limp, hoarse stadium would dispute that point.

TWO NEW RECORDS

Thirty-nine times Trull threw and 19 times he connected for 204 yards in all, for two new marks in the Southwest Conference record book, for a whole head full of gray hairs on Darrell Royal's noggin.

Elkins grabbed 12 of the passes for 151 yards, and that gave him a new conference record too.

At the end of his afternoon of heroics, Trull owned the new Southwest Conference career pass completion record with 276, topping the mark set by SMU's Fred Benners by 10 a dozen years ago. He also took full possession of the career passing yardage record with 3,598 yards, surpassing Bobby Layne's old mark of 3,585 yards. And get this—Layne set his mark over a four-year period. Trull needed only the equivalent of two seasons.

Elkins's busy afternoon left him with 56 completions, 8 more than Arkansas' Jim Benton caught in setting the mark in 1937.

Baylor coach John Bridgers (seated, wearing cap) surrounded by his key players (left to right): James Ingram, Lawrence Elkins, Dalton Hoffman, Don Trull, and Ken Hodge. Courtesy of Baylor University Athletics.

With those two star-spangled faces making the most of the big plays, the Bears drove to the Texas 12-yard line the first time they got the ball, then boomed right back to the 20, and then faded into nothing until the fourth quarter, when they rolled to the Texas 32 and finally to the 19.

It was when the Bears got close and their No. 1 ranking was threatened that the Longhorns breathed fire, now rushing Trull hard, now making him miss, now slamming his receivers and dropping them in their tracks.

BEARS COULDN'T RUN

As expected, the Bears couldn't run. Their rushing game produced only a net of 6 yards after Trull's 21 yards in losses had been subtracted. The Longhorns punished the Baylor defense for 242 yards rushing, extracted another 60 passing, and thus won the total offensive battle, 302 yards to 210, and had 17 first downs to 13.

Even so, the Bruin defenders, led by stubborn Bobby Crenshaw, James Rust, Ronnie Rogers, and Bobby Maples, fought like cornered grizzlies. They halted the Longhorns short of a touchdown on their first possession for the first time in seven games. They stopped Texas' best first-half drive at the Bruin 5 and forced a field goal attempt, which Crosby missed.

They later forced them to punt again from the Baylor 31, they forced another futile field goal try from the 40, and they finally took the ball away from the Longhorns on a fumble after Texas had pushed to the Baylor 13 in the game's dying moments.

Stockton bobbled the ball at the 13 after the bounding Carlisle had swept around the Baylor right side for 24 yards, apparently icing down the decision for Texas. Only two minutes and four seconds remained when Carlisle got away, and with Texas on the Bruin 13, even the strongest of the Baylor believers began to lose heart.

But then the Longhorn fullback fumbled as he hit at right tackle, and Ken Hodge sucked up the ball. And there the Bears were, a minute and 53 seconds left, 83 yards to cover, and not a soul in the house ready to leave.

TRULL TO ELKINS

This had to be it—the game, the season, the Cotton Bowl. Texas started by jumping offsides. Then Trull did what he did best all afternoon—hit Elkins on the sidelines—and the Bears had maneuvering room at the Baylor 36.

Now Trull was rushed hard by Olen Underwood and Frank Bedrick, and his pass went awry. Again he was rushed, and as he faded, he slipped down on the wet, tricky turf at the Baylor 21. But here the Bears got a break. Well upfield lay a red flag. Texas was ruled guilty of a personal foul, and the Bears were given a first down at the Longhorn 42.

Now Trull tried to hit Elkins, but the pass missed, so he hurled quickly to his tight end, the sure-fingered Hodge. The Bears were on the Texas 31, and Memorial Stadium was a madhouse.

A minute and 11 seconds remained. To stop the clock, Trull straightened and fired the ball into the ground. Then he and the Bears regrouped, and on the next play, he fired to Elkins at the Texas 22. Again he quickly grounded the ball, stopping the clock with 50 seconds remaining.

For the Longhorns and all those who thrive on the "Hook 'em" yell, this was an eternity of torment. The Bears it seemed were not to be stopped—neither by the clock nor by Appleton nor by the other guys in the burnt-orange jerseys.

Now it was fourth down and a yard needed, and Dalton Hoffman drove furiously to the 19, keeping the Bears alive. Again, with 29 seconds left, Trull fired straight at his feet, stopping the clock.

So now, at long last, the moment of truth was at hand . . . Trull fading, Elkins roaming into the end zone. Trull firing, and Carlisle running and running as if his life depended on his steps and then intercepting.

VICTORY ROAR

The Longhorn cannon went off and a Longhorn victory roar split the heavens and Texas stalled out the last precious seconds, letting Carlisle take the snap and simply kneel down.

Earlier, much earlier, the Bears had started as if they intended to trounce the 'Horns, snatch away their reputations, and take control of the conference race.

On the gray, cold afternoon—rain fell later during the combat—Baylor won the flip and chose to receive. On the game's first play, Trull hit Elkins for a gain of 9, and the Baylor trend had been set. When Trull couldn't find Elkins open, the Bears were in trouble.

But it was Texas that was in trouble after the game's second play, as Elkins worked behind Tony King and took Trull's pass for a 34-yard gain to the Texas 37. If the throw had been longer, it would have been a touchdown. Elkins had to wait, and King was able to recover and get him.

Trull fired to Ingram to the 24, then to Hodge to the 19. On fourth down, Hoffman lunged to the 14 for a first down, and Baylor fans were screaming.

But the Longhorns stopped them there, although Elkins made another miraculous, juggling catch at the 12 on third down.

The Longhorns took over at that point. One play later and in the press box, someone wondered out loud, "How many times can your heart stop beating?"

LONGHORNS ATTACK

Now the Longhorns sprang to the attack, driving for one first down to the 32. But a penalty wiped out a 10-yard run by Ford and forced a punt, and Texas had been stopped on its first possession for the first time since the season opener against Tulane.

It was a moral victory for Baylor. Trull and Elkins quickly tried to produce something more tangible.

Starting at the Baylor 27, Trull fired, and Elkins tipped the ball with one hand, then caught it at the 39. From there, the Bears rolled quickly—to the 50, to the 41, then to Elkins at the sideline at the 28. But after slamming to the 20, Dalton Hoffman fumbled and King recovered, the quarter ended, and here comes Texas.

The Longhorns' line blocking suddenly became vicious, rolling the Bear defenders back. Carlisle ran to the 39, Ford and Phillip gored to the 49, then Ford scrambled to the 38. On the option pitchout, Phil Harris found room at left end and ran to the Baylor 21. Phillip blasted to the 16 and Ford to the 10. Then there went Ford again, to the 6.

Just when it appeared the 'Horns had become unstoppable, Crenshaw and Johnny Jessup and Bobby Maples called a halt. On fourth down, Joe Dixon knelt at the 12, and Crosby tried a field goal. The angle was bad, but the kick was almost good. But *almost* didn't count Saturday.

Later in the first half, Texas drove from its own 31 to the Baylor 34 but was stopped again. And then, when the 'Horns were stopped on the third-quarter kickoff after driving from the Texas 24 to the Baylor 31, Baylor partisans began to smile. The Bears weren't moving much, but maybe this was going to be their day after all.

SLOW BUT SURE

The Longhorns found the combination. Eddie Whiddon punted 61 yards and Harris returned to the Texas 40, and when a red flag fell after a Baylor personal foul, the Longhorns were on the Baylor 45.

Carlisle took them in slowly but surely. On third down, the Texas quarterback started right, then stopped and passed back to his left to Dixon, and it was a 16-yard gain to the Baylor 25. Carlisle swept right end to the 19, and Ford bored straight ahead to the 13.

Now things got sticky. Dixon gained nothing at left end. Carlisle went wide and got 3, then went wide again to the 4. That made it fourth and 1, and here came Ford . . . blasting all the way to the Baylor 1. Stockton

Texas' Joe Dixon (21) and Knox Nunnally (88) combine to halt an opposing running back. Courtesy of University of Texas Athletics.

took it from there, Crosby kicked goal, and Texas—after being held scoreless for 43 minutes—finally had the lead. Now, could the Longhorns hold it?

Two possessions later, the Bears tried to retaliate. Trull hit Elkins on a 17-yarder, but on fourth down, Eddie Whiddon tried to fool the Longhorns with a sweep instead of a punt, and end Charley Talbert came from the opposite side and ran him down for no gain.

Texas took over at the 40 and drove to the Baylor 32. Carlisle slipped on third down, and Crosby came in and tried a 50-yard field goal that was low and off target. Starting at the 20, Trull immediately tried to hit Elkins on a long bomb that Hix Green intercepted and returned 21 yards to the Baylor 34. From that point, the Longhorns drove on down to the Baylor 13, where Stockton fumbled and gave the Bears their last big chance.

They almost made it, but not quite. They played a

fine game, and most of the way they gave as good as they got, and at the finish even the victors saluted them. As for the Longhorns, they took all the Bears could muster and remained No. 1. That tells the story.

At the final gun, as the players trudged away, Don Trull and Duke Carlisle paused on the 40-yard line and exchanged congratulations. That was the nation's best quarterback saying a final well-done to the quarterback of the nation's No. 1 team. Quite a pair. Quite a game.

JANUARY 2, 1964
TOP-RANKED TEXAS SMOTHERS NAVY, 28–6

DALLAS, Tex.—Let the word now go forth to all the land: the Texas Longhorns are the undisputed national champions of college football.

On this bright, crisp first day of 1964, before a bedazzled, wonder-struck Cotton Bowl mob of 75,000, the last skeptics went down like the US Navy at Pearl Harbor. As a matter of fact, it was as one-sided as Pearl Harbor. The Longhorns, answering their season's biggest challenge with an almost perfect performance, hit Navy with a withering barrage of passes and won in a walk, 28–6.

Those who came to cheer the year's most heralded player, Navy's Roger Staubach, stayed to sing the praises of Texas' Duke Carlisle. The engineer of the Longhorns' perfect-record team passed for two touchdowns, ran for a third, set a Cotton Bowl total offense record of 267 yards, and won the vote for the game's outstanding back from here to yonder.

Carlisle, fleet receiver Phil Harris, and a raging Longhorn defense simply blew the ambitious Middies out of the tub. Navy made only two big threats all afternoon, both in the second half, and both came against players that were less than Texas' best.

Although the celebrated and gifted Staubach set a Cotton Bowl passing record, hitting 21 of 31 aerials for 228 yards, he and his mates wound up with an empty bag. They got nothing until the fired-up Longhorns got their 28 points and the verdict was well beyond recall.

This was the game that Navy, the nation's second-ranking team, had hoped to use to prove its oft-stated claim—that it really deserved to be recognized as the best team in the country.

Instead, it wound up the most soundly trounced Cotton Bowl loser since Rice whipped Alabama by the identical score 10 years ago, the day Dicky Maegle ran wild.

As the crowning blow, the infantry-minded Longhorns beat the Middies at their own game—passing. With Navy pulling its defense in tight to shut down Texas' hammering ground game, Carlisle simply turned to the aerial buttons, riddling the scattered Navy secondary.

His passes scored the first two touchdowns from long range, and then another shot set up the third score. The passes of relief pitcher Tommy Wade set up the fourth.

Harris, brilliant both in his receiving and in his running after his catches, scored the first two touchdowns, going 58 yards with a Carlisle pass on the game's sixth play, then teaming with the same passer on a 63-yard play six minutes deep in the second quarter.

Carlisle maneuvered through a broken field for 9 yards and the third touchdown with 2:39 left in the first half, and then fullback Harold Philipp got the final score on a 2-yard plunge with 2:40 left in the third period.

Texas went 78 yards in six plays for its first touchdown, 63 yards in one play for the second, 34 yards in seven plays for the third, and 52 yards in six plays for the fourth.

With its reputation by now in shreds, Navy finally started hitting against the Texas reserves and marched

Navy quarterback Roger Staubach (12) tries to escape the grasp of Texas linebacker Tommy Nobis (60). Courtesy of *Dave Campbell's Texas Football*.

75 yards in 14 plays for a fourth-quarter touchdown, scored on a 2-yard run by Staubach with 11:59 remaining in the game.

When the Midshipmen recovered a Texas fumble two plays later and started rolling back into Longhorn land again, Darrell Royal sent his front-liners back into the battle, and they turned back Navy's last big bid at the Longhorn 16.

Late in the game, feisty little sophomore Marvin Kristynik led a group of Texas irregulars down to the Navy 1-yard line as time ran out.

By then, even the superintendent of the naval academy, Admiral Charles Kirkpatrick, was convinced. "They just beat the hell out of us," he said.

Navy wound up with 16 first downs and 213 yards in total offense; Texas with 18 and a whopping 402.

What the figures don't tell, however, is how Carlisle caught the Middies with their defenses pulled in almost a nine-man front, then passed over them for decisive gains. And how the Longhorn defense, which must be one of the great ones in the history of the game, throttled Navy down to a whisper.

This was the Navy team that had been averaging 31.4 points a game, led by a quarterback who had never been stopped. And for this game, Navy threw the book at Texas—reverses, reverse passes, screen passes, tricky handoffs, halfback passes, even a pass to passer Roger Staubach.

Staubach, as feared for his scrambling, breakaway, broken-field runs as for his aerials, was pursued, hounded, chased, and ever contained. He wound up with minus 47 yards rushing as All-American Scott Appleton—rightfully voted the game's outstanding lineman—and Tommy Nobis and George Brucks and David McWilliams and a host of others had a field day.

Navy finished with a minus 14 yards rushing, so tightly did the Longhorns apply the clamps. In other words, the Middies couldn't run a lick, and it if had not been for Staubach's passes, they wouldn't have scratched.

Well, they almost didn't anyway, as the Longhorns proved once again that hully-gully football is no match for Darrell Royal's pound-of-flesh variety. The Longhorn tacklers punished the Middie runners and receivers something awful.

"It wasn't Roger's best day," said a convinced Wayne Hardin wearily.

"I've never been knocked down like that before," said

Tommy Nobis. Courtesy of University of Texas Athletics.

Knox Nunnally. Courtesy of University of Texas Athletics.

Staubach. "Texas hit harder, much harder than anyone else."

However, the crack Middie operator, completing 21 of 31 passes for 228 yards, did set a new bowl record—one of four individual marks broken. Another was tied, and in addition, two team records were broken and another tied.

Texas' first breakthrough came on the game's third play, when Carlisle circled left end and ran for 19 yards to the Texas 42. Three plays later, the thunderbolt hit. Carlisle took one step to his left, then passed right. Harris had broken outside Pat Donnelly. He made a fine over-the-shoulder catch, faked Donnelly so badly the defender fell down, and then set out for touchdown land.

It was such a breathtaking play, the fans sat silent for a couple of seconds, stunned, and then came alive with a full-throated roar.

Staubach got his first taste of what was to come a few plays later when Appleton smeared him for no gain, and then the roof fell in shortly thereafter when Pete Lammons and Knox Nunnally, crashing hard and very fast, dropped him for a 23-yard loss.

So it went for the remainder of the day, with Texas providing both the irresistible force and the immoveable object.

"Texas has a fine team. I don't ever remember seeing a team more deserving of being No. 1," said Wayne Hardin, fully convinced.

So let the word go forth.

TEXAS VS. NAVY: A CLASSIC CASE OF ESPIONAGE

JIM TRINKLE

It was on the annual Southwest Conference press tour prior to the 1973 football season that I first heard the story of how Texas was able to cash in on Navy's signals in the Cotton Bowl game that unfolded on the first day of 1964.

At a dinner arranged for visiting newsmen following UT's press day that August, the conversation at one table turned to football signals and how they worked and how, now and then, they were stolen.

Bill Ellington, at the time a key member of Darrell Royal's UT staff, told me he knew of a game that had taken place some years earlier where stolen signals helped turn a big showdown into a near rout. And then he confided the details.

A few months later, when several SWC teams began fretting about the possibility of someone in the camp of the opposition being able to steal their signals, I asked longtime Fort Worth Star-Telegram *sports columnist Jim Trinkle to research Ellington's tip and write a story on his findings for one of our fall issues.*

The result was the following report, which became a Texas Football *exclusive.*

Dave Campbell

The man stands on the sidelines during the football game. Constant movement around the players' bench obscures him, and he is unnoticed by the crowd. He is busy too. The poor fellow appears to be seized by convulsions. He clutches himself. He thrashes his hands. He rubs his left elbow or slaps his right knee. Obviously he needs a tranquilizer to quiet his nerves.

Not really. He is flashing signals to the field of play, and it is one of the oldest tricks in the game.

Perhaps unbeknownst to him, he is the center of attention to a couple of sets of binoculars zeroed in on him from the press box. Someone is trying to steal his signals. The sign heist is pure espionage—spies attempting to break the code.

"A lot more of that goes on than anybody realizes," says Texas assistant coach Bill Ellington, one of the craftiest signal thieves in college ranks.

Ellington can tell about one of the all-time classic cases of football espionage and how it paid off in a thumping victory for No. 1–ranked Texas over No. 2 challenger Navy in a big Cotton Bowl showdown a decade ago. More about that later.

A brief story appeared early in the 1973 season in the *Arkansas Gazette*, the unofficial "voice" of the Arkansas Razorbacks. At the time the story appeared, the Razorbacks were 0-for-2 and had scored only one touchdown against USC and Oklahoma State. The story said, "The Arkansas football coach on the sideline no longer looks like a refugee from a third-base coaching box. The Porkers now are calling plays by alternating split receivers."

"We switched to keep people from stealing our signals," said Don Trull, who coaches Arkansas' quarterbacks and receivers. "I stole signals from a couple of teams last year. If I can steal them, they can steal them from us."

Baylor, Trull's alma mater, was one target of the former Houston Oiler quarterback's minute observations last fall. Don saw something on the sidelines that Arkansas could use. The Porkers employed his code-busting expertise to win, 31–20, which may seem a shabby way for Trull to treat his "olde skule." But breaking signal codes is as important in football as in baseball.

Nearly all college teams use defensive signals from the sideline. A scratch of the knee or head or a tug at a shirt tells a linebacker which defense to call.

TCU assistant Russell Coffee says fans can observe the semaphore that passes information from sideline to huddle.

"Watch the linebackers between plays," Coffee said. "They nearly always look to the sideline for a signal. Everybody in the Southwest Conference gives defensive signals, and up to this year, nearly all of them gave offensive signals."

Most of them quit making offensive gesticulations because they were getting their brains picked by the press box pirates.

As the *Arkansas Gazette* story noted, the Razorbacks moved from hand signals to a player shuttle system. They since have switched again, using the same player (Larry Brown) to carry in each offensive play.

Some teams use hand signals, Coffee said, "because if you don't have any depth beyond your first 11 people, the No. 1 guys are usually so much better than the ones back of them. If you're shuttling plays, the subs are playing as much as the best players."

But the shuttle eliminates the threat of the press box poacher. Coaches haven't gotten into ESP yet, though some claim to read minds.

Darrell Royal quit using offensive signals at Texas. "I didn't want anybody stealing them," he said. "And I like to call the plays to alert our press box people which way the play is going. It tips them on the flow of the play."

Scouts work best in pairs, because some coaches have two assistants, or an assistant and a player, giving signals. Only one of them, however, is flashing a valid sign. The other is merely going through motions to sidetrack the sign stealers. One scout can't catch all the motions from two signalers.

Sign rustlers never look at the game. Those beady li'l eyes are pinned to the sidelines, particularly to the area near the coach.

"Say it's first and 10," Coffee suggested. "If some guy down there scratches his head and tugs his belt, we write it down. If he puts his hands on his hips on second and 3, we make a note of it. After we get home with the film, we check to see what they did when the guy was making the signs. If a pattern develops—he's given the same signal in the same situations—you have some solid information.'

The late Jim MacKenzie, an Arkansas assistant before becoming Oklahoma's head coach, could tie scouts in knots with baseball signals.

"We never could steal Arkansas' signals," Coffee, a former assistant at Texas, said. "Jim would be giving signs to the line of scrimmage, and Johnny Majors would shoot another batch at the deep secondary. Jim would be doing so many things so fast, there was no way to keep up."

Oklahoma was a soft touch the two years (1964–65) when Gomer Jones was the head coach. Ellington scouted the Sooners for at least 10 years and knew what to look for.

"We had their signals both years Gomer was there." Coffee recalls. "Bill had 'em down cold. Bobby Drake Keith gave their signals, and they were pretty simple."

If a smug Arkansas defender hadn't popped off early in the 1972 game with Texas Tech, the Razorbacks might have won by a more substantial margin than 24–14. Raider quarterback Joe Barnes looked across the line once and saw the linebacker grinning at him like Captain Midnight's tomcat. The Porker couldn't restrain himself.

"You're gonna run a little ol' power sweep left, ain't you, Joe?" he purred. Suddenly Barnes wanted an aspirin and a cold towel.

"He called it right on the button," Barnes told writer Galyn Wilkins of the *Fort Worth Star-Telegram*. "It was awfully suspicious, to say the least."

So the Raiders began tossing out false signs, and Arkansas needed a 17-point surge in the final period to win.

Tech assistant Jack Fligg says, "If we see the coaches on the other sideline talking a lot and making funny motions with their hands, we know they're trying to break down our signals. Then we show some false signals. We change ours frequently."

There's no honor among sign thieves either, see?

"There are several avenues of deception," says Tech head coach Jim Carlen. "If we send in a play with a flanker," he explained, "the other teams figure a pass play is coming, right? So we switch it now and then—send in a pass play with a runner or a flanker in with a running play."

Texas ended its 1960 season in traditional fashion, against the Texas Aggies. Charley Shira, who moved on to become athletic director at Mississippi State, was calling defensive signals for the Longhorns, who used a six-two defense, rushing the inside linebackers on each first down. The Aggies laughed to see such fun.

Coffee recalled, "We rushed those linebackers all afternoon, and their quarterback kept raising up and popping his ends with quick passes. We didn't know if they were stealing our signs or just recognizing our tendencies. Later, we decided they had to be stealing."

Which brings this theme to Wayne Hardin. Hardin once coached Navy to delirious heights and then became Temple's resident genius. He may still lie awake some nights, conjuring dark thoughts of what might have been—if it hadn't been for 1963 Texas and the 1964 Cotton Bowl.

The '63 Longhorns were unbeaten at season's end and ranked No. 1 nationally. Navy was No. 2, beaten only in a huge upset by SMU. So when the Middies arrived in Dallas a few days before the New

Texas quarterback Duke Carlisle (11) launches a pass among a crowd of Navy defenders en route to Texas' 1964 Cotton Bowl victory. Courtesy of *Dave Campbell's Texas Football*.

Year's Day game, Hardin declared that the bowl game was for the national championship.

"Texas is champion and we're the challenger," he said. "When the challenger whips the champion, doesn't that make him No. 1?"

The logic didn't endear Hardin to Darrell Royal, who maintained that the national crown was decided over a 10-game season, not by a single game. Another major coaching figure, unnamed here because he is still active, wasn't in love with Hardin either. He told Texas what every signal from the Navy sideline meant.

Ernie George was Navy's line coach and signaler. He flashed them to the quarterback, who was Roger Staubach, the subsequent Cowboy hero. The Longhorns knew everything about Staubach, including birthmarks. More important, they had every defensive signal the Middies owned.

"We had," Royal will admit today, "a Hungarian lock on 'em."

The Longhorns had three weeks to rehearse the information passed to them by the coach who had broken Navy's code. Royal stationed one of his men with binoculars in the Memorial Stadium press box during practice. Another one impersonated Ernie George on the opposite sideline.

"As soon as he [George's impersonator] gave the signal," Coffee said, "our press box man would tell me on the phone. I was standing next to Jim Pittman. Pitt would give the same signal to [Texas quarterback] Duke Carlisle, who was kneeling in the huddle, looking at Pitt through somebody's legs."

By New Year's Day 1964, the Longhorns had their lines down letter perfect. Only minutes into the game, the Texas coaches knew that their information was good.

"We got 'em," Mike Campbell, Royal's top aide, said and chortled.

"We were just giggling," Coffee said. "We knew what we had was good."

Navy sailed into the trap using a box defense—two safeties and two cornerbacks. The right cornerback jammed the line, ready to rush Texas' wing-T. He also had the responsibility of covering Texas wingback Phil Harris if a pass developed.

Well, he done his dangedest. Harris twice flew past him so fast that the kid caught a chill. Both passes went for long TDs, and by halftime, Texas was winning a laugher, 28–0.

And that, kiddies, was the Great Brain Robbery. The 28–6 romp established Texas' No. 1 claim without argument. Years later, when Staubach was told how Texas was handed the keys to the Navy defense by the anonymous coach, Roger the Dodger snapped, "I always thought he was a [bleep]. That proves it."

Al Conover (on phone) getting his signals straight on the Rice sideline. Courtesy of Rice University Athletics.

But alas, as ye git, so shall ye be got. Texas learned this even before it played Navy. The same season, Arkansas got the goods on Texas at Little Rock.

"Every time we'd blitz," Coffee said, "they'd throw a quick pass to the tight end. Jack Davis [one of Frank Broyles's assistants] was a friend, so we accused him of swiping our signals. He just laughed, so we knew they did it."

But the sword is mightier than the sign, and Texas won anyway, 17–13.

When A&M won the 1967 SWC championship, Lide Huggins of the Aggie coaching staff was one of the architects of A&M's 33–21 victory over Arkansas. Huggins is a Tennessee assistant now.

"Lide knew every signal Arkansas had," said ex-Aggie assistant Ralph Smith, who later became one of Billy Tohill's TCU lieutenants.

"It's not hard picking up signals from a basic offense or defense," said Huggins. "The hard part is getting to our players on the field. If you can just pick up a blitz or man-to-man coverage, it takes a lot of pressure off your offensive line."

He first learned of signal larcenies from another assistant, Huggins said. His tutor was the late Tom Ellis of Texas.

"We used to stay in Tulsa, then drive over to Fayetteville," he said.

"Tom got me onto what was going on because he never carried a notebook. All he had was a tape recorder."

What Ellis said into his tape recorder was bad news to Arkansas.

Lide said, "Last year, we thought Auburn had our signals. [Auburn beat Tennessee, 10–6.] To eliminate that possibility this year, we started subbing people. They would've had to put a man in our huddle to get the signals." Tennessee won, 21–0.

Putting a man into the enemies' huddle isn't so farfetched, at that. Ralph Smith, who coached at Orange High after graduating from A&M, says high schools have gone beyond cracking signal codes. In 1962, some South Texas preps were using walkie-talkies.

Said Smith, "They tap in on your press box. They'd change their walkie-talkie to your frequency and hear every word you said."

When Al Conover, the Rice coach, was an assistant to Bill Peterson at Florida State, the Seminoles took an annual licking from the University of Houston—until 1968, that is.

Writer Giles Tippett, in *Saturday's Children*, tells of the youthful-looking Conover flying into Houston on a scouting mission. When Conover scouted a team, he went all out. He first went to a campus bookstore and bought a Cougar T-shirt, a couple of books, and notepads. Al "passed" as a Houston student, slipped into a practice session, took notes on the Cougar defenses, and left. Score: Florida State 40, Houston 20.

At your next college game, remember that what you see could be the product of another day on another field. All the brain waves don't pass between quarterbacks and flankers.

Observe the men standing near the head coach. If one seems on the edge of epilepsy or dancing to invisible vibes, he's merely talking in what he hopes is an unknown tongue. And is the guy next to him trying to talk turkey to a pom-pom girl?

"You got a 'live' touch and a 'dead' touch," Lide Huggins explained. "Nobody stealing signals knows which one is which."

Which means the "live" one is relaying a genuine signal. The "dead" one is throwing in the phonies. But they may be alternating, and that's why signal thieves drink lots of milk and nibble Rolaids. If they can crack the code, it's worth it.

The victim of what Jim Trinkle termed the "Great Brain Robbery" of New Year's Day 1964, Navy quarterback Roger Staubach, later returned to the city of his misfortune and became one of that city's all-time heroes.

If there was anything gallant and grand that Staubach failed to do during his years in a Dallas Cowboys uniform, I wouldn't know what it might be.

Darrell Royal's Longhorns profited from their own skills and their knowledge of Navy's plans that day to nail down the 1963 national championship. Six years later, they were back on the same gridiron, seeking to certify their claim on still another national crown.

They had a different opponent that day, and as far as I know, they had no special advantage where signals were concerned. But the outcome—although much closer and more dramatic—was the same. The final score: Texas 21, Notre Dame 17.

Royal coached until the end of the 1976 season and then retired. Ellington later succeeded him as UT athletic director for several years and then retired himself. One of the grand guys of both Texas high school and SWC football, he now lives on what he lovingly calls "the Ponderosa"—his ranch near the community of Quinlan in North Texas.

Dave Campbell

NOVEMBER 20, 1966

PONIES WIN 24–22 THRILLER FROM BEARS

DALLAS, Tex.—Those Cardiac Kids from SMU, dead game beyond belief, got off the floor and out of the graveyard in the very last minute of a fantastic struggle here Saturday and came up with the four stunning plays they had to have to defeat Baylor, 24–22, and move within one victory of an uncontested Southwest Conference championship and a trip to the Cotton Bowl. The triumph assured them of no worse than a share of the 1966 crown.

Dennis Partee, whose field goal beat Texas in the last 18 seconds, kicked a 20-yard three-pointer with 15 seconds remaining to win the game and pluck the bloom from one of the greatest comebacks the Bears have ever made.

In those last 60 seconds, the Mustangs piled great play on top of great play. Just when all seemed lost, tackle Ronnye Medlin blocked a Baylor punt, Jerry LeVias turned a short pass into a 27-yard gain, and Mike Livingston ran around right end for 18 yards to the Baylor 3-yard line.

That left it all up to Partee and Dennis the Menace, who earlier had missed twice from longer ranges, to put the Ponies home free.

This truly was a case of snatching victory from the jaws of defeat, but then the Mustangs have become masters of such. They beat Rice in the last 9 seconds and Texas, of course, in the last 18.

SMU's indomitable Jerry LeVias was the first African American scholarship athlete in the Southwest Conference. Courtesy of Southern Methodist University Athletics.

In some ways, this one was the most incredible of all, and certainly it stands now as the most significant. Because this Mustang exercise in the unbelievable, combined with Texas Tech's shocking conquest of Arkansas, left Hayden Fry's forces needing only a victory over TCU next Saturday to nail down their first uncontested championship since 1948.

Even now, with the big stadium dark and the limp, babbling crowd of 30,000 gone elsewhere, the whole thing seems impossible.

Thirteen seconds deep into the second half, SMU moved into a 21-point lead, thanks to a 100-yard kickoff return by Jerry Levias. Remember that name. Baylor heads this morning will throb at the sound of it.

With the Mustangs ahead by three touchdowns and with Pony partisans in the stands cheering wildly as they listened on transistors while Texas Tech moved ahead of Arkansas, the outcome appeared cut and dried. But at that moment, the Bears pulled themselves together and seized control of the game.

Terry Southall was firing on almost every play. He would wind up with a record 29 completions in 50 attempts for a whopping 350 yards and two touchdowns—his greatest day ever and the second-greatest day in SWC history. Two ace receivers, Tommy Smith and Paul Becton, wrapped themselves in glory as well.

Quickly the Bears flashed 58 yards in 6 plays for a touchdown. Running back Richard Defee put the points on the board from 1 yard out. Then right back they came, moving 69 yards in 17 plays for another touchdown, the payoff coming on a 1-yard pass to Becton. Both times the extra point failed—first Bobby Purvis's missed kick, then a failed try for two points. That left it 21–12.

Undismayed, the Bears stopped the Mustangs at the Baylor 12 after a 68-yard Livingston completion to Levias, and with 8:31 left in the game, they scored again. Southall fired the final 36 yards to Smith, Purvis kicked the extra point, and the Bears were within two points of the lead.

They got those on their next possession after stopping the Mustangs at the Baylor 24. On fourth down, Partee tried a 42-yard field goal and missed.

In nine plays, Southall hurried the Bears 44 yards to the SMU 27. There it was fourth down. If there was any wind at that point, it was blowing against the Bears. But the icy-nerved Purvis, atoning for the extra point he had missed after Baylor's first touchdown, calmly swung his foot and sent the ball tumbling end over end through the goal posts and over the crossbar 44 yards away.

Two minutes and 37 seconds remained to play. Baylor was ahead 22–21. SMU supporters, so sure of victory earlier, so thrilled when Texas Tech's victory became official with the Mustangs still holding a 21–12 lead, were speechless. They couldn't believe their eyes.

And yet it soon developed that all that had gone before had merely been window dressing for SMU's last implausible game-winning, heart-stopping gasp.

First they tried to move and couldn't. They then stopped the Bears at the SMU 35, taking time out after every Baylor play. A little more than a minute remained as Southall moved deep to supply the punt that would sew it up and give Baylor its seventh straight victory over SMU.

The punt never got airborne. A towering SMU hero, the rangy Medlen, crashed in and blocked it. With one minute to go, the Mustangs had new life at their own 47.

Now the game unraveled swiftly amid pure bedlam. Livingston, who had failed to complete a single pass in the first half, sent a short one to Levias in the right flat at about the Baylor 45.

That fancy-stepping sophomore, so dangerous in an open field, wheeled toward the sideline a few feet away, then twisted back toward midfield. A Bruin had him and he got away, then he got away again. He was stumbling, lurching, and twisting. At about the Baylor 25, for no reason at all, he fumbled, and after a couple of bounces, the ball wound up in the arms of SMU's Ken Motes. Now the Ponies not only were alive—now they had a good chance.

Quickly Livingston fired to a sideline target, missing but stopping the clock. Twenty-eight seconds remained.

Livingston retreated to throw, fading a bit to his left. Everyone in the big Cotton Bowl playpen knew he had to throw, and Bears growled in on him. But he wheeled, came back to his right, and got away. He found daylight and ran to it—down the sideline 18 yards to the Baylor 3-yard line. Although long-legged Mike ran for 129 yards on the afternoon, those were the biggest of all.

As the ball was placed down on the west hash mark, Baylor asked for time. Eighteen seconds remained. Partee was coming into the game, setting up for a field goal attempt. This had to be for all the marbles.

So they lined up and Partee kicked, and the ball soared high and true, and an official signaled good, and the SMU bench and the Mustangs on the field and the SMU people in the stands went slightly berserk. You've heard about pandemonium reigning? Man, it reigned right then.

In retrospect, it hardly seems possible. But there were witnesses.

JANUARY 1, 1967

GEORGIA STEAMROLLS SMU IN COTTON BOWL

DALLAS, Tex.—They call them the Georgia Bulldogs, which may be a misnomer. They're more like wolves. Ravenous to the very finish, they ripped and tore at sputtery Southern Methodist here Saturday until there was nothing left but a bag of bones, and by then the men from Dixie had exactly what they wanted—a decisive 21–9 victory in this 31st annual Cotton Bowl Classic.

A shattering 74-yard touchdown run on the second play of the game by the most outstanding back on the field, jet-fast tailback Kent Lawrence, gave Georgia the upper hand at the outset, and the Bulldogs never let up.

Lawrence, a 165-pound sophomore who was only a second-teamer most of the season, went on to carve 149 yards out of the SMU hide on 16 carries, and the Bulldogs went on to hand the seven-point underdog Methodists the worst strapping a Southwest Conference representative has suffered in this bowl in 22 years.

Not since Oklahoma A&M flattened a wartime TCU team, 34–0 in 1915, has a conference team been put through a more exciting wringer.

SMU quarterback Mac White on the move against Arkansas. Courtesy of Southern Methodist University Athletics.

FIRST HALF RUGGED

It was a tense, tight, hard-fought contest for the first 30 minutes, and although the Bulldogs over that span gained a 17–9 upper hand, few in the sell-out throng of 75,500 would have predicted Georgia would shut out the Mustangs so completely in the second half.

But Vince Dooley's quick and muscular representatives, the nation's fourth-ranked team, became all-powerful after intermission. In the third quarter, Georgia ran 23 plays from scrimmage and earned eight first downs, while SMU got off 9 plays and earned only one first down.

The Mustangs' single severe threat in the second half became a rather typical exercise. Given fine field position on a Pat Gibson interception, the Mustangs moved on the next play down to the Georgia 2-yard line as Mac White and Larry Jernigan teamed on a 38-yard pass and run play. Jernigan was touchdown bound until he cut back into Georgia traffic. From the Georgia 2, in four plays, the Ponies not only failed to score; they wound up losing 8 yards as Georgia's two tackles, George Patton and Bill Stanfill, and guard Dickie Phillips erected unmovable roadblocks.

Patton, an All-American on some lists this year, later was voted the game's outstanding lineman, so it was a clean sweep for the visitors. They had the most valuable back, the most valuable lineman, and the most valuable end of the scoreboard.

The 149-yard rushing explosion by Lawrence was the second-best afternoon enjoyed by a footman in Cotton Bowl history. Only Dicky Maegle's unforgettable afternoon against Alabama here a dozen years ago (265 in 11 carries) surpassed it. While Lawrence, who hits his hole as quickly as Chris Gilbert and has more speed but less balance, made a runaway of the most valuable back balloting, the Bulldogs were long on quality behind the line—and also quality up front.

A FUNDAMENTAL VICTORY

They simply overwhelmed the Mustangs in football's fundamentals. Georgia scored on touchdown drives of 76 yards in 2 plays, 33 yards in 4 plays, and 59 yards in 13 plays, and sandwiched between the first and second scoring drives was a 28-yard field goal by Bob Etter, the Bulldog placement expert who also kicked true after each touchdown. He did miss a 31-yard field goal effort early in the third quarter, however, and that was about Georgia's only miss of the afternoon. After Lawrence had blistered the Mustangs early with that 74-yard sprint and Etter had kicked his field goal, the Bulldogs scored again with 14:11 left in the half on a 20-yard pass from nifty quarterback Kirby Moore to end Billy Payne.

After dominating the third quarter, they scored again on the second play of the fourth quarter when their superb fullback, 210-pound Ronnie Jenkins, drilled the Mustangs from 4 yards out.

Jenkins was something to see. He's a rip-snorting type, and although the SMU defensive midsection is supposed to be the Mustangs' strength, Jenkins plundered it like a certain fellow named Sherman once plundered old Georgia. He crashed and ripped and powered and bulled straight ahead for 88 yards during the game, and often it seemed that he was getting his 4 and 5 even when the Ponies were hitting him with three and four tacklers.

That was the Georgia strategy—blast 'em with Jenkins between the tackles until their midsection was groggy, then fire the fleet Lawrence at them on a simple quick opener. Or as a change of pace, Moore would fake the run and then flip a pass to one of his ends, Payne or Sandy Johnson. He passed 14 times and completed 6 for 79 yards and handled the offense superbly. So basically the Bulldogs thrived by trumping SMU's most-heralded defensive weapons. Defensively, it was much the same.

SMU's bread-and-butter plays all season were Mac White's stuttery runs inside or outside end. After giving ground early, the Bulldogs started wiping out Mac on his keepers. He wound up with a minus 21 yards on 19 carries, although losses on pass attempts had something to do with that.

Georgia often was able to penetrate SMU's pass protection in critical situations.

With White shut down outside, the Ponies had to turn again to the sensational sophomore who saved them so many times all season, Jerry Levias. And while Jerry made several splendid catches and gave the Bulldogs a scare, he was unable to score any knockouts. He finished with three catches good for 62 yards—not bad, but then, not an ultimate weapon either.

With White throttled and Levias well guarded, Larry Jernigan and Mike Richardson became the workhorses of the Mustang attack. Jernigan rushed for 28 yards and grabbed two passes worth 42 yards. Richardson had 24 yards rushing and 45 catching.

It was Richardson who got the last yard on SMU's one touchdown march, a 72-yard advance put together in 13 plays and scored with 1:14 left in the first half. Levias provided the high octane for that thrust, catching one pass for 23 yards and, four plays later, grabbing another for the same distance.

Dennis Partee, who kicked a 22-yard field goal with 6:17 left in the first quarter after the Ponies had moved 29 yards in 8 plays to the Georgia 5, missed the one extra point conversion he attempted.

Other than the touchdown thrust, the drive that was climaxed by the field goal, and the fourth-quarter advance that was turned back at the Georgia 2, SMU never threatened. Meanwhile, the Bulldogs, who rolled up 363 yards in total offense and gathered 17 first downs, moved the ball consistently.

After Lawrence's flash-footed opening effort had shoved Georgia into a 7–0 lead, the visitors yielded the field goal to SMU, then matched it with one of their own on a 45-yard, 10-play drive that featured a 19-yard Moore pass to Payne—the same combination that later clicked on the 20-yard touchdown pass. That latter thrust, which pushed the Bulldogs into a 17–3 lead, was set up when a Mike Livingston pass was deflected by the rangy Patton and intercepted by Lynn Hughes at the SMU 33.

It was in the third quarter that the Bulldogs established their mastery, as Jenkins steadily bulled for gains up the middle and the visitors controlled the ball. They moved in 10 plays from their own 20 to the SMU 14 before missing a field goal, but a few plays later, they cranked up again, and this time there was no stopping them.

Or catching them. At the finish, Vince Dooley had turned it into a laugher for his troops, letting Patton, a tackle, play tailback. On the game's final play, big George ran 16 yards to the SMU 34. A flag was down on the play and SMU could have asked for a rerun, but the Mustangs didn't.

By then, they had had enough.

SEPTEMBER 17, 1967

MIRACLE-MAKING MUSTANGS STUN AGGIES

COLLEGE STATION, Tex.—The Texas Aggies were back only a short while. Something like 39 seconds. But the defending champion SMU Mustangs were never away.

In a breathless, dramatic, helter-skelter finish that put all those miracles they constructed last year to shame, those crazy Cardiac Kids of Hayden Fry drove 57 yards in just five plays and 32 seconds and defeated the favored Aggies here Saturday, 20–17.

The touchdown that broke the Aggies' backs, to say nothing of their hearts, was scored with all of four—that's right, F-O-U-R—seconds left in the game.

"Last year," quipped SMU's assistant athletic director Lester Jordan, "our record for a tight finish was nine seconds, against Rice. This is a new record, and it's going to be hard to beat."

The most unbelievable Mustang of them all, Jerry LeVias (who else?), scored the winning touchdown. Naturally, Jerry the Jet does everything . . . and even while out of his senses.

Returning A&M's last kickoff of the game, he was knocked groggy.

He played the rest of the game—five plays—on what he called instinct alone. At the finish, he claimed he remembered nothing about the plays both Hayden Fry and Gene Stallings will never forget.

After starting the game by returning the opening kickoff 46 yards, he wound it up by catching Ines Perez's dinky little 6-yard pass in the A&M end zone, even as sophomore Jack Whitmore waved his arms frantically, trying to deflect the ball.

Perez is as implausible as the final score. He's 5-foot-4. Imagine a 5-foot-4-inch quarterback beating a highly favored Aggie team in its own backyard. Unbelievable, but it happened. All through the second half, in big situations, little Ines plundered the Aggie pass defense as if his name were Sammy Baugh or something.

Last year, LeVias beat the Aggies with an 83-yard punt return that he uncorked midway through the fourth quarter. Apparently Jerry, like all the Mustangs, is running a little late this year.

It's a good thing the national television cameras were here, along with 34,000 eyeball witnesses. Otherwise,

Lynn Thornhill was an all-conference guard for SMU in 1966. Courtesy of Southern Methodist University Athletics.

not a soul would have believed it. Heck, they probably don't anyway.

Imagine. With 43 seconds left in the game, the Aggies, who played a very ordinary game start to finish, finally climaxed a tortuous, catch-as-catch-can drive of 83 yards in 10 plays by scoring a touchdown and moving in front, 17–13.

Edd Hargett's 29-yard pass to wingback Bob Long, a beautifully executed play, finally put Texas (the Aggies are back) A&M ahead after all but the most stouthearted of Aggie supporters had given up hope.

When little Charlie Riggs added the extra point, the Aggies moved four points in front—in other words, out of field goal range.

At that point, an observer had to feel a twinge of sympathy for the Mustangs, who, as underdogs picked to finish last in the SWC title chase this year, had played beyond themselves.

They also had played the entire second half without their long, tall quarterback, Mike Livingston, who hurt his knee scoring SMU's first touchdown on a 3-yard scramble late in the second quarter.

But that score, along with Dennis Partee's two field goals, seemed ages ago when Hargett and Long touched off a mighty roar of exultation from the Aggie section by putting Ol' Army ahead by those four points with less than a minute to play.

Now hang on to your hats and listen closely, and you can almost hear the Mustangs making history. They did it in rapid-fire order this way:

A&M linebacker Billy Hobbs, trying to steer his kickoff away from Levias, kicked short but within Levias's reach, and SMU's meal ticket ran in and out of the grasp of four or five Aggies before being downed on the SMU 43. It was a 24-yard return. The clock showed exactly 36 seconds left to play.

As the Mustangs came out of the huddle, the Aggies were anxious but not in a state of panic. Not yet. SMU still had 57 yards to go, and the Mustangs, for reasons known only to themselves, had used up two precious timeouts earlier on the Aggies' touchdown drive, stopping the clock with 1:04 to go and again with 49 seconds to go—and each time when the Aggies desperately wanted the clock stopped.

You see, SMU's strategy is beyond the understanding of mortal man, but what the heck, it works.

Anyway, SMU lined up for a do-or-die effort at its own 43, and at first glance, one would have sworn the Ponies were going to try to make it without a quarterback. But looking closely, there he was—the tiny but deadly Perez.

First play—bull's-eye. Levias caught the sideline shot and cut back to the middle of the field the way he did against Baylor in the last telltale minute last year—and with the same result. They finally wrestled him down on the Aggie 29.

Now Perez let Levias rest while he fired complete to Harold Richardson at the Aggie 12.

Whitmore knocked the receiver down, but by then, he was out of bounds, stopping the clock with 20 seconds left. Perez fired in Whitmore's zone again to sophomore Sam Holden, and suddenly the Mustangs were on the A&M 6-yard line. If you ever have wondered what

Jerry LeVias was inducted into the College Football Hall of Fame in 2003. Courtesy of Southern Methodist University Athletics.

the inside of a tomb is like, you would have known had you been in the Aggie section right then.

Quickly Perez lined them up and passed again—and missed, and that was only the mighty mite's second miss of the entire second half in 11 aerial attempts. I told you he was deadly, didn't I?

"Hold 'em! Hold 'em just a little longer," came a frantic plea from up in Kyle Field's new second deck. Nine seconds showed on the scoreboard clock, and the words were still hanging in the air when Perez rolled to his left. An Aggie came in on him quickly, but he got the ball away—almost a lob. And just before he ran out of the end zone, Levias grabbed the pass and clutched it for all he was worth, and a man in a striped shirt shot his arms skyward, signaling touchdown.

Levias didn't see the signal. By then, he was out cold, but one play too late for Ol' Army.

In the four seconds remaining, the heartbroken Aggies had time only to return the kickoff. By then, no one expected them to do more. To win a game in four seconds requires a miracle, and SWC miracles these days apparently come wrapped only in Red and Blue.

OCTOBER 15, 1967

LONGHORN SUPERSTARS LEAD RALLY

DALLAS, Tex.—It's the Year of the Horns, all right. Has to be. Otherwise, the explosive Oklahoma Sooners, doing just about as they pleased all through the first half, would have battered Texas by two or three touchdowns here on this breezy, overcast Saturday afternoon.

But after surviving on borrowed time, a flubbed Oklahoma field goal, and two end zone interceptions during the first 30 minutes, the stout-hearted Royal men rallied behind the whiplash running of Chris Gilbert and Bill Bradley and shot the frustrated Sooners down in flames, 9–7, before 75,504 witnesses.

After young Rob Layne, son of the immortal Bobby, had finally gotten the Longhorns on the scoreboard with a 35-yard field goal in the third quarter, Bradley and Gilbert blended their many talents and hurried the Horns 84 yards in 10 plays for the decisive fourth-quarter touchdown.

Bradley turned to his own left end and sped the last 7 yards as Gilbert and Teddy Koy supplied the key blocks that opened opportunity's door with 14:19 left to play. Gilbert carried for 29 yards on the drive, and Bradley ran for 22 and passed for another 22.

Chris Gilbert (25) penetrates the Oklahoma line. Courtesy of Cotton Bowl Athletic Association / James D. Smith.

Texas would not have won had Oklahoma's Mike Vachon not missed two field goals—by wide margins—from point-blank range. Each miss came after the Sooners had slammed to the Longhorn 11-yard line, once in the second quarter, when everything was going Oklahoma's way, and the last time with 4:02 left in the game, after the Sooners had marched 69 yards in eight plays amid a fine mixture of consternation and pandemonium in the stands.

That was the last clear call for the Sooners, although they did manage to surge back into Texas territory on a last-gasp, futile dash in the closing seconds. But it would have taken a miracle to save them then. Bradley had seen to that by banging a 46-yard punt out of bounds on the Oklahoma 3-yard line with 1:17 to go.

By foot, by arm, and by shoulder pad, Bradley led the comeback assault on the Big Red from Soonerland. It was an 11-yard Bradley pass to Ragan Gennusa followed immediately by another 11-yarder to Ed Small at the Oklahoma 7-yard line that set up the Texas touchdown, it was a Bradley run that produced the score, and it was a Bradley tackle in the first half that finally nailed Eddie Hinton and staved off a touchdown after that swift Oklahoma back had broken past all other Longhorn defenders on a heart-stopping 33-yard punt return.

Bradley rushed for 86 yards, and so did Gilbert, and Bradley threw for another 74 yards, but all those statistics would have been lost in the wreckage had not the Sooners in the first half kicked opportunity around like it was an old rag doll.

Oklahoma scored the first time it gained possession, booming 78 yards in a mere five plays. Tailback Ronnie Shotts tallied from 2 yards out, and Vachon kicked the extra point. To the wildly cheering Sooner partisans, it seemed they actually outnumbered and out-yelled the Texas backers most of the way; this was going to be easy, easy, easy.

Only thing was, the Sooners neglected to put any more points on the scoreboard.

But never mind. At that point, Oklahoma had 11 first downs, 208 yards in total offense, and seven points. Texas had 6 first downs, 108 yards, and nothing remotely resembling a threat, much less a point.

Two things happened in quick succession that turned the game upside down. Darrell Royal gave his lackluster pupils the woodshed treatment verbally at halftime, and early in the third quarter, Warmack ran off and left the football on the Texas 31, blotting out still another promising Oklahoma drive.

Right then and there, Texas took full control of the proceedings. D. H. Martin recovered, and on their next two possessions, Bradley and associates whipped 141 yards in 20 plays and scored all their nine points. Oklahoma over that span gained exactly 8 yards.

The Longhorns rushed to the Sooner 12, but that signaled a Sooner defensive stand that cost the Horns 5 yards on their next three plays.

So on fourth down, Layne came in for what looked like a rather forlorn try—a 35-yarder that would have to bite into the teeth of that gusty south wind. But lo and behold, his kick sailed high and straight and true. Texas at last was on the scoreboard.

Not only that—the Longhorns now had momentum. When they got the ball back at their own 16 with 4:34 left in the third quarter, there was no stopping them.

Needing a yard on third down, Bradley circled the end and got 15. Two plays later, the incredible Gilbert, who can run only inches off the ground, caught Oklahoma in a stunt and dashed for 21 yards to the OU 39. He was almost gone.

A couple of plays later, Bradley found Small, whose catch was of the unbelievable variety. The tight end was fumbling the ball as he went down, and he was savagely tackled, but somehow he retained possession at the 7.

Bradley wasted no time. He dialed his own number, keeping on a thrust at left end, and scored standing up. Layne missed the extra point, but on this day, it did not matter. Texas was up 9–7, and that is the way the score would stay.

NOVEMBER 5, 1967

AGGIES' HARGETT HARNESSES HOGS

FAYETTEVILLE, Ark.—On a windswept playing field in the chilled Ozarks, facing an old nemesis they had not scored on in 4 years and had not beaten in 10, the young Texas Aggies grandly came of age here Saturday.

Trailing by a touchdown going into the fourth quarter, the Aggies exploded for three touchdowns in the game's final telltale 15 minutes and smashed Arkansas, 33–21, before a Razorback homecoming audience of 41,000.

There was nothing fluky about it. Although they had to fight from behind twice, the Aggies won going away.

Dazzling Edd Hargett, supersophomore Larry Stegent, and a fired-up array of Aggie receivers and defenders kept coming up with big play after big play as the league-leading Cadets won their fourth straight conference game and their most significant yet under Coach Gene Stallings.

To be sure, the victory counts no more in the tight and tense championship chase than the earlier Cadet triumphs over Texas Tech, TCU, and Baylor. But A&M had whipped those teams before—like last year. They had done nothing against Arkansas since Hector was a small pup, and they were favored to lose again this time.

But Hargett, cool and deadly in the clutch, threw three touchdown passes against an Arkansas defense that had surrendered no scoring passes all season, and Stegent rammed for two more touchdowns, and that was enough to knock the regrouping Razorbacks out of the race.

Not since the great 1961 Texas Longhorns put 33 points on the scoreboard against Arkansas—and that was 70 games ago—has a Razorback defense been treated so shamefully. Not only did the Aggies break their scoring drought against the Porkers; they scored more points against them than they had scored in their last eight meetings combined.

If Arkansas' old grads were left popeyed, there was a reason. Never before had a Frank Broyles–coached team lost to A&M.

Hargett threw scoring passes of 3, 12, and 15 yards to Barney Harris, Wendell Housley, and Tommy Maxwell, in that order. Those aerial trips to the payoff window were sandwiched between Stegent's two scoring runs of a yard each.

Arkansas, which played one of its better games of the season in defeat, scored on a 1-yard plunge by versatile David Dickey and twice on passes from Ronny South to Mark Peacock. South's first touchdown throw was a 6-yarder, the second a deflected 19-yarder.

In the final analysis, the Aggies won because they got maximum mileage out of their opportunities. Each time

Texas A&M receiver Tommy Maxwell went on to help the Baltimore Colts win Super Bowl V in 1971. Courtesy of Texas A&M University Athletics.

Barney Harris, a sophomore receiver for A&M in the 1967 season, overcame personal tragedy to contribute to the Aggies' subsequent 1968 Cotton Bowl victory. Courtesy of Texas A&M University Athletics.

the Aggies got inside the Arkansas 40, they scored. The Porkers, on the other hand, were repulsed after getting once to the Aggie 10 and later to the 22.

But don't fault the Arkies. Credit Bill Hobbs, Rolf Krueger, Ross Brupbacher, Grady Allen, Harvey Aschenbeck, and a long line of Aggie defenders who keep getting better by the week.

Two long drives, a 59-yard opening sashay by Arkansas that died at the Aggie 10 and a 90-yard reply by A&M, used up all but 13 seconds of the first quarter, and the big surprise was the way the Aggies were able to move the ball on the ground against the conference's top-ranked defense.

It was primarily a Hargett-Stegent production. Hargett threw one time—23 yards to Tom Buckman—and ran four times for gains of 6, 6, 9, and 8 yards. Stegent pounded away 10 times for a net of 29 yards. After the powerful Housley had picked up a first down at the Arkansas 4, the Porkers put on a stirring goal-line stand, but on fourth down, Stegent went diving over from a yard out.

The Aggies then forced two Razorback punts and had things going their way until Housley, wide open, dropped a pass that would have yielded a first down. The Aggies were forced to punt; the Porkers got the ball at their own 49, and away they went. Facing fourth and 3 at the Aggie

15, South drilled one through the crowd to Peacock at the 5, and Dickey blasted across from there in three tries.

A few moments later, when Steve O'Neal's punt went only 34 yards into the teeth of that strong north wind, the Arkies were in position to take the lead. They wasted no time. With 2:44 showing on the clock, South overcame a first-and-19 situation by hitting Mike Hendren on a 21-yard completion on fourth down. Two more bits of needle-threading, South to Hendren for 9 to the Aggie 6 and South to a wide-open Peacock in the end zone, shoved Arkansas out in front, 14–7.

The Aggies started winning the game in the third quarter when they held the Porkers for the most part while facing that unfriendly breeze. O'Neal's punts did most of the damage. A 46-yarder left Arkansas backed up to its own 16; the next one, a 45-yarder, left the Arkies on their own 1. Bob Long's 22-yard punt return to the 19 gave Hargett just the position he wanted. The drive required two fourth-down conversions, but Hargett ultimately found Barney Harris embarrassingly uncovered in the end zone, and it was an easy 3-yard touchdown to tie the score.

After the Razorbacks countered with a 19-yard TD pass from South to Peacock, it was time for Hargett . . . and Stegent . . . and Housley . . . and all the Aggies. They came like a rush, like the Indians at Little Big Horn.

Stegent returned the kickoff 21 yards, and on first down, Hargett threw to Buckman for 16 yards. The yards came quickly and freely down to the Porker 12. From there, it was sudden death—Hargett hitting Housley on a flip over the middle and the powerful Aggie fullback lowering his shoulder and booming over. The kick failed, and the Aggies trailed, 20–21.

Two plays later, A&M's Winston Beam hit Arkansas runner Glen Hockersmith, forcing a fumble. Maxwell got it, and the Aggies were almost home. Hargett hit Stegent on a 17-yard pass—on third down, naturally—and then on still another third-down play drilled the ball between two Arkies and into Maxwell's hands in the end zone from 15 yards out.

The two-point conversion failed, but now the Aggies were ahead, 26–21; the only question was whether their defense could hold. It could. After yielding two first downs to South and his good right arm, the Cadets snuffed 'em out. After the punt, there went Hargett and Stegent again, this time from the Aggie 47. A 35-yard pass to Stegent moved the Cadets to the Arkansas 16, and just when it appeared the drive had been stopped, Hargett fired to Stegent again, and leaping Larry leaped on to the Arkansas 3. Two plays later, Stegent plunged in and left Arkansas needing 12 points and a miracle to survive. Brupbacher's interception in the final minute, his fifth in three games, ensured there would be no miracle on this day.

So Arkansas is out of the race (1-2-1) and the Aggies are in the big middle of it, with an open date coming up before they take on Rice and Texas in the mad dash for the wire. Until those late returns come in, this sparkling Saturday in the Ozarks must stand as their finest hour.

NOVEMBER 24, 1967

AGGIES SCUTTLE RIVAL LONGHORNS TO GAIN COTTON BOWL BERTH, 10-7

COLLEGE STATION, Tex.—Those incredible, unbelievable Texas Aggies landed on the moon, conquered Mt. Everest, swam the North Sea, and balanced the national budget all in one fell swoop here this historic Thanksgiving Day afternoon. That is, they whipped favored, blood rival Texas, 10–7, which is the same thing, and in so doing, they swept to their first Southwest Conference championship in 11 years and nailed down their first Cotton Bowl berth in two and a half decades. In wildly delirious Aggieland, supreme joy reigns.

Gene Stallings's kings of the comeback road, who played an entire conference campaign with their backs pinned to an unyielding wall, broke the Longhorn spine with one majestic, breathless play—an 80-yard touchdown pass, Edd Hargett to Bob Long.

The knockout blow, scored with 10:55 left in the fourth quarter, wiped out the 7–3 lead Texas had just constructed with a 55-yard, seven-play show of power that reached the payoff window when Bill Bradley faked to big Ted Koy and then followed the sophomore tailback into the Aggie end zone from 2 yards out.

With those two fourth-quarter touchdowns, which came within 16 seconds of each other, canceling each other out, little Charley Riggs's 32-yard field goal was there to provide the difference and put the sky-high Aggies home free.

Riggs's field goal, kicked with 5:36 remaining in the first half, was the direct product of the first of the great Bill Hobbs's two interceptions. When Texas' Bill Bradley tried to pass from the edge of his own goal line, Rolf Krueger burst in on him and deflected the ball, and the swift and sure Hobbs fielded the ball on the Texas 15 and returned it 4 yards.

Four plays later, after the Cadets had been hurled back to the 15 by the fierce Texas defense, Curley Hallman knelt at the 22, Riggs kicked, and the ball eased up to the left upright, hit it, and glanced safely through while a big portion of the largest crowd ever to see these two archrivals play—at least 52,000—went slightly mad.

But that was mild to what they did when the nerveless Hargett drifted back, took his time, and fired deep and true to Long just after the Longhorns had gone ahead in the fourth quarter.

Until that moment, Texas had been slowly but surely gaining control of the game. The first half had belonged to the Aggies, but now the momentum had turned.

LONGHORNS LOSE GILBERT

Unable to cross the A&M 42 in the game's first 30 minutes, Texas had returned to the action full of fire. The Longhorns lost breakaway terror Chris Gilbert for the rest of the afternoon on the second-half kickoff, replaced him with the powerful Koy, and immediately started mauling the Aggies off-tackle.

Gilbert couldn't have done better. Indeed, in the first half, he had not done as well.

Working most of the time behind the effective blocking of big Howard Fest, Koy and Bradley carried the Horns down to the Aggie 26 before grinding to a halt. Rob Layne tried a 43-yard field goal and missed.

Back the Longhorns came to the Aggie 25, and this time, an interception by smooth Tommy Maxwell at the A&M 4-yard line rebuffed them. Bradley had his target, Randy Peschel, running open near the Aggie goal, but he tried to loop the ball instead of drilling it, and Maxwell got there first.

But the next time, there was no holding the orange tide, as Koy battered and ripped and stormed the line as Bradley hit one key pass—a 35-yarder to a wide-open Ed Small to the Aggie 17.

Two plays later, the same Bradley—who on this sunny, breeze-swept afternoon was neither super Bill nor plain Bill—got free around right end for a 7-yard gain, and three plays later, he burst into the end zone. Layne's extra point made it a 7–3 game and cast the biggest wet blanket you ever saw over rebuilt Kyle Field.

But all that did was set the stage for Hargett and Long. After Layne's kickoff to the end zone had been touched down, the Aggies lined up at their own 20, missed on one Hargett incompletion, and then shook down thunder from the skies.

Long, a master receiver, deadly in the clutch—the Aggies' big-play man for seven games and then shut out in the last two—went down and across and got a couple of steps on Bonnie Ehrig.

Hargett laid the ball right there, perfectly. He couldn't have handed the old pigskin in better style. Long caught the ball at chest level, on a dead run, at the Texas 40, and down the west sidelines he went, running for glory, with Texas safety Pat Harkins in frantic pursuit.

SHORT WAIT FOR STALLINGS

Harkins almost had a shot at him at about the 10, but Long changed direction, slanted back toward the middle of the field, and went into the end zone untouched. You couldn't hear yourself think.

It was the kind of play coaches diagram on the blackboard and then spend a lifetime waiting for their pupils to execute properly. Stallings was lucky; he only had to wait three years. And when it came—what a payoff!

That beautiful bomb knocked the Longhorns to their knees. They refused to stay there.

They came rolling back, and Hobbs stopped them with an interception. They came rolling back again, 60 yards in 10 plays to the A&M 15, and Buster Adami stopped them with a brilliant diving interception. They came back still a third time, and Lynn Odom and Grady Allen stalled them by tossing Bradley for a loss of 2 on fourth down at the Texas 49. And they came rolling back one last time in the game's final minute of play, but after driving from their own 30 to the A&M 38, they ran out of downs and time and opportunity.

When Bradley's last pass of the afternoon failed to get a first down, the Aggies took over with six seconds left, a spectator sitting just in front of the press box suffered a heart attack, and Edd Hargett took the snap from center and curled around the ball and then vanished in a flood of bounding, jubilant, whooping Aggie humanity.

This is the town some would rename "Malfunction Junction," but it malfunctioned only for the Royal men today.

Striving for victory that would have assured them a share of the championship, a 5–2 SWC record, and perhaps a Cotton Bowl berth, they ended up instead with their third straight 6–4 season and a finish that can be no better than third. No year of the Horns, that.

Royal put it on the line for his troops before the battle: lose this one and there's no bowl in the Longhorn future this year. They lost even though they won the battle of statistics coming and going. They led in total offense, 344 yards to 277; in rushing, 200 yards to 74; in ball control, 79 plays to 57; in punting, 44.5-yard average to 41.

In the second half, they had a whopping upper hand. They led in first downs, nine to two. They out-rushed the Aggies, 129 yards to a paltry 12. They even out-passed them, 129 yards to 94. And—get this—they ran 52 plays from scrimmage while permitting the Aggies only 20. Unbelievable.

But still they lost, for only the second time in the storied rivalry in 17 years, and the reason they lost goes back to Hargett, Long, and an A&M defense that can find more ways to make big plays than Carter has little bitty pills.

Six times the pressure-proof Aggie defense pilfered the ball away from the enemy—four times with interceptions and twice by forcing fumbles and then recovering—and at the finish, a sad Darrell Royal pointed to those six turnovers as the big difference.

"It was a long day," said Darrell. "Except for that one big play [Hargett to Long], I thought we played

Gene Stallings (in sport coat and tie) heads onto the field after halftime. Courtesy of Texas A&M University Athletics.

an outstanding football game. But you're not going to win against a better or equal team if you give up the ball on turnovers many times. They [the Aggies] didn't reciprocate."

Well, as a matter of fact, the Aggies did lose the ball twice—once on a Hargett fumble (Mike McKinney recovered) and once when Harkins intercepted a Hargett pass, but at the finish, those turnovers were only incidentals.

Texas, meanwhile, could look back and see where victory got away—Hobbs's interception at the Longhorn 11, setting up Riggs's field goal; Grady Allen's recovery of Chris Gilbert's fumble at the Aggie 42, after Texas had moved 35 yards on four plays in staging its best drive of the first half; a Billy Piper recovery of a Koy fumble at the Texas 41 early in the third quarter, when the Longhorns were driving again; Maxwell's interception at the Aggie 4, wiping out a severe Texas threat; Hobbs's second interception at the Texas 27; Adami's tremendous interception at the Aggie 8 late in the fourth quarter, foiling the Longhorns' last push inside the Aggie 20.

All those Aggies were superb defensively. So were Rolf Krueger, Ivan Jones, Harvey Aschenbeck, and Grady Allen. When it took a big play to take the starch out of the Longhorns, they found a way to execute it, except on Texas' scoring drive.

The Longhorns defense played grandly itself, except on the one big bomb. Led by Loyd Wainscott, Jim Williamson, Joel Brame, Harkins, and Leo Brooks, they fought for their lives in the first half, when the Aggie offense was on the move, and they came through.

They turned the Aggies back at the Texas 13 early in the game, after Hargett had escorted his team 63 yards in seven plays (a 43-yard pass to—you guessed it—Long was the big gainer) and watched as Riggs missed a field goal attempt. They stopped the Aggies on fourth down at their 30 after A&M had moved 40 yards in 8 plays.

They made the Maroon settle for the field goal after Hobbs's interception had given A&M a first down at the Texas 11.

"I'm sure proud of our defense," said Royals.

But even at that, he wasn't as proud as his young adversary. Stallings won it all for his alma mater in just three years, and he coached the Aggies to their first conquest of the hated Horns in 11 long years, since Bear Bryant's '56 A&M team beat Texas in Austin. One of the captains of the '56 Aggie team was a guy named Gene Stallings.

For young Gene, '56 was nothing to compare with '67. "I've never been prouder of a football team in all my life," he said. "This has got to be the happiest moment of my athletic life. Our players displayed a lot of class."

This came from the coach who 10 weeks ago, on this same field, before a national television audience, watched his favored Aggies blow a conference game to SMU with four seconds to play.

The Aggies lost that day because, in the clutch, they had no defense. The touchdown that beat them was scored at the south end of the field. Today they had both the defense and the game's last touchdown, and it too was scored at the south end.

The final facts and figures gave Hargett 9 completions in 17 attempts for 203 yards. Long caught 4 of them for 143 yards, and Barney Harris got 3 for 37. Willing Larry Stegent got 80 yards on 22 carries. Thirty-one of them came on one gallop around left end—A&M's longest run of this season. Although Steve O'Neal, the conference's leading punter, was out-kicked by Bradley for the afternoon, he shook the Longhorns with one beautiful 45-yarder that hit in the end zone and then rolled back out to the Texas 1, where Danny Schneider and Burney Harris killed it.

It was from that perilous position that the Longhorns were operating when Hobbs intercepted the pass that set up Riggs's eighth field goal of the season, the one that set a new Aggie team record and provided the difference in the game Ol' Army just had to have.

Bradley also left a punt dying on the A&M 1, but the Fightin' Farmers got out of the hole unscathed. When a mistake would have been fatal, A&M refused to err.

Bradley punted for a 44.5-yard average, ran for 44 yards, and passed for 134 (8 completions in 21 tries, with 4 interceptions). Gilbert rushed for 51 yards, Koy for 75 on 23 carries. Peschel caught two passes for 25 yards, Ragan Gennusa two for 28, and Tom Higgins two for 37.

But long after those figures have been forgotten, old and young Aggies will still be talking about Hargett and Long and Hobbs and Gene Stallings, about the '67 A&M team and how it finally beat Texas and won the championship and claimed the right to meet Bear Bryant's Alabama team in the Cotton Bowl. On Thanksgiving Day 1967, they made the earth move.

THE GENE STALLINGS STORY

I am one of those few sportswriters still alive who actually went to hot and dry Junction that summer day in 1954 as a member of that season's Southwest Conference press tour. We started that season meeting with Rice coach Jess Neely and the Owls, and under normal circumstances, we next would have gone to College Station, Texas A&M's home base and longtime campus. But A&M had a new football coach that year—none other than famous Paul (Bear) Bryant. And that first season, Bryant wanted his players to do their training away from any distractions or prying eyes. There were precious few prying eyes in Junction.

So instead of going to College Station that year, my first as the new sports editor of the *Waco Tribune-Herald*, we went to Austin to get the lowdown on the Longhorns and football coach Ed Price. We spent the next night in Austin, then got up at first daylight, drove to Fredericksburg for breakfast at the old Admiral Nimitz Hotel, and then drove on to Junction.

We found Bryant sending his inheritance through their paces on a fairly level field that looked to be filled with gravel and some grass burrs. But I heard no complaints, although Mickey Herskowitz, a member of the *Houston Post*'s sports staff in those days and whose assignment was to cover Bryant's activities, assured us that some candidates for the team were leaving late at night—just slipping away. As A&M's sports information director in those days, Jones Ramsey, often said, "We went to Junction in three buses and came back in one."

We writers on that press tour were all abuzz. Bryant was new to the SWC. He was magnetic; he was exciting. What would he do or say next? Personally, I had never met Bryant. I knew of Don Watson, one of the "Junction Boys," because he was from Franklin, down the road from Waco, and he had been a big scoring threat at Franklin, one of the teams we had covered on high school Friday night football. But Gene Stallings? He was just another name on Bryant's football roster to me.

But he didn't stay that long. Although Bryant's team lost its first game that 1954 season (41–9 to non-SWC member Texas Tech, which became a member of the SWC in football in 1960), I remember Bryant started shuffling his players around, and one player he singled out for his play and effort against the Red Raiders was "that skinny kid named Gene Stallings—he played really hard. We can win with him," Bryant said, as best I can remember.

But I got to know Stallings in a more personal way when he became coach of Texas A&M football in 1965. Darrell Royal was in his heyday then, just two seasons removed from a national championship in 1963 and four seasons away from winning another national crown in 1969. (The "Big Shootout" in Fayetteville, remember?) But that 1965 season, using the 1–9 team he had inherited from Hank Foldberg, Stallings used a special play he had put in just for the Texas game: The QB faked a handoff to a player running wide left, then as Texas' defense closed in on the QB, he fired a lateral to the player he had just faked to. The receiver caught the ball after it had bounced just above his shoe tops and acted as if the play had been a pass, killing the play. But as a lateral, the play was still alive, and the player straightened and threw a deep pass to a streaking receiver, Dude McLean, who was wide open. It was an easy touchdown. Texas came back to win the game, 21–17, but Royal praised the "special pass" as one of the "most original" he had ever seen.

I covered that Thanksgiving Day football game played at Kyle Field that afternoon, just as I covered several of the games played and won by the Aggies in 1967, when Stallings's team lost its first four games (to SMU, Purdue, LSU, and Florida State) and then did not lose another game. I was fortunate enough to get to cover the SMU loss and the A&M victories over Baylor, 21–3, at Kyle Field; Arkansas, 33–21, at Fayetteville; Rice, 18–3, at Rice Stadium; and Texas, 10–7, at Kyle Field.

Then SWC champions over SWC runner-up Texas Tech, the Aggies went to the Cotton Bowl, and on an impossible-to-forget, bitterly cold day, they defeated visiting Alabama's Crimson Tide, armed with quarterback Kenny Stabler (later a celebrated NFL quarterback) and Stallings's old mentor Bear Bryant, 20–16. After the final whistle, Bryant came across the gridiron and hoisted Stallings to his shoulders, much to the delight of the wildly celebrating A&M fans. I was fortunate enough to get to cover that game. It was A&M's first SWC football championship since the university's undefeated football team in 1956 in the third year of Bryant's tenure at Texas A&M.

A&M's consensus All-SWC players that year included wide receiver Bob Long and QB Edd Hargett and, on defense, end Grady Allen, tackle Rolf Krueger, and linebacker Bill Hobbs. A lot of the SWC press corps thought that A&M running back Wendell Housley also should have been on that All-SWC selection.

Texas A&M's youthful head coach Gene Stallings, one of Bear Bryant's "Junction Boys." Courtesy of Texas A&M University Athletics.

One other thing happened at A&M during Stallings's coaching days there. One day after A&M's spring football game, Stallings sponsored a media golf tournament (the better to get coverage on that spring game) and then invited some people that night, including the press guys, to his home for a meal and fellowship. Among those he invited was A&M's president at the time, Earl Rudder. For those who are not familiar with World War history, Earl Rudder is a native of West Texas and one of the monumental heroes of World War II, starting with the invasion of Normandy. Being a veteran of World War II myself (14th Armored Division, fought in France and Germany), I considered it a real honor to get to talk to Earl Rudder. I still do.

I have one lasting memory of Stallings as coach of the Texas A&M football: In 1968, the athletic faculty representatives of all SWC members met for their usual spring meetings in Fort Worth in mid-May. Several of the SWC members came to those meetings determined to charge Stallings with recruiting violations—maybe eager to put A&M on probation as they had done to Bear Bryant and the Aggies in the spring meetings in 1955. Members of the SWC press corps set up camp in Fort Worth in droves.

Among those who were there were Bob Galt of the *Dallas Times Herald* (now defunct) and yours truly. All of us were working furiously to find out what really was going on in those meetings.

But I had a decisive advantage. An A&M friend of mine also had a friend close to Stallings, and because of that pipeline, I had the inside track. And I was keeping Galt (now deceased) informed too. When it was all over and Stallings and A&M had managed to get off the hook, Galt and I were able to get an advance scoop. As a result, one of the faculty representatives accused us of having bugged the SWC faculty meetings. That's the only time I've ever been accused of doing such a thing.

As for Stallings, he moved on from his job at A&M to Tom Landry's staff with the Dallas Cowboys in 1972, where he coached the secondary; then to the St. Louis-Phoenix Cardinals in 1986; and finally to head coach of the Alabama Crimson Tide in 1990. In his first attempt, he directed Alabama to a coveted victory over Auburn, and in 1992, he coached the Crimson Tide to the ultimate: a perfect 13–0 season climaxed by a 34–13 victory over heavily favored Miami in the 1993 Sugar Bowl, giving Alabama its first national football championship since the days of Bear Bryant in 1979.

Stallings continued to coach the Crimson Tide before retiring after the 1996 season (there were several more great seasons but no more national titles). He was voted SEC Coach of the Year twice, and he was inducted into the College Football Hall of Fame in 2010. He was named a Distinguished Alumnus of Texas A&M in 2000, has been voted into the Texas Sports Hall of Fame, and was presented with the Legends Award by the All-Sports Association of Dallas in 2001. He has also served on the Texas A&M Board of Regents.

He now lives with his wife, Ruth Ann (they were married after his graduation from A&M), and they have had five children (one, John Mark, is deceased after being born with Down syndrome, and because of that development, Stallings became involved in a number of projects promoting better education and quality of life for the developmentally disabled). The retired coach and his wife now live on a working cattle ranch in Powderly, near his childhood town of Paris, Texas.

JANUARY 2, 1968

AGGIES AMBUSH ALABAMA, WIN COTTON BOWL, 20–16

DALLAS, Tex.—The incredible Texas Aggies, who opened the football season by losing to a pint-sized quarterback, closed it in delicious and delirious fashion here Monday by upsetting one of football's giants, the Alabama Crimson Tide, and its legendary coach, who walks only in 12-league boots.

A sellout mob of 75,000 frost-bitten witnesses was treated not only to a classic Cotton Bowl battle that A&M finally won, 20–16, but also to an unforgettable sight—a beaten Bear Bryant meeting his triumphant pupil, Gene Stallings, at midfield and hoisting the happy Aggie coach onto his shoulder in a final, bittersweet salute.

And that was the way the day ended, the Aggies on top of the world and Stallings riding high on his idol-mentor's shoulder. "This is the biggest victory I've ever had," Gene said, beaming.

This is known as going from the ridiculous to the sublime in one short season. This also is known as bringing in the new year with the most delightful Aggie joke of them all. Gene Stallings wound up the season by beating Darrell Royal and Bear Bryant back to back, and this is only slightly less difficult than making water sprint uphill.

The Aggies did it the same way they won the Southwest Conference—by getting beat in the figures while making the big plays that paid off on the scoreboard. And all the while, they played like a team that hadn't been to the Cotton Bowl in 25 years—which, as a matter of fact, they hadn't.

Cool Edd Hargett, voted the game's outstanding back, passed for two touchdowns and 143 yards, fullback Wendell Housley thundered for one touchdown, and linebacker Bill Hobbs and Alabama reject Curley Hallman led a raging defense that gave the Southwest Conference a victory in its own Cotton Bowl for the first time in three years. Hobbs later was voted the game's outstanding lineman.

The Aggies got off the floor and beat 'Bama at its own game, turning interceptions and fumbles into the keys that unlocked the door to victory.

Tommy Maxwell's pass interception—one of three the Aggies managed—set up A&M's first touchdown and an Alabama fumble set up the second one, and from start to finish, the Aggies took the ball away from their touchdown-favored visitors five times on miscues while giving it up only once.

The result was A&M's first bowl victory since John Kimbrough and associates out-tugged Fordham in the Cotton Bowl back in football's stone age of 1941. The result also was A&M's seventh straight victory of the season, but only its first, of course, of 1968. First thing you know, someone will be saying this is the Year of the Aggies.

After the tricky and deadly Kenny (Snake) Stabler had directed the Crimson Tide 80 yards to a seven-point advantage in the first quarter, Hargett hurled touchdown passes of 13 yards to blue-ribbon sophomore Larry Stegent and 7 yards to Tommy Maxwell in the first half.

Barney Harris, a sticky-fingered sophomore who became a hero amid personal tragedy, set up A&M's first touchdown by taking a Hargett shot, evading two 'Bama tacklers, and turning the play into a 28-yard gain to the Tide 15. Three plays later, Stegent drifted free in the left flat, took Edd's pass, and squirmed into the end zone, pulling away from All-American Booby Johns en route.

Harris typified A&M's total dedication. The San Antonio product's father died Saturday. Barney was with the grieving family all weekend. He attended the funeral Monday morning and then, at the family's urging, caught a plane to Dallas.

He was in uniform for the kickoff, he caught passes

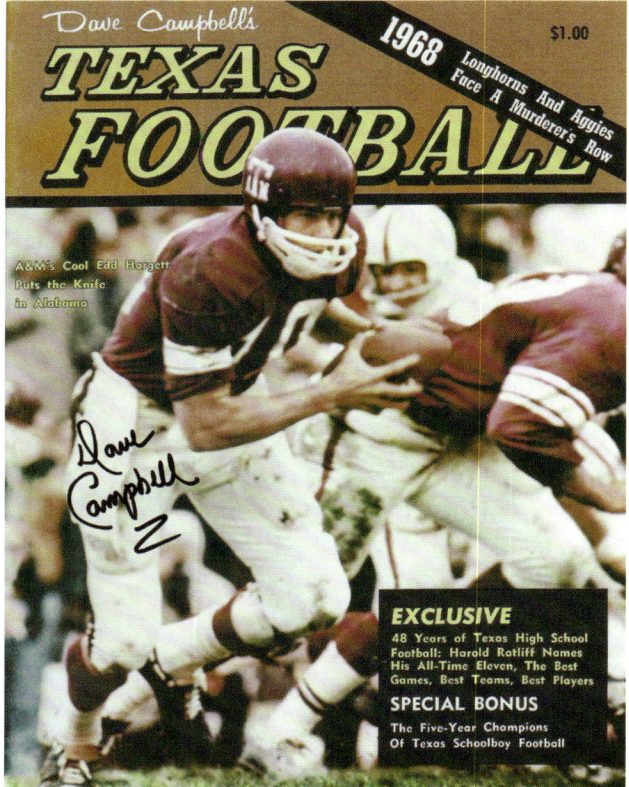

Edd Hargett's cool-headed play in the 1968 Cotton Bowl led the Aggies to victory over Bear Bryant, Kenny Stabler, and Alabama. It also landed him on the cover of the 1968 magazine. Courtesy of *Dave Campbell's Texas Football*.

that helped fuel two touchdown drives, he was down under punts like a demon all afternoon, and after the game was over, the team voted to give two "game balls" away instead of the customary one—one to Stallings and one to Barney Harris.

Alabama, moving 56 yards in 11 plays to the A&M 19 immediately after the Aggies had scored their first touchdown, took a 10–7 lead on Steve Davis's 36-yard field goal with 14:56 left in the second quarter.

Hargett's bullet pass to Maxwell erased the Tide's 10–7 lead with 16 seconds left in the half, climaxing a drive that carried 56 yards in eight plays. It was a Hargett production throughout, pieced together on completions of 17 yards to Bob Long, 21 yards to tom Buckman, and 14 yards to Stegent, who made a tumbling, bobbling, hair-raising catch at the 'Bama 7. After Stegent's catch, Maxwell's touchdown grab was almost anticlimactic.

But not quite. Touchdowns against Alabama on this gray but star-spangled afternoon were never anticlimactic.

The unflappable Aggie quarterback then directed the Fighting Farmers to a 20–10 advantage with 8:32 left in the third quarter as Housley plundered the Alabama midsection for 33 of the 52 yards needed to get the touchdown.

The final 20 yards came on one splendid burst between left guard and left tackle. The big and strong Housley, injured much of the season and running as if he intended to make up lost time, was through the line before 'Bama knew he had the ball, and when Tide defenders Eddie Propst and David Bodwell tried to flag him down in the secondary, Housley just got a little lower and little stronger and bulled on to the end zone. Charlie Riggs, who kicked true after the first Aggie touchdown and missed after the second, added the 20th point.

Stabler brought 'Bama right back, getting a touchdown in nine plays, and although fullback David Chatwood was engulfed by the angry Aggie defense 3 yards short of the payoff window on a two-point conversion attempt, A&M was only four points ahead and vulnerable as the game moved into its last 18 minutes.

That's when the wide-ranging Hobbs rallied the Aggie defense, snuffed out Stabler's most lethal endeavors, and finally, in the fading moments, shook off what could have been a demoralizing 25-yard fourth-down penalty and stopped the Crimson Tide short and took the ball and the victory away.

The penalty came with 2:47 remaining, after the Aggies apparently had smeared receiver Ed Morgan on the Alabama 20 on fourth down, far short of first-down territory. But a red flag fell upfield, an Aggie was ruled guilty of defensive holding, and Stabler and his terrible swift sword got new life on the 'Bama 44.

Giving Kenney the Snake a second opportunity is like reentering the lion's den. A man—or a team—can get hurt that way. The Aggies almost did.

Stabler, who completed 16 of 26 passes for 179 yards and scored two touchdowns himself on runs of 3 and 7 yards, quickly passed to Perry Willis for 7 and All-American Dennis Homan for 14—and there the Crimson Tide was on the Aggie 35, blowin' and goin'.

A&M's massed thousands, so jubilant a moment earlier, so confident of victory, were fit to be tied. This was Dallas-Green Bay all over again, and no need to say which was Green Bay.

Then the never-quit Aggie defense, which was due a break, got a beauty. Homan, normally as sure-handed as Willie Mays, sped into the clear at the Aggie 15, reached for a perfect Stabler peg—and let the possible touchdown throw bounce off his fingers.

A&M needed no more help. Stabler tried a shot to Richard Brewer, and Hallman broke it up. Then the Snake came back with a pass to Hunter Husband, and Hobbs was waiting for the receiver at the A&M 29—4 yards short of a first down—and Hobbs didn't miss.

The Aggies took the ball and ran some tantalizingly slow quarterback sneaks. Then with 31 seconds left, Steve O'Neal kicked 38 yards to Homan, and when the Alabama safety retreated, trying to find running room, the raging Stegent came in like the cold north wind and blew him down.

So 'Bama started back on its own end of the field with a few seconds left, and Stabler tried one long desperation pass and Hallman intercepted it—his second interception of the game, by the way—and then the Aggies whooped and hollered. Now they knew they were home free. The dam burst and the noise came.

From the start, it was one of those football rarities—a game with a classic buildup that never disappointed through ebb and flow, point and counterpoint.

Although Alabama prevailed in the final statistics—14 to 33 in first downs and 314 yards to 257 in total offense—the Bryant men were never inside the Aggie 20 except on those occasions when they put points on the scoreboard. Several times they sabotaged themselves with illegal-receiver-downfield penalties; other times the quick-reacting, swarming Aggies handed them the bad plays that short-circuited their drives.

Stabler was always a menace. Although he lost the ball on the game's first maneuver on a busted play that gave the Aggies possession on Alabama's 28, he came right back four plays later—after the Aggies had been stopped on the 'Bama 26—and directed his team 80 yards in 10 plays (and two penalties) to a touchdown.

A pass to the fleet Homan up the middle gained 14, and after red flags twice had given the Alabamans first downs, Stabler carried over himself from the 3. Davis added the extra point.

On the long drive that paid off in Davis's field goal, Stabler had pass completions of 11 and 13 yards, and it was his fake that enabled Martin to squirt up the middle for 18 to the Aggie 23. But then Buster Adami, Billy Kubecks, Rolf Krueger, Hobbs, Harvy Aschenbeck, Grady Allen, Jimmy Piper, and Ivan Jones rose up and refused to let the Crimson Tide roll on. That became a trend. Those Aggie defensive names kept bobbing up when the going got tough and the chips got blue.

It was Maxwell who stole Stabler's pass that set up A&M's first touchdown. It was Piper who recovered the fumble at the A&M 48 that set up the second. It was the entire right side of the Aggie defensive line that refused to yield a yard on third and 1 late in the game, making Alabama punt when 'Bama didn't want to punt at all. And it was steady Steve O'Neal who kept punting the ball high and far (10 times, 41-yard average) when good punting was vital to the Aggie cause.

The second half was played to the tune of a different drummer. In the first half, it had been aerial warfare pure and simple. A&M got 13 points during those first 30 minutes of combat but only 12 yards net rushing. Hargett's passes (10 of 21 for 133 yards) and the catches of Stegent, Long, Buckman, and Maxwell got them there.

In the second half, Hargett switched strategy. He turned to his infantry. In the game's final 30 minutes, he threw only one pass (a 10-yarder to Harris on the winning touchdown drive). While 'Bama waited for the pass, Edd sent Housley thundering straight ahead on quick hitters (seven carries for 52 yards) and ran an option on which he and Stegent bruised the Tide's flanks. That also controlled the ball and ate up the time.

Only once during the second half did Alabama threaten to engulf A&M, as the handicappers had expected. After A&M had taken its 20–10 lead, Stabler and his mates got their revenge yardage in big chunks. Chatwood got 20 up the middle on a trap. When the Aggies plugged that hole, Stabler hurled a 19-yarder to Danny Ford. Later he hit Homan on a quick slant in from the flanker post, and Denny turned it into a 22-yard play to the Aggie 7. Ross Brupbacher staved off the touchdown for a moment by flagging down Homan, but Stabler faked and kept at left tackle and went in standing up two plays later.

But the try for two points failed, and so did everything else 'Bama tried, even some shotgun formation stuff late in the game.

Meanwhile, the Aggies played defense, stuck to their knittin', and played ball control, and they might even have gotten some insurance points had Housley not fumbled with 8:15 left at the Alabama 22.

But that just helped set the stage for the tension and

Gene Stallings, hoisted off the ground at midfield by his lifelong mentor, Bear Bryant, at the conclusion of A&M's victory over 'Bama in the 1968 Cotton Bowl. Courtesy of Texas A&M University Athletics.

drama that was to come at the finish, when 'Bama made its last drive and the Aggies made their last great stand and won the game and walked off winners. And Bear Bryant came out to midfield and picked up Gene Stallings and gave him the symbolic victory ride young Gene will never forget. Neither will the Aggies.

NOVEMBER 23, 1969

MUSTANGS HOLD OFF FIGHTING BEARS, 12–6: DARYL DOGGETT PACES PONY WIN

On a day that will long live in infamy in Columbus, Ohio, the scrappy Baylor Bears almost made a little history in Waco, Texas, themselves. They came within 18 yards and an extra point Saturday of beating the SMU Mustangs and winning their first game of the 1969 season.

They didn't win it, of course. Hayden Fry's forces won, 12–6, ending their 3–7 season on a high note of sorts after combining to best advantage the darting runs of mini-Mustang Daryl Doggett, the short passes of Chuck Hixson, and a ball-hawking defense that held off the attacking Bears in the last minute when it counted the most.

As a Baylor Stadium crowd of about 20,000 focused its full attention on the south end of the arena, the Bears took a cue from their aroused defense and drove 39 yards to the SMU 18 as the clock started to run down. But alas, that was their high-water mark.

Two bombing runs failed, the last crucial one being broken up in the end zone on a nice play by Mike Jordan, and instead of acquiring the last few yards they needed to give Coach Bill Beall his first Baylor victory, they were forced to surrender both hope and possession.

In terms of coming close, this was Baylor's best performance in conference play. This was the first time the Bears have managed to keep a league opponent worried and anxious for the entire game. SMU constructed its victory total with bits and pieces—a 5-yard touchdown run by Hixson, an extra point by Chipper Johnson, a 52-yard field goal by Johnson, and finally a safety donated by Bruin quarterback Laney Cook late in the fourth quarter when the Bears opted for some deep strategy.

The strategy worked—sort of. It got the Bears out of a deep hole and led to their final opportunity, which they almost cashed. But that was the story of their day—a long series of almosts. "One of these days," said a not-altogether-unhappy Bill Beall, "that thing's going to turn around for us."

One of their finest moments took shape at the Baylor 6 as the clock showed just a bit more than six minutes to play. It was a 10–6 game by then; SMU, with the wind at its back, had moved from its own 43 to the Baylor 15 on seven plays, the biggest one being a 16-yard pass from Hixson to tight end Fleming. A pass failed but then the determined Doggett bolted on a trap to the 10, then to the 6.

It was fourth and 1. If the Mustangs got a first down there, it was all over. They turned to their little meal ticket once more, and this time the Bears were ready for him. Doggett, blocked at right tackle, tried to spin away to the outside, and Miller, Marsh, and Serafin ganged up on him for no gain. The Bears were still alive.

That set the stage for a curious and unexpected bit of strategy four plays later. On fourth and 9, the Bears scorned the punt and sent Laney Cook to take the center snap. Cook faded and looked over the field for a moment only to see if he could spot an open receiver, and when nothing tempting met his eye, he knelt in the end zone for a safety.

While the scoreboard blinked out another two points for the Mustangs, Ed Marsh, the nation's No. 1 kicker, stood at the Baylor 20 and boomed out a 61-yarder into that stiff south breeze. SMU clipped on the return and wound up back at its 17. Marsh's superb punt and the savage play of the defense on the next three plays gave the Bears their final chance. Bicky Lesser's punt was a poor one, but it came wrapped in a lucky package. It rolled and rolled, forcing the Bears to take over on their own 43.

Stuart hit Huggins, a nervy little rascal who is all heart, for three passes totaling 37 yards as the Bears found themselves with a first down at the SMU 20. A minute and 44 seconds remained. Two plays later, Huggins twisted for 2 more yards on a halfback draw, but the Bears had gone as far as they could go.

IT WAS A DARK AND STORMY NIGHT

With all due apologies to comic strip genius Charles Schulz and his unique creation *Peanuts*, that night in Fayetteville, Arkansas, was truly dark and stormy. And I was there to interview Arkansas football coach Frank Broyles and several of his more talented Razorbacks, who had just wrapped up spring football practice.

This was in May 1960. A new magazine was coming off the drawing board in Waco, a publication that would be called *Texas Football*. My share of the coverage of the eight Southwest Conference schools was Rice, Texas A&M, Baylor, and Arkansas, and all the copy for the magazine had been written, except for that pertaining to the Razorbacks.

The agreement we had for that evening was that I would fly to Fayetteville and check into the historic Mountain Inn Hotel. Broyles would fly back to Fayetteville after a speaking engagement at a coaching clinic in the Midwest, then swing by the Mountain Inn and pick me up for dinner, where I would have time to get my interview.

Only problem was, a whopper of a thunderstorm had blown into the Fayetteville area that evening. All of us at the Mountain Inn were ordered to come down to the hotel lobby; it would be safer there. As for the chances of Broyles's plane being on time? Well, good luck.

But he did make it—maybe a little late, but not by much. He wheeled by the hotel, picked me up, and told me we would just go to his home for the dinner his wife, Barbara, had prepared. All told, I got a great steak dinner and a good interview, and then Broyles took me back to the hotel.

It was only months later, in a story written for the *Saturday Evening Post* by the *Houston Post*'s outstanding sportswriter Jack Gallagher, that I found out the rest of that story. In taking me to his home that night, Broyles had permitted me to intrude on his and Barbara's wedding anniversary.

And so it went with *Texas Football*'s coverage of the Arkansas Razorbacks. Indeed, largely at the behest of several Razorback officials, I launched a companion magazine, *Arkansas Football*, in 1963. *Arkansas Football* enjoyed years of success, especially during the Broyles era, when the Texas-Arkansas rivalry was almost beyond words.

As Mickey Herskowitz wrote in his outstanding story in the 1966 issue of *Texas Football*, this had become a rivalry matching teams coached by good friends but fierce rivals Broyles and Darrel Royal,

"built not by tradition or interstate commerce but on the excellence of the teams involved and the high treasure for which they invariably compete."

The 1965 nationally televised game, he wrote, "was the *Mona Lisa*," and sports page historians concluded that "it was the most exciting game ever played between Southwestern Conference teams, on a national stage, watched by so many, with so much to be gained or lost."

In Herskowitz's story, in which he noted that the 1960, 1962, and 1964 games were final-second spellbinders that decided SWC championships, he declared the 1965 game had topped them all. Arkansas, playing on home turf, had taken advantage of Texas turnovers to jump in front, 20–0. The Longhorns had answered with a throbbing comeback of its own that won the game for the Razorbacks in the last 100 seconds, 27–20.

My headline for the Herskowitz story in the magazine read "A Classic Series, and a Game for the Ages."

Forty-four years after the fact, I would have to say that those words have the ring of truth, but they were written in haste. Four years later, the 1969 Texas-Arkansas game—the "Big Shootout," as it has become known in both conversation and memory—was incomparably bigger.

Indeed, I still count that 1969 thriller—No. 1 Texas against No. 2 Arkansas; won late in the game by the Longhorns, 15–14; played on a special December 6 stage in Fayetteville that was preordered by a major network for a national television audience and personally viewed by US President Richard Nixon, famed evangelist Billy Graham, and everyone else who could get a ticket—as the best football game I ever saw.

I was fortunate enough to see and write about all those Texas-Arkansas classics other than the 1960 game, and I also was in the press box for all the meaningful games involving those two teams for the next 10 seasons. Then I started missing them as other teams commanded center stage, but I made sure to be on hand on December 4, 1976, at Texas when both Royal and Broyles announced their retirements.

Texas won that game, 29–12, but the score seemed almost unimportant. Two coaching giants of college football were leaving

> the stage. If you were a sportswriter, you didn't want to miss that moment.
>
> Those two men, and their teams, had meant so much to the Southwest Conference in their salad days of coaching, and the grand old league wouldn't have been the same without them.
>
> And consequently, I doubt Texas Football would have been the same either.
>
> Times have changed, of course. Arkansas moved to the Southeastern Conference in 1992, and we discontinued Arkansas Football. The Razorbacks now have been gone from the Texas Football scene for going on two decades, and thus the "50-year" lists (best coaches, players, etc.) featured in this 50th anniversary edition do not include the Razorbacks.
>
> But in no way have we forgotten them.

DECEMBER 9, 1969

LONGHORNS CAPTURE 15–14 THRILLER OVER ARKANSAS IN "GAME OF THE CENTURY"

FAYETTEVILLE, Ark.—Staggered, desperate, its dream of a national championship almost in eclipse, Texas scratched and clawed its way back from the very edge of the abyss here Saturday and in the ebbing moments courageously secured the 15–14 victory that broke Arkansas' heart.

There might have been even less difference between the two teams than the score indicates.

Arkansas led for the first 56 minutes in this game of games, then was fatally gored by an improbable 44-yard fourth-down pass, perfectly thrown by superhero James Street and caught brilliantly by Randy Peschel at the Arkansas 13. The pass set up the touchdown that won the game for Texas. Jim Bertelsen scored it on a 2-yard plunge.

The pressure-proof, top-ranked Longhorns, once behind by 14 points, pulled even at last with 3:58 left when Bertelsen drove into the end zone. Then Happy Feller, the most appropriately named Longhorn of them all, kicked the extra point that sacked it all up for Texas—the No. 1 ranking, the Southwest Conference championship, the perfect 10 season, and the Cotton Bowl date with an eager and powerful Notre Dame.

This one was tighter than the bark on a tree. Of all the millions of witnesses—the 44,000 in jam-packed Razorback Stadium and the massive television audience—the man who might have appreciated the thin line between victor and vanquished most of all was the most distinguished member of the breathless Fayetteville crowd, President of the United States Richard M. Nixon. He's been involved in a few close ones himself.

The No. 2–ranked Razorbacks, whose defense surely played beyond itself against the nation's most relentless, punishing offense, saw everything go down the drain— "the chance of a lifetime," they had called it—because of just four or five big plays.

They lost one touchdown that would have made all the difference—a 26-yard scoring pass from Bill Montgomery to Chuck Dicus late in the first quarter—because of a red flag (offensive interference).

They gambled—foolishly, perhaps—and lost with 10½ minutes left in the fourth quarter when they passed on third down from the Texas 8-yard line and saw Texas' Danny Lester make a game-saving end zone interception. The Razorbacks led at that moment by 14–8, and they were in point-blank field goal range, and those were three points that would have won the game for them.

"A field goal then would have killed us," a jubilant Darrel Royal was to say at the finish.

But most of all, the fired-up, gung-ho Razorbacks lost because they couldn't keep James Street down. Almost by himself, the gutty Texas quarterback, a blithe

Jim Bertelsen (35) carries off tackle, in need of a replacement jersey. Courtesy of University of Texas Athletics.

spirit but a cool customer when the chips are piled high, plucked a victory from the ashes of defeat.

He scrambled 42 yards for a touchdown on the first play of the fourth quarter when the Longhorns were sagging, 14 points down.

He squirmed across on the two-point conversion play that followed, putting Texas in position to win the game.

And finally, on a dramatic fourth-down test of nerve and skills, with 4:47 left in the game, with Texas having to come up with 3 yards or succumb, he fired the 44-yard bomb that an equally nerveless Peschel grabbed at the Arkansas 13-yard line just before he fell out of bounds in the arms of defenders Jerry Moore and Dennis Berner.

That bomb tore open the game. Bertelsen scored from the 2-yard line two plays later, after Ted Koy had blistered the Arkansas defense for the first 11 yards.

Feller kicked Texas' winning point, and a chill deeper than that brought in by the soft north wind settled over the fearful Razorback rooters.

But they weren't through. No one thought that. By then, the sullen gray skies had lowered until they formed a tight little umbrella over the stadium, temperatures were dropping, and the Razorbacks faced the wind, but no one thought of leaving.

They had three minutes and 38 seconds of playing time and they faced 80 yards of enemy grass, but a field goal still would win it for them. A 50- or 60-yard drive might do it, and Montgomery had been moving them well.

In a similar situation—almost identical, in fact—the Porkers in 1965 had answered a Texas comeback with a comeback of their own and had won the game (27–24) and the No. 1 ranking.

You know such thoughts surged through Arkansas memories as the Porkers lined up for their final thrust. Surely the Longhorns remembered too. This was the final moment of truth.

You must admit, the Razorbacks died hard. They moved 41 yards in nine plays as Montgomery passed artfully to Dicus and to tough Bill Burnett. They moved to the Texas 39. A few more yards might do it. A minute and 51 seconds remained.

And then Texas supplied the noose. As the Longhorn front four applied pressure, Montgomery sprinted

Cool-as-a-cucumber Texas quarterback James Street. Courtesy of University of Texas Athletics.

right, looking for John Rees, who got a step on the Texas defender, then cut for the sideline. Montgomery threw. The Longhorns' Tom Campbell—son of Mike Campbell, the architect of the clutch-playing Texas defense—reached in front of Rees and pulled the ball away.

As one official signaled an interception, the Longhorn bench erupted in ecstasy, sure now that victory was theirs. Back upfield, the broken, crestfallen Razorbacks moved silently to the bench. Texas used up two plays in stalling out the clock, cementing one of its greatest comebacks ever.

The Longhorns had proved themselves in the fourth quarter when it counted.

The final score, and the way it was wrapped up, represented irony compounded. In 1965, Arkansas won because Texas couldn't stop the Porkers' final fourth-quarter thrust. In 1964, Arkansas won when Texas tried for a two-point conversion and missed.

This time, the Longhorns made the two-point play and choked off the Arkansas comeback when the game was up for grabs, and in so doing, the Longhorns won one of their sweetest victories of all time.

And one of the most memorable, for all seemed lost for the Longhorns as the clock ticked in the fourth quarter.

The comeback arrived with a jolt when, backing up to pass at the Arkansas 42, Street suddenly shot forward, escaping a covey of defenders. He stumbled, regained his balance, broke away to his right, and suddenly was long gone. It was a 42-yard touchdown run that not only climaxed the 80-yard, nine-play drive but also shocked the Longhorns to life.

When Street also cashed in on the two-point conversion try, you knew the Longhorns were back in the game to stay.

Dead ahead was that ill-fated Arkansas drive, the one engineered so smartly by Montgomery, which carried from the Razorback 20 to the Texas 8 before Lester intervened just in the nick of time. Dicus had catches of 20 and 21 yards on that drive and Rees had a 13-yarder, but Lester had the biggest catch of them all.

The biggest, that is, until Street, facing a fourth-and-3 situation, raced out to his left, stopped, and fired deep to Peschel—the only receiver out on the play.

It was an incredible gamble—foolish if it failed. Nor were the Porkers fooled. Peschel got a step his two defenders, but that was all, and when the ball came down, they were right there with him at the edge of the boundary on the east side. Somehow Peschel made the catch amid the tangle of arms at the Arkansas 13. Bertelsen's short scoring burst two plays later was almost anticlimactic. So was Feller's kick.

Thus the Longhorns won it with a pass, which they often scorn. And then they sealed it 10 plays later with Tom Campbell's interception at the Texas 21—their second interception and only the second stolen pass Montgomery has given up since the Baylor game back in early October. But those two came precisely at the wrong time.

"I'll never forget this game as long as I live," said a vastly disappointed Montgomery at the finish. Neither will all those who were there.

STREET WOULD TAKE ON ARKANSAS EVERY WEEK
DAVID CASSTEVENS

FAYETTEVILLE, Ark.—Danny Lester flashed the biggest smile his face would allow. Bobby Mitchell kissed a fur-coated blonde. And the emotion-wound Texas Longhorns trotted across a rain-soaked Arkansas Astroturf here Saturday afternoon, cramming into college football's most crowded, most jubilant dressing room.

Inside was Richard M. Nixon, the Reverend Billy Graham, sportswriters from Phoenix to Philly, and TV cameras that had viewed the Longhorns 15-14 comeback win over the relentless Razorbacks, Texas over Arkansas—like Truman over Dewey. It was a double take never to be forgotten.

When the tense, pressure-cooker shootout was over, everyone was glad the No. 3–ranked Hogs were now a year removed. Everyone but quarterback James Street, that is.

"Heck, I wish we could play them every week," Street said flatly. "They're such a great team. They test your offense and defense and make you play the very best you can."

Only the absurdly confident or the crazy could ask for another nerve-fraying fracas. But Street is the absurdly confident. After all, he's never lost a game for Texas while starting at quarterback—that's 19 straight for him now.

This 19th game, an epic unfolded before a nationwide TV audience, was never out of reach, said Street. Not even in the fourth quarter, down 14-0, with Penn State imagining the thrill of becoming the new No. 1.

"NEVER FELT OUT OF IT"

"We felt like we were never out of it—I knew we could come back," Street said. "Turnovers kept hurting us. But you have to attribute them to their great defense. And we were lucky to stop them like we did there at the last."

What silenced the Hog-calling was a pass interception by Tom Campbell with only 1:13 remaining after quarterback Bill Montgomery had spurred the Big Red into field goal range.

That was a monumental play—it was a turning point. But there were many. "The turning point?" questioned beaming Darrell Royal.

"Gosh, how do you single out any one? Was it our fumble there early? Or was it Peschel's [Randy] big fourth-down catch, or was it James Street scrambling when we didn't have any points on the board?

"I didn't think two touchdowns would win it," he added. "We had to make one or two minor adjustments at halftime. I told them that we could draw x's and o's for an hour and a half, but it boiled down to being aggressive. We felt like in the first half they were more aggressive than us."

Royal had praise, most of it for Arkansas—their readiness, their talent. "We were just looking for crumbs out there for a while," he admitted. "Arkansas is as good a team as we are. And probably they played a little better today. Montgomery certainly impressed me, and Burnett [Bill] ran well. They're a great offensive and defensive team."

GREAT COMEBACK

But it was Texas' relentless comeback that will be savored, talked about, relived, and second-guessed. With four minutes remaining, the Longhorns cashed in what one Chicago writer termed "the biggest gamble I've seen in football."

Texas trailed, 14–3, and staring at them was a fourth-and-3 situation at the UT 43-yard line. Rather than try to punch out the needed steps, Street rifled a deep pass to Peschel, who slithered between two defenders for the 44-yard completion. Two plays later, Texas notched the winning touchdown.

A hard call to make? "We all drew straws to see who would call it," Royal joked. "Not really. It was an agreement by several of us."

Street was more definite: "Coach Royal called it. It was just another great call. He did it because we had been running our option, and that's our strength. We felt like they were expecting it. They support it [the option] real fast with their defensive backs."

STREET SAW SIGNAL

"It was just a great catch. All I saw was the referee give the signal," said Street, jutting both hands high in the air. "Then I thought we'd score for sure."

For Peschel, the catch-or-perish play must have been a frightening thing—at least an unexpected call—but it wasn't. "I felt like I could catch it," said Peschel.

"When we got in the huddle, James called the play and said, 'Randy, you know that's to you—just get behind him and run like hell.' I got the step on him.

"If the halfback had stayed with me, I was supposed to cut in and get the first down. We had to have that."

Texas got it, the winning touchdown and a berth in the Cotton Bowl to meet highly ranked Notre Dame. "We know Notre Dame is a good team and we feel very fortunate to play them," said a straight-faced Street.

About that time, Frank Erwin of the University Board of Regents congratulated James.

"Did we have you worried?" Street questioned Erwin.

"You're mighty right you did," came the reply.

Sir James broke into a broad grin. Nineteen straight has been such fun.

"Are you ready for Notre Dame?" Nixon asked in his dressing room visit.

"This was one of the great games of all time," Nixon said. "I said at halftime that both teams were going to score in the second half, and I also said I thought what would determine it would be whether Texas could move the ball in the fourth quarter.

"The wire services will name Texas the No. 1 team, and this is a great honor in the 100th year of college football. The fact that you won a tough game and the fact that you didn't lose your cool and didn't quit makes you deserving of No. 1."

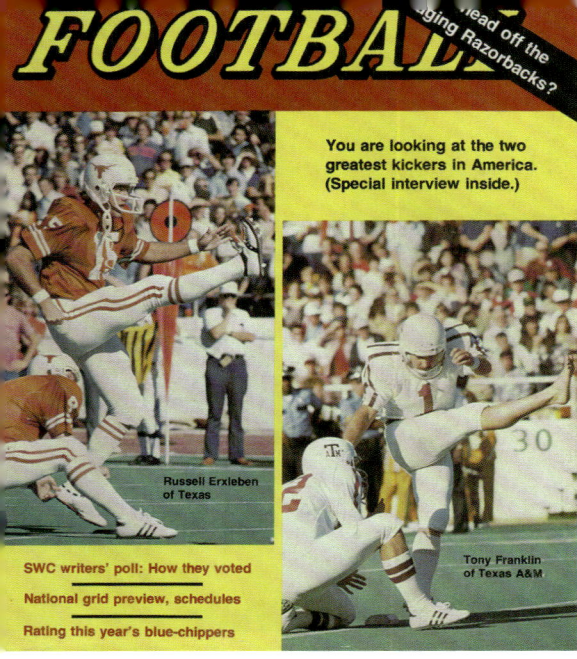

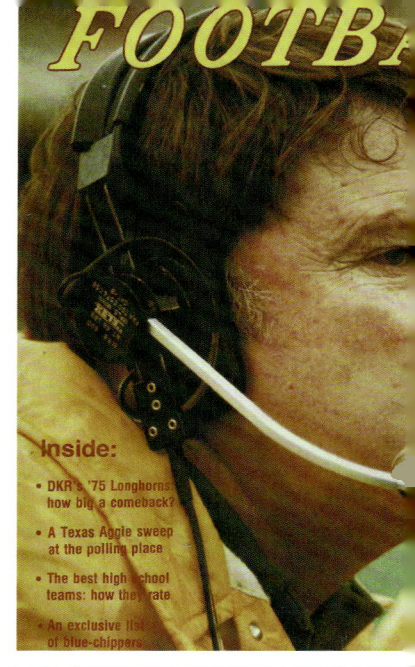
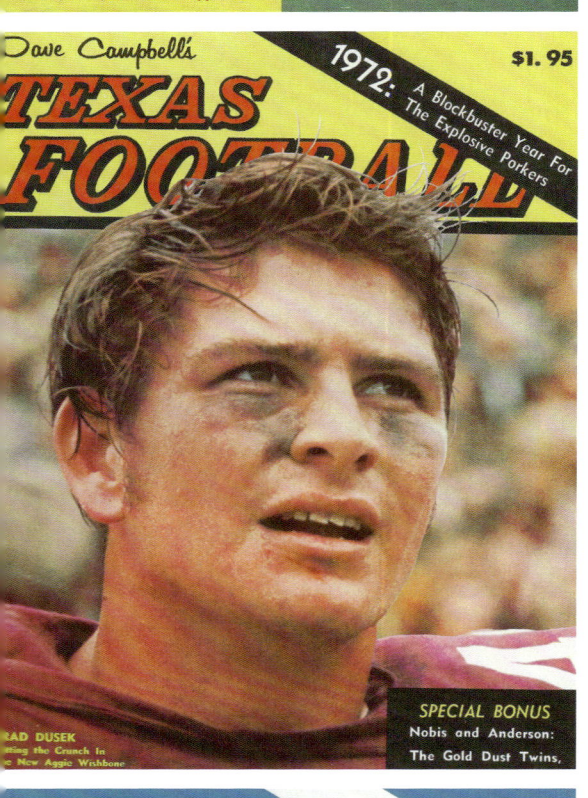
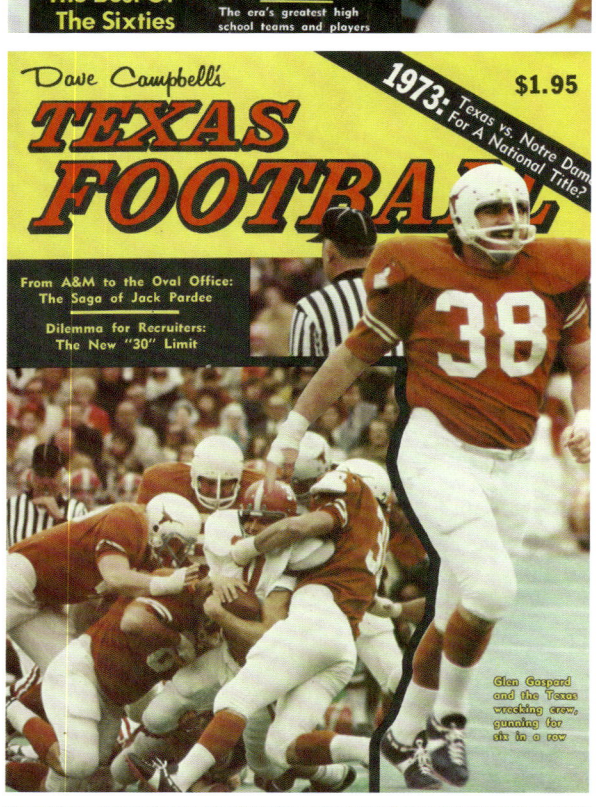

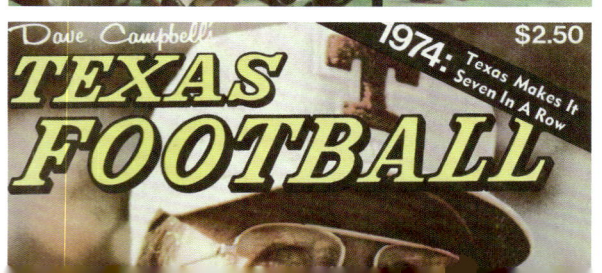

3
THE TYLER ROSE AND THE HOUSTON VEER
1970–1979

The Southwest Conference has never stood taller than it did on the first day of 1970, the first day of the new decade. The conference had emerged from college football's centennial year (1969) boasting the nation's top-ranked team, which had just won the "Big Shootout," the most spotlighted game in league history—perhaps, because of its special circumstances, the most spotlighted game in the history of the college game itself.

Texas was No. 1 in the nation, fresh from its remarkable comeback victory over No. 2–ranked Arkansas, and preparing to take on the most glamorous team in football, the Fighting Irish of Notre Dame, who would at last break their long boycott of the college bowl season. That is the way the seventies began.

The decade ended in noteworthy fashion too, with the league's newest member—the University of Houston—representing the conference against Notre Dame in the Cotton Bowl's infamous "Chicken Soup" game, so dubbed for the warm, healing bowl of the stuff that supposedly fortified an ill Joe Montana at a critical point in the game, which occurred in the midst of the worst ice storm Dallas had seen in thirty years. And along the way, Texas' Earl Campbell, the "Tyler Rose," would earn offensive player of the decade honors while racking up an astounding 4,442 rushing yards during his collegiate career.

JANUARY 2, 1970

STEERS' WISHBONE-T PERFORMS MIRACLE AGAIN TO STUN "LUCK OF THE IRISH," 21–17

DALLAS, Tex.—Those intrepid Texas Longhorns, masters of the fourth quarter, finally conquered the gallant Fighting Irish of Notre Dame, 21–17, here Thursday and began the seventies on the same nerve-jangling note they wound up the sixties—as the pressure-proof kings of college football.

As the tension mounted and the clock unwound and the shadows lengthened across the Cotton Bowl's battle-scarred turf, the Longhorns relentlessly drove 76 yards in 17 plays for the touchdown that spelled the difference in this epic struggle, surely one of the grandest in the 34-year history of the Cotton Bowl Classic.

With a minute and eight seconds left on the clock, halfback Billy Dale plunged the last of those bitterly contested 76 yards, and the Longhorns went ahead to stay. On the west sideline, a wide smile lit up the face of Freddy Steinmark, that brave young cancer victim who stood erect on crutches throughout the furious battle, urging his teammates on.

After winning their fifth straight bowl victory, the Longhorns gave the game ball to Steinmark, who had started their first 10 games at safety before being hospitalized for amputation of his cancerous left leg.

The Longhorns had pledged to win this one for Freddy, and they did, but not before the fired-up Irish had pushed them to the brink, even as Arkansas did less than three weeks ago. Indeed, there were times when this sun-splashed game, played before an overflow crowd of 73,000 (including former president Lyndon B. Johnson) and a television audience of millions, seemed to be following the very game plot that dominated that unforgettable shootout in Fayetteville.

Just as on December 6, Texas got behind early. And again James Street brought the Longhorns back with an 11-point fourth quarter. And again he set up the winning touchdown with a dramatic fourth-down pass, a pressure-packed 8-yarder that Cotton Speyrer carefully plucked off the grass-tops at the Notre Dame 2-yard line. And again Tom Campbell reached up and intercepted a desperation enemy pass that put the final wraps on victory.

Campbell's fateful grab of Irish quarterback Joe Theismann's aerial at the Texas 14-yard line came with only 29 seconds left to play and put an end to a last-gasp Notre Dame push that had reached the Texas 39.

In getting their 20th straight victory and the 500th of their 77 years of football, the Longhorns were forced to make not one comeback but two—and both of them came in the fourth quarter and both consisted of long, time-consuming, dramatic drives, when to err would have been fatal. Texas didn't err.

The first drive carried 77 yards, required 18 plays, and reached the payoff station with 10:05 left in the game, when Ted Koy, knocked senseless earlier and forced to miss a quarter of the action, returned to the battle and circled his own left end from the 3. Happy Feller, accurate as always, kicked the point that put Texas ahead for the first time, 14–10.

Notre Dame's answer was a furious burst that flamed 80 yards in eight plays. Theismann, who completed passes of 11 and 14 yards and then ran for an 11-yard gain while directing Notre Dame past the midfield mark, wound up the thrust by throwing a 24-yard touchdown pass to Jim Yoder with 6:52 left to play.

Scott Hempel kicked the extra point, and Notre Dame went back in front, 17–14, setting the stage for the game's most dramatic and torturous drive, the drive that finally turned everything around for Texas.

Earlier, in the second quarter, the Longhorns had moved 74 yards in nine plays for the first touchdown as Jim Bertelsen did some fine running, Street some

James Street (16) was the Longhorns' field general in the 1970 Cotton Bowl win over Notre Dame. Courtesy of Cotton Bowl Athletic Association / James D. Smith.

productive passing, and Steve Worster some devastating blocking. Bertelsen scored that touchdown from the 1-yard line with 11:12 left in the first half, and Feller kicked the extra point.

Then on the bullish, 18-play power display that netted the Longhorns their second touchdown, Worster had been the heavy-duty guy, smashing forward 34 steps on seven carries and again blocking ferociously. His running (20 carries for 155 yards, his best figures of the season) and blocking were to win him the game's Most Valuable Offensive Player award.

But now, with 6:47 left in the game and a national title hanging in the balance, and with Notre Dame perhaps overly conscious of Worster and his big-thunder charges, Street started attacking with all his weapons.

Bertelsen ran for 4, then Street passed for the first time since midway of the third quarter, and his 17-yard aerial stuck in Cotton Speyrer's hands just before he stepped out of bounds. Worster ran for 7 and Bertelsen ran for 4 to the Notre Dame 44.

Worster got 4 more and then Koy, returning to the action after his lengthy stay on the sidelines, followed Bertelsen's crushing block and sped to the 28.

Now things got extremely sticky. Koy got a pair, Bertelsen got 4, and Worster plunged up the middle for 2. Fourth and 2—a crisis. Texas took time out, and Street jogged to the sidelines to confer with Darrell Royal as the clock stayed still at 4:26.

The battle resumed. Street pitched out to Koy on the option play; and big Ted met the game's most valuable defensive player, raging Notre Dame linebacker Bob Olson, at about the 19; and somehow Koy carried him the 1 yard and 1 foot that Texas had to have to retain possession.

So it was first down at the 18, and the Irish defense was still full of fight. Fred Swendsen broke through and threw Koy for a loss of a yard. Bertelsen scrambled off the tackle in heavy traffic and got 4, then swept right end and fought his way past two tacklers to the 10.

There it was: fourth and 2—another crisis. Again the 'Horns called time. Again Street conferred with Royal as the huge throng, caught up in the mounting drama, waited in hushed expectation. Time left: 2:26.

Now the Longhorns broke their huddle and Street bowed under, ready for the snap. He rolled left as a Notre Dame lineman applied pressure. Speyrer maneuvered in the left flat and Street threw—low, perhaps too short. Speyrer came back to meet the ball, dove under

Fourth and 2 with 2:26 left to play: Royal and Street on the sidelines. Courtesy of Cotton Bowl Athletic Association / James D. Smith.

it, and made a sparkling, game-saving, rolling catch at the Notre Dame 2.

Dale scored two plays later, and Campbell made his interception three plays later, and it was all over.

But what a game it had been.

Eventually the Irish defense, which had been limiting opponents to 85 yards aground, was to give way, surrendering 25 first downs and 333 yards to the Longhorns infantry and 448 in total offense, and Notre Dame coach Ara Parseghian was to admit that never had one of his teams faced such a powerful backfield.

Notre Dame, with all those traditions behind it, is something special, and the Irish died hard and oh, so slowly. They gave it a terrific try; the Longhorns gave it a better one. Freddy Steinmark knew they would.

JANUARY 12, 1970

AUSTIN, Tex.—Various signs here and there declared that they were No. 1, and so did the printed programs, but up there on the screen, the guys in the orange shirts looked like Ned and those other guys in the first reader. Fumble, fumble, fumble. Sloppy, sloppy, sloppy. The ball would go squirting away, an enemy jersey would come up with the fumble, and then the camera would focus on Darrell Royal pacing the sideline—frowning deeply, saying things under his breath—and right then you would know why they say a single picture is worth a thousand words.

And all the while, the audience, more than 4,000 strong, laughed and laughed. This was at the banquet given Monday night for Darrell Royal's national champions, and this was a case of the Longhorns poking fun at themselves. It made for a neat change of pace, just as the banquet itself did. You know how these things usually go: long, boring, stilted, formal speeches and more pats on the back than a guy can count. "That," said Darrell Royal at the outset, "is what I *don't* want in the way of a banquet this year."

So this one was different, although there were a few pats on the back, all right—plus a wire of congratulations from the White House along with a message of regret that Mr. President couldn't be there. (One was reminded of a Notre Dame player's wisecrack, "Apparently he doesn't think he has the Texas vote sacked up yet.") But that was all right. If Mr. Nixon couldn't make it, LBJ and Lady Bird could and did. There they were, sitting at the head table, enjoying that special film of Longhorn boo-boos as much as everyone else. Later on, Mrs. Johnson presented to Longhorns tri-captains James Street, Ted Koy, and Glen

I presented the Grantland Rice trophy to the team captains. Courtesy of the *Waco Tribune-Herald*.

Halsell the Associated Press's gleaming piece of hardware designating them as 1969 national champions.

But mainly, it was a night for western attire, barbecue, delicious flashbacks to an unforgettable season, and laughs. Jack Blanton, president of UT Ex-Students, said he sure was glad the season was finally over: "As a human being, I simply couldn't stand many more games like those last two. Denton Cooley told me last week that lately, his cardiovascular business has been great."

Royal also had some interesting things to say about some of his Longhorns: "I'll say this for Tom Campbell: he sure knows how to end a game." It was Campbell, of course, who came up with the victory-sealing interceptions late in the fourth quarter against both Arkansas and Notre Dame. When he got to Cotton Speyrer, Royal didn't simply hand him his award; he tossed it to him—low, of course, like Street's pass in the Cotton Bowl. And Speyrer went down on one knee to catch it as the crowd laughed.

Amid the jokes, the laughter, the fun, the films, and the trophies, there was one poignant moment when the crowd was hushed. Royal was handing out the letter jackets to the Longhorns. The next two players, he said, would come to the stage together: Scott Henderson and Fred Steinmark.

Unaided, a slim, cheerful, awesomely courageous figure—face split by a grin—hobbled across the stage, big Scott Henderson at his side, and the applause started in the back of the big coliseum and swept forward and overshadowed anything else that drew applause Monday night. On and on the applause went, and there wasn't a dry eye in the house.

The ovation for Freddy Steinmark continued until Royal held up a hand so he could continue.

Unforgettable.

SEPTEMBER 29, 1970

ON SECOND THOUGHT

Someone asked Jim Carlen the other day what he missed most about West Virginia, and the new Texas Tech coach replied, "Not getting to play VMI this week."

Replacing Virginia Military with the Texas Longhorns does rank as one of football's more ill-advised trades, and about the only way a coach could hope to come out in good shape on that one is by having a combination of the Detroit Lions and LA Rams at his disposal.

Carlen doesn't.

He has a team of very average football players for the most part (with some notable exceptions such as Ken Perkins and Larry Molinare and Johnny Odom), but it is a team that was well drilled for the Texas game and played with great enthusiasm. At the finish, both Darrell Royal and the record audience felt this was a team definitely on the come.

Well, maybe not *this* team, although it will be a mild surprise if the Raiders don't finish above .500. Such a record is within the Raiders' reach—that is, if they play as they did against Texas. But they don't have the overall speed or offensive line skills or the breakaway backs to have an outstanding team.

Tech's time will come later. This year's time belongs to Texas. If you are a football fan, you owe it to yourself to see the Longhorns at least once before the season ends. This has to be one of the better teams of our time.

Better than last year? Well, really it is just an extension of last year, although there is a new quarterback. They also have a new passing scheme; they are using halfbacks coming out of the backfield and roaming as primary targets in open spaces over the middle. And they have changed up many of their blocking patterns.

The result can be devastating. On the eve of battle, California thought it had a good team, and as a matter of fact, it was good enough last weekend to beat Indiana, 56–14. Texas merely toyed with California.

Texas Tech was an entirely different cup of tea. Their defense was much better schooled, and they refused to panic and wilt under pressure. They made Texas earn everything it got, which was plenty.

Behind by 14 points at the end of the first quarter, the Raiders made it a 14–13 game by halftime. Not many teams can come back like that against Texas. And if quarterback Charles Napper, on the opening play of the fourth quarter, had rifled his 35-yard pass to wide-open David May instead of floating it, the Raiders would have had a touchdown and would have been within a two-point conversion of gaining a 21–21 tie.

Much earlier, in the first quarter, Perkins returned a punt 35 yards to the Texas 30, but a clipping penalty rubbed out the yardage and set Tech back to its 19. Three plays later, Texas scored. "That clip was a 12-point play," Tech athletic director J. T. King noted. "We're ready to go in for a score, and instead they get the touchdown."

So things could have gone better for the Raiders than the final score of 35–13 indicated. But the consensus of press box row was that Tech went into the game well prepared and played up to the limit of its ability, and no one could ask for more. "No," Carlen said, "I really can't be disappointed in anything except the final score."

Maybe he changed his mind a few minutes later after seeing the game film for the first time. He didn't say. Apparently he felt Tech got a bad call on the clipping penalty, and all the writers who sat with Carlen through the film showing left the room pretty well convinced that Texas offensive tackle Bobby Wuensch had been permitted to jump the snap of the ball something like 20 or 25 times.

But none of those developments should obscure the main fact: once the Longhorns got really aroused, Tech wasn't about to win. Texas just put the cold steel to them, and there was little Tech could do about it, and that was a sight a man owes it to himself to see.

Watching the film as the Longhorns broke the back of his team's fiercely resisting defense in the second half, Carlen had some interesting comments.

"This boy makes the difference, fellows," he said at one point as Eddie Phillips faked masterfully and then carried for 14 yards. And later, "I'll tell you, those two halfbacks [Jim Bertelsen, Billy Dale] can block." And still later, "You can't stunt against Texas because you're going to be off-balance when you reach [Steve] Wooster, and you aren't going to stop Wooster with an arm tackle. You've got to really hit him."

What will it take to beat Texas?

"First, you've got to have phenomenal defensive end play," the Tech coach suggested. "On offense, you've got to have a quarterback who can run and one who can throw, and you've got to be able to protect the passer. So I'd say you've got to have a superteam."

NOVEMBER 4, 1972
JEFFREY GETS BACK ON TRACK

FORT WORTH, Tex.—The very best thing of all is that there were witnesses. Otherwise, not a single solitary soul would believe it.

You see, right out there in broad daylight before 22,925 spectators, an impossible dream disguised as the Baylor football team turned a TCU homecoming into a nightmare without end for the Frogs and their old grads here Saturday while roaring off with a 42–9 victory.

Yes, you read it right: 42 for Baylor, 9 for TCU. And yes, that's the most points a Baylor football team has ever scored in Fort Worth. And yes, that's the most points and the worst defeat the Bears have ever put on the Frogs in league play, going back to the year TCU was admitted to the SWC—1922. And yes, that's only 7 fewer points than Baylor scored in *all* its conference games a year ago.

For the Baylor thousands who were there, it was a little like opening a piggy bank and finding a million dollars. They didn't want to leave the premises. Most of them didn't. They adjourned to the vicinity of the Baylor dressing room, and there they stood around waiting for their heroes to appear so they could give them a few hundred rousing hurrahs. Some of them are probably still there.

Only in 1910, when Baylor beat TCU 52–0, and in 1915, when the Bears triumphed 51–0, in games played in Waco, have the wearers of the green and gold scored more points against the Frogs, and those games hardly count. In those days, both schools were just learning what football is all about. Now the Bears know.

The Frogs were supposed to win by 4 points. They usually beat the Bears anywhere from 4 to 44. They had clubbed Baylor every blessed time in Fort Worth since 1954 and every blessed time in Waco since 1963, and more often than not, they had pounded them like a drum.

This time the drum pounded back. And kept pounding. Baylor scored the kind of landslide that the man in the White House hopes he scores Tuesday. The longer it went on, the worse it got. You kept expecting a towel to be thrown in from the TCU bench.

"They just whipped us every way you can whip a football team," summed up TCU coach Billy Tohill. The defeat, TCU's second in conference play, knocked the Frogs from title contention.

Grant Teaff's intrepid troopers, beautifully prepared, actually had to come from behind. TCU led 7–0 with 7:22 left in the first quarter, thanks to a 25-yard drive following a Baylor fumble.

Then the Bears turned them every way but loose. They were in front at halftime by 14–7, led at the three-quarter pole by 21–9, and then gushed for 21 more points in the fourth quarter even though Teaff sent in his reserves.

By that time, the regulars were on the bench, whooping it up and thinking about Texas. The Longhorns (4–0) come to Baylor Stadium Saturday for a showdown that athletic director Jack Patterson said "will draw standing room only." If the Bears can find a way to win that one, they will have a delicious shot at a berth in the Cotton Bowl. Fantastic!

Gary Lacy, running with verve and velocity, scored two of Baylor's touchdowns on runs of 1 and 2 yards. Fleet Billy Wilson scored another on a 3-yard burst. Randy Cavender tallied from the 1, Ray Harper from the 2, and Neal Jeffrey hit Kenny Townsend with a 1-yard scoring toss.

Kicker Mike Conradt made six straight extra points during the Bears' fun-filled afternoon and took three shots at long-range field goals but missed each time.

This was a victory pegged to the slashing runs of Lacy and Wilson, the scorching overhead work of Jeffrey, and that old Baylor reliable—defense.

TCU couldn't drive a lick on that defense. Would you believe the Frogs finished the afternoon with *six*

Charles Dancer. Courtesy of Baylor University Athletics.

Roger Goree. Courtesy of Baylor University Athletics.

first downs? They gained 109 yards rushing and only 44 through the air. Baylor held Mike Luttrell to a mere 31 yards on 11 carries (although one was a 3-yard touchdown). They picked off a whopping six interceptions. And apart from their one touchdown surge, the Frogs were never inside the Baylor 20.

In short, so sticky was the work of Joe Johnson, Coy Zunker, Mike Black, Roger Goree, Ed Taylor, John Oliver, Millard Neely, and every other green shirt, the Frogs couldn't sustain anything on the ground, got behind, and had to start throwing, and that just opened the floodgates.

Tommy Stewart intercepted one of Perry Senn's passes and returned it 32 yards to the TCU 4-yard line to set up a touchdown. Derrel Luce picked off another and took it 18 yards to the 1, leading to another score. And Dan Drake, who pilfered a pair, set up the final Bruin touchdown with a steal at the Frog 34.

The other interceptions were by Dwayne Trammell and Roger Goree, and Goree added an extra twist to his. After snitching a pass at the Baylor 45, he lateraled to Stewart and did some blocking as his teammate sped back to the TCU 35. That Roger sure likes to get in on all the action. First thing you know, he'll think he's a blocking back.

In addition to all that larceny, Black and Paul Savage recovered fumbles for the Bears, which means TCU wound up suffering eight turnovers.

When the game was in doubt, however, it was the pinpoint passing of Jeffrey that did TCU in. Cool-hand Neal completed 15 of 24 passes for 206 yards—his best performance of the season—and those throws set up Baylor's first three touchdowns.

On the first one, Jeffrey threw 11 yards to Gene Wilson, 23 yards to Charles Dancer, and 15 yards to Brian Kilgore at the TCU 2. Two plays later, Lacy went over from the 1 for the equalizer after TCU turned that early turnover into a score.

The fumble came on a misdirected pitch from Jeffrey to Billy Wilson, recovered by the Frogs' Ed Robinson, who played a fine defensive game, along with Dede Terveen and Lyle Blackwood. After the recovery, Billy Sadler broke for 16 yards to the Baylor 9, and Luttrell scored two plays later.

After tying the score with 8:37 left in the half, the Bears rolled 80 yards on 12 plays on their next possession. Jeffrey again did the blitz work, throwing 21 yards to Lester Ealey, 15 yards to Dancer, 16 yards to Kilgore to the TCU 7, and then 6 yards to Dancer at the 1.

Dancer, who caught three passes for 44 yards, made a marvelous grab, taking the ball away from David McGinniss a step inside the boundary. On the payoff play, Jeffrey faked neatly to Lacy, then flipped to Townsend, who was open at the back edge of the end zone.

The Bears also scored on their first possession of the second half, driving 66 yards in 11 plays as Jeffrey completed passes to Ealey, Lacy, and Kilgore for a total of 40 yards. Then Kilgore zipped 12 yards to the 3 on an inside reverse, setting up Billy Wilson's touchdown run on the next play.

NOVEMBER 18, 1972
RAIDERS GET SUN BOWL SPOT

WACO, Tex.—Sun Bowl–bound Texas Tech eased past Baylor 13–7 here Saturday on a shivery, sunless afternoon as the Bears made mistake after mistake after mistake. But the worst mistake they made didn't appear to be a mistake at the time.

With 9:20 still remaining in the opening quarter, the Bears knocked Tech tailback Doug McCutchen out of the game. His replacement, sophomore Cliff Hoskins, came in and did things to the Baylor defense that were beyond the reach even of Texas' mighty Roosevelt Leaks.

Hoskins, a rancher's son from George West who weighs 196 and runs like he weighs 296, rushed for a whopping 204 yards, including a 3-yard blast late in the third quarter that produced Tech's only touchdown. Hoskins had carried only 14 times all season before Saturday. But against the Bears, he looked as irresistible as an idea whose time has come.

Hoskins set up Tech's touchdown with a 31-yard burst to the Baylor 13. Fullback James Mosley, another of Tech's hard runners, gouged out 3 yards and then Hoskins devoured the remaining distance in two gulps, giving the Raiders a 13–0 advantage that was more than enough to withstand Baylor's fourth-quarter rally.

The Bears finally did get on the scoreboard, driving 76 yards in 13 plays and scoring with 12:14 left in the game as Neal Jeffrey threw 15 yards to Brian Kilgore, but they never got beyond their own 23 the rest of the way, as Tech did just what Texas did a week ago—played ball control as the clock ran down—and Baylor partisans among the crowd of 18,000 slowly gave up hope.

After the Bears scored their touchdown, the Red Raiders ran 24 plays plus a punt plus a field goal attempt that the Bears blocked, and over that span, the Bears ran 4 plays for a net of 2 yards. In that period of keep-away, Hoskins ran 19 times for 99 yards and left the Sun Bowl representatives who were watching on high from the press box breathing a sigh of relief. They had invited Tech unofficially to their El Paso Classic even before the opening kickoff, and their faces would have matched the color of Rudolph's nose if the Bears had managed to flatten the men from West Texas.

Don Rives went on from Tech to play linebacker for the Chicago Bears for five seasons. Courtesy of Texas Tech University Athletics.

What we will never know is whether Grant Teaff's men might have done just that—if they had not been so generous. They were generous to a fault.

Five fumbles the Bears lost. Plus two interceptions. Plus a couple of dropped passes. At the finish, Don Grimes's 21- and 34-yard field goals were there to make the difference in Tech's favor, and the Red Raiders had to move only 34 yards to kick them.

The wonder of it is that the score wasn't much more one-sided. There is a double explanation: in the first half, the Red Raiders darn near matched the Bears mistake for mistake (although they didn't commit their four turnovers in their own end of the field, and they made none at all in the second half), and Baylor's defense, with one exception, played a bristling brand of ball when its goal line was threatened.

Derrel Luce recovered two fumbles and blocked a field goal, Mike Wilder and Coy Zunker also covered fumbles, and Roger Goree, Paul Savage, and several other defenders played like gangbusters at times. But those errors left them facing a summit they couldn't conquer.

The Bears fumbled away the first kickoff they received, drew a major penalty on the first play they ran from scrimmage, threw an interception on the first pass they tried, got their first punt partially blocked, and fumbled away the first punt they tried to field.

Put all that together and you get two Tech field goals, and at the finish, those were the field goals that decided the game, giving the Red Raiders their eighth victory in 10 starts (with Arkansas still to be played), their fourth victory in six conference games, and their second visit to the Sun Bowl in the three years Jim Carlen has been at the switch.

"Naturally, we are proud to be going to the Sun Bowl," Carlen said after the game and the formal announcement that it will be Tech versus North Carolina in the El Paso game December 20. He continued, "It is a compliment to both our coaches and players. And the Sun Bowl is near enough to Lubbock for our fans to make the trip easily."

Carlen said the Red Raiders actually had their choice of bowls, with the Liberty and Peach Bowls also tendering unofficial invitations.

In picking up only their second victory ever in Waco (both on their last two trips, both with Carlen at the helm), the Raiders rolled for 20 first downs and 347 yards in total offense and kept the ball for 78 plays compared to 63 for the Bears.

All of which actually reflect Baylor's bumbling start. The Raiders ran 14 plays and kicked a field goal before the Bears gained so much as a yard, and over that span, Baylor lost a fumble, threw an interception, and committed three penalties.

Andre Tillman would go to Miami in the second round of the 1974 NFL draft. Courtesy of Texas Tech University Athletics.

At the finish, Baylor had 19 first downs and 273 total yards. Once the Bears got going, they moved the ball fairly well. They flubbed their first, second, and fourth possessions with turnovers. But on eight possessions, they drove the ball across midfield. Apart from their scoring drive, their most promising venture was a 10-play, 48-yard thrust to the Tech 10 in the second quarter. Jeffrey lost the handle at that spot, and Don Rives recovered for Tech.

For the second Saturday in a row, Jeffrey will want to sponge the game from his memory. Certainly the defeat should not be put at his door—he made some good plays, threw some passes that should have been caught, and often moved the team well—but he did end up losing two fumbles and throwing two interceptions, just as he did against Texas.

Probably troubled by an elbow he injured last week, Jeffrey managed 5 completions in 16 attempts for 60 yards. Baylor's usual leaders overland—Gary Lacy, Billy Wilson, and Gene Wilson—produced mostly modest gains (27, 22, and 36 yards, respectively). Thus the steadily improving sophomore Brian Kilgore stepped forward to spur the offense, rushing for 76 yards on 10 carries and making three catches for another 42, including the Bears' touchdown.

Freshman fullback Pat McNeil also had his busiest afternoon, carrying seven times for 39 yards and refusing to yield easily.

Hoskins was easily Tech's leading weapon. Mosley rumbled for 54 yards, Joe Barnes for 37, and McCutchen for 31 before his injury. Barnes completed only one pass for 18 yards, and that one, to Andre Tillman, was terminated by a fumble, which Baylor recovered.

Tech wound up losing the ball on fumbles at the Baylor 18-, 31-, and 37-yard lines (twice). The Bears' turnovers occurred at their own 29, 23, 44, and 34 and at the Tech 10, 38, and 41.

BILL YEOMAN: "MR. VEER"

Bill Yeoman came late to the old Southwest Conference and stayed around to put University of Houston football on the map.

I first was able to meet the tall and humorous Yeoman when the Cougars were admitted to the conference as a team eligible to compete for the SWC football championship in 1976. The Southwest Conference football press tour included the University of Houston for the first time that year (probably in August, because by then, teams were allowed to play 11 games in the regular season rather than just 10).

As a matter of fact, Houston had done so well in several of its previous seasons, that I decided to put Yeoman and his quarterback, Bubba McGallion, on the cover of the 1976 *Texas Football* magazine. And I hired Jack Gallagher—a great sportswriter, a good friend, and a member of the *Houston Post* sports staff—to write the lead story about Yeoman and his team in the summer magazine that year.

We found Yeoman to be a great interview—candid, knowledgeable, quick to answer questions, and downright funny at times. He had an unusual way of summing up things, be it an appraisal of the talents of one of his players or his team overall or what the Cougars would be facing in their first season of competition against the "big boys" of the famous SWC, home of quite a few national football champions going back to 1935, when undefeated SMU beat undefeated TCU and nailed down that mythical honor, known then as the Knute Rockne Trophy. (SMU went on to the Rose Bowl and lost by a touchdown to Stanford, and TCU went to the Sugar Bowl and beat LSU, 3–2. So TCU and SMU, with identical 12–1 records, then both claimed the national championship.)

As I remember it, Yeoman told us he thought the Cougars would be competitive, but after all, they had only posted a 2–8 record the previous season. So there was no reason for him to go out too far on what could be a very fragile limb.

So all he and the Cougars did that season was win it all—the Southwest Conference and the Cotton Bowl, enabling the Cougars to wind up being ranked No. 4 by the wire services. And Maryland, coached by Jerry Claiborne (former Texas A&M assistant coach under Bear Bryant), a team that had been undefeated, ranked No. 2 nationally and was hoping to defeat Houston and win the national championship, fell back to No. 8.

Incidentally, Bubba McGallion was Houston's senior quarterback that year, but when the season started, sophomore Danny Davis had become the starter. Davis continued to hold down that position all the all way to the Cotton Bowl and the victory over Maryland, and I imagine he would have been the consensus choice for All-SWC quarterback if Rice's Tommy Kramer had not had such a terrific season. Kramer became the consensus choice for All-American quarterback that season, although Houston beat Rice in the city showdown, 42–20.

Bill Yeoman is a midwesterner who made his way to Texas (Texas A&M) in 1945, then to West Point (as an Army Cadet in 1946–48, playing center on the football team and winning second-team All-America recognition on the famous Glenn Davis-Doc Blanchard duo), then to Michigan State as an assistant football coach, and then—his final stop—to the University of Houston.

And all he did there, coaching the Cougars from 1962 to 1986, was direct the Cougars to four SWC football championships and establish himself as the winningest football coach in school history, posting an overall record of 160-108-8 and a 51-35-2 mark as a coach in the SWC.

Courtesy of *Dave Campbell's Texas Football*.

Bill Yeoman and his players hoist the 1976 conference trophy. Wilson Whitley (78), winner of the 1976 Lombardi Award, looks on. Courtesy of University of Houston Athletics.

Yeoman's Cougars became nationally famous for their high-scoring offense. Many insiders credit him with revolutionizing college football, developing and then exploiting all the advantages offered by the veer option. Using the veer, the Cougars led the nation in total offense for three consecutive seasons in the late 1960s. As a result, the Cougars started winning games against well-respected opponents in highly respected conferences: 56 points against Kentucky in 1966, 37 points against Michigan State in 1967, 74 points against Mississippi State in 1969, and 42 points against Syracuse and 53 points against Florida State in 1970. They twice rampaged against defensive-minded Virginia Tech, scoring 56 points in 1971 and 54 in '73.

By then, Yeoman and his coaching staff were also getting a leg up on a lot of schools by recruiting and signing black athletes to play football for UH. According to one source, Yeoman was the first football coach at a predominately white school in Texas to sign a black football player (the sensational Warren McVea from San Antonio, who signed with Houston in 1964).

But it was the game in 1968 that proved to make all the difference. In 1968, with Darrell Royal's Longhorns using the wishbone offense for the first time, the Cougars went to Austin and played the Longhorns to something of a standstill. The scoreboard read 20-20 after the last shot had been fired. According to those in the know, "If we're going to play 'em, they should be in the Southwest Conference and recruiting under the same rules that we do," Royal reportedly said.

That 1976 season, the Cougars lost only to Florida in a nonconference and to Arkansas in conference combat. They wound up tied for the title with Steve Sloan's Texas Tech Red Raiders, but Houston had gone to Lubbock that season and defeated Texas Tech, 27-19, and thus won the right to go to the Cotton Bowl and the bowl game against Maryland.

I covered three Cougar games that fall: the season-opening game in Waco against Baylor (23-5, an upset), a Houston victory in Austin over Texas (30-0, a huge upset; teams just didn't hold the Longhorns scoreless in those days, but the Cougars did—to the amazement of all of us), and the Cotton Bowl victory over Maryland.

Houston won the SWC football crown again in 1978, but I didn't get to cover that Cotton Bowl game. A hard freeze made the road to Dallas icy and slippery (the wind-chill factor was a minus 6 degrees), and I decided to stay home in Waco and watch the game on television. That was the game where the Cougars got well in front of Notre Dame (a

Yeoman with Elmo Wright. Courtesy of University of Houston Athletics.

22-point lead starting the final period), but then Irish quarterback Joe Montana, thawed out by the warm soup his coaches had given him, engineered an unbelievable Notre Dame comeback in the fourth quarter. Notre Dame scored on the last play of the game, Dallas native Joe Unis went in to kick the game-winning extra point, and the Irish won, 35–34.

Houston won still another SWC crown in 1979 and defeated Nebraska in the 1980 Cotton Bowl, 17–14. But I didn't see that one. I was in Atlanta, Georgia, covering Baylor's upset victory over Clemson in the Peach Bowl.

In 1984, Bill Yeoman directed his Cougars to a tie with SMU for the conference football title and a fourth trip to the Cotton Bowl to play Boston College. Houston defeated SMU, the home team for that game, 42–28, to win the Cotton Bowl trip. I did get to cover that scoring duel, which wound up with Boston College holding the upper hand, 45–28. UH's Earl Allen raced 98 yards on a kickoff return for a touchdown (the longest such return in Cotton Bowl history), but the game ultimately belonged to Heisman Trophy–winning Boston College quarterback Doug Flutie, who threw for three TDs in leading his team to victory.

Yeoman retired after the 1986 season and was replaced by Texas A&M-Washington Redskins gridiron hero Jack Pardee. A six-man football standout in West Texas, Pardee was one of Bear Bryant's "Junction Boys" at A&M and a 1956 All-American linebacker.

Yeoman has since been inducted into the University Hall of Honor (1998), the College Football Hall of Fame (2001), and the Texas Sports Hall of Fame (2003).

In the Bill Yeoman coaching era, the Cougars finished four times ranked in the AP top 10 and 11 times in the AP or UPI top 20. He coached 46 players who won All-America recognition by one or more All-America entities and sent 69 of his players to the pros. In recognition of his great 25-year tenure at the University of Houston, the Cougars have unveiled a statue of Yeoman this season on the UH campus. One of his greatest players was wide receiver Elmo Wright, who went on to fame in the NFL.

Said current big-winning Cougar head coach Tom Herman recently, "Coach Yeoman has been a great resource for me. He's in the building at least a few times a week. We usually take the time for me to pick his brain on some things."

It must be paying good dividends, since the Cougars opened their 2016 season upsetting Big 12 Conference favorite Oklahoma, one of the teams favored to make college football's Final Four in the 2016 season.

JANUARY 2, 1973
HORNS RALLY TO SINK TIDE

DALLAS, Tex.—Whether by trick or treat or tainted touchdown, Darrell Royal still has Bear Bryant's number.

Royal's Longhorns, behind by 10 points at halftime, used the bullish power of Rosey Leaks and the artful runs of Alan Lowry to stage a scorching comeback that swept them to a 17–13 victory over the Crimson Tide here on a cold, gray New Year's Day in the 37th annual Cotton Bowl Classic.

A capacity audience of 72,032 saw Lowry scoot 3 and 34 yards for the touchdowns that the Southwest Conference champions needed to overtake Alabama and protect DKR's record against the Bear. Royal has never lost to Bryant, and their teams now have met four times.

In their first meeting, in 1957, when Bryant was still at Texas A&M, Royal added a couple of new plays to the Texas arsenal (dubbed "Aggie keep" and "Aggie pitch"), and they helped the Longhorns score a 9–7 upset. When Royal and Texas upset Bryan's No. 1-ranked Crimson Tide in the 1965 Orange Bowl game, the Longhorns treated viewers to one of the finest goal-line stands ever staged as they turned back Joe Namath and friends. On Monday, the road to victory was paved by some tricky Lowry footwork that was too slick even for the guys in the striped shirts, who missed the sight of the Texas quarterback stepping out of bounds on his second touchdown run.

This was in the fourth quarter, with 'Bama leading by three points, 13–10, and Texas driving. Indeed, Texas spent the final 30 minutes of the game driving, driving, driving as Leaks gained most of his 120 yards (on 25 carries) and Lowry, voted the game's top offensive player, kept moving the chains with his runs and passes. He wound up with 117 yards rushing on 16 carries and 61 yards overhead on 5 completions.

The Longhorns scored on their final possession of the third quarter, marching 59 yards in 15 plays. On their next possession, they stormed down to the Alabama 26, where they just missed on a fourth-and-1 situation. The next time opportunity knocked for them, they drove to the 'Bama 33 and then tried a long-range field goal that missed.

Alabama then produced some fireworks of its own briefly, moving into Texas territory. But when lethal Terry Davis, probably the best-passing wishbone operator of them all, whistled a 34-yard aerial to the Texas end zone, trying for a quick touchdown strike to Wayne Wheeler, Texas defender Terry Melaneon intercepted the throw, aborted the drive, and flashed a green light for Texas' payoff drive.

So the Longhorns went to work at their own 20. They had been moving steadily on the bruising runs from tackle to tackle by the powerful Leaks, but 'Bama after a while started watching for Leaks. So Lowry started faking to Rosey and running or throwing. He threw to Pay Kelly for 20 yards and then to Julius Whittier, his tight end, for 16. Two smashes at the Alabama midsection gained 8; it was third and 2 at the Crimson Tide 34.

Now Lowry faked beautifully, fooling every son of Dixie in sight, and as he tucked the ball away and spun around left end, nothing but daylight yawned in front of him. As the Tide's pursuit came across, using the angle it had on him to try to head him off, he did some fancy footwork about the 11-yard line right at the boundary, got the one good block he needed from tight end Rick Davis, and went across standing up.

The officials on the spot signaled a touchdown. They had missed what the television cameras saw and kept showing to a nationwide audience on instant replay—that Lowry's foot had kicked up the chalk on the west sideline 12 yards upfield. "There's no question he stepped out of bounds," one of the television commentators later said in answering a question on the subject from the press box.

It probably wouldn't have mattered—not the way

Alan Lowry, who switched to quarterback for his senior year at Texas, tries to escape the Baylor line. Courtesy of University of Texas Athletics.

the Longhorns were moving by then. And in the last four minutes, Texas was in position to kick two field goals, and two would have won the game. At the finish, a gracious Bryant was saying it out loud: the team that deserved to win did win.

After Lowry had scored and Billy Schott had kicked the extra point, Alabama tried to fashion a comeback and got as far as the Texas 43-yard line. There, with 1:36 left in the game, facing a fourth-and-1 situation, Davis called on his best runner, swift Wilbur Jackson, to get the vital yard. He didn't come close; Randy Braband, voted the game's best defender, broke into the 'Bama backfield and met Jackson solidly at the 44 and dumped him for a yard loss. The ball went over, and Texas used the remaining time in marching down to the Crimson Tide 12-yard line.

The big play on that last sashay was Lowry's 34-yard burst to the Alabama 11. When it counted, the visitors simply couldn't cope with both Lowry and Leaks, and they couldn't do a lot with that Texas defense.

Alabama was never inside the Texas 30 in the second half as the Longhorns played a punishing brand of keep-away. The Crimson Tide would sustain nothing overland. Only the swift Jackson (64 yards on 10 carries), who turned one pitchout into a devastating 31-yard touchdown run late in the first quarter, really dented Texas' defense against the run. Heralded 'Bama fullback Steve Bisceglia got 30 yards on 11 carries, Joe LaBue got 15 yards, and Terry Davis got 20.

Stymied aground, the Tide had to go aloft for much of its yardage, and although Davis often threw beautifully (10 completions in 17 attempts for 174 yards)—and late in the second quarter blistered the Longhorns with a 67-yard, 6-play drive that consumed only 1:28 on the clock and paid off in a field goal—he finally ran out of magic upstairs. Melancon helped short-circuit him, grabbing two interceptions.

It was almost two games rolled into one, Alabama winning the first one and Texas the second.

Alabama used an interception on the third play of the game at midfield to launch its first drive. After six plays had gained 17 yards, Greg Gantt set a Cotton Bowl distance record by kicking a 50-yard field goal for the visitors.

Late in the first quarter, another Lowry pass was picked off by the same thief, Steve Wade, and returned 42 yards to the Texas 31. Jackson used LaBue's great block to get outside right end, and there simply was no catching him. So with 4:49 still left in the first quarter, 'Bama had a 10–0 lead.

Texas retaliated with a time-consuming march of 71 yards in 15 plays down to the Alabama 8. Actually, the Longhorns got to the 3, but Mike Washington then threw Don Ealey for a 5-yard loss, and Texas had to settle for Billy Schott's 24-yard field goal.

Late in the second quarter, Schott missed a field goal from the Alabama 22—something he hardly ever does—after Texas had rolled from its own 41 to the enemy 15. Taking over on their own 20, Bryant's men took to the air. Davis completed a 10-yarder to LaBue, a 31-yarder to Dexter Wood, a 9-yarder to Wood, and then caught a 13-yard pass himself on a trick play that carried the ball to the Texas 13. Bill Davis then kicked a 30-yard field goal with three seconds left, putting 'Bama in control 13–3.

But the Crimson Tide knew it hadn't heard the last of Lowry or Leaks and that bone-bruising Texas defense, and the longer the game went, the more decisive it got. Texas wound up leading in first downs, 20 to 15; in total offense, 378 yards to 324; and in ball control, 80 plays to 60.

On Texas' first touchdown drive, which used up more than 7 minutes of the third quarter, Leaks carried 9 times for 37 yards. Actually, Alabama had Texas stopped on the first series of the drive, but an offside penalty gave Texas a first down at midfield, and the 'Horns made the most of the reprieve. With the ball on the Alabama 3-yard line, Lowry faked to his inside runners and then kept the ball himself and raced across inside left end.

That made it a 13–10 game, and for the Crimson Tide, defeat was just around the corner. They should have recognized it. They haven't won a bowl game now since 1966. Chances are, when they do win one, it won't be against Texas.

NOVEMBER 9, 1974

MIRACULOUS BRUINS STAMPEDE STEERS

WACO, Tex.—Mr. Webster, back to the drawing board. Your dictionary is woefully incomplete. It does not yet contain a word to properly describe what the fantastic, intrepid, absolutely mind-boggling Baylor Bears did on a cold, gray, delicious, delightful Saturday afternoon here November 9, 1974.

What the Baylor Bears did was defeat Texas, 34–24. Say it fast, and it sounds routine. So say it slow, slow, slow. Because there was nothing routine about it.

Listen, this was a game that will burn in memory for at least an eon or two—certainly for all those 43,100 witnesses who huddled under umbrellas for the first two quarters and then started shoving them aside as a miracle began unfolding before their very eyes. The skies could have fallen in the second half and breathless Baylor fans wouldn't have noticed. As a matter of fact, I'm not sure the skies didn't fall.

At halftime in this knucks-down battle for survival in the SWC's zany championship chase, the highly favored Longhorns were doing exactly what they had been expected to do—they were beating the Bears like a drum. At halftime they were ahead, 24–7.

And then, in perhaps the most memorable 30 minutes in Baylor's long football history, the Bears

Receivers Alcy Jackson (left) and Ricky Thompson (right) played key roles in the Bears' 1974 victory over the Longhorns. Courtesy of Baylor University Athletics.

—scored 27 points while holding the explosive Longhorns without a single point;

—moved into a tie for the Southwest Conference lead with the Texas Aggies, who lost Saturday to SMU, and thus jumped into the big middle of the madhouse scramble for a berth in the Cotton Bowl;

—defeated Darrell Royal for the first time in his long stay at Texas and beat the 'Horns for the first time in 18 years;

—scored more points than any Baylor team has *ever* scored against Texas, in a football series that goes back to 1901, and scored more points against a Royal team than any conference team has managed since Rice also got 34 way back in 1958; and

—held Texas' earth-scorching wishbone, which went into the game as the nation's third-hottest offense in rushing, to a mere 52 yards overland in the last two quarters, a paltry 84 yards in total offense in that span, and a single sashay into Baylor territory.

Let Bruin quarterback Neal Jeffrey sum it up, because of all Baylor's many heroes Saturday, Neal Jeffrey deserves to be heard first. "This was the biggest and the best," Neal said. "All those four years of work paid off. We were down in the valley, and now we're on the mountain."

All Jeffrey did against Baylor's old nemesis was run for one touchdown, throw touchdown passes of 69 and 54 yards, complete 20 of 31 passes for a shattering 351 yards, and guide the poised Bears to touchdowns or field goals on five of their six meaningful possessions in the telltale second half.

"Jeffrey's a super passer, and he throws real well under pressure," said Texas' All-American tackle candidate, 250-pound Doug English, admiringly.

Jeffrey threw the 69-yarder to Alcy Jackson early in the first quarter. Then after scoring himself early in the third period, he hurled a 54-yard touchdown to Ricky Thompson, who, like Alcy, doubles as a performer in the spring for Clyde Hart's track team. Actually, the passes weren't bombs, but the receivers turned them into bombs with their nifty running.

Roosevelt Leaks (46) tries to break past Arkansas defenders. Courtesy of University of Texas Athletics.

Phillip Kent ran 6 yards for Baylor's fourth touchdown of the game, the one that put the Bears ahead to stay, and Bubba Hicks provided the final six points with field goals of 35 and 25 yards.

Bubba also kicked four extra points, but it was his field goals, made under intense fourth-quarter pressure, that moved the Bears beyond Texas' reach.

Gracious as always in defeat, Darrell Royal went to the Baylor dressing room after the game, congratulated the Bears on their victory, and told them to keep on going all the way to the Cotton Bowl.

"Baylor played an outstanding game, and they deserved to win," Royal told newsmen. And to the Bears themselves, he said, "You had a chance to quit and you never did. You took the fight to us. Don't look back . . . go all the way."

That was a dressing room made up of "immensely proud" Bruins, said an immensely proud Grant Teaff, who became the first Baylor coach to beat Texas since Sam Boyd's Sugar Bowl–bound Bears did it in 1956. "They weren't all that emotional, but they were very happy," said Teaff. "They remind me of a bunch of champions."

The Bears scored on the fourth play of the game as Jeffrey threw a short spot pass to Jackson, who quickly turned it into a 69-yard TD thunderbolt.

Suddenly, with just a minute and 45 seconds gone, the Bears had six points, and Hicks quickly made it seven. That didn't faze Texas. The Longhorns regrouped, grabbed a Baylor fumble, and started blistering the Bears.

Texas' answer for that opening Baylor salvo was a numbing barrage that went touchdown, touchdown, field goal, touchdown. Billy Schott kicked all the extra points, the Texas band struck up all the winning marches, and Baylor faces just got longer and longer.

Ah, but deliverance was only an intermission away.

A blocked punt turned the momentum. Texas put the ball in play to start the third quarter, and the Bears,

Baylor quarterback Neal Jeffrey helped guide his team to crucial victories over Texas and SMU during the Bears' SWC championship season in 1974. Courtesy of Baylor University Athletics.

having adjusted their defense a bit and with 6-foot-3, 255-pound Leslie Benson inserted at middle guard to provide more muscle, shut the wishbone down. Derrel Luce stacked up Roosevelt Leaks on the first play for no gain, and it was a sign of things to come.

On fourth down, Texas punter Mike Dean got the snap, and even as he swung his foot, Bears were all over him. Reserve rover Johnny Greene blocked the punt, and linebacker Johnny Slaughter fell on the ball for Baylor at the Texas 17, and the Bears scored from there in seven plays. The tide had turned, and it stayed turned.

Texas responded with a drive of 12 plays that carried 57 yards to the Baylor 23—the only significant Longhorn drive of the second half. Leaks got the final first down at the Baylor 26, but then the Baylor defense got ferocious. Three plays gained 3 yards, and on fourth down, Schott tried a field goal and his kick sailed wide.

And then the Bears really shifted into high gear. With each down, they gained momentum and confidence. An 8-yard pass to Pat McNiel yielded a first down at the Baylor 33, and tailback Steve Beaird carried to the 46. And then, look out! Jeffrey threw to Thompson, who juked a defender, weaved and wagged, and broke into the clear. Fred Sarchet had a final crack at him and couldn't catch him. It was a 54-yard play, and Hicks's extra point made it a 24–21 game with 52 seconds left in the third quarter.

The word for what developed in the stands at that moment is spelled b-e-d-l-a-m.

Texas moved from its own 10 to the 34 before defender Ron Burns blasted Longhorn quarterback Marty Akins as he tried to hand off, and Tim Black recovered the resulting fumble. Jeffrey got his high-as-a-kite teammates out in front in just four plays.

Beaird caught a swing pass, eluded a tackler, and ran for 12 yards to the Texas 21. But he hurt his knee in going down and had to leave the action. Cleveland Franklin, seeing his first duty since the Arkansas game, replaced him and promptly gouged to the 15 before Kent got loose on an inside reverse and gained 9 yards to the 6. The Bears then called the same play, Kent scored, and Hicks calmly made the extra point to make it a 28–24 game. In the stands, it was bedlam redoubled.

With Baylor ahead in the fourth quarter, Akins went back to the option. But now he was facing Bears of a different mood. The Baylor strategy called for the cornerback, usually Burns, to flatten Akins quickly while the defensive end took care of the pitch man. When Akins tried to option, the ball went flying wildly, and Marty lost 16 yards in recovering. On fourth down, Dean's punt carried only 23 yards, and the Bears took over on the Texas 27.

Jeffrey quickly hurled a 13-yard pass to Jackson and

then an 11-yarder to Kent, setting up Hicks for a 35-yard field goal with 9:38 to play. Behind by seven points, the Longhorns could only win now with a touchdown and two-point conversion.

They didn't come close. They notched one first down on Leaks's power running, but when they tried the option again, Tommy Turnipseede dropped halfback Raymond Clayborn for a loss of 7, and once more, Dean had to punt.

The Bears took over on their own 12 (after a clipping penalty) with 7:04 to go and rolled to two first downs on Jeffrey passes to Jackson before having to punt. Bill Moore's 40-yarder set the Longhorns back to their own 17, and they never escaped the trap. Turnipseede intercepted Akins and returned 9 yards to the Texas 34, and Jeffrey threw a 20-yard pass to Kent that made it easy for Hicks to kick a 25-yarder with 43 seconds left, removing all doubt.

There was just enough time left for Scooter Reed to intercept still another Texas pass, this one by Mike Presley, and return to the Longhorn 6-yard line. By then, all those jubilant Baylor fans were off somewhere in football's seventh heaven.

The Bears won for the fifth time in their last six outings. Two hours after the final gun, with the stadium empty and darkness closing in, the scoreboard lights still said it all: Baylor 34, Visitors 24. At last report, they planned to let those scoreboard lights burn all night. "After 18 years," said one old Baylor grad, "how sweet it is."

NOVEMBER 24, 1974
AMAZIN' BEARS CORRAL MUSTANGS

DALLAS, Tex.—All of SMU's horses and all of SMU's men could not stay Steve Beaird and the valiant Baylor Bears from making their appointed rounds on a damp, windy, and altogether successful Saturday afternoon in the Cotton Bowl. After they had made those rounds, to the great delight of a majority of 40,168 witnesses, they had strapped the talented Mustangs 31–14, shattered records left and right, and moved within one short step of winning their first Southwest Conference football championship in 50 years.

All they need now to wrap up their most successful season in half a century is to defeat Rice here next Saturday afternoon.

Such a victory would give them a 6–1 record in conference play, and that would pay off in either an uncontested title and trip to the Cotton Bowl Classic on New Year's Day or a share of the crown with Texas A&M. All that confusion will evaporate on Friday in Austin, when the Texas Aggies and Texas Longhorns renew the league's foremost blood rivalry.

This year, that rivalry will unfold amid Baylor-flavored cries of "Sic 'em Horns" and "Hook 'em Horns." Because if the Longhorns do win that game and the Bears do beat Rice, Grant Teaff's intrepid youngsters will be home free, kings of the mountain, definitely No. 1 in the SWC. Saturday in Dallas they moved closer.

The Bears finally caught the idle Aggies in the league standings on a day when the clouds were sullen and Bruin partisans were nervous and tireless. Steve Beaird was in a mood to run, run, run.

Stormin' Steve ran for three touchdowns, the first two on 19- and 7-yard spurts right up the SMU middle through daylight—opened by Aubrey Schulz's fantastic blocking against 260-pound Louie Kelcher and others—and those three scoring gallops pushed Steve's total for the season to 15, or 1 more than the immortal Wesley Bradshaw scored in setting the old Baylor record back in 1922.

But Beaird, who slashed the Mustangs 26 times for 133 as his mom watched proudly wearing orange

Steve Beaird. Courtesy of Baylor University Athletics.

Grant Teaff coached at Baylor from 1972 to 1992 and was named Southwest Conference Coach of the Year six times. Courtesy of Baylor University Athletics.

and white, was just the busiest of the record breakers Saturday.

Poised, cool, no-mistakes Neal Jeffrey completed his first 7 passes of the afternoon and 11 of 17 for the game for Baylor's all-time aerial king. Neal now had thrown for 4,224 yards in his three years as a Baylor Bear, and that moves him ahead of his boyhood idol, All-American Don Trull, who hurled for 4,143 yards at Baylor from 1961 to '63. And just as he had done against Marty Akins of Texas, Jeffrey outdistanced SMU's dangerous Ricky Wesson in their head-to-head battle for supremacy at quarterback.

When Beaird wasn't running through the Mustangs and Jeffrey wasn't throwing over them, Don Bockhorn and Bubba Hicks were kicking them into the decisive defeat they had hoped to avoid in what was their final game of the season.

Bockhorn's contribution was a whopper, a 59-yard field goal kicked with 8:04 left in the third quarter—four plays after the Bears had recovered the only fumble the Mustangs lost of the six they put on the ground during the game.

That wind-aided bulls-eye, both coaches later agreed, was probably the game's turning point. Ironically, it's the only field goal Bockhorn has kicked this season. Usually he leaves such chores to Bubba Hicks, who delivered in such telling fashion against Texas and Texas Tech. But Bockhorn has the strongest leg on the team, which he uses in supplying kickoffs that go out of the end zone, and Grant Teaff knew if anyone on the Baylor team had a chance from 59 yards out, Don did. "I just had a feeling," said Grant.

Baylor was working with a 14–7 advantage when Bockhorn stepped back to kick, but SMU had surged

SMU's Louie Kelcher was a Consensus All-American in 1974; he played with San Diego and was selected for the Pro Bowl three times. Courtesy of Southern Methodist University Athletics.

89 yards in 11 plays just before intermission time to get its touchdown, and at that stage, the Mustangs were still full of fight and giving the Bears a hard time.

Bockhorn's monumental boot, second longest in conference history and longer by 7 yards than the field goal former record holder Terry Cozby kicked against SMU in 1969, returned momentum to the Bears, and they never surrendered it again.

They scored touchdowns on two of their next three possessions, and Bubba Hicks kicked true after each, giving him 4 perfect kicks for the afternoon and making his conversion total for the season read 26 out of 26. First thing you know, someone's going to start calling Bubba Mr. Automatic.

Also first thing you know, Bubba's going to set a new Baylor single-season conversion record. Hank Dickerson set the current mark of 26 in 1949; Bubba, of course, tied Hank's mark Saturday.

Amid all that record-book stuff, the Bears stayed busy winning their fourth game in a row, something they had not done since 1963, and their seventh game in their last eight outings. And for a change, they didn't leave Teaff or their adoring fans with such moist palms this time. They not only won the fourth quarter; they also won the other three. They led from pole to pole while handing the Mustangs a defeat that compared favorably in decisiveness with the lacings SMU suffered at the hands of Ohio State (28–9) and Texas (35–15).

"Baylor was just outstanding," said SMU grid boss Dave Smith. "They played every phase of the game in championship style. I don't think anybody we've played—Ohio State, Texas, anyone—had controlled a game with us like Baylor did today."

Right from the outset, the Bears played as if they would like to play more often on Cotton Bowl turf—for instance, on New Year's Day. They barged 80 yards in six plays for a touchdown on their second possession, then went 66 yards in nine plays for another touchdown scored late in the second quarter.

The Bears gave up not a single pass interception and fumbled only once. That one lost fumble came on their first possession, on the game's second play, just after Jeffrey had thrown a 19-yard completion to Phillip Kent. Kent bobbled when hit hard by Ronnie Robertson, and end Mark Cones recovered for SMU at the Baylor 39.

So actually, you say, the Bears started with a crisis. Not really. The Mustangs gained only 2 yards in three cracks at the Baylor defense, and John Dunlap's bid for a 52-yard field goal, kicked with a 17-mile-an-hour breeze at his back, didn't come close. As Dave Smith later said, "The defensive phase of Baylor's game was outstanding." The Mustangs did not get a first down until their fourth possession of the game.

Rescued by their defense, the Bears turned to Beaird and his blockers up front. "That's the best job anyone's done on Kelcher this season—by far the best job. Baylor's really going down the middle and they work well together," said SMU publicist Bob Condrun with admiration.

With Schulz leading the way, the blockers blocked and Beaird ran . . . for 30 yards off left tackle, then for 5, then for 13 on an option carry around right end. Jeffrey

Kenny Harrison (15) was a constant downfield threat for SMU. Courtesy of Southern Methodist University Athletics.

broke the pattern briefly, throwing an 11-yard pass to Ricky Thompson to the SMU 19, and then there went Steve again, flying along like a bowling ball, crossing the goal line standing up. The drive went 80 yards, and Beaird gained 68 of it.

The Bears played conservatively for a while, letting their defense (led once again by Derrel Luce, Joe Johnson, Tim Black, Ron Burns, and Flynn Bucy) muffle the Mustangs by dealing them a succession of bad third-down plays. Then the Bears opened full throttle again.

Jeffrey threw to Kent for 12, to Thompson for 11, and to Beaird for 5. Facing a third-and-5 situation at the SMU 38, Jeffrey faked to Beaird, then threw to Kent for a 23-yard gain to the SMU 15. SMU linebacker Ted Thompson had Kent stopped on a counterplay for a 5-yard loss, but the swift Bruin pulled away and turned it into an 8-yard gain. Then Beaird broke to daylight up the middle again and zipped 7 yards for a touchdown.

In the press box, an SMU man muttered, "I'll bet Mickey Early's getting tired of missing Beaird down there on the goal line."

That touchdown went on the scoreboard with 3:07 left in the first half. When the Mustangs clipped on the ensuing kickoff, they had to start at their own 11-yard line. They came out throwing—which looked like good strategy for Baylor. The Bruin picket line figured to pick off one of Wesson's aerials and maybe give the Bears field position for more points before intermission. But it didn't work out that way.

Wesson missed a pass, then ran for 19. Wayne Morris, a multitalented back who had been averaging 5 yards a carry, could get only 17 yards on 11 carries against the Bears Saturday, but 10 of them came on a run that sustained that particular SMU drive. Three plays later, with the drive bogging down, Wesson completed a 25-yard strike to Kenny Harrison, then a 16-yarder to Freeman Johns. Then with 20 seconds showing on the clock, he threw quickly to Johns again, and the Mustang receiver fielded the throw a yard deep in the end zone. So suddenly,

Oscar Roan. Courtesy of Southern Methodist University Athletics.

the Mustangs were back in the game, having moved 89 yards in a matter of two minutes and 51 seconds.

Baylor got nothing on its first possession of the third quarter, but when fullback David Bostick fumbled at the SMU 44, Joe Johnson recovered for the Bears, and green-and-gold banners started waving. But the Bears went nowhere. So on what looked for all the world like a hopeless one-in-a-million shot, Bockhorn lined up and kicked at a field goal from 59 yards away . . . and lo, the ball flew and flew and went on through the uprights.

Armed with that 10-point lead, the Baylor defense got the ball right back for Jeffrey and company at the Baylor 36, and that time, they hit all the right buttons. Alcy Jackson caught a 25-yard pass, Beaird ran for 8, and Jeffrey surprised them by running for 11 himself. The yardage came harder now, inside the SMU 20, but Beaird gouged out a first down on a fourth-down try at the Mustang 9, and three plays later, fullback Pat McNeil went around left end and just refused to go down until he had made it to the end zone. Hicks's kick made it 24–7.

SMU retaliated strongly, with speedster Tennell Atkins returning the kickoff 57 yards to the Baylor 42 before Ron Burns, the last Bruin with a shot at him, sent him sprawling. That threat flamed out when Scooter Reed intercepted Wesson's pass in the end zone on the final play of the third quarter.

The Ponies went all the way: 45 yards on eight plays—on their next possession, however. The key play and the big gainer was a 28-yard Wesson pass on which tight end Oscar Roan made an unbelievable diving catch at the Baylor 13-yard line. Wayne Morris got the final yard, and Ted Thompson kicked the extra point.

SMU still had time—if the Mustangs could hold the Bears. They couldn't. Jeffrey whipped his troops 80 yards in nine plays for the touchdown that sacked it up while chewing up the clock. On that drive, Alcy Jackson artfully turned a 15-yard pass into a 35-yard gain, Kent caught an 11-yarder, and Beaird ran for 7, 12, and finally the last 2 yards.

At the finish, Baylor's No. 2 backfield—quarterback Mark Jackson, tailback Cleveland Franklin, fullback Mike Ebow, and wingback Brian Kilgore—was in the game and not doing badly at all. The Bears boomed from their own 21 to the SMU 21 before the clock closed them out, and on that drive, Franklin had excellent runs of 9 and 18 yards.

After scorching the defenses at Texas, Texas A&M, and Arkansas, Wesson, the SWC's third-leading rusher, found the Baylor defense ready for him. He could get only 42 yards on 14 carries. Upstairs, he completed 8 of 19 shots for 134 yards but gave up two interceptions—to Reed and Ken Quesenberry. Bostick, the big fullback, led SMU's footmen with 89 yards on 19 carries. Other than Beaird's 133, Baylor profited from Kent's 39 yards of rushing and McNeil's 29. Kent also caught four passes for 65 yards, Alcy Jackson two for 60, and Ricky Thompson two for 23.

Beaird's big day pushed his season rushing total to a league-leading 970 yards. Already he is Baylor's leading rusher for a single season. If he can get 30 yards against Rice, he will become the school's first 1,000-yard runner ever.

A hand-lettered sign posted on the outskirts of Waco Saturday morning admonished Baylor travelers to the Dallas game: "Last one leaving Waco turn off the lights."

Steve Beaird wasn't the last Bruin out of Waco. But he sure turned out the lights on the Mustangs.

DECEMBER 1, 1974

BEARS UNDISPUTED IN SWC

WACO, Tex.—On a telltale afternoon of frozen fingers and frosted toes, the red-hot Baylor Bears kept that rendezvous with destiny here Saturday.

They swept past the Rice Owls 24–3 and became undisputed football champions of the Southwest Conference for the first time in half a century.

The victory left Grant Teaff's unbelievable Bears alone at the summit with a 6–1 conference record—one full game ahead of Texas and Texas A&M, the two teams that tied for second.

Having peeled away 50 years of failure and frustration, the Bears whooped and hollered their way into the dressing room, where Field Scovell, chairman of the board of the Cotton Bowl Classic and chairman of the bowl's selection committee, said the words Baylor fans have been aching to hear for more than three decades.

"Gentlemen, I congratulate you for being the undisputed conference champions," said Scovell, "and I'm happy to invite you to the Cotton Bowl. Now I just want to know one thing—are you coming?"

The Bears' roar of acceptance shook the dressing room walls.

That bit of formality made the matchup complete. It will be Baylor versus Penn State, the champions of the East, in the 39th annual Cotton Bowl Classic on New Year's Day.

The Bears finally conquered the SWC summit in a game watched by 40,100 fans, most of them adoring Baylor partisans who through the years have gathered time after time in hopes of seeing the Bears finally nail down the "Big One," only to see them fall short.

But this time, they made it with room to spare, and although the afternoon's chill deepened as the game wore on, few fans left. Obviously they wanted to soak up all the delicious sights and sounds of the historic occasion before going off to hunt for Cotton Bowl tickets.

The undisputed championship and Cotton Bowl invitation crowned a stunning comeback engineered this year by coach Grant Teaff, and Baylor was quick to reward the achievement.

Athletic director Jack Patterson announced even before Saturday's final gun that Teaff was being given a new five-year contract. The new salary terms were not disclosed.

"We feel this is merely a small vote of thanks for the tremendous job he and his coaching staff have done in the three years he has been at Baylor University," said Patterson, "and we want the entire world to know just how proud we are. And we want to assure him that we want to make this a quality job."

Grant Teaff celebrates Baylor's 1974 conference title, their first since 1924. Courtesy of *Dave Campbell's Texas Football*.

In Teaff's three years on the job, the Bears have recorded 5–6, 2–9, and 8–3 seasons. He was named Southwest Conference and Texas senior college Coach of the Year in 1972 and is considered a sure bet to win similar honors again this year and to make a strong run at national Coach of the Year recognition.

Winless last season in conference play, the Bears became the first team since Rice of 1936–37 to go from the SWC basement to the throne room in back-to-back seasons.

"What can I say? I was very proud of them," said Teaff after the Bears had demolished the Owls and then had romped to their dressing room through a tunnel that had been lined with cotton bolls by some enterprising Baylor fan. Teaff led the team in prayer before personally going from player to player, thanking him individually.

The game itself, played on a sunny afternoon where the chill factor was 20 degrees, was Baylor all the way. The Bears led at halftime, 14–0, after touchdown runs of 20 yards by tailback Steve Beaird and 10 yards by fullback Pat McNeil, and after Rice had managed a field goal on its first possession of the third quarter, the Bears scored 10 more points on quarterback Mark Jackson's 13-yard run and Bubba Hicks's 35-yard field goal.

Beaird rushed for 134 yards, sending his season total to 1,104 yards and wrapping up the SWC rushing championship. He also became Baylor's first 1,000-yard runner in history.

Baylor's all-conference center Aubrey Schutz could have been speaking for Beaird, quarterback Neal Jeffrey, himself, Teaff, and all those jubilant frozen fans. "It's a great way to end the season—I mean, the regular season," he said.

It's a season that will burn in Baylor memories forever.

JANUARY 2, 1975

SECOND HALF SPELLS DOOM FOR CHAMPION BU BEARS

DALLAS, Tex.—Yipes! So *that's* what a Nittany Lion is. And that's what he can do when he gets riled. And when a bunch of them get riled—well, yipes again!

They got riled in the second half of the 39th Cotton Bowl Classic here New Year's Day and left Baylor's promised land in shocking disarray. Scoring 38 points in the game's final 30 minutes, they butchered the Bears 41–20 and turned an afternoon of high promise into the new year's first bad hangover.

In short, Cinderella got mugged.

A chilled audience of 67,500 saw Baylor's impossible dream last just 30 minutes too long. The Bears, typically spirited and resolute, went to rest at halftime owning a 7–3 upper hand, and at that moment, there were a lot of reasons to think Baylor's first undisputed Southwest Conference championship in 50 years was going to be crowned by the school's first Cotton Bowl victory in history.

But in jest, a veteran of SWC press boxes previewed what was waiting just around the corner.

"There's good news and bad news for Baylor," he said. "The good news is that the Bears are leading, 7 to 3. The bad news is that they decided to go ahead and play the second half."

If the second half amounted to Penn State's reprieve, the Nittany Lions promptly made the most of it. They scored five touchdowns and a field goal on their seven possessions of the final 30 minutes, and the only reason they didn't get a sixth touchdown on that one unproductive possession is because they got nailed by a sharp-eyed official on a 64-yard TD play, and instead of getting six points, they drew not one red flag but two and wound up getting the equivalent of an 88-yard penalty.

But that play might also have been the turning point—at least, it was that play that got the Nittany

Lions riled. "Yeah, I'd have to say that's when we got fire in our eyes," said freshman wingback Jimmy Cefalo, who is the sweetest-running—and catching—freshman you ever will see.

Cefalo, tight end Dan Natalo, fullback Tom Donchez, and quarterback Tom Shuman, a guy with a slingshot arm, just crumpled what had been a stingy, clutch-playing Baylor defense and left it on the short end of almost everything it tried.

Shuman was supposed to be one of the better passers the Nittany Lions have had, but heck, nobody said anything about him being another Sammy Baugh. He throws spirals, he throws them with authority, and he throws them long and right on the money. He turned Baylor's pass defense wrong side out.

The 6-foot-1, 194-pound senior completed 10 of his 20 passes for a scorching 226 yards, only 5 yards off the Cotton Bowl aerial record, and he also ran for a touchdown, wrapping up outstanding offensive player honors for the second year in a row. Last year, he won such honors in guiding Penn State to an Orange Bowl victory over LSU.

Baylor safety Ken Quesenberry prevented a Penn State sweep by winning outstanding defensive player honors. Kenny was a sensation for almost 40 minutes, before being sidelined with a knee injury. The voters had to notice what happened to the Baylor defense when Kenny went out. What happened was the defense went to pot.

The Nittany Lions also had their defensive heroes—linebacker Chris Devlin, tackle Mike Hartenstine, safety Mike Johnson, and tackle John Quinn in particular—but towering over all was Shuman, the offensive triggerman. The guy was simply devastating in his marksmanship in the second half. The Lions gave him plenty of time to throw, and Cefalo and Natale in particular turned his humming bullets into demoralizing big gainers. Meanwhile, Donchez, the big fullback, ravaged the Bears overland, and Joe Paterno's bounce-back kids just kept moving those stakes. And rolling up the points.

Actually, what happened to Baylor on this windy Wednesday now has happened to four of Penn State's bowl opponents. Kansas in the '69 Orange Bowl, Texas in the '72 Cotton Bowl, LSU in the '74 Orange Bowl, and now Baylor in the '75 Cotton Bowl—all led at halftime and then became Nittany Lion knockout victims in the second half.

The difference was that Penn State's late landslide buried Baylor more completely than the others, indeed more completely in terms of points allowed than any team in Cotton Bowl history. However, Penn State's record-setting last touchdown was a bit of a fluke—scored with two seconds left on the clock and long after school had let out.

With sophomore Mark Jackson engineering smartly, the Bears had just rolled 70 yards in 10 plays and scored their third touchdown of the game on Jackson's 11-yard pass to Ricky Thompson with 14 seconds left. When the two-point conversion try failed, that made it a 34–20 game.

But still full of fight, the Bears tried for one last miracle. The effort blew up in their faces. They tried an onside kick, a bouncer delivered on a slant toward the east sideline. As the Bears rushed toward the ball, hoping to recover, Penn State linebacker Joe Jackson rushed forward and fielded the ball on the bounce and never missed a step. All the Bears were still headed south while Jackson was going north at full speed with the ball tucked under his arm. It was a 50-yard touchdown play that consumed 12 seconds on the clock. When John Reihner kicked the extra point, which was Penn State's 41st point, the old Cotton Bowl scoring record, which had belonged to Texas (Texas 40, Missouri 27 in '46), went down the drain.

Those were the easiest points the Nittany Lions got, although at times they did get their yardage in alarming gulps. Starting with their final possession of the first half, they moved 77 yards in 14 plays and produced a 25-yard field goal (kicked by Chris Bahr); then in the second half, they drove 80 yards in 9 plays, 52 yards in just 2 plays, 68 yards in 9 plays, 18 yards in 5 plays, and 50 yards on the kickoff return, and all those drives culminated in touchdowns. For good measure, Bahr also kicked another field goal, a 33-yarder that climaxed a 54-yard, 8-play drive.

Donchez, who rampaged for 116 yards on 25 carries, scored the first Penn State touchdown on a 1-yard run. Shuman threw 48 yards to Cefalo for the Nittany Lions' second TD, and then Cefalo ran 3 yards in scoring his second touchdown of the day. Shuman snaked 2 yards on a keeper for the visitors' fourth touchdown of the day, and Jackson supplied the capper with his spring with two seconds remaining.

At times, Baylor moved the ball well, especially in the first half, but the Bears couldn't come up with enough equalizers. What they did come up with were three touchdown drives: 84 yards in 11 plays, with stout Steve Beaird going the final 4 yards with 4:13 remaining in the first period; then 55 yards in 4 plays, with Neal Jeffrey hurling a 35-yard touchdown pass to Ricky Thompson with 4:23 left in the third period; and finally the 70-yard, 10-play march at the end of the game, which Mark Jackson engineered and climaxed with his 11-yard touchdown throw to Thompson again.

Baylor not only held the upper hand at halftime; the Bears also moved back ahead 14–10 when Jeffrey threw the 35-yarder to Thompson. During that stretch, so many good things were happening to the Bears that it appeared they still might win, despite Penn State's mounting momentum.

In the first half, the Nittany Lions had boomed from their own 25 to the Baylor 11 on their first possession—and then had missed a close-in field goal attempt. They gained possession on the Baylor 23 on a pass interception and got nothing out of it. They repeatedly came up with some long gainers in the first half—Cefalos's 23-yard carry on their second play of the game; a 22-yard pass to Donchez on Shuman's first aerial attempt; Shuman completions of 13, 15, 12, and 19 yards; and some rumbling runs by Donchez that picked up 13 and 14 yards.

But all they got out of all that wave-making was Bahr's 25-yard field goal, kicked with 1:13 left in the first half.

And then in the second half, after Shuman had hit Natale on 42- and 20-yard aerial strikes in setting up Donchez' 1-yard scoring lunge with 10:46 left in the third quarter, and after the Bears had misfired on their first offensive effort of the second half, the game's most spectacular near miss unfolded.

Penn State had started on its own 19, and Donchez had whirled for 22 yards. But soon it was third and 15, and Shuman went back to throw. He hit Donchez on a screen pass, with a convoy of blockers in front of him, and the big fullback rolled down the field like a runaway express. All the way he went—64 yards to the payoff station—apparently pushing the Lions into a 17–7 lead. But wait, a flag was down. And when he saw the flag, Shuman picked it up and hurled it away in anger and disgust. When he did that, a second flag promptly fell. It was double no-no, first for an illegal block downfield (ruled offensive pass interference) and then for unsportsmanlike conduct, and while the Lions fretted and fumed, the man in the stripes marched the ball all the way back to the Penn State 12-yard line. From here they punted.

But wait—Baylor's run of good fortune still wasn't over. The Bears got the ball at their own 45, and when Jeffrey was blitzed on a pass attempt, a Lion came in late on the play, and Penn State was docked another 15. And then two plays later, Thompson ran a deep pattern and got a step behind Mike Johnson. Jeffrey's pass was a good one, but Johnson got a hand on it and deflected it—right into Thompson's hands for a touchdown.

Bubba Hicks's second conversion kick of the game pushed Baylor back ahead 14–10.

"Man, all the weird things that have happened to Penn State—I couldn't figure it," said one neutral in the press box. And then I looked around, and there was Billy Graham wearing a green scarf.

Alas, that was the high-water mark for the green, the gold, the scarf, and the Bears.

Quesenberry had been hurt on Donchez' long touchdown run that didn't count. Facing a juggled Baylor secondary, Shuman went to work in earnest. And as Cefalo said later, after the double penalty, the Lions got fire in their eyes. Suddenly there was no holding them. Shuman sent Cefalo racing down the east sideline on a deep pattern while his pass protection gave him plenty of time to throw. When Cefalo got clear behind two Baylor defenders, Shuman hit him perfectly. It was an easy touchdown, pushing the Lions back ahead.

And this time they stayed ahead.

Baylor's tackling got sloppy as the game wore on, and the Lions took full advantage. Soph Neil Hutton (79 yards on 12 carries) ignited their next touchdown march with a 17-yard thrust, and Cefalo kept it going with a 21-yard romp on a reverse that carried to the Baylor 16. Donchez carried to the 3, and Cefalo got the final 3. Reihner's kick made it 24–14, and lights were getting dim for Baylor.

They had to punt in short order, and Penn State used the next possession to march 54 yards to the Baylor 16. The big gainers included a 14-yard run by Hutton and a 34-yard aerial strike, Shuman to Cefalo. On fourth down, Bahr kicked a 33-yard field goal with 6:17 left in the game.

So for the Bears, it was now or never. It was never. Jeffrey's first pass was intercepted by Mike Johnson and returned to the Baylor 18, and five plays later, Shuman annexed the final 2 yards. Reihner kicked the extra point, and it was all over.

Making his first appearance, Baylor's Mark Jackson gave the Bears reason to think good thoughts about '75. He ran for 16, then threw to Sam Harper for 15 and 14 yards, and finally he and Ricky Thompson teamed on a beautifully executed 11-yard play that produced Baylor's final touchdown of an unforgettable season. But too little and too late. And too much Joe Jackson on the onside kick that followed.

As much as anything, the Nittany Lions snuffed out Baylor's little big man, Steve Beaird, in the second half,

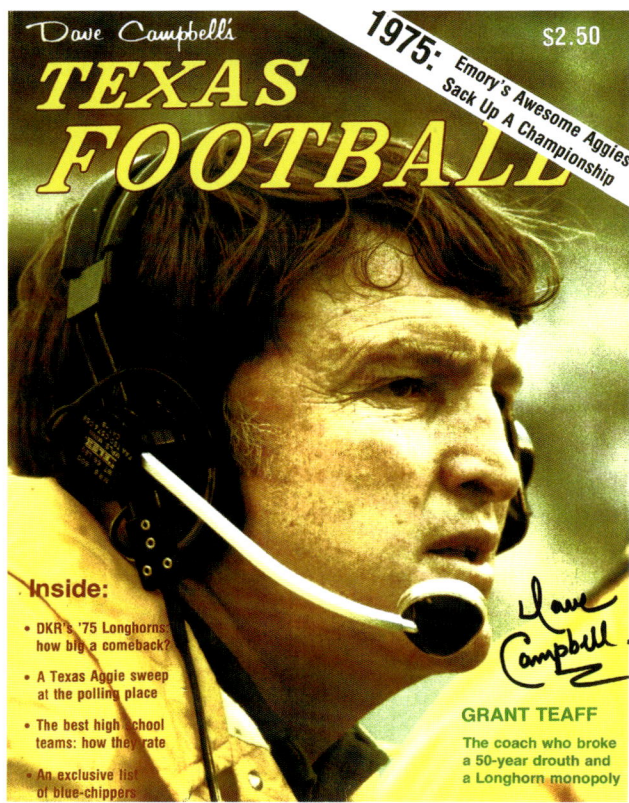

Courtesy of *Dave Campbell's Texas Football*.

which eliminated Bruin hopes for ball control—or anything close to it. Beaird rushed for 72 yards on 14 carries in the first half but could get only 12 yards on 7 carries in the game's final 30 minutes. "I couldn't believe that little rascal, the way he was running against us in the first half," said Penn State ace Greg Murphy. "But in the second half, I guess we just got down on his level."

Stout Steve hit the Lions repeatedly for good gainers in the early going, and on Baylor's first scoring march, he touched off the thrust with a 20-yard burst right up the middle. He carried 8 times on that 11-play drive for a net of 49 yards, and his last carry, a 4-yard job against a massed defense, put the Bears in front.

But the Lions eventually found the handle on Steve. And the second half arrived, and the second half is their half. In those final 30 minutes, they rampaged for 284 yards in total offense (139 rushing and 145 passing), plus the 50-yard touchdown run on the kick return, while holding Baylor to 160 yards in total offense. And 70 of that came on the Bruin scoring drive produced after the issue had been settled.

Combining blitzes with good coverage, the Lions managed to muffle Jeffrey's guns most of the time. He had to settle for 7 completions on 19 attempts for 135 yards. Thompson, Harpy, and Alcy Jackson made the best catches. Other than Beaird, only Pat McNeil (8 carries for 36 yards) and Mark Jackson (3 for 18) rushed in double figures. Jeffrey lamented Baylor's inability to rally one last time for a fourth-quarter victory. "I guess our luck finally caught up with us," he said.

But Grant Teaff summed up best. "We played a fine football team. They're well coached, poised, and experienced. They took it away from us in the fourth quarter, when that's been ours. But don't be ashamed of the loss," he told his players. "You're still the Southwest Conference champions. You learn something from everything."

Shuman was generous in victory. "Baylor was a good team," he said. "They weren't that physical and they weren't big. But they were a good, aggressive team."

A good, aggressive team that finally got a stirred-up Lion—a Nittany Lion, that is—by the tail and couldn't turn loose. As Teaff said, you learn from everything. Next time, guys, make the season 30 minutes shorter.

SEPTEMBER 12, 1976

INSPIRED COUGARS UTILIZE SECOND-HALF COMEBACK TO DEAL DAZED BEARS 23–5 DEFEAT IN OPENER

WACO, Tex.—After waiting 5 years and 30 minutes, the Houston Cougars joined the Southwest Conference here Saturday afternoon with a bang—well, actually, joined it with multiple bangs: bang, bang, bang, bang, bang. Add up all those bangs and a shocking score emerges: Houston 23, Baylor 5.

Trailing the favored, title-minded Bears by five points at the end of the first half, the lean, mean, unfazed Cougars came back after intermission and just poured the cold steel to the dazed, rapidly tiring Bears as all the Baylor partisans in the Baylor Stadium crowd of 37,500 looked on with growing bewilderment and disappointment.

No telling what the regional television audience looked on with, but all those Big Red fans back in Houston, watching in their living rooms, must have been delighted, jubilant, ecstatic. As far as they were concerned, the story writers couldn't have come up with a better script for this one in Hollywood.

Lordy, the longer it went, the worse it got, and finally, with a mere three seconds left on the scoreboard clock, the still-hungry Cougars called a time out, then ran one more play and scored a touchdown, leaving the Bears down by 18 and most red of face. Talk about embarrassing . . .

Redshirt sophomore quarterback Danny Davis directed the Houston comeback and scored the first touchdown put on the board by a Cougar team in Southwest Conference play. Davis's artful 4-yard ramble climaxed a 9-play, 45-yard journey that pushed the Cougars ahead at 6–5 with 6:07 remaining in the third quarter. Although more than 20 minutes of playing time remained, the Bears, who played with a strange lack of emotion on offense, were never really in the game again. Or at least, they were never in Houston territory. Not once.

Houston's second-half comeback, which mainly marched straight ahead on quick openers and counters

Danny Davis was inducted into the University of Houston Athletics Hall of Honor in 2002. Courtesy of University of Houston Athletics.

featuring the brute-strength runs of fullbacks John Housman and Charles Lynch, was aided and abetted by some bad Baylor decisions and bad Baylor turnovers. After it was all over, it was difficult to remember that the Bears had staged a truly outstanding, crowd-arousing goal-line stand in the first half and had almost staged another great one in the fourth quarter.

Leading by that single point at 6–5, Bill Yeoman's fired-up pupils gained possession with 3:48 remaining in the third quarter when Anthony Francis intercepted Mark Jackson's underthrown pass at the Houston 13. From that point, Davis directed his messengers of victory straight down the field, most of the time clipping off the yardage in big bursts, until they nailed a first down at the Bruin 2-yard line.

Then Housman squirmed for a yard. Randy Love hit the middle and got nothing. Houston hit the middle and got the same nothing. So it was fourth and 1 at the 1, and the game was still very much up for grabs, and then Dyral Thomas went right, cut inside, and just did clear to the Baylor end zone. Lennard Coplin added the extra point that moved the Cougars ahead, 13–5, and from that point, the Bears faded like a spent morning glory. They never got beyond their own 40-yard line the rest of the warm, sun-splashed afternoon.

Houston's final insurance points included a 22-yard field goal by Coplin, which came after Cougar linebacker David Hodge intercepted a foolishly thrown Mark Jackson pass and returned it 19 yards to the Baylor 28 and a 5-yard touchdown run by Thomas scored with those three ticks of the clock to play. For the Cougars on their day of destiny, there was nothing like being sure.

At the finish, the Bears not only were dead tired; they also were still looking for their first touchdown of this bicentennial year.

Their first points came gift wrapped. Facing a fourth-and-2 situation at their own 28 early in the opening quarter, the Cougars moved into punt formation, with Chuck Brown snapping to punter Jay Wyatt. Brown was too strong. His snap sailed over Wyatt's head and bounded back into the Cougar end zone, where Wyatt, after one false start, recovered for a safety.

For the Bears, so far so good, although if they had been lucky, the payoff would have been greater. They had almost blocked Wyatt's first punt of the game. But the next time they had a return on, which meant they made contact and then started dropping back to block as soon as the ball was snapped. Thus there was no pressure on Wyatt as he chased the ball down, and when he fumbled on his first recovery attempt in the end zone, there was no Bruin there to grab the ball for a touchdown.

Even so, the Bears took the ensuing free kick and marched from their own 42 to the Houston 11, and while no one would have believed it at the time, that, friends and neighbors, was as close as they were to get to the Houston end zone the entire afternoon.

Facing a third-and-5 situation, they lost their momentum when Mark Jackson, looking to pass, was blindsided and fumbled. Baylor guard Rell Tipton came out of the pileup with the recovery back on the UH 19, and Lester Belrose then kicked a 36-yard field goal, giving the Bears a 5-point advantage.

It looked as if they would pad it in the second quarter when they marched 54 yards in 9 plays to the Houston 14, but on third and 1, Mark Jackson and freshmen center Arland Thompson failed to make connections on the exchange, and Houston's Grady Ebesnsberger came up with the recovery.

Offensively, that was it for the Bears, who wound up with 13 first downs, 176 total yards rushing, 235 yards in total offense, and a bad case of Wilson Whitley–itis. They also lost two of six fumbles and surrendered two interceptions, and in the telltale second half, they were badly whipped along the line of scrimmage, almost constantly on offense, and too often on defense.

Now and then they would break off a good run—Mark Jackson had runs of 13, 13, 10, and 10 yards; soph fullback Steve Howell had a 23-yarder; and newcomer Gary Blair had a 20-yard burst—but they were unable to sustain a drive or control the ball. The massive, hard-charging Whitley and teammates David Hodge, Vincent Greenwood, Paul Humphreys, Frederick Snell, Don Sebastian, and Anthony Francis had a lot to do with that, of course.

With the offense saddled with a case of the blahs, the Bruin defense had to hold the fort, and it held well all through the first half. The most glittering moment came late in the second quarter, after the Cougars had moved from midfield to the Baylor 11 in seven plays. Then Alois Blackwell hit very quick up the middle to the 5. Davis tried to roll, and Flynn Bucy knocked him down back on the 7. Blackwell bolted up the middle again to the 2—it was fourth and 1 at the Baylor 2-yard line. And Blackwell, trying to get those last 36 inches, got nary an inch as Mike Nelms and Shane Nelson dropped him like a stone.

The Bruin defense also held on Houston's first possession of the third quarter. Then with the Bears marching (from their own 20 to their own 45 in three plays), Mark Jackson ran a keeper, got in deep trouble, tried to option to a trailing halfback, and succeeded only in turning the ball over to the Cougars' Mark Mohr at the Baylor 45.

Houston ripped up those 45 yards in nine plays, the muscular Housman getting the first 9 and Davis the last 5. Trying for a two-point conversion, Davis threw accurately to flanker Robert Lavergne in the end zone, but the receiver dropped the ball. That was about the last thing the Cougars dropped the rest of the afternoon.

With Blair bursting for 20 yards up the Cougar middle, the Bears drove out to midfield on their next possession. Then on first down, Jackson tried for a home run. His long throw aimed toward sophomore wingback Greg Hawthorne was underthrown, and Francis intercepted at the 13 as the Baylor receiver, for some reason, really made no effort to break up the catch.

Facing 87 yards of real estate, the Cougars started fitfully, netting a single yard on their first two plays. Then in what Grant Teaff later called one of the game's big, big plays, Davis completed a 22-yard pass to Don Bass over the middle, preserving the drive.

At one point, a 5-yard penalty made the Cougars pause, but they quickly were on their way again—Davis bolting for 11, Lynch for 14, and Thomas for 12 to the Bruin 13-yard line. Housman and Thomas moved the ball on to the 2, at which point the Bruin defense almost snuffed 'em out. But not quite.

That 16-play drive left the Bruin defense gasping, and it really had only one other bright moment left—when it stopped a Houston drive short at the Baylor 5 following Hodge's interception and return and forced Coplin to go for the field goal. At the finish, the Cougars were in full command.

Houston's statistics—16 first downs, 254 yards rushing, 301 yards in total offense with no turnovers—were impressive enough, as were the figures for Housman (16 carries, 85 yards) and Lynch (7 runs, 44 yards). Davis ran for 48 yards but was erratic overhead. Blair had 68 yards for Baylor, Jackson 55. Jackson really had little chance to pass. A Cougar was always draped around his neck or pawing his face.

Defensively, the Bears seemed to put their best foot forward when soph nose guard Gary Johnson was on the prowl, and when Johnson had to sit out part of the action in the second half, Houston found the going much easier. Bruin linebackers Shane Nelson and Jerry Harrison got in some good licks, Flynn Bucy was sturdy, and the secondary—especially Nelms, Ron Burns, and Gary Green—were tough. But all too often in the second half, the Bears were guilty of some very sloppy tackling.

"We simply got out-footballed in the fourth quarter," a glum Grant Teaff capsuled the long afternoon. "When you play good competition like we did today, you must win it in the fourth quarter. We didn't and they did.

Gary Johnson. Courtesy of Baylor University Athletics.

"We had good momentum in the first half and our defense played super. We couldn't hold on to the football in the second half and they won it."

So the new kid on the SWC block, after waiting so long, promptly made the most of his first opportunity to go to the head of the class. Probably several conference teams will be along to put him in his place before the '76 race is over, but not the Baylor Bears. For the Bears, it's back to the old drawing board while the Cougars and SMU Mustangs take over the league lead. Yipes!

NOVEMBER 2, 1976
ON SECOND THOUGHT

Doug Ethridge is the coach of the Port Neches-Groves football team that overcame a number of formidable obstacles last year to win the Class 4A state title. The other day, Ethridge was talking football with Bill Ellington, a member of Darrell Royal's staff at Texas. "You know, Bill," Ethridge said, "sometimes it seems a team just has to be destined."

It is beginning to appear that Texas Tech might be the destined team in the Southwest Conference this year, much as Baylor was in 1974, as Texas A&M was in '67, and SMU in '66. All three kept winning when the form chart said they had no business winning.

You look at Steve Sloan's Red Raiders, and you have to wonder. They have an excellent offensive line and a truly outstanding quarterback. But several other teams can match them in running backs and receivers, and as Royal himself noted yesterday, Houston is stronger physically on defense than Tech. So is A&M, so is Arkansas, and so, for that matter, is Texas. The Red Raiders don't have a Wilson Whitley, a Brad Shearer, a Jimmy Dean, or Arkansas' defensive speed.

But the team that stands 6–0 and ranks fifth in the nation and is off to its best start in 38 years is not Houston or Arkansas or A&M or Texas. The team that is stirring up the echoes is Texas Tech, which once again Saturday played like a team that is "destined."

Coming from behind to beat the aroused Longhorns by three points, the Red Raiders moved into an enviable position. They alone of all the SWC teams have Texas and Texas A&M behind them. The way the Aggies have been playing and the way the Longhorns played Saturday, that is no small thing.

Nor was the way the Red Raiders performed on third down against Texas a small thing. Their offense repeatedly came through in those situations, just as their defense turned back the 'Horns in clutch moments. And the way a team plays on third down, experts say, separates champions from also-rans.

The Red Raider who had a hand in most of those key third-down plays was Rodney Allison. But not all of them.

It was Larry Dupre's interception of a Mike Cordaro pass on third down that set up Tech's first touchdown. Dupre, son of a former Baylor football hero, became the darling of the High Plains on Saturday with his pass defense and touchdown-saving tackles against Longhorn speedster Johnny (Lam) Jones.

Dupre's first big play came on Texas' second possession. On a third and 8, he picked off a Cordaro pass over the middle and returned it 23 yards to the 13, and Tech scored three plays later.

In the second quarter, with Texas up 14–7, one of Rodney Allison's pitchouts was batted back toward the Tech end zone and recovered by UT's Raymond Clayborn at the Tech 30. If the Longhorns had turned that

John Wesley "Lam" Jones's speed made him dangerous any time he got his hands on the ball. He won a gold medal as a member of the 4 × 100 meter relay team at the 1976 Summer Olympics in Montreal. Courtesy of University of Texas Athletics.

Running back Larry Isaac was inducted into the Red Raider Hall of Fame in 2014. Courtesy of Texas Tech University Athletics.

opportunity into a touchdown, well, who knows what might have happened?

As it was, the Longhorns got to the Tech 20, then lost yardage on three straight snaps, and the key play was on third down. Ted Constanzo went back to pass, and Harold Buell sacked him for a 15-yard loss to the Tech 46. Although he had a 15-mph wind at his back, Russell Erxleben missed the long field goal attempt, and at the finish, Texas still trailed by a field goal.

Allison, on the other hand, thrived on those third-down situations. On the first one he faced in the opening quarter, needing 19 yards to move the chains, he threw a 23-yard completion to Sammy Williams.

As the play-by-play chart of Tech's scoring drives shows, Allison and the Red Raiders were close to flawless on third down:

With 8:56 left in the first half and Tech trailing by seven, the Raiders started at their own 20. On third and 3, Allison handed off to flanker Brian Nelson on an inside reverse, and Nelson gained 7 to keep the drive alive. On third and 22 from the Tech 22, Allison bolted up the middle on a quarterback draw for 33 yards. On third and 1 from the Texas 37, Billy Taylor gained 2. Finally, at the end of the drive on the Texas 18, Taylor's halfback pass fell incomplete, and Brian Hall kicked a 34-yard field goal into the wind, which turned out to be the winning margin.

In the third quarter, with Texas up 21–10, the Raiders drove 80 yards in 17 plays for a touchdown, coming through on third downs with gains of 12, 11, and 8 yards.

Finally, trailing 28–24 in the fourth quarter, Allison and friends staged a 76-yard march that put them ahead to stay, converting three more third downs along the way. The first was the backbreaker for the 'Horns, as Allison avoided a sack and ran 22 yards on third and 7.

Later, Larry Isaac converted a pair of third and 2s to put the Red Raiders on the doorstep, and Billy Taylor did a fourth-down swan dive for the touchdown after Texas stopped Allison three times inside the 2.

At the finish, Tech led in snaps (90 to 66), in first downs, total yards, and time of possession, but mainly the Red Raiders led in third-down conversions, and that enabled them to lead where it counted most—on the scoreboard.

The way they kept doing it, you could almost say they were destined. I'll bet the Longhorns thought so.

NOVEMBER 7, 1976

RELENTLESS COOGS HUMILIATE HAPLESS LONGHORNS, 30–0

AUSTIN, Tex.—The University of Houston Cougars, ravenous to a fault here Saturday afternoon, not only bit the hand that sponsored them in their successful battle for Southwest Conference membership five years ago; they went on and gnawed Texas' arm off clean to the shoulder. And then went to work on Bevo's liver, gizzard, and horns.

It was downright shocking, the way the championship-minded Cougars pushed the former SWC rulers around. The final score was Houston 30, Texas 0, and it could have been worse. It could have been Houston by 45 to zip.

Indeed, if all Bevo lost was an arm, he was lucky. But there are 77,809 Memorial Stadium witnesses who will tell you he lost more.

He lost his second game in the race for the title, and that virtually spells elimination.

He lost his 42-game Memorial Stadium winning streak.

He suffered the worst defeat in conference play that *any* Texas team has suffered since Darrell Royal first arrived at Forty Acres 20 seasons ago. Only a 39–7 loss to Ole Miss in the 1958 Sugar Bowl would be a lower point for a Royal team at Texas.

He was shut down to a mere 24 yards rushing Saturday, and that is absolutely the most meager total since they started keeping football statistics at Texas more than a half a century ago.

On a day when the winds blew, the crowds booed, and Houston romped, there were Texas negatives by the score, but lest ye forget, for each Longhorn negative, there was a Cougar positive, and most of these positives they flat went out and earned. Danny Davis, Wilson Whitley, Vincent Greenwood, and chums had themselves the kind of day Houston will want to bronze and send to the Smithsonian.

"We were not in the football game—ever, at any point," Darrell Royal told it like it was in the postmortems. "We were totally dominated."

Victorious coach Bill Yeoman decided his Cougars "were fortunate—we got super play out of our young men." Among them the gargantuan Wilson Whitley, who feasted on a straight diet of prime beef.

"There was never any doubt in our minds," said Whitley. "We knew we could get the orange mountain, but we had to make the people in the stands believe it."

OK, Wilson, they believe it. Boy, they believe it.

Alois Blackwell scored Houston's first touchdown on a 7-yard run, Charles Lynch scored the second on a 1-yard plunge, Danny Davis scored the third on a 28-yard toe dance down the east sideline, and Lennard Coplin punctuated those trips to the payoff window with three successful conversions and three field goals. His field goals were for 30, 20, and 32 yards.

Coplin missed another three-point effort from the 15, and split end Don Bass dropped a touchdown pass, but never mind—such misses tend to be forgotten when your defense is never permitting your opponent to get inside your 20-yard line.

On the Longhorns' second possession of the afternoon, Raymond Clayborn grabbed Danny Davis's fumble at the Houston 35, and in four plays, the orange shirts drove to the Houston 24. On the fifth play, Ted Constanzo threw a high hard one that wound up in Houston safety Elvis Bradley's hands at the 1-yard line. Bradley returned to the Houston 21, the Cougars promptly drove 79 yards in their next 17 plays for the touchdown that Blackwell scored from the 7, and from that moment on, lights started going out for Texas.

In the first half, Royal's representatives got inside Cougar territory one more time, taking over a punt at the Houston 38 and then being forced back to the 45 on the next three plays before having to punt. On their sixth possession of the second half, they drove from their own 27 to the Houston 46 before a game official mercifully called the whole thing to a halt.

Otherwise, friends and neighbors, the 'Horns went nowhere. Royal used three quarterbacks—starter Ted Constanzo, backup Mike Cordaro, and freshman Mark McBath—and finally he went back to Cordaro, but the results were as slim and none. The Cougars limited their opponents to eight first downs and 121 yards of total offense on 54 plays, and five times they sacked UT quarterbacks for losses that added up to 32 yards. "Our quarterbacking? I don't know what else we can do," Royal answered the question that is now on Texas tongues everywhere.

Plagued by a holdover case of Tech fever and badly weakened by the loss of the Campbell boys (fullback Earl Campbell and defensive end Tim Campbell did not suit up Saturday), Royal looked in vain for others to take up some slack. One thing DKR now knows for sure: you don't spell relief C-o-u-g-a-r-s.

In running their own conference record to 5–1 (with only Tech and Rice left to play in SWC combat), the Cougars played a lot of defense in the first half and then a lot of both defense *and* offense in the last 30 minutes. They led at intermission, 10–0, thanks to that 79-yard TD drive on their second possession and Coplin's 30-yard field goal kicked with only 36 seconds left in the second quarter.

But it took a Longhorn fumble (Johnny Lam's bobble at the Texas 15) to get the Cougars on the board for the second time just before halftime, and the way the Cougars were dropping passes and misfiring at critical moments, while netting a mere 88 yards in total offense on 36 plays, it looked as if Texas might have a chance, if only the 'Horns could find a spark.

But they couldn't. Meanwhile, the Cougars kept their own powder dry, and all through the final two periods they romped and stomped, rolling up 13 first downs, 194 yards rushing, and another 88 overhead. Houston in the second half rolled up 282 yards in total offense on 44 plays; Texas only 68 yards on 24 tries. In the second quarter, Texas netted exactly 2 yards.

In those last 30 minutes, the Cougars had touchdown drives of 65 yards in 11 plays and 80 yards in 7 plays, they made another fumble recovery (at the Texas 22) serve as a launching pad for Coplin's second field goal of the afternoon, and they drove 59 yards in 12 plays before turning to the same kicker for a third field goal.

Heck, even the nation's leading punter, the fabulous Russell Erxleben, got outkicked. Houston's Jay Wyatt averaged 46.8 yards on five punts; Erxleben (who did have one 80-yarder with a strong wind at his back) averaged 43.9 on eight boots.

The capacity crowd, the eighth sellout since Memorial Stadium was expanded to its present capacity, saw the game start in zany fashion. Texas won the toss and elected to defend the south goal. Houston elected to kick off *into* that strong south wind, which was gusting up to 25 mph. So Kenny Hatfield kicked off, and his kick was so high, Texas tight end Joe Samford got the ball after signaling for a fair catch at the Texas 18. That should have been a telltale clue right there that things were going to follow an unusual course, and did they ever.

Constanzo, who could complete no passes the week before against Tech, completed the first one he tried—for 17 yards—against the Coogs, but it was the pass he threw several minutes later, after Clayborn had recovered Davis's fumble at the UH 35, that yanked Texas right out of the driver's seat. Bradley's interception turned the momentum Houston's way, and the Cougars never relinquished it again.

On that first touchdown drive, Texas provided one helping hand; it was third and 6 at the Houston 26. Davis threw an incompletion, but on the play, the Longhorns were offside. Given a new chance on a third-and-1 situation, Davis got his first down on a keeper, and Houston then rolled on to touchdown town.

Blackwell carried six times for 24 yards, and on one critical fourth-down play—fourth and 8 at the Texas 28—Davis threw a 15-yard completion to Don Bass. A Longhorn hit late on the play, the ball was moved on to the Texas 7, and Blackwell scored on the next play, taking Davis's neatly executed option toss into the end zone.

With Houston leading by seven points and going nowhere fast, Texas tried to get something going from deep in its own end of the field late in the second quarter and promptly got burned. Jonny Lam fumbled on a draw play, David Hodge recovered for Houston at the Texas 15, and the Cougars cashed in on Coplin's 20-yard field goal with 36 seconds left. Even so, the 'Horns were lucky. Bass dropped a touchdown pass in the end zone just before Coplin kicked true.

Jimmy Walker, standing in for Earl Campbell for the afternoon, fumbled on the first play of the third quarter, and Robert Oglesby covered the ball for UH at the Texas 22. The Cougars in five plays drove down to the Texas 1-yard line, but a third-down play aimed at Brad Shearer cost them a yard, and Bill Yeoman decided to take no chances. He sent Coplin out to do his thing from the 10, and once again Coplin kicked true.

The Cougars then scored on three of their next four possessions and removed all doubt. Davis completed passes of 9, 22, and 16 yards and then ran 11 yards for a first down to the Texas 15 while getting the Cougars into position for Coplin to kick a 32-yard field goal and boost their margin to 16–0.

The next time they got the ball, they drove 65 yards for a touchdown, with Davis firing 16 yards to Eddie Foster and 13 to Robert Lavergne while keeping the Texas defense off balance. With the ball at the Texas 20, Dyral Thomas broke on a slanting play over left guard. He ran to the Texas 7 and fumbled, and the ball rolled off sharply to the right—and straight into Cougar Rickey Maddox's hands. It was that kind of day for Houston.

Lynch scored from the 1 three plays later, and Coplin made it 23–0. Darrell royal decided to try a new hand at the switchboard. He turned to freshman Mark McBath for the first time this season. On third down, McBath fumbled straight up into the air, and Wilson Whitley speared the pigskin at the Texas 22. The Cougars messed up that opportunity, Coplin missing a field goal effort from the 15, but they went all the way on their next possession. Lynch got loose down the sideline on a 30-yard scamper and then Davis closed it out with a 28-yard run.

Houston's final figures—19 first downs, 370 yards in total offense—put a spotlight on several Cougars. Thomas got 64 yards, Lynch 61, Blackwell 52, and Davis 46, and Davis completed 7 of his 16 passes for 103 yards. Johnny Lam paced what ground attack Texas had with 22 yards on 14 carries, but wherever Johnny went, Greenwood and Whitley (and others) were sure to go. Cordaro got 57 yards overhead on four completions, and Constanzo had 40 yards on three strikes.

So at the finish, the Tower remained dark. It was Texas' first loss at home since TCU defeated the 'Horns in November of 1967, it was the first shutout ever handed to the Texas wishbone in conference play, and it was only Texas' second shutout in the Longhorns' last 150 outings.

DARRELL ROYAL'S FINAL DAY AS COACH

The rumors were thick that week leading up to the final game of the 1976 Southwest Conference football season, and most of them were insisting that Darrell Royal was about to hang up his hat as UT's head coach.

Texas and Arkansas would be wrapping up disappointing seasons on the night of December 4 in Austin as national television cameras looked on. Royal had been the Longhorns' head coach for 20 (mostly glorious) seasons. He had won more games, more championships, and more bowl contests than any SWC coach in history. A lot of fans, especially those who had come on board after Royal's first UT campaign in 1957, couldn't imagine a Longhorn team without him.

The rumors at the beginning of the week claimed DKR's famous rival and close friend, Arkansas' Frank Broyles, also would end his coaching career that night in Austin. There weren't many who believed that talk either.

But then a few days later, before his team left for Texas, Broyles confirmed the rumors. He had decided to step down after 19 seasons and 144 victories with the Razorbacks.

So that Saturday, all football roads led to UT's Memorial Stadium. With Broyles leaving and Royal maybe leaving, it promised to be an occasion a sportswriter would remember for the rest of his life.

That afternoon, Royal met with the UT Athletic Council and informed its members of his decision to retire from active coaching ranks. That night, he directed the Longhorns from the coaching lines for the last time. Later on, in his customary meeting with the press, he talked about his decision, his last day, his memories—a lot of things.

Texas Football *was there for the game and then for Royal's final press conference. This is how it was.*

The entire day, Darrell Royal said, "seemed so confused, so hurried." He and his wife, Edith, left their home and spent Friday night at a downtown hotel, seeking a little peace and quiet from the ringing telephone. But the demands of time caught up with them early Saturday, and from then on, it was one mad gallop.

Edith had just washed her hair at the hotel room that morning and was getting ready to give it the hair-dryer treatment when Royal told her, "Come on, we've got to run." She said she grabbed the hair dryer, wrapped a towel around her hair, turban fashion, and took off right through the hotel lobby—towel, hair dryer, and all. And that's the way she spent her day, rushing with Royal hither and yon. She never did find the time to go back and fiddle with her hair, as women like to do.

Someone finally asked her if she wouldn't like to replace the towel with a scarf. She did. That afternoon, she found the time to take off the scarf. She found her hair was perfectly dry—and a mess. The only thing to do, she said, was wash it again and start over. Which she did.

"For the first time in 25 years, I didn't talk to the football team after the pregame meal. I didn't make it over there," Royal observed later. "My assistants had to do it. I even blew that."

A young woman asked Royal to autograph her Texas-Arkansas game program after the final whistle, after Texas had won DKR's last game 29–12. As he obliged her, she said, "You know, Mr. Royal, you have been my only coach since I was eight years old."

Now the tumult and the shouting had died away, the captains and the kings had departed. And Royal, in keeping with a tradition first started in 1961, had joined the newspaper guys at famed Room 2001 of an Austin motel to discuss the just-completed game.

Only this time, precious little of the conversation concerned the game or the mechanics of victory. The conversation instead concerned the man behind the victory, the man behind a record 167 victories at Texas over the last 20 years.

When did he decide to quit? Why now? What will be his role in the selection of the new UT coach? What will he do tomorrow?

"I'll go tape my TV show," he said. "But I'll tell you one thing I'm not going to do. I'm not going to go look at that game film."

The final day, he admitted, had been tougher than he had anticipated. "You never know until it gets on top of you. But yes, it was different than I had anticipated."

He had found himself brushing away the tears, he said, when he realized he was putting on the headset for the last time. And he had led the team personally out of the chute Saturday night, something he had never done before. Nor had he ever before given the "Hook 'em" sign before the game as the Longhorn band played.

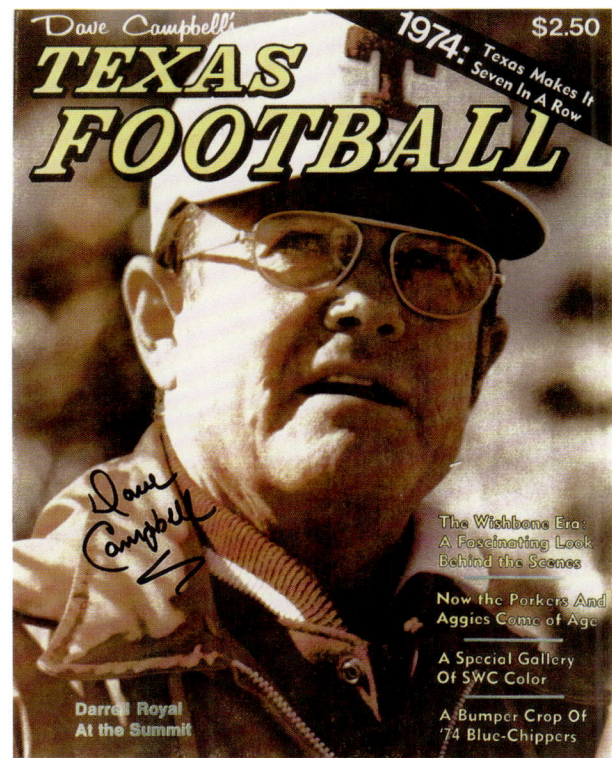

Courtesy of *Dave Campbell's Texas Football.*

Well, you don't just turn your back on 20 years—20 good years—and walk away and not feel it. The Longhorns felt it as much as their coach in those final hours.

The story of Frank Broyles's impending exit had broken at midweek in Arkansas, so the Razorbacks, the visiting team, had time to get adjusted to the idea. Through my field glasses, the Razorback bench Saturday night appeared almost routine. Not quite, but almost.

The raw emotions belonged to Texas.

At one point, a Longhorn player confided later, senior cocaptain Billy Gordon had burst out, "Look, this is his last game. Let's move."

At the midnight press conference, the questions kept coming back to a central theme: Why? And why now? Could he give some reasons—list them one, two, three, four?

"I don't have it organized that well," Royal told the group. "But as I told the guys in the dressing room right after the game, throughout my career, I've tried to study people who were in advance of me, about 10 years in advance of me. I remember I studied Ray Graves when he was a chief assistant [at Georgia Tech] and when I still aspired to be a chief assistant. I started watching the top ones. Then as I moved up, I studied head coaches in advance of me. Then those going through retirement. And I think that's been helpful.

"I can't follow them totally, of course. I have to follow my own gut instincts. I have to have some judgment of my own. I've always felt I wanted to quit before I was totally spent. I wanted to quit while there was still a little ham on the bone. I didn't want to overstay my time."

He was especially grateful, he said, that "throughout my coaching career, I've never had to coach under pressure. Never had to work under pressure. Of course, I've always known you had to win, but I've never been in a situation where I had to make a decision to please someone else. All the pressure has been self-imposed."

That pressure could be fierce: "Man, every time I'd lose a game, I'd hurt. I'd finally get to sleep and wake up and be hot as a burning match, aching and hurting. I don't like to hurt. I guess you think about quitting after anything like that.

"I can't say I came to the decision at any set time or for any set reason. I wouldn't want to pinpoint a time. But I've been thinking about it for years."

Age and health had nothing to do with his decision: "I don't think I'm too old, I really don't. My health is good. But I became a head coach when I was 28 years old... best as I can remember, I was the youngest head coach in the country. That didn't last long because Terry Brennan was named at Notre Dame and he was younger, but for a while, I was the youngest. But it's really not how old you are as it is how many years you've been under the gun, so to speak. A guy who hadn't been a head coach that long would have a lot more bullets left.

"I'm going to continue in athletics and I'm going to continue speaking out," Royal said. "And there are those of you who know how opinionated I am, and it seems like I get a little more opinionated as I get older. But I had to get a certain age before I felt I could speak up. Before I could talk at the table. That was the way I was brought up. And now [having put in his time], I think you're kind of shirking your duty if you don't speak up."

Are things much different than when he first started?

"I'd hate to paint a dark cloud," he replied. "There have been many changes, drastic changes. Things that used to get by with a phone call now take an original and 15 carbons."

Now that his coaching career was over, would he make some comparisons? No, he wouldn't.

Darrell Royal made a stopover at the Waco airport on his way to Dallas for a Texas-OU game in the mid-1960s. I was able to get a quick interview with him. Courtesy of Dave Campbell.

How about picking out some players who got the very most out of their ability?

"I don't want to do that either.... Marvin Kristynik damn sure would be an entry. Tommy Nobis would be a great one. He had great ability, but he sapped it. He sapped it all. But there—I've already named two, and I wasn't going to name any."

The questions and answers went on and on. The room was crowded, the air was informal; it was a nostalgic time. A lot of these people had been down a long road together. Nobody really wanted the session to end.

So DKR talked of many things . . .

The job offers that have tempted him over the years: "The only one that lingered at all was the first time I was contacted by Oklahoma, and they'll throw up when I say that."

On whether his team's final performance against Arkansas was its best of the season: "Well, I don't know—we played pretty good against Oklahoma until we left it on the ground. And I wasn't surprised when they [OU] missed the point either. I feel the old guy with the sheet and sickle said, 'Hey, they're not going to make that extra point. That would be too much.'"

On the pro offers he's had: "I've been contacted by some pro teams, and I swear to you, I couldn't tell you which ones. I looked around and saw where those people lived and I said, 'No way. I love Austin. This is where I want to live.' If I had a satchel full of money and could live anywhere in the world, I'd pick Austin, Texas. Oh, I'd visit other places, but I'd always come back to Austin."

On telling his staff of his retirement plans: "I asked the staff to come into the locker room right after the game and I told 'em. That was probably the hardest part of it. Because that leaves them in limbo. I thought about that a long time, but it was inevitable. I finally came to realize I would always have a staff [to leave in limbo], but you have to have the feeling you're walking out on them."

His best coaching performances? "We had some seasons when we were 3-3 or 4-4 and finished up good. That's when it's tough. I think you learn to coach more in adverse situations. I've learned that I learn more from getting beat than from winning."

Did he achieve all his goals? "I'm not a goal setter. I just do the best I can, running here and there, stomping out the fires. I've always just tried to do my best."

On whether he had recommended his top aide, Mike Campbell, as his successor: "I'd rather not talk about that. I'm not trying to be coy, and I sometimes think you can hurt a person more by not saying anything—by saying 'No comment'—but in this case, I think it's best for me not to say anything, and I just hope that is not misinterpreted. I love Mike Campbell like a brother. I've been with him 21 years. If I had to go in a dark alley and pick someone to stick with me, Mike would be one of the first ones I'd pick."

He recalled his experience as a 12-year-old hitchhiking to Childress, Texas, to see FDR. His father didn't know that he was ducking out of school for the trip. He hitchhiked there, worked his way "between those legs right up to where I could touch the iron" of the railroad, saw and heard FDR, and then hitchhiked back home. A friend of his father's picked him up on the highway. He expected his father to find out, but he never did.

He said he told the story to LBJ years later. "I told him it was in 1936. He told me, 'No, that's wrong, it couldn't have been in '36.' I thought it was, but I said, 'Well, I guess I'm wrong on that, Mr. President.'

"But when I got back to the office, I got on the WATS line and called the Childress newspaper and asked them when FDR came through there on the train, and they told me in 1936. But I never did tell Mr. Johnson."

He was asked to single out his most memorable moments.

"I can't pick out a most memorable. I think on the good things—my whole career. I think of it as a happy one. I do know the most stinging defeat was in '65 up at Fayetteville. But overall, I've had an unusual career, and not all of it was my own doing. For instance, I haven't been involved with a losing team since I was a junior in high school, and certainly I wasn't the reason for all that. I'm proud of that, but what I'm saying is, I've had an unusual career.

"I've enjoyed it, I really have. It's like Floyd Tillman wrote in his songs, 'I've dwelled with kings, I've dwelled with bums, I'm in your church, I'm in your slums.' I've enjoyed knowing the janitors and the parking lot attendants, and I've enjoyed knowing the president of the United States.

"I never dreamed I'd have the experiences I've had. They haven't all been pleasant, but I wouldn't take anything for them."

The press conference broke up shortly before 2 a.m. There was more small talk after that as Royal and his wife got up to leave, and some of the guys asked him to autograph their press box stubs, and emotions ran close to the surface.

"Coach," Texas sports information director Jones Ramsey finally said, grasping Royal's hand, "it's been a little bit of heaven."

Darrell Royal laughed, and then he and his wife stepped out into the night and were gone—his longest day was done, and the Royal football era at Texas was over.

No one ever really doubted that if Darrell Royal had had his way, longtime defensive coordinator Mike Campbell, a member of his original UT staff, would have succeeded him as Texas' new head coach. Campbell appeared to be eminently qualified.

But Royal didn't have his way. By then, two powerful UT regents, the late Frank Erwin and the late Allan Shivers, were determined that athletic director Royal would not be permitted to handpick the new coach. When all the dust had settled, Wyoming coach Fred Akers (a former UT assistant on Royal's staff) had the job, and Mike Campbell was out.

Royal stayed on as athletic director for a few years and then moved from the athletic department to become special assistant to the UT president. Campbell, meanwhile, became a special fundraiser for UT athletics.

Royal left behind a record achievement not likely to be equaled by any UT football coach—and probably not by any SWC football coach—in our lifetime. The Royal era of 1957–76: truly it was royal.

In 1983, the National Football Foundation and Hall of Fame did a most appropriate thing: it inducted both Darrell Royal and Arkansas athletic director Frank Broyles into its ranks. They won their fame as coaches together; it was only right that they enter the Hall of Fame together.

Dave Campbell

JANUARY 2, 1977

COUGARS IN TALL COTTON: HOUSTON CAPS INAUGURAL YEAR IN STYLE

DALLAS, Tex.—The young Houston Cougar who made the play that simply had to be made to save Houston's bacon late in the fourth quarter at the frozen Cotton Bowl Saturday can't tell you how he did it. Or how close he came to failure.

Danny Davis is his name, and the music he inspired on that play sounded better to Bill Yeoman and all those red-capped Cougar partisans in the stands than anything another Danny Davis and the Nashville Brass will ever produce.

The situation was this: Houston had gotten so far out in front of undefeated, untied, favored, national championship–minded Maryland that at halftime, the game had become a laugher. Houston was leading 27–7, and cynics were making all kinds of bad jokes about the caliber of Atlantic Coast football. And then, 25 minutes and several Cougar turnovers later, the score was Houston 27, Maryland 21. And even Bill Yeoman's palms were a little sweaty—and on an afternoon when the chill factor was so low, it was obscene.

With 4:54 left to play, facing a third and 4 from his own 11-yard line, Danny Davis went back to pass. Terrapins came in all over him. One got a hunk of his shirt. A couple of them appeared to have him cold. But as Davis was going down, he somehow, someway got off a pass to Robert Lavergne, who made a catch just inside the boundary at the Houston 24 for a first down. Reprieved, the Cougars drove on down the field, kicked a field goal with 18 seconds remaining, and nailed down one of their most delicious victories ever.

But tell us, Danny, how did you do it?

Danny Davis is one of those guys who truly lets his deeds speak for him. He uses words softly, and if you don't listen carefully, you'll miss his entire conversation. He described the make-or-break play matter-of-factly without making it any big deal. "We had an out-right called," he said. "I figured he'd be open because Lavergne runs excellent patterns. He was open."

How close were you to getting trapped, Danny?

"I don't really remember. I'll have to check the film to see."

Robert Lavergne knows it was close: "The regular pattern calls for me to go 15 to 18 yards downfield. On this one, I just had to come back a little farther because I saw he was in trouble. I didn't think he was going to get the ball away, really. It was a must for us to make that first down. If we don't, we have to punt into the wind, and by then they had the momentum. We knew we had to do something—to keep the ball and run out the clock."

Did he know when he got the ball that he had the first down? "Yeah, I knew," he said and grinned. "The crowd told me that."

That was the only pass senior flanker Robert Lavergne caught all day. "But hey, that could very easily been the biggest play of the game," agreed Bill Yeoman. "That kinda turned it back our way. That catch was absolutely super. And Danny did a great job of getting the pass off under extreme pressure."

In the dressing room, surrounded by yelling, excited, all-smiles Cougars, Yeoman was a happy man. But a rather tired one. He answered a barrage of questions while standing up, then sat down to answer the same questions all over again. Once, he paused for an unconcealed yawn. Someone brought him word that his wife was on the bus outside and did he want the bus to go without him? "No, tell them I'll be there as soon as I can," he said.

"What happened there in the second half?" someone asked him. Did the Cougars suffer a letdown, permitting the Terrapins to come storming back?

"Hey, this [Maryland] team won 11 football games

A clutch pass by Danny Davis (4) kept Houston's Cotton Bowl dreams alive in 1977. Courtesy of University of Houston Athletics.

this year. They've got a heckuva team. They've got excellent people, and they're well coached. Heavens, friend, I just think our team did a super job against a team that was as good as they were. It really impressed me the way Maryland played. They have great character.

"Was I concerned at the end? Listen. I was concerned when we took the field in the first quarter. And now that it's over, I don't know of anything that could be more gratifying. I am so happy that we could play and win the Cotton Bowl game, regardless of what else transpired. I think we should be ranked at least fourth" (Maryland was ranked fourth coming in to the game).

Maryland also went into the game with a defense that ranked third in the nation against scoring (giving up 116 yards per game to enemy ball carriers) and second nationally in total defense (giving up an average of 211 yards per contest). The Terps had not been scored on in more than 12 quarters, and they had not given up a touchdown to the rush in more than five games.

Houston drove 80 yards in 11 plays for a touchdown the second time it had the ball and scored from 11 yards out on a rushing play. The Cougars rushed for 144 yards in the first quarter alone. Two of their runners, Alois Blackwell (22 carries for 149 yards) and Dyral Thomas (14 carries for 104 yards), frequently made the Terrapin defense look foolish. The Cougars carved out 428 yards in total offense. Did any of this surprise Yeoman?

No, it didn't. Maryland used basically an eight-man front, he noted. "You get those eight guys up there and they make a mistake, there's not much behind them," he said. "And also I remember we used to go play Georgia and Ole Miss, and they would be in the top five or six defensives, and we'd get 400 or 500 yards. So no, it didn't shock me."

What was his thinking in going for the field goal at the

end of the game, with 23 seconds showing on the clock, Maryland out of time outs, and the Cougars encamped on the Terp 12-yard line? Most observers expected Yeoman to take no chance on a blocked field goal that could be returned the length of the field, à la the Vikings against the Los Angeles Rams in the NFL playoffs. But he surprised them. He sent Leonard Coplan into the game, and Coplan kicked true, and that was that.

"Hey," Yeoman said, grinning, "we were only six points ahead. With a field goal, we have a chance to win the game and maybe get to laugh and giggle for 12 whole seconds before it ends." Which they did.

OCTOBER 16, 1977

BU'S COMEBACK FALLS SHORT: FIRST-HALF MISTAKES LEFT BEARS WITH 28-POINT DEFICIT

MARK MCFARLANE

WACO, Tex.—For the longest time Saturday afternoon at Baylor Stadium, a determined bunch of Baylor Bears seemed on the verge of pulling off their greatest comeback victory since that memorable day against Texas in 1974.

No, the Bruins didn't quite make it, but their second-half heroics stirred up fond memories nonetheless and left favored Texas A&M clinging to a 38–31 victory at the suspenseful end.

With the Bears making mistakes at every turn, the Aggies powered their way to a seemingly insurmountable 35–7 lead late in the second quarter. But Baylor pushed across a touchdown just before halftime, exploded for 14 more points early in the third quarter, and amazingly enough, trailed only 35–28 with plenty of time left for victory.

Though their comeback bid fell short in the final minute of play, the Bears still felt it was a day of accomplishment.

"We came back in the second half and proved to those folks [the Aggies] what we're made of," Baylor defensive end Allen Stone said in the postgame dressing room. "At halftime, I looked up at the scoreboard and just couldn't believe we were 21 points behind. They weren't beating us on the line of scrimmage. We just decided that we were not going to keep making those stupid mistakes we made in the first half."

Interceptions led to the first and fifth A&M touchdowns, while a roughing-the-passer penalty set up the fourth Aggie score. A 72-yard run by David Brothers and a 61-yard touchdown pass from quarterback David Walker to uncovered end Darrell Smith accounted for the Aggies' second and third tallies.

All of those scores came in the first half, but the Bears never lost their cool.

"We just stayed with our basic game plan in the second half," explained BU coach Grant Teaff. "I told the team at halftime that I really felt like we had a chance to come back and win. I wasn't just saying that, but I really believed it. We had a chance to win it and didn't, but you can't take anything away from our comeback.

"Obviously, their passing game killed us [Walker threw three TD passes in the first half], and they were able to break that long run on us. But we turned the ball over too much."

The Bears' only encouraging sign in the first half was the explosive running of fullback Steve Howell, who broke on runs of 67 and 55 yards to set up both Baylor touchdowns.

"They had the safety taking the pitch man on our outside veer play," explained Howell, who carried only three times in the game, "and all I had to do was turn upfield. They [both runs] were on the same play. I just got good blocking."

It was an alert defensive play by Stone that really put the Bears' comeback plans into action in the second half.

With A&M leading 35–21 early in the third quarter, Stone grabbed a midair fumble by Walker on the Aggie 26-yard line and returned it to the 3-yard line to set up Baylor's fourth touchdown.

"Walker ran the option and tried to give the ball to Woodard," Stone said, "but there was some indecision, and George didn't take it. The ball popped up into my hands. I almost didn't know what to do with it. I've never been accused of having great speed. I was really trying to score. . . . I don't know if it looked that way or not."

Speed or no speed, Stone's electrifying play put the Bears back in contention. Even their ecstatic fans could sense a possible victory.

But the Aggies had other plans in the critical fourth quarter, and it was their defense that came up with the big plays.

With the Bears trailing by only seven points and driving at midfield with 2:23 left to play, blitzing Aggie linebacker Floyd Randle caused freshman quarterback Scott Smith to fumble, and teammate Jacob Green recovered at the BU 26-yard line.

The Bears' got one final chance moments later, but Smith, under heavy pressure again, had his pass intercepted by Aggie safety Kenneth Taylor.

"You just can't make the mistakes we did and expect to win," Smith admitted. "They blitzed a lot, but that's their style. You can usually see them coming, but I just threw to the wrong man on that last interception. When your quarterback throws an interception, it just kind of takes the wind out of you."

Said Howell of Smith's competitive performance, "Scott had a lot of pressure on him. But that's the way the Aggies like to play defense. I thought he did a good job. He'll be back, don't worry. And next time, he'll know how to handle the pressure better."

A&M's barefoot kicker Tony Franklin set an NCAA record in 1976 with a 65-yard field goal against Baylor. Courtesy of Texas A&M University Athletics.

Baylor cornerback Scooter Reed took the blame for the Aggies' 61-yard touchdown pass play in the second quarter as split end Darrell Smith broke 25 yards into the open field before catching Walker's pass.

"The play was misread by everyone," Reed said. "But it was my responsibility. They ran a regular option play, and I took the pitch man. The end came out to block and then took off.

"We worked so hard all week on stopping the run. That's all they had been doing in the past. They surprised us with all the passes they threw.

"I don't think this is as good an Aggie team as past ones. They're just not as physical, but it's still a good rivalry that we have going."

OCTOBER 16, 1977
LONGHORNS GUN DOWN ARKANSAS, 13–9

FAYETTEVILLE, Ark.—It was No. 2 Texas versus No. 8 Arkansas—played before the national television cameras with the stands full and both teams undefeated and emotions running wild. Veteran observers of the classic series were looking back and remembering 1969 and calling this not another Big Shootout but rather "Little Shootout No. 1."

It doesn't matter what you call it, Big Shootout or Little Shootout, it came out the same way. Facing a ton of pressure and a relentless wind, Texas made the long drive it had to make in the fourth quarter to overtake the Razorbacks and win the game and escape with all the marbles, the prestige, and the national ranking. Just like in 1969.

The final score was 13–9 with the Longhorns winning the game by staging an 80-yard, eight-play drive that reached the end zone with 4:31 left to play and with all those Arkies in the crowd of 44,296 slowly chewing up their fingernails.

Johnny (Ham) Jones took a cleverly executed option pitchout from quarterback Randy McEachern and circled left end for the final yard of the telltale drive, scoring the only touchdown of the bitterly waged struggle.

Ham Jones finished what Earl Campbell started and carried on for most of this beautiful Saturday afternoon in the Ozarks. Remember that name Earl Campbell. Arkansas heads throb today at the sound of it.

In a game of crashing tackles, marvelous kicking, and nerve-stretching ebb and flow, the bombastic running of the Earl of Texas gave the Longhorns their winning edge. It was Campbell who set up Ham Jones's payoff punch with a 28-yard run on a screen pass that carried to within a step of the Arkansas end zone.

Just as in 1969, the infantry-oriented Longhorns used passes to unlock the door to fourth-quarter victory. McEachern, the nation's most celebrated and successful third-team quarterback, had completed only one pass when the Longhorns took over on their own 20 with 8:36 left in the game. And then he completed three straight passes without a miss.

Facing a crucial third-and-4 situation at his own 26, he hit Ham Jones for a first down at the Texas 40, then completed a 31-yarder to a well-covered Alfred Jackson on the next play. Then came the fateful screen pass to Earl Campbell that set up the score and shattered the Razorbacks.

After Campbell's scorching run, you just knew that Texas was going to win, and it did, and now the Longhorns are 5–0 for the season and 2–9 in conference play, Earl Campbell is well on his way to winning the Heisman Trophy, and the Longhorns certainly could be well on their way to winning the Southwest Conference championship. The team that beats them is going to have to be a great one. They proved that here Saturday.

Campbell, a marked man throughout, nonetheless ravaged Arkansas' inspired defense for 188 yards on 34 carries and became the Southwest Conference's all-time leading footman. His whopping yardage total, achieved before an audience of millions and all those Heisman voters, left him with a career rushing total of 3,386 yards. The old record belonged to Arkansas' Dickey Morton, who got 3,317 yards in three seasons. Campbell, of course, is now playing in his fourth season.

"Campbell is outstanding. He's completely outstanding. A lot of times we'd just miss him at the line of scrimmage. It's unbelievable some of the cuts he made," said Arkansas tackle Dan Hampton, who joined linebacker Larry Jackson, backs Patrick Martin and Howard Sampson, and end Cornelius Smith in heading up a Porker defense that played as well as any Arkie could have hoped until the fourth quarter's moment of truth.

The wind, which was whistling in from out of the north, made this something of a chess game for the longest time. Texas got the wind early and used it to get

Brad Shearer was a consensus All-American lineman for Texas in 1977. Courtesy of University of Texas Athletics.

six points. Arkansas got it in the second quarter and used it to tie the score. Texas had it again for the third quarter and lost its advantage amid a flurry of fumbles, so in the final stanza, the Longhorns just threw caution to the winds and won the game.

A week ago in the Oklahoma game, Texas' matchless fool, Russell Erxleben, gave the Longhorns a slight but decisive edge. Erxleben again performed wondrously well—field goals of 58 and 52 yards kicked while Texas enjoyed the blessing of the 20-mile-an-hour wind and a punting average of 47.7 yards—but Arkansas' Steve Little actually bested him a bit because Erxleben also missed on one close-in attempt that could have cost Texas the game.

Know what Little did? He kicked a simple 33-yard field goal with 10:30 left in the second quarter, and then with 3:30 left, he stepped back and put his foot into the ball and sent it soaring through the uprights from 67 yards away. That's right, 67 yards. The kick matched the NCAA record first set by Erxleben two weeks ago.

Erxleben's field goals had come after modest advances of 9 yards in 3 plays and 16 yards in 4 plays. Little kicked true after a 64-yard advance in 11 plays, then 14 yards in 6 plays.

Then the Arkansas kicker untied the game and put the Razorbacks ahead for the first time with a 25-yard placement that climaxed a 13-play, 55-yard drive that carried to the Texas 8-yard line late in the third quarter. That was Arkansas' deepest advance of the afternoon, and as it turned out, the failure to acquire those final 8 yards of real estate cost the Razorbacks the game.

It was an understandable failure, however. With Brad Shearer, Steve McMichael, Dwight Jefferson, Lance Taylor, Johnnie Johnson, Glenn Blackwood, and Ricky Churchman constantly attacking anything that moved in Razorback red, Arkansas was able to move only in fits and starts. The Longhorn first-team defense, after five games, still had not surrendered a touchdown.

At the finish, Porker coach Lou Holtz second-guessed himself. The Porkers went into the game armed with a big-play offense that had been exploiting wide-open football, both overland and overhead. But they turned conservative against the Longhorns, especially after going ahead.

"Texas made a lot of good plays. That was the difference in the game," said Holtz. "Yes, the screen pass to Campbell was a critical play. He made a great move on it. When you look back, had we known they would score, we would have opened up the offense when we led, 9–6. But with the wind at our back, we didn't expect them to drive 80 yards on us. As it turned out, we should have played more wide open in the fourth quarter."

Ben Cowins, Arkansas' terrible swift sword who was the conference's leading ball carrier before Saturday, several times came within a step of breaking all the way. But always that one last Longhorn would be there to bring him down. He did finish with 94 yards on 24 carries, and he played exceedingly well.

But Earl Campbell played better.

Arkansas managed to break even in first downs (14 to 14), but thanks to Campbell's bullish rushes, usually touched off by a deep handoff in the I formation, Texas led in total offense (334 yards to 256) and in ball control in the fateful fourth quarter, when Arkansas owned the wind advantage. Arkansas quarterback Ron Calcagni was never able to hit the big pass when it mattered most.

It appeared for a while that fumbles (the Longhorns bobbled three times and lost all three in Razorback country) would finally put Texas down for the count. Only thing is, the Longhorns wouldn't stay down.

Thus Fred Akers, an old Razorback himself, carried the day on his first visit back to his old stomping grounds, and when it was all over, the Longhorns gave him the game ball and went flying back to Austin with a victory in their hip pocket.

Just like in 1969.

The first half was a battle of hard knocks, short drives, and long kicks and ended appropriately at 6–6.

Just as the Razorbacks came out of their dressing room to start the game, a bright sun burst through cloud cover and red-dominated stands took it as a favorable omen and set up a throaty roar of approval.

But it was Texas that scored first.

Such could have been anticipated because the Longhorns won the opening toss and elected to put that 20-mile-an-hour wind to their backs. As expected, Erxleben kicked out of the end zone; as expected, Arkansas had an early difficulty moving the football; as expected, Texas inherited great field position for its first possession when Little's punt into that whistling wind carried only 26 yards to midfield.

Campbell got 4 at left guard, Ham Jones earned a couple, and then Texas tried a fooler—running Ham Jones on an end-around. For a moment, he had gobs of daylight, then Pat Martin and Larry Jackson got there, holding him to a 3-yard gain and forcing Fred Akers to call for Erxleben.

Texas' trusty right foot stood at the Arkansas 48 and kicked true from 58 yards away.

Arkansas, on its second possession, did what it had to do—it gouged out a couple of first downs, putting nothing on the scoreboard but using up a little time. Calcagni ran for 12, then Cowins for 14, and Little's punt four plays later turned the ball over to Texas back on the Longhorn 14.

The Longhorns passed for one first down but then had to punt. Erxleben's boot rode the wind for 59 yards, and when Arkansas clipped on the return, the flag fell, the official stepped off the yardage, and the Razorbacks had to start from their own 7-yard line. All that added up to a big plus for Texas.

The Razorbacks did hack out one first down, using up more time, but a delay penalty on third and 2 at their own 26 cost them dearly, forcing a punt. Little's 28-yard kick gave Texas the ball at the UT 49.

Campbell almost broke on the first play, finding daylight at left tackle, then cutting back for 10 yards. Howard Sampson's tackle saved a touchdown. Two passes fell incomplete, and the swarming Hogs held Campbell for a 6-yard gain to the 35, so here was Erxleben again, kicking from the 42 and kicking true.

The 52-yarder, kicked with a minute left in the first quarter, left Texas with a 6–0 lead. But for the Razorbacks, relief was just around the corner.

Starting at their own 20, they ran three plays into the wind, and their third one was the charm. In that one, Calcagni faked and then kept the ball himself, broke tackles, and ran 23 yards, moving the Hogs into Texas territory for the first time.

Calcagni three plays later broke a solid tackle by Morgan Copeland and got the 3 yards he needed to get a first down and keep Arkansas' opportunity alive. The Porkers drove on down, using a well-executed double screen to Roland Sale to gain 29 yards to the Texas 19, but things got sticky there, and on fourth down, Steve Little kicked true from 33 yards away. The Porkers were on the scoreboard for the first time.

They got there again after finally snuffing out Texas' best drive of the first half. That one started at the Texas 20 and carried to the Razorback 29 and featured deep handoffs to Campbell from the I formation. A safe play, it enabled big Earl to wait for his blocking to develop and simply run to daylight, which he did as only Campbell can do. He ran for 7, then for 16, then for 6, then for 7, then for 11—and all those redcoats in the stands suddenly grew very quiet indeed.

But then, surprisingly, Texas moved from the I to the veer—and bogged down. And when Erxleben tried to kick a field goal into the wind from 41 yards away, Patrick Martin broke through quickly to block the kick, and Cornelius Smith picked up the ball and returned 13 yards to the Porker 37.

From there, Arkansas moved 14 yards in six plays to the Texas 49 and then lined up in what most witnesses expected to be a long, valiant, but futile field goal attempt from 67 yards away.

But no! Little's kick just kept going and going and dropped over the crossbar with a couple of feet to spare, and a big "3" went up on the scoreboard as the fans roared.

Late in the second quarter, the Porkers gained possessions at midfield after a 25-yard punt into the wind by Erxleben. But after a 12-yard pass to Sales, the Porkers bogged down, and on fourth down, with 60 seconds left in the first half, Little tried a 60-yard field goal. The kick was long enough but wide.

The trend then completely flip-flopped in the second half, the team facing the wind managing to grab a scoreboard edge. And Texas faced the wind last.

Fumbles stopped Texas for the longest. The first one came on the Longhorns' first possession of the third quarter, at a time when Fred Akers's troops had moved to the Porker 37—virtually point-blank range for Erxleben when he kicked with the wind. But Earl Campbell bobbled away that chance, Cornelius Smith recovered, and the Porkers moved smartly downfield—55 yards in 13 plays to the Texas 8-yard line before Little kicked a 25-yard field goal, moving the Hogs ahead on the scoreboard for the first time.

The big play on that drive was a 14-yard scamper by Cowins to the Texas 14 on a fourth-and-1 challenge. Glenn Blackwood finally flagged down the speeding Cowins, saving the touchdown.

That great Texas defense then tightened, and Little had to come in and do his thing with 5:45 left in the third quarter. Even so, Arkansas had used up 6:47 of the third quarter going into the wind; it looked like possibly a decisive development.

Texas' answering challenge moved out to midfield, but a 16-yard penalty forced a punt. The Razorbacks failed to gain and had to punt themselves, and the Longhorns regained possession at midfield and moved to the Arkansas 34 before McEachern's option pitchout to Ham Jones miscarried, and Jimmy Walker recovered for the Porkers.

Arkansas was on the move just before the end of the third quarter, but a fumbled exchange on a snap at the Arkansas 47 turned the ball back over to the Longhorns. By then, the Porkers were without their No. 1 center, Rick Shumaker, who had jammed his neck four plays earlier, and with the new center, Mike Burlingame, in there, the Porkers suffered.

But never mind, Campbell broke on a scorching 30-yard run, then fumbled when hit by Sampson, and the ball was easily recovered by Larry Jackson at the Arkansas 12.

Off the hook one minute, the Porkers immediately got back on it the next. Little had to punt, and his 52-yarder was counterpunched 49 yards by Johnnie Johnson to the Arkansas 21. Stan Williams, an Arkansas walk-on, finally made the tackle.

Then the strangest thing happened. Texas got a motion penalty and had to call on Erxleben for a field goal from the 15, and Erxleben, the guy who can kick field goals from the next county, missed a 25-yarder. Arkansas' 9–5 lead remained intact with 11:53 left in the game and the Porkers now enjoying the wind advantage. Momentum belonged to the Hogs.

But not for long. Arkansas drove for one first down, then Little punted 56 yards into the end zone. Texas started on its own 20, 80 yards away from deliverance with 8:36 left on the scoreboard clock.

Deliverance began taking shape three plays later. Facing a third-and-4 situation, McEachern took his time and hit Ham Jones in the flat for a 14-yard gain to the 40. Giving the Porkers no time to recover, he faded again and fired deep to Alfred Jackson, and although Alfred was well covered, he came up with the ball at the Arkansas 29.

The final breakthrough came two plays later. McEachern faded again and Campbell delayed, then moved out into the left flat. McEachern got him the ball on the screen, a Porker tried to make a quick tackle and missed, and blocking carried Campbell the rest of the way—all the way to the Arkansas 1-yard line.

Amid the solemn sounds of silence, broken only by a few Longhorn shouts of exultation, McEachern gave the ball to Ham Jones on an option play to the left. Ham went into the end zone standing up, Erxleben kicked true, and Texas was ahead to stay with 4:31 left in the game.

Arkansas' final answering volley fell far short. In the final moments, the Hogs died with hardly a squeal of protest as the Longhorns hogged the ball themselves. By then, they had pretty well convinced all witnesses that this Texas team could be on its way to greater things.

NOVEMBER 26, 1977

LONGHORNS' COTTON BOWL EXPRESS SMOTHERS AGGIES

COLLEGE STATION, Tex.—Texas A&M has a huge thing called a cyclotron, which is used to smash atoms. It is buried underground, encased in lead, and surrounded by concrete walls 6 to 8 feet thick.

If the thing ever gets out of control, it still can do no more damage to the Aggies than Texas' Earl Campbell and Randy McEachern did here Saturday.

McEachern threw for four touchdowns, and Campbell ran for a whopping 222 yards and scored three times as the No. 1–ranked Longhorns splintered the Aggies, 57–28, and wrapped up an undisputed Southwest Conference championship and a chance to play Notre Dame in the Cotton Bowl on January 2.

Not only was that the most points Texas has ever put on the scoreboard in this ancient blood rivalry; that was the most points a Texas A&M team has ever surrendered. Ever.

And it took place on hallowed Aggie ground, before a record Kyle Field audience of 57,443, and most of the witnesses were Aggies. They came expecting A&M to make it close or maybe even beat the hated Longhorns and knock them off their national pinnacle and out of the Cotton Bowl.

The Aggies really didn't come close, although they did score the first time they got the football, and they did pull to within two touchdowns of Fred Akers's atom smashers, at 40–28, with 17½ minutes left in the game.

But Campbell and McEachern then finished what they had started, and a game that had teetered all afternoon between classic and rout finally became an orange-flavored runaway.

In the game's last 15 minutes, the Aggies managed only one trip across midfield and two first downs in five

Earl Campbell, the "Tyler Rose." Courtesy of University of Texas Athletics.

possessions. By then, Texas had that 18-mile-an-hour wind at its back and was romping and stomping.

Campbell saved his best for last. In the final regular-season game of his UT career, he not only rushed for more yardage than in any previous game; he probably nailed down the national rushing and scoring championships.

Heck, he even caught a 60-yard touchdown pass. That was too much. It so stunned the Aggies that they didn't recover until the game was out of hand.

Emory Bellard's wishboning warriors had surged 70 yards on 11 plays after taking the opening kickoff, and the way they were revved up, with the multitude cheering them on, why, visions of an upset started appearing before Aggie eyes all over Kyle Field.

And then Texas turned Earl loose. He ran for 18 yards around right end, and then three plays later, with his team facing third and 11, he got free down the west sideline and McEachern hit him perfectly—and boom, it was a 60-yard touchdown that left Kyle Field as quiet as midnight.

Then on their next four possessions, the Longhorns went 51 yards in 2 plays, 20 yards in 3 plays, 22 in 6, and 59 in 10, all ending in touchdowns. This was the story of the tortoise and the hare, only this time, the hare won from here to yonder.

The Longhorns would drift along for a moment and then they would strike and make it look so easy. In scoring that record point total, they needed only 19 minutes and 26 seconds. Six of their scoring drives consumed less than three minutes, and three were over in fewer than 60 seconds.

It was an afternoon that Longhorn partisans will never forget. Campbell scored on that 60-yard catch and run, then on runs of 4 and 23 yards. Johnny (Ham) Jones had a 4-yard touchdown run. And McEachern—who remembers that he began the year as a third-stringer?—added touchdown passes of 9 and 12 yards to acrobatic Alfred Jackson and a 37-yarder to the world's fastest Longhorn (and possibly the world's fastest footballer), Johnny (Lam) Jones.

Finally, with 7:04 left in the game, Steve McMichael kicked a 48-yard field goal. McMichael was standing in for the Texas siege gun, Russell Erxleben, who suited up but did not play. The Longhorns obviously didn't need Erx. But they might against Notre Dame, and by then his injured leg ought to be ready.

Emory Bellard coached at Texas A&M from 1972 to 1978, compiling a 48–27 record. Courtesy of Texas Sports Hall of Fame.

Russell Erxleben (15) shares the NCAA record for longest field goal (67 yards) with Steve Little of Arkansas and Joe Williams of Wichita State. Courtesy of University of Texas Athletics.

The Aggies—routed, embarrassed, and shell-shocked—did manage some consolation. They scored more points than anyone else has against that lip-busting, gang-tackling Texas defense. They scored four times overland against a unit that had allowed only one rushing touchdown all season. And they earned a bid to face Southern Cal in Houston's Bluebonnet Bowl on New Year's Eve.

Curtis Dickey scored A&M's first touchdown with a 7-yard run that climaxed that game-opening sashay of 70 yards in 11 plays. Then George Woodard, all 265 pounds of him, scored on a pair of 1-yard plunges that sandwiched an 8-yard scoring scamper by quarterback David Walker.

"I thought we moved the football pretty good. We just couldn't stop them," said Bellard, who saw a personal two-game winning streak over Texas ripped asunder by the Campbell-McEachern typhoon.

The Aggies wound up with 16 first downs, 186 yards rushing (81 by Woodard on 25 carries and 58 by Walker on 14), and 103 yards passing.

But while A&M gained 4.1 yards per play, Texas averaged 7.2 on an identical number of snaps (70) while rolling up 20 first downs and 506 yards of total offense (334 rushing, 172 passing).

Looking back on an aerial display that put him in the UT record book alongside old Longhorn hero Clyde Littlefield (four TD passes against Daniel Baker College in 1915), McEachern could only shake his head. "I never imagined it would ever come to this," he said. "If you had told me before the season that I would throw that many TD passes in the biggest game of the year, I never would have believed it."

The Aggies can believe it. But in pinpointing the villain of the piece, they looked first at Earl Campbell.

Earl Campbell (20), looking for a hole in the Oklahoma line. Courtesy of University of Texas Athletics.

"In the third quarter, if we could have stopped them just one time," said Walker. "But then Earl Campbell went on his way."

And when Earl goes on his way, look out. At the half, he had 88 yards on 14 carries and had scored twice. Then A&M, owning the wind, kicked off to start the third quarter, and things went like this:

Campbell at right guard, no gain. Quick pitch to Campbell around left end, 11 yards. Campbell again for 4 yards, then Campbell around left end for 59 yards to the A&M 6, with safety Kenneth Tayler making the tackle that staved off a touchdown. But not for long, because on the next play, Campbell went through a crowd for a touchdown, dragging Eddie Heath the last couple of yards.

In five plays the Longhorns moved 80 yards against the wind for the touchdown that gave them a 40–14 advantage, and Campbell gained every blessed yard.

All told, his 222 yards overland gave him 1,744 for the season and 4,443 for his career.

"This is the way I would like for it to have ended," said Campbell. "I don't know if this was my best game. I try not to judge those things. In one more game, I'll let you know."

So that's 11 down and 1 big one to go for the Longhorns. Next stop: Big D. Up to this moment, the cyclotron couldn't have done any better.

LONGHORNS' CAMPBELL WINS HEISMAN
DECEMBER 8, 1977

NEW YORK, N.Y.—University of Texas running back Earl Campbell won college football's greatest prize, the Heisman Trophy, Thursday night, climaxing a poor-boy saga that began in the rose fields of East Texas and ended in triumph amid the rich glitter of New York.

Campbell, a 6-foot-1, 220-pound senior and the driving force of the nation's top-ranked football team, accepted the coveted 13½-inch-high bronze statue from the University of Chicago's Jay Berwanger, who won the first Heisman Trophy in 1935.

The presentation, which became a television special for the first time ever, unfolded before an audience of football notables and University of Texas athletic officials and partisans who had gathered at the New York Hilton in anticipation of just such a triumph.

The record-breaking Longhorn ball carrier won over Notre Dame end Ken MacAfee and Oklahoma State running back Terry Miller. They were the top three in ballots cast by more than 1,000 Heisman electors from coast to coast.

"I will do everything in my power to represent the Heisman Trophy well," Campbell said in accepting the award before a cheering audience of 1,400 that included his beaming 54-year-old mother, Ann, who arrived in New York Wednesday night as part of a Tyler delegation. Earl is the fifth of her 11 children.

Appropriately, Earl wore a yellow rose pinned to his lapel. "I hope this rose is from Tyler," he said and grinned.

Looking toward his mother as he accepted the trophy, Campbell said, "When I was a kid and in trouble, I used to say, 'Momma, I'm in trouble.'" After a pause, he added, "So Momma, I'm in trouble. I don't know what to say."

But his achievements in the arena already had spoken eloquently for him, so eloquently that his selection was really no great surprise.

However, at a later press conference, Campbell told reporters, "I can't tell you how afraid I was that something would go wrong. I'm too happy to cry and too happy to smile."

But smile he did as the photographers' flashbulbs crackled and popped.

"You made my Christmas a lot better, and you made my momma's a lot better," he told the reporters.

Said Ann Campbell, "I'm just happy for Earl. We've been sweating this thing out for a long time."

Campbell called winning the award "a dream come true."

"When I was injured last year and in the training room," he said, "I read where Tony Dorsett had won the Heisman. And I said, 'Someday, *I'm* going to win it.'"

Earlier in the evening, in an awards ceremony expanded to include Downtown Athletic Club honors in six categories, Campbell also was named college football's best running back over LSU's Charles Alexander and Oklahoma State's Terry Miller.

In other categories, Chris Ward of Ohio State was named best offensive lineman over Mark Donahue of Michigan and Ken MacAfee of Notre Dame, MacAfee was named best end over Wes Chandler of Florida and Ozzie Newsome of Alabama, Ross Browner of Notre Dame was named best defensive lineman over Brad Shearer of Texas and Art Still of Kentucky, Jerry Robinson of UCLA was named best linebacker over Tom Cousineau of Ohio State and Gary Spani of Kansas State, and Zac Henderson of Oklahoma was named top defensive back over Luther Bradley of Notre Dame and Dennis Thurman of Southern California.

Campbell's immense reputation preceded him to New York. At a Wednesday night gathering of former Heisman winners, the Tyler Rose clearly was the choice of most. Georgia's Frank Sinkwich; Auburn's Pat Sullivan; Oklahoma's Steve Owens; Wisconsin's Alan Ameche; Michigan's Tom Harmon; UCLA's Gary Beban; Florida's Steve Spurrier; Navy's Joe Bellino; Ohio State's Howard "Hopalong" Cassady and Vic Janowicz; Notre Dame's Leon Hart, Johnny Lujack, Angelo Bertelli, and John Huarte; Yale's Larry Kelley; Texas A&M's John David Crow; and the University of Chicago's Jay Berwanger all had come to New York for the Heisman ceremonies, and most were predicting Earl Campbell would be the winner.

He became the Southwest Conference's fourth winner and, in so doing, broke a 20-year drought. The SWC had not had a winner since Crow in 1957. TCU's Davey O'Brien won in 1938 and SMU's Doak Walker in 1948.

A&M's John Kimbrough (1940) and TCU's Jim Swink (1955) finished second in the Heisman voting; SMU's Doak Walker (1947, '49), SMU's

Campbell won accolade after accolade—many from opposing coaches—during his Heisman year. Courtesy of University of Texas Athletics.

Earl Campbell (center), Coach Fred Akers (left), and Earl's mother, Ann Campbell, at the 1977 Heisman Trophy dinner. Ann is wearing the yellow rose given to her by my wife, Reba, upon arriving at the venue for the awards ceremony. Courtesy of *Dave Campbell's Texas Football*.

Don Meredith (1959), and Texas' James Saxton (1961) and Roosevelt Leaks (1973) all finished third; and TCU's Sam Baugh (1936), Baylor's Don Trull (1963), Texas Tech's Donny Anderson (1965), and Texas' Steve Worster (1970) finished fourth.

Campbell, all-state at Tyler John Tyler in 1973, when he led his team to the Class 4A state title, was recognized as a rare talent from the start, and he immediately started living up to the billing by winning a starting job as a freshman.

As long ago as last spring, when most eyes were focused on players elsewhere, Houston coach Bill Yeoman hinted that Campbell could be headed for just the kind of season he had.

"Earl Campbell is the one player in the conference who can almost dominate a game by himself," Yeoman said.

And dominate he did. "You don't ever stop an Earl Campbell; you just survive him," Oklahoma defensive chief Larry Lacewell once said.

This year, no one has survived him. Or Texas.

Campbell truly saved his best for last—both in his last season at Texas and in his last game against Texas A&M.

As a freshman in 1974, he rushed for 928 yards, and as a sophomore he led the conference with 1,118 yards, earning All-America honors on the coaches' team.

But this year, he was coming off a star-crossed junior season in which he sat out four games with injuries and missed so much time in others that he was limited to 653 yards.

Several months after that season, he was up to 242 pounds, and there was some doubt in Texas circles if he would ever run again like the Campbell of old. His leg injury, some said, might be a chronic thing. Others thought he had lost some of his original flaming desire.

They didn't know Earl Campbell.

New coach Fred Akers told him to lose 20 pounds and get ready to carry the football in a new multiple offense, the veer and I. At 220 pounds, he moved at his old speed and quickness but without loss of power. Only those who saw him take pitchouts, rev up to full speed (4.6 in the 40), and turn the corner can appreciate the awesome

Courtesy of University of Texas Athletics.

sight of Campbell thundering down on cornerbacks, linebackers, and safeties.

Since last spring, a small wooden plaque had adorned a wall in his dorm room. "Keep me going, Lord," it reads, and by midseason, it was obvious that the deeply religious Campbell, like the Longhorns, was going, going, gone.

After rushing for a mere 87 yards in Texas' opening-game runaway against Boston College, he started fashioning 100-yard performances Saturday after Saturday for 10 consecutive Saturdays in all.

But vastly more important, he made the game-breaking plays Texas needed to construct the only perfect regular-season record in major college football this year.

His 24-yard scoring run was the only touchdown in Texas' tight and tingly 13–6 upset of Oklahoma. His 28-yard run on a screen pass set up the winning touchdown late in the fourth quarter against Arkansas in the game that ultimately proved to be the difference between first and second place in the SWC title chase. His 58-yard touchdown run against SMU turned what had been a close and hard-fought game into a romp.

Texas was leading Houston by only a point in the third quarter when Campbell broke loose on a 43-yard touchdown run, then on his next carry, he went 40 more to the 1-foot line, putting the Cougars down for the count. He had back-to-back runs of 43 and 25 yards on a 55-yard touchdown drive that started Baylor on the road to ruin.

But as noted earlier, it was against A&M that Earl Campbell, called "The Man" by his teammates, became Superman. He had his finest day ever, rushing for 222 yards, scoring four times, and catching the first touchdown pass of his star-spangled career.

At the end, he had a career total of 4,443 yards rushing—best in SWC history and fifth-most in NCAA annals—and 1977 national supremacy in rushing (1,744 yards, also an SWC record), scoring (114 points on 19 touchdowns), and all-purpose running (1,855 yards).

And the University of Texas had its first Heisman Trophy winner.

Several weeks ago, a reporter asked Ann Campbell if she would have been disappointed if Earl had never played football.

"If Earl had never played a foot of football, he'd still be the same to me," she said. "He's just a quiet, calm little boy who grew up in the sand."

Thursday night at the plush, extravagant, gaily decorated New York Hilton in the heart of Manhattan, before a black-tie audience of dozens of football notables from all over, before a national television audience of millions, that little boy who grew up in the sand of East Texas accepted the trophy that established his place as one of college football's immortals.

JANUARY 2, 1979

LUCK OF THE IRISH

HOLLIS BIDDLE

DALLAS, Tex.—Leprechauns and four-leaf clovers broke through a painful blanket of ice that covered the Cotton Bowl Monday afternoon, and when those dark, gray, snow clouds finally blew away, the scoreboard was shining with a 35–34 victory in favor of Notre Dame over Houston.

It was as though some Hollywood scriptwriters had turned those Notre Dame omen-from-the-skies jokes into reality.

Ailing Irish quarterback Joe Montana came out of the sick bay in the fourth period to become the triggerman in the three-touchdown explosion that shattered the broken Cougar hearts into a thousand pieces.

A *three-hour* epic in the 43rd, frigid Cotton Bowl Classic came down to the final play of the game, and it is in those situations that the Irish are always better prepared.

The dramatic setting had Notre Dame pressed on the Houston 8-yard line and just two seconds showing on the stopped scoreboard clock.

Montana rolled right and whizzed a strike into the arms of Kris Haines, who had wrestled free of the Cougar defenders on a down-and-out pattern midway on the end zone sideline. There was instant doubt about whether he had control and was in bounds completely, but the officials promptly removed the cloud of suspense.

This TD tied the count at 34 all. And then Irish kicker Joe Unis had to kick correctly two times before getting the final tally. Notre Dame was offsides on his first try, and he had to go again from the 8, which he did without a flaw.

Less than a *minute* earlier, Houston was holding on to a 34–28 lead and could have possibly pulled out of danger.

The Cougars were in their final possession and trying to eat away the clock when a *big* decision time came. Facing fourth and 6 at his 24, coach Bill Yeoman called on punter Jay Wyatt, who poked a 21-yarder into the gusting 30-mph winds. This was not a bad punt considering the windy elements that kept both teams pinned in the south end zone all day.

Norte Dame was offsides on the punt. And after Houston took the penalty to the 29, Yeoman and his Coogs elected to gamble and go for the first down.

Wham—second-team linebacker Rob Crable met Houston back Emmett King in the middle hole for absolutely not an inch gained.

It was Notre Dame's time to shine with 28 seconds left and 29 yards to go.

Montana rolled right for 11 and passed to Haines for 10 at the 8-yard line as the breathless Cougars called a time out to collect their senses and the team's defenses. It didn't work.

Montana wasted four seconds on an incomplete pass to Haines, but they came right back with the same call, and "Bingo!" went the scoreboard.

Just eight minutes earlier (7:37 left in the game), Houston was walking easy with a 34–12 lead and was about to hand Notre Dame its second-worst loss in its bowl history.

Tony Belden got in the first lick that changed the tide when he got through to block a Wyatt punt, and Steve Cichy snared the elusive ice cube ball and had a free path to the goal line. Montana threw to Vegas Ferguson for two points, and the skies began to clear.

Houston began to go conservative, cautious, and nervous, and the collapse kept coming and coming.

Wyatt punted 28 yards to the Houston 39, and it took Montana five plays to get eight more points. The score was now Houston 34, Notre Dame 28, and you could just about get the feeling you knew what would eventually happen. And it did.

Montana, in a recall vote, snatched the game's outstanding offensive player award away from Houston's Danny Davis on the final ballot.

Joe, who has now directed two straight Irish victories in the Cotton Bowl, finished the day with 26 yards rushing and 13 of 34 passes for 163 yards. He was intercepted four times, and his performance was not all that great until the clutch time came.

Montana couldn't answer the bell to start the second half because of a week-long bout with the flu. But Dan Devine was forced to call on his gutsy senior when the Cougars were about to make a mockery of that famed golden-domed legend.

Houston won an early race against frostbite by keeping their hands and noses pressed to the Notre Dame end zone six times in the first three periods. All of those came after the Coogs had spotted the Irish a couple of touchdowns on some bobbled balls that were just too cold to handle.

An instant name change to "Ice Bowl" was coined quickly Monday morning, when Dallas experienced its worst winter blast in 30 years and a blanket of thick ice covered every seat in the arena.

There were 39,500 empty seats too, as the fickle elected to take other means of watching football on the first day of 1979. For those 32,000 attending, their first chore was picking away the ice from their folding chairs before sitting down. A steady exodus started trickling from the grounds late in the first period, and those nonbelievers will have a pretty good hangover after the Irish's unbelievable comeback.

The painful 20-degree temperatures and knifing 30-mph gusts made it appear the game would be played with an icicle instead of a football. There was no sure handle at any time.

Ground crews had to work on the Cotton Bowl's artificial turf late into New Year's Eve and early Monday morning to get the ice off the field. Their party tools consisted of steel sweepers and road graders.

The conditions were enough to boggle minds, and it did as the game started on a confusing note. The officials misread the signals, and at one time, both teams were lining up with a football on the tee. A double kickoff was prevented, however, and Notre Dame's Randy Harrison got things rolling with a 56-yard kickoff return to the Houston 34.

That Houston mountain on defense stymied the Irish on their first try and shut down their running game most of the day.

Houston generated a good drive on its first try before Emmett King fumbled—the first of six Cougar bobbles and the first of three they lost. Jay Case got the recovery, and Notre Dame drove 66 yards for its first score in nine plays.

Whoops! Houston's Terry Elston fumbled the kickoff, and Notre Dame had a punch-in 25-yard TD on the way. Montana scored the first TD, and Pete Buchanan got the second for a 12–0 lead as both extra point tries were botched.

The wind and cold made the long center snaps almost impossible to control.

Houston, guided by the expertise of Davis on offense and the massive David Hodge on defense, then got under way to a giant lead of 34–12 before Montana rose again.

The Cougars needed only 164 total yards to get the seven scores adding up to 34.

First of all, a Houston punt hit a Notre Dame player in flight, and Chuck Brown recovered at the Notre Dame 12.

Davis wound up passing 15 yards to Willis Adams for the score that got Houston back in the game.

Hodge, who was voted the game's outstanding defensive player on a first ballot, recovered a fumble to set up a 21-yard TD drive capped by Randy Love on a fourth-down plunge from the 1.

Danny Davis (4) hands off to Alois Blackwell (32). Courtesy of University of Houston Athletics.

Interceptions by Kenny Hatfield and Steve Bradham worked the Cougars for a pair of field goals by Hatfield. These strikes were from 21 and 34 yards out and gave the Cougars a 20–12 halftime edge.

Hatfield almost missed the ball on his 34-yarder, but the driving wind carried the ball just over the crossbar for three points.

Davis put on a dazzling show in the third period as Houston capitalized on two punting misfires by Notre Dame to score twice more.

First, a bad punt gave Houston possession at the Irish 38, and the Coogs scored in seven plays. Davis took it in from the 2.

Randy Harrison blocked the next Irish punt at the 19, and Davis eventually scored from the 12.

Injuries to All-American linebacker Rob Golic and punter Joe Restic and Montana's illness hampered the Irish game plan all day until the chips were down.

Hodge took his defensive honors in a runaway with six tackles, nine assists, a fumble recovery, and a pass interception. Hosea Taylor, Leonard Mitchell, Grady Ebensberger, Robert Oglesby, and Steve Bradham were solid as usual up front.

Davis, in a close footrace, led all rushers for the day with 76 yards in 19 attempts. King added 74, Love had 73, and Jerome Heavens led the Irish with 71.

The aggregate 69-point total was the highest in Cotton Bowl history, winding out a 33-year-old record, and it was just fitting that Notre Dame would come out on the long end.

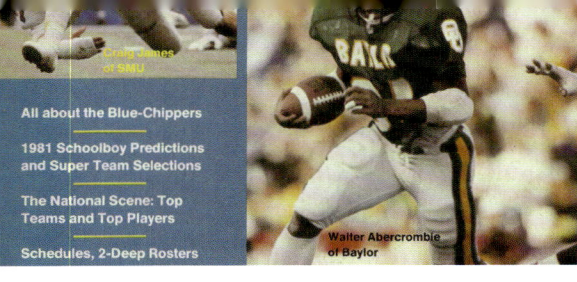

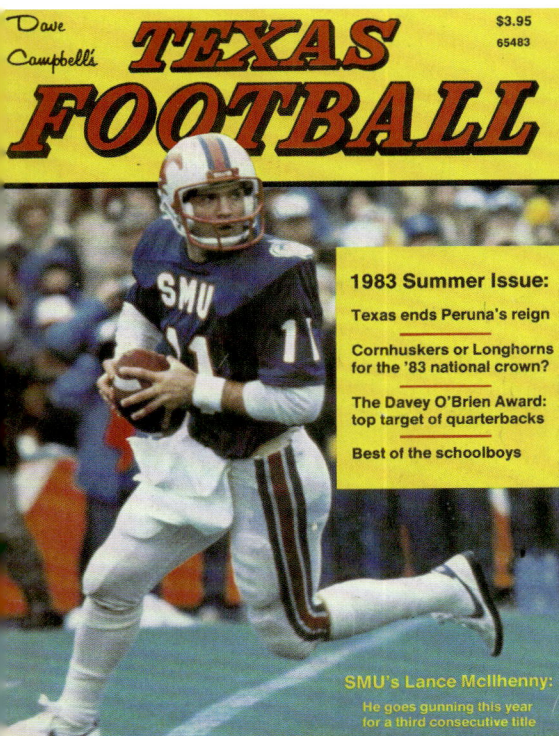
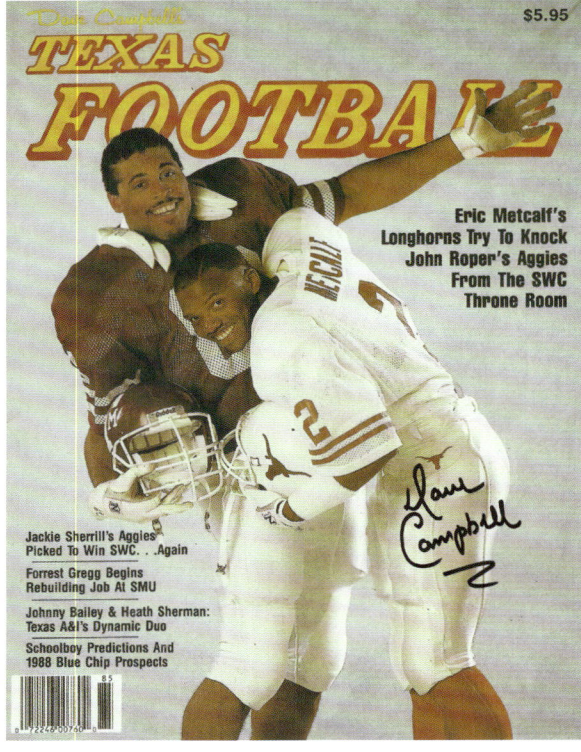

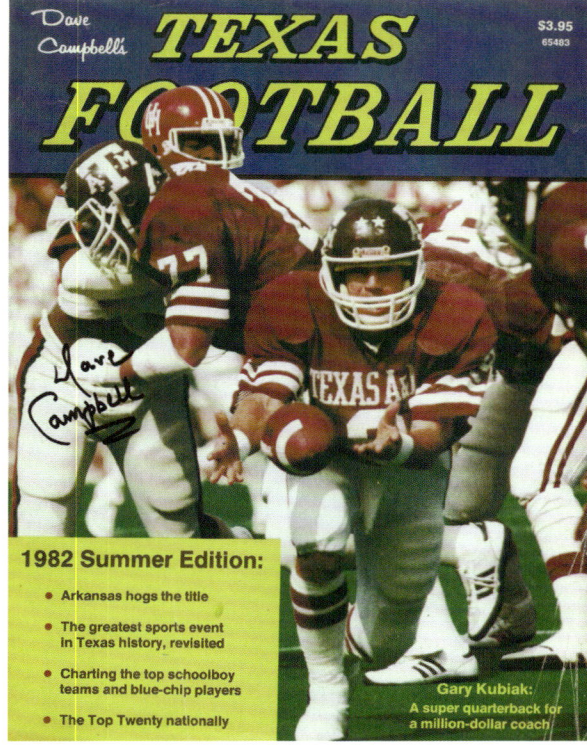
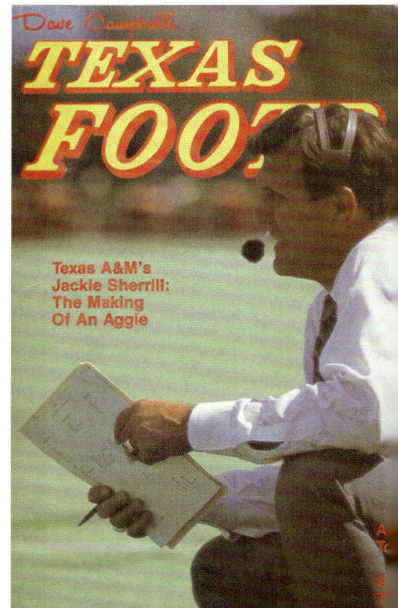

4
NEW FACES, CHANGING TIMES
1980–1989

I guess it's no secret that I'm a Waco boy, so I couldn't help getting at least a little bit excited when the '80s opened with a Baylor Southwest Conference championship and a trip to the 1981 Cotton Bowl. The Bears' celebration was made possible, in large part, by the stellar efforts of a young linebacker named Mike Singletary, a three-time All-SWC and two-time All-American selection. Under the guidance of mentor Grant Teaff, who had taken over a Baylor team in 1972 that was 7-43-1 for the previous five seasons, the Bears became a force to be reckoned with in the SWC, earning invitations to three more bowl games during the decade.

But it wasn't all about Baylor during the '80s, of course. During this time, SWC fans learned the phrases "Frog Fever" and "Pony Express," as Texas Christian, under the leadership

Baylor's outstanding linebacker Mike Singletary was drafted by Chicago in 1981 and became one of the "Monsters of the Midway." He was inducted into the Pro Football Hall of Fame in 1998. Courtesy of Baylor University Athletics.

of Jim Wacker, and Southern Methodist, with Ron Meyer at the helm, assembled some impressive teams that included players like the Mustangs' Eric Dickerson and Lance McIlhenny and the Horned Frogs' Kenneth Davis. Sadly, much of these teams' progress would be stymied by NCAA penalties for recruiting and other rules violations. Jackie Sherrill's Aggies would also feel the sting of NCAA sanctions.

Notwithstanding all that, there was a lot of exciting football during the 1980s. After Baylor's 30–2 defeat at the hands of the Crimson Tide in the 1981 Cotton Bowl, Texas would avenge the loss the following year with a 14–12 victory over Bryant's team. In the 1985 edition, Doug Flutie's air attack with Boston College would prove too much for Bill Yeoman's Cougars, and the Aggies would stop Auburn and its star running back Bo Jackson, 36–16, the following year. Texas A&M won two more conference titles—in 1986 and 1988—which would set up Cotton Bowl clashes with Ohio State (lost 28–12) and Notre Dame (won 35–10), respectively.

SEPTEMBER 29, 1980

AN AWESOME LUBBOCK EFFORT BY THE BEARS

LUBBOCK, Tex.—As a man who was there at ground level, who could hear the collisions and almost feel the shock waves, Grant Teaff just knew his Bears were playing extremely well on defense against Texas Tech in Lubbock Saturday night.

But really, Teaff said Sunday, he had no idea.

"Looking at it on film, it was a lot more awesome than I thought. We just completely dominated the line of scrimmage. Maybe it's happened before, but I can't ever remember when our front four played as well as this front four played Saturday night."

Because that front four played such a wipeout game against the Red Raiders, the Bears were able to prevail in their own personal Jinx City on a day when upset was the name of the game from sea to shining sea.

Let us count the names: Oklahoma, LSU, Florida State, Washington, Kansas, Michigan, North Carolina State, Ole Miss, Iowa, Auburn—all favored to win Saturday and all upset. And while for such lopsided favorites as Arkansas and Houston the day turned out to be victorious, it was a darned near thing.

However, at chilly and wet Jones Stadium, it was Baylor 11, Texas Tech 3, and I doubt there was a one of the 48,539 eyewitnesses who left the premises late Saturday night saying the Bears didn't deserve what they got. Maybe they deserved more.

"If it hadn't been wet," said A&M assistant coach R. C. Slocum, who was there to scout the Red Raiders, "I believe Baylor would have scored a lot more. They're so quick, so fast. A lot of times you could see they were just about to break something big, and the footing or the wet ball would mess them up."

GOOD GRADE TO BRING HOME

Grading the film of a Baylor victory earned in Lubbock was a new experience for Teaff. None of his Baylor teams had never won at Jones Stadium before. No Baylor team had won there since 1966. And no Baylor team playing there or elsewhere has ever done what those Bears did Saturday night: they held Tech to a minus 36 yards rushing for the game, and on 21 plays they dropped the Raiders for losses totaling 121 yards.

If Teaff had looked carefully at the fine print on that film, he probably would have found some wording on it somewhere, wording that read "Compliments of the front four."

Charles Benson. Courtesy of Baylor University Athletics.

Their names are Charles Benson, Max McGeary, Tommy Tabor, and Joe Campbell, and for one night, at least, they were supermen in green wearing seven-league boots. The first two are ends, the other two are tackles, and here is what they did against Tech, as tabulated by Baylor coaches Sunday in the actual film breakdown:

Benson, 6-foot-3, 245, a sophomore, was in on 14 tackles, and 7 of them resulted in losses of 30 yards for the Red Raiders. He also broke up three passes. "We've had some pretty good ends here in my time," said Teaff, "but never, ever, have we had an end play as well as Charles Benson did Saturday night."

McGeary, 6-foot-2, 219, a senior, had eight solo tackles, assists on two others, and five tackles behind the line for losses totaling 12 yards, and he also broke up a pass and partially blocked a Tech field goal attempt. When the field goal was blocked, press box observers credited the deed to cornerback Thomas Earl Young, but on the plane ride home after the game, Young said he didn't come close—that the credit belonged to McGeary. And the film verified it. So McGeary now has 12 blocked kicks for his Baylor career—five punts, four field goals, and three extra points. He has to be leading the world in blocked kicks.

Joe Campbell, 6-foot-0, 254, a senior, had nine tackles, four of them resulting in Tech losses.

And Tommy Tabor, 6-foot-3, 259, a junior, was in on four tackles, one of them a stop that gave Tech a 7-yard loss.

SUPERLATIVE EFFORTS ON DEFENSE

"Charles Benson was just unreal, awesome. But our entire front four proved they could play with anybody, I believe. And I think it should be pointed out that one reason we got so many quarterback sacks was because we were getting great coverage in the secondary. That was giving Tech's quarterbacks so many problems that our linemen were able to get to them. It was a team effort in every sense of the word," said Teaff.

"Lester Ward and Doak Field also had excellent games at linebacker. In fact, one reason Mike Singletary [middle linebacker] had fewer tackles than usual is because Tech wasn't getting that many runners to the line of scrimmage for him to tackle."

All last week, Teaff had said Baylor's defensive play and performance in the kicking game would decide the outcome.

The Bears were out of sight defensively. And the kicking game? They won a decided edge there too, although Tech's reputation for a first-rate kicking game is well established.

Punter Maury Buford, to be sure, out-punted Baylor's Ron Stowe, 47.2 yards to 39.2, but those figures represent only the tip of the iceberg. Baylor returned Buford's 10 punts a total of 74 yards. Tech returned Stowe's punts a mere 6 yards. Tech gave up four points (two safeties) when two different deep-snap men sailed their snaps over Buford's head and out of the end zone. Baylor had no such breakdowns. The Raider culprits blamed the wet ball for their problems. Teaff wonders

Texas Tech punter Maury Buford (7) tries to get his kick over the outstretched arms of Baylor defenders. Courtesy of Texas Tech University Athletics.

if that field goal McGeary partially blocked early in the first quarter didn't have something to do with them.

"You know, we blocked one of their punts last year [at Baylor Stadium], and then Max partially blocked the field goal, and I think that might have gotten their attention," he said. "A lot of people are so afraid of our punt-block potential that it gives them problems."

The positive returns from the defense and kicking game were so gaudy that it was easy to overlook some good things the offense did.

To be sure, this was hardly a star-spangled show by the offense. Going into the game, the Bruins had ranked No. 2 nationally (behind Nebraska) in total offense with an average of 616 yards per game. Tech held them to 273 yards, dropping their season average of 502 yards.

But Teaff didn't expect any 616-yard outbursts. Tech is one of the league's better defensive teams. North Carolina, a Gator Bowl winner over Michigan last December, found that out in an earlier game this season in Lubbock.

"Except for the three missed scoring opportunities, I was pretty pleased with the offense as a whole," said Teaff. "I think you have to give Tech a lot of credit. They're big and strong. They stopped us more than we stopped ourselves. And you know, whenever they had us backed up deep, we didn't take any chances."

But he did agree Baylor's third-down conversion record was terrible (only 3 of 18 tries), that the split ends had a bad night, and that starting quarterback Jay Jeffrey was "not as sharp on his passing as he has been." Three times Bruin backs were open for touchdown throws, but the ball did not get to them. On the other hand, the Bears did not fumble or throw an interception in their end of the field either, and in view of the playing conditions, there is much to be said for that.

Teaff singled out three of his offensive performers in particular: "Someone suggested to me Sunday that the Tech game might have been Walter Abercrombie's worst [13 carries for 19 yards, two catches for 27 yards]. I told the guy it probably was his best, and I meant it. Walter simply was superb. I'm talking about his blocking. On just about every long run Dennis Gentry made against Tech, Walter was there making the clearing block. Dennis gained 119 yards, and Walter might have been responsible for 110 of that. He's one of the most unselfish backs I've ever had, and I know he's the best blocking back I've ever had.

"Gentry did just what we wanted him to. The way we had our game plan designed, he was supposed to have the opportunity to get some big yardage, and that's exactly what happened.

"And then there was Mike Brannan. Mike went in at quarterback there in the fourth quarter and executed well while taking us to our touchdown. He gained some confidence in himself. I think the week before, against West Texas State, Mike proved to himself that he finally is over his knee surgery physically. Against Tech he proved he is over the surgery psychologically. His experience is very valuable to us. It was very valuable to us Saturday night."

Teaff did not rule out the possibility that Brannan could start at quarterback against Houston Saturday night at Baylor Stadium. Let's see, now—Houston is another one of those jinx teams for Baylor. The Bears have not beaten the Cougars since they joined the SWC. Last year, in fact, the Bears only got five first downs against the Coogs and only two in the second half. Talk about your defense!

JANUARY 2, 1981

TURNOVERS BLOW BAYLOR OUT OF GAME

DALLAS, Tex.—All those 74,281 football fans who turned out for the 45th annual Cotton Bowl Classic here New Year's Day saw two things that were perfection itself—the weather and the Alabama defense.

Perhaps the order should be reversed. The Alabama defense was better than the weather, and the weather was absolutely gorgeous.

The fans also saw one thing that was remarkably imperfect—the Baylor offense. Well, make that two imperfect things, because Baylor's punt-return game also was fatally flawed.

With that in mind, does anyone have to tell you who won Thursday's long-awaited battle between Alabama's celebrated Bear and Baylor's ambitious Bears? Alabama's Bear—head coach Bear Bryant and his quick-as-a-snake Crimson Tide—won the game, and won it from here to yonder.

The scoreboard's final reading favored Bryant and Alabama, 30–2, and those are cruel figures to drop on a Baylor team that had enjoyed so many favorable figures during the regular season.

But in all truth, the Bears brought a lot of it on themselves. Alabama brought the rest. For much of Thursday afternoon, the Bears found that trying to move against the Tide was about like standing on some lonely beach and trying to hold back the tide.

Wherever Baylor's vaunted running backs went, Tide defenders were sure to follow—closely. Indeed, they often showed up in the Bears' own backfield, and as a result, Baylor could net only 54 yards overland.

The major thorn was Alabama tackle Warren Lyles, who had eight tackles, including five for 26 yards in losses. Lyles was an easy choice as the game's top defensive player.

Still, Alabama's runners often had their problems too. Baylor's defense did not play all that badly for most of the game.

But whatever chance Grant Teaff's representatives had of turning the game into a near-even battle vanished when the Southwest Conference champions developed a bad case of the turnovers.

The Bears lost four of five fumbles and suffered three interceptions, and they picked the most gosh-awful time and place to make some of those turnovers—for instance, the Baylor 13-yard line, the Baylor 25, and the Alabama 8. And two of Alabama's touchdown drives followed interceptions.

"Turnovers—that's the story in a nutshell," said a glum Teaff when it was all over.

Quarterback Jay Jeffrey echoed his coach: "The darn turnovers just killed us. When it came time to move, we could make a mistake and kill ourselves. All year we avoided the errors, and then today we had enough for a whole season."

Certainly turnovers were a significant part of Baylor's second straight one-sided defeat in the Cotton Bowl Classic (the Bears lost to Penn State, 41–20, on New Year's Day of 1975). But the way the Crimson Tide played defense, Alabama's chances for victory would have been excellent even if Baylor had bobbled nary a time.

Bryant's iron curtain was just too strong, too quick, too well-schooled, too deadly for the best offense in Baylor's 81-year history. The Bears could block 'em for an instant—but they wouldn't stay blocked.

As a result, quarterbacks Jeffrey and David Mangrum operated under a relentless pressure, Bryant's veterans roiled in truly like a Crimson Tide, and runners Walter Abercrombie and Dennis Gentry, the two leading footmen in the SWC, had to try to run through holes that simply were not there.

The guys from 'Bama had it easier—not a lot, but somewhat. They had a hard time sustaining much of anything for a long time, but thanks to a few big plays and those Baylor turnovers, they didn't have to sustain all that much to dominate the scoreboard.

Actually, Alabama didn't exactly overwhelm the scoreboard for the game's first 45 minutes. But they were never behind and never appeared in any real danger of falling behind—except maybe near the end of the first quarter, after they had grabbed a 6–0 margin on field goals of 29 and 28 yards by Hawaiian import Peter Kim.

But then, for the first time, the Bruin offense started showing some life. It moved 71 yards in four plays (the big play was a 50-yard pass interference call against Alabama) before Gentry lost a fumble at the Alabama 8-yard line.

Two plays later, Bruin tackle Tommy Tabor trapped Alabama's second-team quarterback Walter Lewis in the end zone, giving Baylor a safety and forcing 'Bama to make a free kick from the 20.

Gerald McNeil returned the punt brilliantly for 30 yards before being dropped by Mike Clements at the Alabama 37. Thus the Bears started with delicious field position. If they could have pushed to the pay window there, they could have moved in front.

Alas, Jeffrey's first-down aerial fell into the arms of Alabama's Jeremiah Castille, who returned 10 yards to the Alabama 24, and from that point the Tide rolled 78 yards in seven plays for a touchdown.

Baylor was never that much in the game again, and at the finish the Bears still could show only the lone safety for eight quarters of play against the men from Tuscaloosa (Alabama blanked Baylor in 1979, 45–0).

"I thought we had a touchdown when I started to throw," Jeffrey said about the momentum-turning interception. "Mike Fisher was wide open. But I got hit [by standout tackle Byron Braggs] as I threw, and the ball was short and intercepted."

After that it was all 'Bama—but grudgingly so—through three quarters. Going into the final period, the Crimson Tide led only 16–2, and the Bears still had a chance.

But Alabama rallied at the finish instead.

Solid senior quarterback Don Jacobs, who played most of the game and played well, scored from a yard out with 6:54 left in the game, winding up a nine-play, 37-yard drive, and Mark Nix got the final 3 yards of a seven-play, 66-yard drive with 1:15 remaining on the clock.

But those touchdowns were scored after the Baylor defense had sort of worn out. The points 'Bama scored earlier—Kim's Cotton Bowl record–tying field goals of 29, 28, and 42 yards and halfback Major Ogilvie's 1-yard scoring run that came at the end of the 75-yard march in the second quarter—were earned against a Bruin defense that was still full of fire and fight and playing for keeps.

Ogilvie, the game's leading rusher with 74 yards on 15 carries, was also his team's most valuable offensive player in a bowl victory for the second year in a row. And when he dived into the end zone with 13:26 to play in the second period, he made a little bit of history, becoming the first player in NCAA history to rush for a touchdown in a bowl game for four straight seasons.

Interestingly, Alabama's two most heralded players, Ogilvie and All-American defensive end E. J. Junior, described the Bears as perhaps the best team the Crimson Tide played this season.

"Baylor is the best team we played, including Notre Dame," said Junior, who was in on 10 tackles and also recovered a fumble. "Baylor didn't quit; they kept coming at us. Don't look at the score. We had 10 or 11 days to prepare, and we just wanted it more."

Ogilvie said he was surprised "that our defense shut them down like that, but I know our coach had some good schemes. Baylor is one of the best teams we played this year, if not the best. Physically, they were the toughest."

In all truth, the Bears did do some impressive things, especially on defense. But they also kept digging a hole for themselves with their miscues.

On their final possession, for example, a holding penalty wiped out a 9-yard run by Gentry and set Baylor back to its own 17-yard line, and the punt that followed put Alabama in business at the Tide 39-yard line. Alabama used that good field position to drive to the Baylor 15-yard line in seven plays, with a pass from Jacobs to fullback Billy Jackson for 20 yards and a 12-yard run by Joe Carter doing most of the damage.

But then Baylor's defense proved for the first time that it came to play. 'Bama advanced exactly 3 yards on its next three plays and had to turn to Kim to salvage three points out of the opportunity.

The Bears got a full taste of that fierce 'Bama defense on their next possession. The Bears started at their own 22 and lost 9 yards in three plays, and Ron Stowe's punt turned the ball back over to the Crimson Tide at the Baylor 48.

It was on that series, incidentally, that Abercrombie got his first chance to run with the football. But he got the ball at the end of a poorly executed option play and had to make a fine play to retain possession and lose only 6 yards. It was a sign of things to come.

At the end of the game, the SWC's leading rusher had been dealt his poorest hand of the season—9 yards rushing on eight carries and 4 yards on two pass receptions.

To say that Alabama was ready for Walter Abercrombie would be a very large understatement.

"It seemed like every time we came out of the huddle, they were able to adjust to what we just did," he said. "My job is not to coach, and I don't know why I didn't get the ball more. This is the fewest number of carries I've had since I've been at Baylor, but the options just were not there. We finally stopped using them at the half."

With Abercrombie snuffed out, Jeffrey became Baylor's leading ball carrier, finishing with 18 yards on 8 carries. Gentry managed 17 yards on 11 carries, and as noted earlier, the Bears had to settle for 54 yards in 35 rushing attempts and 158 yards on 62 plays in total offense.

Baylor had been averaging 440 yards per game in total offense and 296 yards rushing. But they hadn't been going against defenses such as Alabama either.

With Alabama poised at the Baylor 48 on its second possession of the game, things looked bleak for the Bears. But the Baylor defense quickly forced a punt. Woody Umphrey booted a low spiral that Gerald McNeild fielded on the fly at the Baylor's 5-yard line and returned to the 12, where Mike Pitts blasted him loose from the football and Russ Wood recovered.

And guess what? The Bruin defense, led by Doak Field, Lester Ward, and Thomas Earl Young, became an iron curtain itself, limiting the Tide to a meager 2 yards in three plays. Kim had to come in to kick, and again, he kicked true.

Baylor then got back in the game. Jeffrey aimed a long pass that Fisher might have caught, but Ricky Tucker and Mike Clements were called for interference. After the 50-yard penalty, Jeffrey's running and passing (a 10-yarder to Gentry) got the Bears to the Alabama 15, where it was first down.

But on the next play, disaster struck. Gentry went around left end, and defensive back Jim Bob Harris almost obliterated him, sending Dennis one way and the ball another. Randy Scott recovered for 'Bama at the Tide 8-yard line.

Two plays later, Tabor sacked Lewis for the safety, and two plays after that, Jeffrey threw the pass that Castille picked off, and there went 'Bama on a touchdown drive.

Linnie Patrick (45 yards on 12 carries) got it started with some nifty running on four straight carries, but the big play was a 49-yard pass from Jacobs to Jesse Bendross that carried to the Baylor 4. Ogilvie scored two plays later from the 1-yard line.

Baylor never got out of its own end of the field for the remainder of the first half, and Alabama twice drove inside the Baylor 40, only to get rebuffed.

So at the half, it was a 13–2 game and the Bears were still very much in it. And when they stopped the Tide on its first possession of the third quarter and then gouged out two first downs on their first chance, things started looking up. But that was an illusion.

First the Crimson Tide got an interception, then McNeil fumbled another punt—this one at the Baylor 25. And although the Tide couldn't move on three tries from the 25, Kim kicked his third field goal, from the 32, and Alabama was in front, 16–2.

Later, Teaff sought to explain the usually sure-handed McNeil's problem. "Part of it was he dislocated two fingers in practice last week and he had the two taped together," Teaff said.

With the Bears behind by 14 points, David Mangrum made his first appearance at quarterback for the Bears. He ran three straight times, losing a fumble on the third time and turning the ball over to 'Bama on the Baylor 33. Thomas Earl Young got the ball back for Baylor by grabbing a fourth-down Alabama fumble at the 29. That was Alabama's only turnover of the game.

Mangrum then directed the Bears 31 yards in nine plays to the Crimson Tide 40 before being stopped, and he had the team back in 'Bama territory on Baylor's next possession when one of his bullet passes deflected off a receiver's fingers and into the willing hands of Jim Bob Harris.

That proved to be the blow that killed the Bears. The Baylor defense went back onto the field, but it walked back to the battle line that time, and a voice in the press box noted, "Those guys have about had it."

Later, linebacker Doak Field admitted as much. "The defense let down," he said. "The Baylor defense wasn't the defense we showed during the regular season."

Even so, it limited 'Bama to 17 first downs, 241 yards rushing, and 339 yards in total offense while often laboring under highly unfavorable conditions. And the Tide got 132 of those yards, and 14 points, in the fourth quarter.

Ogilvie's 12-yard run, a 19-yard burst by Jackson, and a 12-yarder by Joe Jones were the big gainers in the 57-yard drive that boosted the score to 23–2. The Tide's final scoring thrust was mainly the work of Joe Carter, who turned a simple option pitchout into a 56-yard burst around right end against the dead-tired Bruin defenders.

In the final minute and 18 seconds, Jeffrey escorted the Bears 52 yards in seven plays to the Alabama 28 before the clock closed him out. Baylor's final play of a remarkable season was a long pass into the end zone that Radar Holt almost caught. But against Bryant's Crimson Tide, almost is not good enough.

"I felt we could play with them defensively, and we did," Teaff summed up. "They had one long run in the fourth quarter and a long pass in the first half. Other than those, we more or less held them to three field goals. It was a disappointing loss, but I told our players one game does not a season make. We can't forget all the good things we accomplished this year."

Bear Bryant, as usual, had the last word: "We made some mistakes, but they forced us into some of those. However, I guess you could say we forced them into some too. Baylor has a fine football team. I'm just as tickled about winning this game as I am about winning the national championship."

Aw, Bear, not really. But he has put career victory No. 306 in the record book. Another nine and he'll move past Amos Alonzo Stagg as football's winningest coach of all time. Judging his Tide by the way it played on the first day of 1981, he ought to get those nine victories before the year is out.

OCTOBER 11, 1981

SOONER OR LATER: RELENTLESS TEXAS PRESSURE CRUSHES OU, 34–14

DALLAS, Tex.—You put even a hard-shell pecan in a nutcracker and squeeze and squeeze and squeeze, and what happens? Sooner or later, the pecan splits open, right? Hard-as-flint Texas put the proud, favored Oklahoma Sooners in a nutcracker Saturday and put on the big squeeze, and the way the Sooners split open left even the Longhorn fans wonderfully bedazzled.

Those fans came to this annual bloodletting at the Cotton Bowl hoping, deep down, that their favorites might find a way to win a tight, tense game. They never expected to bury the Sooners. But bury them the Longhorns did.

Underdogs by three points, they virtually gave the Sooners two touchdowns in the first half and then whipped them to a frazzle in the second half and won going away, 34–14, before a sellout crowd of 75,587 and a national television audience.

It was Texas' biggest point spree against an Oklahoma team since 1970 and tied for the third-highest score run-up by a Longhorn team against the Sooners since 1904. Can you believe that?

What makes it so difficult to believe is that the Longhorns did it while using a Neanderthal offense. They used no finesse; they did nothing fancy. They just put the cold steel to the Sooners, especially in the second half when they scored on five of their seven possessions, fumbled away another opportunity at the Oklahoma 13-yard line, and limited the Sooners to one unproductive trip across the midfield stripe.

Lordy, once the Longhorns got rolling, it was overwhelming, even if it was plain vanilla.

It was Jam Jones right and Jam Jones left and Jam Jones up the middle, and now and then it was a Rick McIvor pass hitting the rather inept Sooner secondary where it hurt.

Jones—and that's A. J. Jones, if you want his formal name—sent his 206 pounds of fury crashing into the Sooner defense a whopping 36 times and finished with 134 yards and one touchdown. McIvor threw 13 passes and completed 6 of them for 127 yards and two touchdowns—a 36-yard scoring shot to Maurice McCloney and a 4-yard payoff toss to Lawrence Sampleton.

Rodney Tate scored Texas' final touchdown on a 17-yard run with 10 seconds left in the game. The Longhorns' remaining points came courtesy of 34- and 22-yard field goals kicked by Raul Allegre, plus four conversions kicked by the same Mexico City native.

Thirty-one of those points came in the final 30 minutes, after Oklahoma had scored touchdowns in each of the first two quarters and snatched a 14–3 halftime

Lawrence Sampleton (87). Courtesy of University of Texas Athletics.

All-American tackle Terry Tausch (79) tending the line as placekicker John Goodson (95) puts the PAT through Oklahoma's uprights. Courtesy of University of Texas Athletics.

lead. Chet Winters scored Oklahoma's first touchdown, bolting a single yard with the game only a minute and one second old, and Oklahoma's leading footman, Stanley (Steamer) Wilson, scored the other touchdown on a 1-yard plunge with 5:12 left in the second quarter. Wilson finished with 85 yards on 23 carries, but no other Sooner runner had as many as 50 yards.

Oklahoma's first touchdown was almost a gift. Texas' John Walker fumbled the opening kickoff, and John Truitt recovered for the Sooners on the Texas 16, and Oklahoma scored in three plays.

The second Sooner touchdown moved a mere 34 yards in seven plays and also was set in motion by a Texas fumble—one of four the Longhorns lost during the afternoon. See how easy Texas made things for the Sooners in the first half?

But the tide turned abruptly in the second half. Oklahoma started making the mistakes and Texas started cashing in—again, by using straight power football that the tiring Sooners found irresistible. In the final 30 minutes, Jam Jones carried the first five times for Texas—on 14 of 22 snaps in the third quarter and on 24 of 40 snaps until the game was out of Oklahoma's reach.

"Our defense forgot we still had a game to play," said Oklahoma's All-American offensive guard Terry Crouch. "UT started moving the ball, and our defense lost its composure. They got caught up in all the pageantry. Then they started getting awed by Texas."

At the half, Oklahoma had the upper hand in first downs, total yardage, and points scored, but Texas' All-American offensive tackle Terry Tausch saw something else. "We were behind, but they were getting tired," Terry observed after the game. "We've worked hard, and it paid off in the third and fourth quarters. I came out in the second half and felt like I hadn't even played yet."

Apparently his fellow offensive linemen felt the same way, and so did the defense; thus the game broke open in this fashion:

Texas accepted the third-quarter kickoff and drove 80 yards in 10 plays for its first touchdown, with Jones carrying eight times for 31 yards and McIvor completing a 39-yard pass to McCloney on a pivotal third-down play that carried to the Oklahoma 3-yard line. Jones plunged the final yard with 10:55 left in the third quarter, and Allegre's kick made it a 14–10 game.

When Oklahoma's Wilson fumbled on the Sooners' first play following the kickoff, destructive Kenneth Sims recovered for Texas at the Sooner 6-yard line. Texas could get but 2 yards in three tries, but Allegre's 22-yard field goal narrowed Oklahoma's lead to 14–13.

On possession No. 3 of the third quarter, Texas drove 69 yards in nine plays, with Jones carrying four times and McIvor completing a 13-yard pass to fullback Carl Robinson, evading a hard Sooner rush, faking a run, and then throwing to a wide-open McClooney for 36 yards and a go-ahead touchdown. Oklahoma really never recovered after that.

Still, Texas refused to let up. The Longhorns drove 42 yards in 12 plays for more points on their next possession. Michael Keeling's 27-yard punt left Texas with great field position, and the Longhorns used the strong running of Jones and John Walker to hack out three first downs to the Oklahoma 8. Three plays later, McIvor faked a handoff to Jones, then threw to a wide-open Sampleton for the score.

With 7:54 left in the game, end Kiki DeAyala blindsided Sooner quarterback Kelly Phelps, forcing a fumble at the Oklahoma 19 that Eric Holle recovered for Texas, but McIvor fumbled away that chance three plays later. However, with the game winding down, former Tulsa schoolboy star Jeff Leiding, a Texas linebacker, intercepted Phelps's pass and returned 12 yards to the Oklahoma 22, and Tate, also a former Oklahoma schoolboy star, scored from the 17 on fourth down, although the Longhorns, in all truth, were just trying to run out the clock.

In the final 30 minutes, Texas gained the upper hand in first downs, 11 to 3; in rushing, 123 yards to 64; in passing, 102 yards to 0 (Oklahoma did not complete a pass during the game); in total offense, 225 yards to 64; and in offensive plays, 44 to 23. "It was like two different games," said Texas coach Fred Akers, whose team whipped the Sooners for the fourth time in Akers's five years on the coaching lines.

"Our kids showed a lot of will, a lot of heart to come back like they did in the second half. Credit our offensive line and the hard running, especially by Jam. And that was real pressure playing by a young quarterback."

Sooner coach Barry Switzer, who saw his team sink to a 1-2-1 record for the season, thought Texas' ability "to make two fantastic third-down plays and our inability to make the fourth-down plays" made the difference.

Switzer referred to McIvor's 39-yard pass to McClooney that set up the Longhorns' first touchdown and the same passer's 36-yard throw to the same receiver that produced the second touchdown. The first came on a third-and-6 situation, the second on a third and 15.

"We stopped those two third-down plays, and they're punting instead of scoring touchdowns," said Switzer.

Oklahoma suffered a spectacular fourth-down failure in each half.

The first came on the Sooners' second possession of the game. They had grabbed John Walker's kickoff bobble and scored right off the bat, and then with six minutes left in the first quarter, they were threatening to score again. They had moved 33 yards in nine plays to the Texas 24, where it was fourth and inches needed for a first down. Phelps tried to sneak for the distance, and Texas' Mark Weber hammered him down hard, yielding not a single inch.

Texas took over at its 27 and drove 56 yards in six plays to the Sooner 17 before Allegre kicked his first field goal, a 34-yarder. The big play on that drive was a 27-yard pass from McIvor to Carl Robinson.

Oklahoma's other notable fourth-down failure came with 5:45 left in the third quarter, with the Sooners trying to protect a 14–13 lead. After surrendering the 80-yard touchdown drive to Texas at the start of the second half and then setting up Allegre's 22-yard field goal with Wilson's fumble at the 6, they started moving from their own 20 and advanced 53 yards in eight plays to the UT 27. There they needed a yard on fourth down. Phelps, who went all the way at quarterback for Oklahoma and played well most of the time, tried to hand the ball to Steamer Wilson, but Holle knocked down Wilson before he could get the ball. Then Sims engulfed Phelps back on the 32 for a 5-yard loss.

For the overwhelmed Sooners, it was time to turn out the lights. And for Longhorn fans, it was time to be shouting "We're No. 1! We're No. 1!" And they may well be.

But you can take it from wide receiver Donnie Little, who looked ahead to Texas' next game in Fayetteville and told Texas governor William Clements, "Come to Arkansas next week. You ain't seen nothing yet."

OCTOBER 25, 1981

SMU GETS BOOT FROM TEXAS, 9–7

IRVING, Tex.—Tenth-ranked Texas used a fierce defense and its Mexican connection to whip undefeated, eighth-ranked SMU, 9–7, here Saturday afternoon and throw the race for the Southwest Conference championship into a perfect snarl.

The verdict not only knocked the Mustangs from the ranks of the nation's perfect-record teams; it also marked the earliest date since the SWC began round-robin play that every team in the league has had at least one conference defeat.

And that, friends and neighbors, is going all the way back to 1934. And that also means the 1981 race is virtually wide open, although Saturday's developments left Texas, SMU, and Texas A&M all virtually tied for first place, each with one defeat.

But the race is barely half over.

A Texas Stadium crowd of more than 60,777 saw the Longhorn defense, as tough as tempered steel, put shackles on an SMU offense that had been leading the conference both in rushing and in total offense, one that had ranked third in the nation in scoring by averaging 39 points a game.

But except for one lightning bolt in the fourth quarter, when SMU's quarterback Lance McIlhenny hooked up with swift wide receiver Jackie Wilson on a 70-yard touchdown pass, the Mustangs simply found Kenneth Sims and friends more than they could overcome.

While that McIlhenny-to-Wilson connection was a stunner, the Longhorns' Mexican connection was just a bit better. Two points better.

That connection is named Raúl Allegre, and his three field goals Saturday—a 32-yarder kicked early in the first quarter, another 32-yarder kicked late in the third quarter, and the decisive 52-yarder kicked early in the fourth quarter—added up to all the scoring the Longhorns could contrive.

Allegre is a native of Coahuila, Mexico, and he came to Shelton, Washington, high school as part of an exchange program. His goal: learn English. But somewhere along the way, he also learned to kick field goals, and after

Eric Dickerson (19) confounded tacklers throughout the Southwest Conference during his playing career at SMU, 1979–82. Courtesy of Southern Methodist University Athletics.

spending two years at the University of Montana and then transferring to the University of Texas, he proved to the Mustangs Saturday that he has learned his lessons well.

Although Allegre once kicked a 54-yarder for Montana, his shorter kicks at Texas Stadium left Longhorn grid boss Fred Akers feeling on top of the world.

"The result was as satisfying as any I can remember," said the embattled Akers, who keeps reading about how his job is in jeopardy. "It was certainly a big win coming off of last week [when Arkansas just dismembered Texas, 42–11]. This puts us back in the hunt."

The Longhorns had the kind of field position to beat SMU as badly as Arkansas beat Texas, but remember—this Texas offense just barely lives up to the name. For much of the time, it was just gosh-awful against SMU, although, of course, the Mustang defense had something to do with that.

"We saw a truly great defensive game today," analyzed SMU coach Ron Meyer at the finish. "Field position was the key the whole time."

And Texas, thanks to some great punting at times by John Goodson (he had kicks of 53, 54, and 57 yards, and one of his punts went out of bounds at the SMU 3-yard line) and the intimidating presence of Sims and a few others, had field position from the word *go*.

Sims knocked SMU's great tailback Eric Dickerson loose from the football on the third play of the game and recovered the fumble himself at the SMU 21-yard line. Although Texas could gain only 5 yards on its next three plays, Allegre was able to put the 'Horns in front with the first field goal, kicked with 12:19 still remaining in the first quarter.

It was a sign of things to come.

Except for that one touchdown pass, Sims and William Graham and Bruce Scholtz and Mark Weber and Jeff Leiding had an answer for just about everything the explosive Mustangs tried, and more often than not, the answer was delivered in a violent, crushing fashion.

Sims had 11 solo tackles (15 stops in all), and 6 of his tackles resulted in 22 yards of losses for the Mustangs. Graham was in on 12 tackles—9 of them unassisted—and he supplied the final crusher against the Mustangs, going high to intercept McIlhenny's long desperation bid for victory in the final seconds. Weber was in on 9 tackles and also recovered a fumble; Scholtz had 9 stops, and 3 of them were behind the line of scrimmage; and Leiding was in on 10 tackles and also had an interception.

Faced with such a conspiracy of defense, the Mustangs could get but 78 yards rushing and 205 yards in

Kenneth Sims (77), Bruce Scholtz (51), and Jeff Leiding (60) contributed to the fierce Texas defense in the early 1980s. Courtesy of University of Texas Athletics.

total offense. They had been averaging 296.2 yards rushing and 398.8 yards in total offense.

Eric Dickerson, the conference's leading rusher with an average of 135.3 yards per game, managed all of 33 yards on 13 carries—and had those fumbles. Craig James, averaging 99 yards rushing per game, could get but 56 yards on 17 trips. After his several sacks had been averaged in, McIlhenny finished with minus 31 yards overland.

Truly, daylight was in short supply for Ron Meyer's flying red horses Saturday.

In almost as short supply, that is, as field position. In the first half, the Mustangs began their offensive efforts at their own 19-, 19-, 3-, 20-, 17-, 13-, and 33-yard lines—and only twice did they cross midfield, and never did they get beyond the Texas 35. In the second half, they started at their own 9-, 20-, 22-, 23-, 20-, 41-, 27-, and 28-yard lines, and except for the touchdown pass, they never crossed that field.

"The Texas defense was simply outstanding. It seemed that on every play their line had great support from the linebackers and defensive backs," said Craig James. Added McIlhenny, who managed to complete 5 of 15 passes while throwing most of the time under relentless pressure, "Field position killed us. We started so many times inside the 20. Things they were doing and throwing at us defeated our game plan. We just couldn't get the running game on track all day."

Texas, meanwhile, had just as much trouble on offense, but thanks to much more favorable field position, the Longhorns—and Allegre—managed to win the day. Texas could get but six first downs, only 133 yards rushing, and only 44 yards passing. Quarterback Rick McIvor could complete only 3 of 11 passes. Texas' leading footman, tailback A. J. Jones, could get but 68 yards. And much of the time, remember, the Longhorns were beginning their maneuvers near midfield or inside SMU territory.

But the Longhorns were already ahead by a 3–0 margin, and play had moved to the midpoint of the second quarter before Texas managed its initial first down of the game. And the 'Horns only had two first downs at halftime. On their first four possessions of the game, it was one, two, three, kick, and that routine continued for the most part throughout the afternoon. But five of those times, that kick was a field goal attempt by Allegre, and three of those kicks were good, and so the 'Horns survived.

Quarterback Lance McIlhenny led SMU to two Southwest Conference championships. Courtesy of Southern Methodist University Athletics.

"I had been sick and didn't practice all week," said Allegre, a civil engineering student who carries a grade-point average of 3.41. "I came out and kicked some yesterday and a little before the game. That was all the practice I had."

In his case, maybe no practice makes near perfect.

After kicking his first-quarter field goal, he did miss with 40 seconds left before intermission, after the Longhorns had moved 17 yards in seven plays to the SMU 33. That was a 50-yard try and fell far short.

On Texas' second possession of the second half, the Longhorns started at their own 47 and drove to the SMU 8-yard line in five plays as substitute tailback Rodney Tate—Texas' fastest back, who gained 55 yards for the afternoon—had runs of 23, 12, and 5 yards. But then, typically, the Longhorns started fouling up, and Allegre wound up trying to kick a field goal from the 27 and missed.

That was his last miss.

After Leiding had intercepted a McIlhenny pass at the SMU 32 and Mike Luck had fumbled the opportunity right back at the Mustang 22, Dickerson committed his second fumble on a fourth-and-1 play at the SMU 42. Weber recovered for Texas, and the 'Horns drove 27 yards in five plays before Allegre kicked a 32-yard field goal with 18 seconds left in the third quarter. The key play on that drive was a pass of 28 yards from the erratic McIvor to Maurice McCloney. McCloney fumbled at the end of his catch and run at the SMU 14 but managed to get the ball back after a mad scramble.

The Longhorns started their next possession at the SMU 39 after Craig James, filling in as the Mustangs' punter for the injured Eric Kaifes, shanked a kick and got only 21 yards out of it. Although Texas could get but 4 yards in three plays, Allegre went back to the kicking line and booted true from 52 yards away.

So the Longhorns had a 9–0 margin with 11:37 left in the game, and then SMU—for the only time during the game—showed just how explosive it can be. Two runs by Dickerson gained a first down out to the SMU 30. Then McIlhenny faked a handoff, faded, and threw deep. Jackie Wilson got two steps behind Vance Bedford, made the catch without breaking stride, and ran untouched to the end zone. Eddie Garcia kicked the extra point.

"We were in a man coverage, and I bumped him and he broke. I saw the football and just fell down as I cut. It was a good pass and a good catch," said Bedford, who then added, "I had confidence all along that we would get enough points to win. It meant too much."

He was right. SMU got one more first down the rest of the way, but the Longhorns got three quarterback sacks, and finally they got Graham's interception to seal everything with 28 seconds left. For Texas, it was a case of doing what comes naturally. The Longhorns have not lost to the Mustangs in Dallas since 1965, and they did not lose here Saturday, and as a result, it looks now like a wide-open race to the wire.

JANUARY 2, 1982

TEXAS TIPS TIDE, 14–12: STEERS' COTTON BOWL COMEBACK FOILS ALABAMA

DALLAS, Tex.—The jinx still lives, even unto 1982. And Alabama's Crimson Tide still has not defeated Alabama coach Bear Bryant's old nemesis, the Texas Longhorns.

For their latest failure, they can blame the most improbable of New Year's Day bowl heroes, once unwanted Texas quarterback Robert Brewer.

Down by 10 points and virtually written off as a hopeless case, the Brewer-sparked Longhorns staged not one but two electrifying touchdown drives in the fourth quarter to defeat the Tide and break the old Bear's heart, 14–12, here Friday in the 46th annual Cotton Bowl Classic.

On those fateful touchdown drives, forged against the nation's No. 3 team, Brewer did things nobody ever dreamed he could do when he was a high school quarterback just up the road in the Dallas suburb of Richardson, where major college recruiters managed to ignore him en masse.

Cold shouldered, he decided to walk on at Texas, his daddy's alma mater, and there he began his Longhorn career as the team's seventh-ranking quarterback. But in the fourth quarter of this savagely contested showdown Friday, with the shadows beginning to lengthen on a cool but sunny afternoon, with 'Bama battling to give Bryant a chance at just one more national championship, young Robert Brewer proved his right to be called No. 1. He made plays that would have challenged even the talents of such former Texas quarterbacking greats as Bobby Layne and James Street.

He scored Texas' first touchdown on an adroit 30-yard bolt up the middle after scattering the normally bullet-proof Tide defense with a series of artful passes.

One of those passes, an 8-yarder to flanker Donnie Little, produced the initial first down in the eight-play, 60-yard scoring drive. But it was the third play of the next series that perhaps turned the tide against the Tide.

Facing a critical third-and-17 situation at the Texas 44, Brewer ignored the bodies crashing down all about him and winged a 26-yard strike that little Herkie Walls fielded between two defenders at the Alabama 30-yard line.

Three plays later, on a third-and-10 challenge, Brewer called time out and visited a moment on the sideline with Texas coach Fred Akers. He then went back to the battle line, took the snap, dropped back a step or two as if to pass, and then raced forward through acres of daylight all the way to the end zone.

"Robert was alert and saw that our third-down play was not as good as their third-down defense. So he called time out. I called the play. It was a hell of a play," said Akers.

It was also the longest Cotton Bowl run from scrimmage since 1977.

That touchdown, scored with 10:22 left in the game, brought all those Longhorn partisans packed into the Cotton Bowl throng of 73,243 roaring to their feet. After enduring three quarters of close calls and frustration, the Longhorns were all a quiver, as if goaded by an electric prod. They sensed Alabama was a tiring team. They remembered their own traditions, especially against Bryant and the Crimson Tide, and they caught the sweet smell of victory in the air.

Brewer again almost did it all himself.

The Longhorns got the ball back at their own 20 with 5:59 left in the game. Two passes fell incomplete; it was third and 10, now or perhaps never.

Back again went Brewer to pass, and here came the raging Tide, which earlier had been so successful in sacking the Texas quarterback in crucial situations. This time he beat them.

Just before the sack arrived, he floated a ball deep and true across the field toward the east sideline, where

During Fred Akers's tenure as coach of the Texas Longhorns, 1977–86, he posted two undefeated regular seasons and notched two conference championships. Courtesy of University of Texas Athletics.

big tight end Lawrence Sampleton and an Alabama defender were running stride for stride. The defender was right there. But it was a soft pass, easily catchable, and Sampleton is 6-foot-6, 234 pounds, and strong. He won the battle for possession and fell to earth with a first down at the Alabama 43—a fantastic 37-yard gain.

Most witnesses realized then that Texas was going to get no worse than a game-tying field goal out of this last big opportunity. But a field goal was not on Texas' mind. Fullback Terry Orr lost a yard, but Brewer immediately got 10 on a pass to Rodney Tate, and then Orr went diving for a first down at the 31. Here came the sack pack again, led by relentless end Russ Wood, dropping Brewer for a loss of 6 yards. But Brewer's reply was overwhelming—a 19-yard pass to Sampleton in the left flat. The fired-up Sampleton caught the ball at about the 24 and carried the defender all the way to the 18 before going down.

Two plays later, Brewer went upstairs again, hitting Little for a first down at the 8.

And then, almost before the Tide could get its bearings, Brewer was giving the ball to the fast, bullish, 220-pound Orr on a trap up the middle. The Abilene sophomore found his hole, cut to the left against the grain, and went into the end zone standing up, winding up the 11-play, 80-yard, game-winning drive.

Brewer, voted the game's most valuable offensive player, accounted for 136 of the 154 yards Texas actually had to gain to score its two touchdowns. He completed his last four passes on the game's decisive drive for 76 yards.

After Orr scored his touchdown, Texas partisans exploded with a roar that resounded like a clap of thunder on a steamy afternoon. Disbelieving underdogs at the start, they were ahead of the Tide at last. Kicker Raúl Allegre's conversion gave them a 14–10 margin—out of field goal range. And now only 2:05 remained.

Well, that could have been enough. Joey Jones fielded Allegre's kickoff and returned it 61 yards—a record Cotton Bowl return—and until sophomore Mike Luck broke through the Alabama blocking wall and cut him down, Longhorn hearts stood still.

The clock showed 1:54 left, and 'Bama was at the Texas 38—plenty of time and not much distance for a team armed with the likes of Walter Lewis.

Now what you must understand is that what Robert Brewer did for Texas on the first day of the new year, Walter Lewis almost did for Alabama. Lewis, a sophomore whose main contribution in the Cotton Bowl game last year resulted in Baylor's only points (a safety that came about when Bruin tackle Tommy Tabor trapped Lewis in the 'Bama end zone), is not the first black quarterback Bryant has had at Alabama, but he is the first black quarterback to make much of an impact.

Friday, he made about as much of an impact as Texas and Fred Akers could stand. He took over at starting quarterback, Alan Gray had fumbled away 'Bama's first big threat at the Texas 9-yard line, and on the team's third possession, he made the big runs and threw the passes that devoured most of the yardage on the seven-play, 82-yard touchdown drive. The touchdown itself was scored on a 6-yard throw from Lewis to Jesse Bendross, and it came as the young passer, strong of arm and hiccup quick, scrambled around—first out of this Longhorn's arms and then away from that one.

On that drive, Lewis had a 17-yard run, a 37-yard completion to tight end Bart Krout, and a 6-yard run that came just before he threw for the touchdown, scored with 8:49 left in the second quarter. Peter Kim kicked the extra point.

Then late in the third quarter, still holding that 7–0 advantage, the Tide gained great field position at the Alabama 48, and Lewis quickly hustled them down to the Texas 7-yard line. He did it mainly with four plays—a 22-yard run on which he almost broke for a touchdown, a 6-yard run, a big third-down 16-yard completion to the elusive Bendross, and finally a little shovel pass that Krout turned into a 7-yard gain to the 7.

But Krout's run left Alabama facing fourth down and still needing 2 yards for new life, so here came Kim to kick the field goal that gave Bryant's guys their 10-point lead with 12:27 left in the game.

But Brewer and Little and Walls and Sampleton and Orr had had answers for all that, of course, and now Texas had a four-point lead, but Alabama, after Jones's great return, had the ball at the Longhorn 38 with just enough time. Walter Lewis, the early game hero who had been forced to yield center stage to Robert Brewer, was going to emerge as top gun after all.

Only he didn't.

On the telltale first-down play, 'Bama tried to get everything in one huge, all-consuming gulp. Lewis retreated and then fired deep—into double coverage on end Tim Clark at the goal line. Texas strong safety William Graham timed his move just right and intercepted at the Texas 1-yard line.

Alabama had two timeouts left and used them to give the Longhorns one more anxious moment. They left the orange shirts facing a fourth-down, must-punt situation from their own 4-yard line with 56 seconds left.

John Goodson, who had almost suffered a couple of blocked punts earlier in the game, went deep into his end zone; fielded the snap; raced right, devouring a few precious seconds; and then stepped out of the end zone, deliberately giving Alabama a safety but winning the privilege of making a free kick from his own 20.

If the Tide could have returned that kick deep into Texas territory, Kim could have won that game with a last-second field goal. But the return only reached the Alabama 40, and two plays later, Walter Lewis went down at the 41 as the clock ticked off its final second.

Texas won the game by playing mistake-free

Texas defensive end Kiki DeAyala takes down an Aggie quarterback. Courtesy of University of Texas Athletics.

Some happy Baylor fans, including one of my daughters, cheer the Bears as they upset unbeaten, No. 5 Arkansas in Waco, November 6, 1982. Courtesy of *Dave Campbell's Texas Football Magazine*.

football—no turnovers. Alabama was guilty of only two turnovers but both were devastating—Gray's fumble after a first-down 6-yard run to the Texas 9-yard line early in the game and Graham's brilliant interception with less than two minutes left.

Gray directed his team 71 yards in nine plays on Alabama's first possession before short-circuiting the drive himself. Tackle Ralph Darnell recovered the loose pigskin, and upstairs in the press box, Texas publicity man Jones Ramsey remarked to his Alabama counterpart Charley Thornton, "That fumble was recovered by [Kenneth] Sims's replacement."

Sims, the Longhorns' greatest defender, missed the game because of a knee injury but nevertheless made his presence felt on the sideline, constantly calling on his teammates to find the keys to victory. And finally they did.

Texas, which finished with 21 first downs, 158 yards rushing, and 359 yards in total offense, seldom failed to earn at least one first down when it gained possession, but in the first half, it could only count advances to the Alabama 30- and 27-yard lines as its best moves. The Tide defense, paced by linebacker Robbie Jones—voted the game's top defensive player—was just too tough when it counted. Finally, with 78 seconds left before intermission, Allegre tried a 50-yard field goal that hung in the wind and fell short.

Alabama also found itself able to gain ground consistently in the first two quarters, moving into Texas territory on its first three possessions. But only the 82-yard thrust climaxed by Lewis's touchdown throw to Bendross paid dividends.

In the second half, however, the Tide got inside the Texas 40 only on the trip that yielded Kim's field goal. In those final 30 minutes, ends Eric Holle and Kiki DeAyala and linebackers Jeff Leiding and Bruce Scholtz kept making plays that rubbed out 'Bama's best efforts.

Lewis, with 79 rushing and 122 yards upstairs, was

'Bama's biggest producer. Bendross caught five of his passes for 78 yards.

Darryl Clark paced Texas' rushing with 58 yards, and A. J. Jones had 57. Brewer completed 12 of 21 passes for 201 yards, with Little catching 7 of them for 92 yards.

Although Alabama finished with 15 first downs and 307 yards in total offense, Bryant's team could get only five first downs and 106 of those yards in the final 30 minutes. "I thought it was a great second-half performance by our defensive unit," said Akers, who started the season under fire from unhappy exes and ended the season with the praise of Bear Bryant ringing in his ears.

"I would like to congratulate coach Akers," said the Alabama legend. "He and his staff and players did a great job. They dominated the fourth quarter and did everything they needed to do to win the game in the final minutes. They just whipped us in the fourth quarter. They're a very well-coached team."

And how about that "Texas jinx," Coach? After all, the Longhorns have never lost in football to Alabama, and they stand 7-1-1 against Bryant-coached teams (3–0 in their last bowl meetings with Alabama and Bryant).

"Naw, I don't think there is a Texas whammy on Alabama," Bryant replied. "Their players and coaches beat us—not a whammy."

If there was a whammy Friday, it came embodied in a once unknown kid named Robert Brewer.

NOVEMBER 21, 1982

PONIES LAND IN COTTON AFTER 17–17 STANDOFF WITH HOGS

IRVING, Tex.—Forced to settle for a come-from-behind 17–17 tie with Arkansas at Texas Stadium Saturday afternoon, the No. 2–ranked SMU Mustangs lost their perfect record for 1982 but won everything else—mainly, an undisputed Southwest Conference championship and a trip to the Cotton Bowl.

The Mustangs, pressure proof to the very end, staged an 80-yard touchdown drive late in the fourth quarter to get the points they needed to pull even with the fired-up Razorbacks, nail down their title, and win the right to play once-beaten Pittsburgh in Big D on New Year's Day.

Although the enormously disappointed Razorbacks still have a game to play against Texas in Austin on December 4, they did not leave the field completely empty-handed. They won an invitation to the Bluebonnet Bowl, where they probably will play Florida on New Year's Eve.

The outright championship was SMU's second in a row. Thus the Mustangs became the first Southwest Conference team to win back-to-back undisputed crowns since Texas in 1972–73 and the first private school in the conference to manage that feat since an earlier breed of Mustangs won in 1947–48.

Cool, poised Lance McIlhenny directed the long SMU drive that made all the difference. He threw the passes—including one that resulted in a hotly disputed interference call against Arkansas—that gained most of the yardage. And he scored the touchdown on the eighth play of that drive, squirming across from 2 yards out and enabling SMU's great seniors to realize their season-long dream of successfully defending their title and winning the bowl trip that was denied them a year ago because SMU was on NCAA probation.

Apparently, it takes a probation to stop the Mustangs. Certainly 10 teams couldn't do it this year. And while the Razorbacks did manage to hold them to a draw, they almost failed too. In the last minute and a half, with the score tied at 17 all, the Mustangs drove 52 yards in six plays to get into position for Jeff Harrell to try to win

Eric Dickerson plunders the Arkansas defense. Courtesy of Southern Methodist University Athletics.

the game with a 52-yard field goal with seven seconds left on the clock.

Harrell's effort was way short. If it had been good, that would have been too much. But all that did was prove that coach Bobby Collins's guys are human after all. They don't always get what they want. But they do seem to get what they have to have.

Once again destiny suited up for them Saturday, as it did in their close, hard-fought games against TCU, Baylor, Texas, and Texas Tech. And when it meant the most, destiny took a decisive hand—in the form of a whopping 40-yard pass interference penalty that Porker coach Lou Holtz and his players will go to their graves claiming was a bad call.

To set the stage, Arkansas had just marched 76 yards in 15 plays before getting a 27-yard field goal from Martin Smith, and then on its very next possession, it had chugged 77 yards in 15 plays to break the 10–10 tie and move out in front by seven points.

Gary Anderson scored the touchdown, his second of the game, on a fine 3-yard run after setting up the touchdown with a marvelous catch of a 24-yard pass at the SMU 5-yard line.

Behind by seven points with six minutes left to play, the Mustangs went back on the attack from their own 20. On their two previous possessions, they had gained 7 yards on three plays and been forced to punt, then they had gained 6 yards on three plays and punted again. One more such exercise in futility would spell curtains for the Red and Blue.

On first down, McIlhenny kept the ball himself on SMU's deadly option play and gained 6 yards. But then here came Arkansas end Bobby Shantz breaking through to toss Eric Dickerson for a 4-yard loss.

So it was third and 8 at the SMU 22, and just about everything—the game, the season, the championship, the Cotton Bowl trip—was riding on the next play. McIlhenny took the snap, took a step back, and quickly threw a pass to Bobby Leach, who was running what coaches call a "fade" route.

The defender was right there when the ball got there, but Leach managed to make the catch at the SMU 43 a split second before he went out of bounds. It was a close call.

The next one was even closer—and much more controversial.

SMU mentor Bobby Collins celebrates another Mustang win. Courtesy of Southern Methodist University Athletics.

McIlhenny backed up, faked a short pass to the right, then threw deep toward end Jackie Wilson, who was speeding down the west sideline. Nathan Jones had him well covered. The ball appeared to be too tall for both receiver and defender. If so, an "uncatchable pass" does not elicit a flag, but a flag went down. It was thrown by Horton Nesrsta, a former Rice football star who now lives at Marble Falls.

"From where I stood, it was offensive pass interference all the way," said Holtz. "When he threw the flag, I thought it was 15 yards and loss of down. Our guy was going for the ball with both hands in the air. Their receiver had his hands on Jones's back. Did the official offer an explanation? He said it was pass interference on our guy. That was it."

Later, Holtz called it one of the most "blatant" cases of offensive pass interference he had ever seen.

Said Jones through his tears in the dressing room, "All I saw was the flag when I got up. I thought it was on him. I went over and asked the official if it was on me and he said, 'Yeah.' I was reaching for the ball with both hands. Neither one of us could have caught it, but I would have caught it before he would have. The ball went 2 or 3 inches over my hands."

Jones, a sophomore from Texarkana, said he was trying to make a play on the ball until Wilson stepped on the calf of his leg, forcing him to slow down.

According to one reporter who was standing on the sideline near the play, an official came running up and said, "Was it offensive interference?" And Nesrsta replied, "No, defensive."

When first interviewed in the dressing room, Wilson said, "I can't say it was a catchable ball. He had me covered all the way. When I first saw the flag—well, at first I thought it had to be on him. Then it got real quiet, and I didn't know what the call was going to be. He slowed down and stuck his hand in [trying to reach the ball], and then I just shot up his back."

Later on, Wilson declared, "I thought it was a proper call. I was going all out for the ball and the defender was blocking me. Just in case, I was screaming and hollering and pointing at him, and that helped the ref throw the flag. I know that it was a big play, and I'm just happy it went our way."

Russell Carter. Courtesy of Southern Methodist University Athletics.

Having won that decision at the Arkansas 17-yard line, the Mustangs turned first to Dickerson to get a first down at the 7, and then the plucky McIlhenny gained the last 7 yards all by himself on two carries.

Bobby Collins could have gotten greedy and gone for two points and a victory that would have preserved the Mustangs' perfect record and perhaps their chance to yet wind up No. 1 after the bowl games. But he sent Jeff Harrell out to tie the game with a simple conversion.

"We didn't give the two-point [conversion] very much thought," he said later. "We thought there was enough time left in the game to where our defense could stop them and get the ball back for us. It almost worked out too.

"I have to give a lot of credit to Arkansas," he added. "They played a tremendous ball game."

Arkansas, which enjoyed delicious field position for much of the first half, scored first by driving 50 yards in 10 plays on its second possession of the game. A superb 32-yard punt return by the elusive Anderson enabled them to start at midfield, and they kept chugging away until they reached their promised land.

Tom Jones, who quarterbacked Arkansas most of the way, had a pair of completions on that drive, a 15-yard personal foul call against SMU also helped, and Jessie Clark's 3-yard plunge on a fourth-and-1 crisis saved the drive at the SMU 9. Anderson then took a pitchout and scored standing up from the 3. Smith's kick left Arkansas with a seven-point lead with 4:05 left in the opening quarter.

A few moments later, Billy Ray Smith grabbed a Dickerson fumble at the SMU 47, and Arkansas drove 37 yards in six plays to the SMU 10 before having to summon Smith for a short field goal attempt. Mustang cornerback Russell Carter came roaring in to block the kick cleanly, and at the finish, that muffed opportunity was there to haunt the Porkers.

SMU finally started punching all the right buttons with 9:28 left in the first half. The Mustangs started at their own 35 and reached the Arkansas end zone five minutes and 31 seconds later, after McIlhenny had completed a 13-yard pass to Gary Smith and then had saved everything with a rather miraculous 21-yard run to the Arkansas 38 on a third-and-17 situation.

The Mustangs had to overcome another severe challenge on that drive on a fourth-down play at the Arkansas 29. Dickerson got loose on a 12-yard scamper around left end, and then that same explosive Mustang scored the touchdown himself three plays later on a 6-yard run around the same side.

SMU moved ahead for the first time on its first possession of the second half, driving 41 yards in 11 plays before getting a career-best 49-yard field goal from Harrell. McIlhenny—who else?—also made the big plays on that drive, completing an 11-yard pass to Gary Smith and then getting loose for a 7-yard gain on a third-and-3 challenge at the Arkansas 45. Another 12-yard shot to Smith got the Mustangs down to the Arkansas 27, but on the next third-down play, Billy Ray Smith sacked McIlhenny for an 8-yard loss, forcing Harrell to do his thing. Which he did.

But when the Razorbacks staged those two long, time-consuming drives—76 yards in 15 plays that used up 6 minutes and 28 seconds before Smith kicked his 27-yard field goal and then 77 yards in 15 plays that knocked 7 minutes and 4 seconds off the clock before

Craig James makes tracks against Arkansas. Courtesy of Southern Methodist University Athletics.

Anderson's touchdown run moved the Hogs ahead—it appeared the Mustangs finally had run out of miracles.

But McIlhenny and Leach and miracles just seem to go together, and when they got together there in the final moments and combined with that controversial 40-yard penalty, the Mustangs had all they needed to win the tie that they were hailing as a "victory" at the finish.

Incidentally, for the Mustangs to sew up a crown and a Cotton Bowl trip with a tie on the scoreboard at the end of the season is almost, for them, doing what comes naturally. They did the same thing in 1947, tying TCU, 19–19, and finishing 9-0-1 for the season, and then they did the very same thing again the next year, tying the Frogs, 7–7, in their season finale.

"I have mixed emotions about not being 11–0, but we accomplished our number-one goal of going to the Cotton Bowl," said Craig James, who had 72 yards on 15 carries and also punted for a 47.5-yard average. He finished with 938 yards rushing for the season and with 3,742 yards for his career—third best in conference history.

Although forced to settle for fewer than 100 yards in his farewell appearance at Texas Stadium (he had 81 yards on 18 tries), Dickerson finished as the league's new all-time career rushing champion. He had 4,450 yards for his four years at SMU, or 7 more yards than Earl Campbell gained in the same number of years for the Texas Longhorns. However, Dickerson failed in his attempt to break Campbell's single-season rushing mark of 1,744 yards. He finished with 1,617 yards for 1982.

"We didn't win, but we didn't lose either. I hope people remember that," the Mustangs' great meal-ticket tailback said at the finish. "Arkansas deserves a lot of credit. They and Baylor were the toughest defenses we played all year."

On the other side of the field, Arkansas' Anderson was brilliant in what the Hogs took as a defeat. He rushed for 37 yards, caught five passes for another 82 steps, and returned three punts for 35 yards.

"We played a good game," he said. "They got the big break [the penalty] at the end that decided it. The official called what he saw. I guess it was a good call. He made it. Our hopes of the Cotton Bowl are gone. We'll never have another shot at it."

Darryl Bowles wound up as Arkansas' leading

footman, getting 53 yards on just eight carries. Tom Jones completed 7 of his 15 passes for 76 yards, and Arkansas' No. 2 quarterback Brad Taylor had 2 of 3, including a 45-yard strike to swift Derek Holloway that did much to get the Hogs into position for Smith's game-tying 27-yard field goal kicked on the final play of the third quarter. Taylor also punted four times for a 48.5-yard average, and Holloway returned three kickoffs for 93 yards as Arkansas got a little the better of it in the kicking game.

But nobody got the better of Lance McIlhenny, who rushed for 43 yards and completed seven of his nine passes for 98 yards. Although Arkansas had more first downs (20 to 16) and more total offense (330 yards to SMU's 294), more offensive snaps (75 to 59) and more time of possession, McIlhenny's presence equalized the books for the Mustangs.

"We're a little disappointed about the national ranking [maybe falling in the polls because of the tie], but we'll easily settle for the tie and the Cotton Bowl," said Sir Lance, putting everything in perspective. "It will be such a relief to go down to Austin for the Texas-Arkansas game and just relax and be a spectator instead of having to worry about the game."

JANUARY 2, 1985
FLUTIE'S FOOT SOLDIERS OVERRUN UH, 45–28: HEISMAN TROPHY WINNER CHECKED, COOGS CHECKMATED

DALLAS, Tex.—It turns out the Boston College Eagles not only can fly high; they also can run low and exceedingly well. And while they can strike like a terrible swift sword while making the most of Heisman Trophy winner Doug Flutie's arm, they can romp and stomp even after Flutie has been stopped.

They proved all that here Tuesday in the 49th annual Cotton Bowl Classic, which as usual was played in weather best associated with the North Pole. A crowd of 56,522 braved the elements, at least for a while.

With the temperature reading 32 degrees and the wind-chill factor pegged at 10 degrees, the Eagles survived a third-quarter scare and buried the Cougars, 45–28.

Although Flutie the magician could manage but two completions for a mere 14 yards during the final 30 minutes of combat, BC still rolled up the most points ever scored in a Cotton Bowl game.

Of course, the nimble Eagle quarterback earlier had burned Bill Yeoman's team with three first-half touchdown passes while tying a 47-year-old record for the number of touchdown passes in a Cotton Bowl game. He also had set up a fourth touchdown with a 27-yard run to the Houston 2-yard line.

When fullback Steve Strachan crashed over for a touchdown on the next play, the Eagles moved out in front of the Cougars, 31–7, with fewer than two minutes left in the first half.

Then for the next 20 minutes—until the clock showed a bit more than 11 minutes left in the game—the Cougars played like Yeoman had hoped they would play all afternoon.

They drove for a pair of touchdowns and turned an interception into an instant third score and made it a 31–28 game. But then, just as things were getting tight, tense, and *very* interesting, they went from snarling big cats back to kittens and wound up in the same sad shape as Texas and TCU—beaten to a frazzle on bowl day.

Texas lost to Iowa, 55–17. TCU lost to West Virginia, 31–14. Houston lost to Boston College, 45–28. However you spell *relief*, the Southwest Conference can use some.

"Flutie is just an excellent football player, an excellent athlete," summed up a weary Yeoman. "But it's obvious Boston College has more than just Flutie."

Flutie opened the scoring with a 63-yard touchdown pass to flanker Kelvin Martin the second time the Eagles gained possession and then fired an 8-yard touchdown strike to tailback Troy Stradford and a 13-yarder to split end Gerard Phelan before intermission. But the visitors turned more and more to Stradford, Strachan, and their revved-up offensive line as the game moved into the telltale stages.

Stradford, a 5-foot-8, 183-pound junior with speed, rushed for a whopping 196 yards on 20 carries while taking advantage of some good holes up front and some erratic Cougar tackling.

Strachan carried 23 times for 91 yards, scored two touchdowns on runs of 2 and 4 yards, and out-polled the more celebrated Flutie in balloting for the game's top offensive player.

Stradford saved his best for last. With the Eagles out in front by a 38–28 margin with fewer than four minutes left, he got loose on a 37-yard run to the Cougar 18-yard line and then scored on an end run on the next play, leaving the Cougars down, out, and frozen stiff.

They had no one but themselves to blame for many of their problems. To be sure, they had their delicious moments—Earl Allen's 98-yard kickoff return for Houston's first touchdown and a new Cotton Bowl kickoff return record, a 38-yard Gerald Landry pass to tight end Carl Hilton followed three plays later by a 15-yard touchdown pass to wideout Larry Shepherd for Houston's second touchdown (scored with 22 seconds left in the first half), a 33-yard catch and run by Hilton followed by a 33-yard run by fullback Raymond Tate that set up Tate's 2-yard touchdown run in the third quarter, and finally, with 3:10 left in the third quarter, an interception and 26-yard touchdown return by free safety Audrey McMillian.

McMillian's return of a pass Flutie should never have thrown—he was about to be sacked by end Gerald

Houston defensive end T. J. Turner (95) recorded 52 tackles in his freshman year, the most for a first-year player in school history. Courtesy of University of Houston Athletics.

Turner and threw in desperation—brought the Cougars to within three points of a tie, and left Yeoman's representatives with enough momentum for three teams.

And when they got the ball the next time early in the fourth quarter, it appeared they would use that momentum well.

Landry, who had a few good moments and a lot of bad ones, came up with one of his good ones: a 14-yard scrambling run to the Houston 48. Tate then broke several tackles and ran to the BC 30. The Cougars were on the move.

And then they weren't. Because a flag fell on Tate's run, a Cougar was ruled guilty of a clip, the run was rubbed out, and Houston was penalized back to the UH 38-yard line. Then came a holding penalty. Good-bye, momentum.

Punting into that cold north wind, Lonnie Stokes managed only a 12-yarder. The Eagles took over at the Houston 43, and while the Cougars managed to get off that hook momentarily when Flutie missed connections with a wide-open Phelan (it would have been an easy touchdown), there was no stopping them after the next Cougar punt.

Starting at the UH 44 that time, the Eagles stayed strictly with their infantry for nine plays while driving for the touchdown that put them 10 points ahead. Strahan carried six times for 31 of those yards, usually inside the tackles, often behind the blocking of tackle Mark McDonald, who gave Cougar standout T. J. Turner a hard time.

"When it was 31–28, I was kind of encouraged," said Yeoman. "But then we got those penalties. That was pretty severe and at a point when our momentum was great."

But the Cougars hurt themselves so often with poor execution, poor tackling, silly mistakes that resulted in penalties, and flagrant breakdowns in what had been a good pass defense that they really did not deserve to win.

They were both lucky and unlucky.

They were lucky in the second quarter when the Eagles zoomed from their own 2-yard line to the UH 24 and then Stradford fumbled the ball forward all the way to the Cougar 1-yard line, where UH cornerback Greg Purell recovered to stave off disaster.

But they were unlucky later in that quarter when a deflected pass hit a Cougar who was prone on the ground. The ball bounced up, and cornerback Todd Russell intercepted for BC and returned 14 yards to the Houston 39. The Eagles scored in six plays.

"I think Flutie is everything everyone expected, but he's got a great cast with him," said Cougar defensive coordinator Don Todd, who saw his pupils surrender 533 yards, a new Cotton Bowl total offense record (BC's 353 yards overland was the second-highest infantry total for a Cotton Bowl team).

"That offensive line was the best we've come up against all year," continued Todd. "They really know how to protect him."

The final figures gave Flutie 180 yards on 13 completions and 37 attempts for the three touchdowns, but he also surrendered two interceptions. "I was able to grip the ball [despite the cold], but it was hard to judge the wind," said the Heisman winner. "On the first interception, I just didn't put enough on the ball. But with the wind I also overthrew some open receivers. It was not one of my better days."

But it was good enough, especially when his rushing total (51 yards on just four carries, and most of those carries came at highly opportune times) is considered.

Cougar turnovers contributed to BC's early splurge. A fumble by running back Mat Pierson at the Houston 28 resulted in a four-play Eagle touchdown drive in the first quarter. An interception by Tony Thursman gave the visitors possession at the UH 15, and they used that opportunity to get a 31-yard field goal from Kevin Snow late in the first quarter.

Snow also kicked true after each of the Eagles' six touchdowns—a new record in that department.

The Cougars finished with 15 first downs, 187 yards rushing, and 154 passing. Landry was 9 for 29 with one touchdown and two interceptions and was sacked four times. He missed the first 9 aerial attempts, and some of them were aimed at receivers who were wide open.

In short, playing in the Flutie shadow, the nervous Landry was hardly at his best, but the Eagle defense deserves ample credit too.

Boston College coach Jack Bicknell, jubilant in victory, suggested the "very slippery" turf hurt Landry and the Cougars more than it did the Eagles, but he also applauded his defense, which was paced by defensive MVP Bill Romanowski, who had 11 solo tackles.

"Everything with us has always been offense, offense, offense and Flutie, Flutie, Flutie," he said. "But the defense showed today they could really play well too. We have a lot of good players on our team."

They had too many good ones on New Year's Day for the Cougars.

JANUARY 2, 1986

A&M SMOTHERS BO JACKSON, AUBURN, 36–16

DALLAS, Tex.—The hairy-chested Texas Aggies brought in the new year here Wednesday in much the same fashion they wound up the old one, with a slam and a bang that added up to a huge victory on the scoreboard and a "Gee, ain't we got fun?" celebration in the stands.

Bidding for a high place in the final polls that will establish 1985 college football's Top Ten, the Aggies demolished Auburn, 36–16, in the Cotton Bowl's golden anniversary game, which was played, appropriately enough, in golden sunshine.

A crowd of 73,137, made up for the most part of A&M partisans joyously on hand to watch their favorites play in the Big D's big bowl for the first time in 18 years, saw the Aggies give Auburn a beating that now and then must have reminded them of what coach Jackie Sherrill's team gave Texas in its regular season finale.

However, that was not quite the case.

The Aggies turned the Longhorns every which way but loose in routing them, 42–10. They dominated the line of scrimmage both on offense and on defense against Auburn (as they did against Texas), they made a marvelous goal-line stand against Auburn (as they did against Texas), and they made a bushel of big plays offensively against the Tigers (as they did against the Longhorns).

But the game did not really get out of hand until fairly late in the fourth quarter when Kevin Murray directed his associates to a pair of touchdowns that left the Tigers as stone-cold dead as the Baylor Bears left another band of Tigers (LSU variety) from the SEC in last week's Liberty Bowl.

The SEC may want to try a different breed of cat against Southwest Conference teams in future bowl games. Apparently Tigers just won't do.

But in the early moments of the fourth quarter, the Auburn Tigers were far from dead. They trailed the Aggies by only five points (21–16), and they were camped at the A&M 6-yard line after a cross-country drive of 88 yards that used up at least seven minutes on the clock.

They had a first down, and brother, were they on the prowl.

Heisman Trophy winner Bo Jackson—and yes, he's all a Heisman winner is supposed to be—smashed a left tackle and drove to the 2-yard line. It appeared to be only a matter of seconds and another play before Auburn would be ahead, despite A&M's obvious superiority in a number of departments.

Then Jackson cracked the middle and went nowhere. Linebacker Todd Howard chilled him for no gain.

Again the Tigers turned to their famous meal ticket, and again he went nowhere. That time noseguard Sammy O'Brient stopped him.

So it was fourth down, and the Tigers were at the A&M 2-yard line, and the Cotton Bowl game was hanging in the balance. After a pause for a timeout, the Tigers went to Bo one more time.

And guess what? The best-known Jackson on the field was stopped for a 1-yard loss by the most-unknown Jackson in sight. Aggie freshman linebacker Basil Jackson, a steal from Hammond, Louisiana, got Bo in his sights and downed him just like a big-game hunter bagging his prey.

The ball went over. The Tigers were never the same again.

Oh, on their next possession, they did get back down to the Aggie 28, where it was fourth and 2. Again they gave the ball to Bo. That time defensive back Wayne Asberry and linebacker Johnny Holland brought him crashing down for a 1-yard loss, and after that, it was all A&M. And I mean all.

On that long-distance drive that died at the A&M 3, the Tigers drove 91 yards in 18 plays and used up almost 8 minutes of playing time—and got nothing. On the next drive, they got 21 yards in 7 plays; they got down to four-down territory but got nothing again.

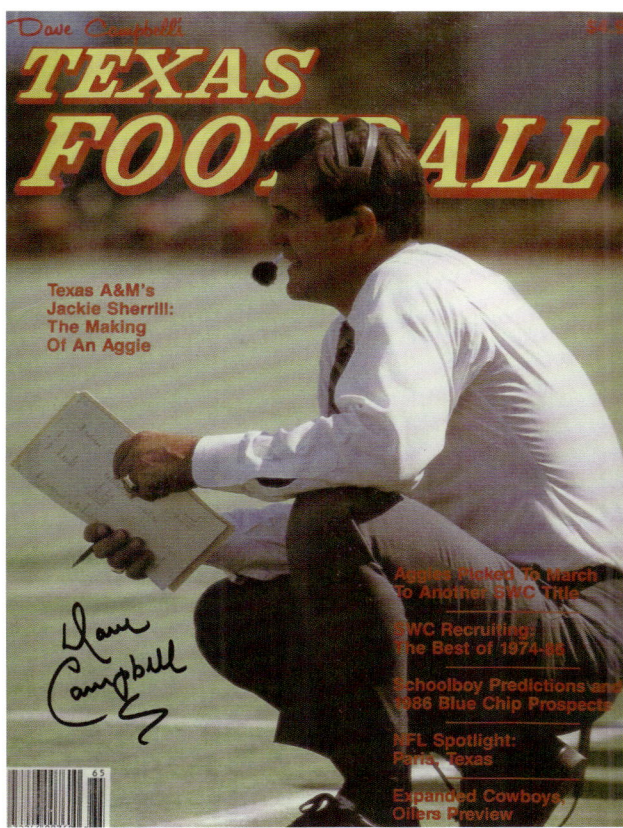

Head coach Jackie Sherrill came to Texas A&M from Pitt in 1982. Courtesy of *Dave Campbell's Texas Football*.

A&M quarterback Kevin Murray (14) turned in an outstanding passing performance against Auburn in the 1986 Cotton bowl. Courtesy of Texas A&M University Athletics.

If you say Texas A&M's defense won this 50th Cotton Bowl Classic, who can argue with you?

But that would be most unfair. Because Murray and Keith Woodside and Anthony Toney and Rod Bernstine were just out of sight themselves.

They were so out of sight, they caused press box voters to split their ballots so many ways that Bo Jackson wound up winning recognition as the game's outstanding offensive player. Since Bo rushed 31 times (a new Cotton Bowl record) for 129 yards and scored both of Auburn's touchdowns—the first on a 5-yard run and the second on an absolutely brilliant 73-yard run after catching a screen pass—he was hardly an undeserving winner. Without Bo, the Tigers might as well have stayed home.

But Murray was sensational. Shaking off the early fumble he lost that set up Auburn's first touchdown (a three-play, 21-yard drive that reached the scoreboard with 13:52 left in the first quarter), Murray had one of the greatest games any Cotton Bowl quarterback has ever had.

He completed 16 of 26 passes for a whopping 292 yards—a new Cotton Bowl record (Notre Dame's Joe Theismann had the old mark of 231). His total offense figure of 283 yards ranks No. 2 on the Cotton Bowl's all-time list, second only to Eddie Phillips of Texas (1971). He threw for one touchdown and overshadowed Auburn's two quarterbacks—starter Pat Washington and reserve Jeff Burger, who played all the second half—by such a large margin that it was almost unfair.

It was the threat posed by Murray's lethal arm that opened the way for most of the good running the Aggies did—186 yards in all, with Toney getting 72 yards and scoring twice on runs of 1 and 21 yards, with Harry Johnson getting loose on an 11-yard scoring jaunt, with

Woodside breaking away on a 22-yard touchdown run, with Roger Vick getting 67 yards on 15 carries.

And when Murray did fake and throw, often it was Bernstine who was wide open to catch the ball and then do something with it. The big and rapid tight end from Bryan had six catches for 108 yards, and most of them were crucial catches.

Woodside also sparked as a receiver, making three grabs for 88 yards. One of his catches started off as a stumbling run after a short catch in a crowd and wound up as a 41-yard gain that set up a 26-yard field goal kicked by Scott Slater late in the second quarter. Then late in the game, after the Aggies had made their two big defensive stands, he followed up on a 37-yard catch and run by Bernstine with a screen pass catch that he turned into a 38-yard sideline-to-sideline spectacular that carried to the Auburn 4-yard line. Two plays later, following a penalty, he caught a 9-yard touchdown pass.

The Aggies went 31 yards in five plays following the recovery of a fumbled punt for their first touchdown, 64 yards in five plays for their third, 72 yards in nine plays for their fourth, and just 11 yards in four plays for their last touchdown, which was scored with just three seconds left in the game.

That touchdown was set up by Domingo Bryant's second pass interception of the game. Domingo also stole an Auburn pass early in the second half to set up another Aggie score. Those two interceptions, along with the 10 tackles he made (7 unassisted), enabled him to win honors as the game's top defensive player. Holland was second in that particular voting.

If you're wondering why Scott Slater kicked A&M's 26-yard field goal late in the second quarter following a 51-yard, 5-play drive, it's because No. 1 kicker Eric Franklin had misfired on the extra point attempt following the Aggies' first touchdown and then misfired again on a 26-yard field goal attempt following a 73-yard, 12-play drive in the second quarter.

Because of Franklin's first miss, the Aggies had to keep trying to make up the difference with two-point conversion attempts. Only one succeeded, late in the game, following the touchdown pass to Woodside. The Aggies faked the kick and gave the ball instead to Bernstine on a direct snap, and the big guy (234 pounds) powered over from a wingback position, thus climaxing the biggest day he's ever had for A&M.

But again, Franklin's flubbed extra point conversion followed by those unsuccessful two-point conversion tries left the Aggies vulnerable. Thus although A&M was completely dominating play, Auburn was able to take a 13–12 lead when Bo Jackson got loose after catching a screen pass. Although the Aggies regained the lead with Slater's field goal and widened their margin to 21–13 early in the third period following a Bryant interception and Toney's 21-yard touchdown run, Auburn retaliated with a 72-yard, 11-play drive that led to Chris Johnson's 26-yard field goal and made the score 21–16.

And that was the way the scoreboard read when Bo came prowling down at the Aggie goal line in the decisive fourth quarter—and when that fired up Aggie defense said, "No, Bo, this is as far as you go."

"We just got together and said this is it, we've got to stop them here," O'Brient said later. "They ran the play over right guard, and we had it stopped all the way. We came into the game knowing we had to stop Bo Jackson to have a chance to beat them. I guess we didn't completely stop him, but except for a big play or two, we didn't do too bad."

They convinced Bo and also Auburn coach Pat Dye. Said Bo, "A&M deserved to win. They have a very physical defense, and they were really fired up."

Dye said the Aggies have "an outstanding team," and he noted the winners "got big plays both off the run and the pass. They had the great goal-line stand, and they whipped us on fourth and short. We were in the game until they completed that screen pass [to Woodside] late in the game. We had plenty of chances, but give A&M credit."

Right now, all over Dallas, Aggie partisans are doing just that.

OCTOBER 19, 1986

A&M QUARTERBACK SCORED EVERYTHING BAYLOR THREW AT HIM

COLLEGE STATION, Tex.—In the moment of truth in the game that came labeled as the Southwest Conference's great showdown of the football season, the awful truth for Baylor was that the Bears had no adequate answer for Texas A&M quarterback Kevin Murray.

The Aggie junior with the rifle arm that is oh so quick rescued the league's reeling defending champions after they had fallen behind by 17 points, and he just kept making big play after big play until he finally got his team dead even with a few seconds less than four minutes left in the game.

And then junior Scott Slater came on to kick the extra point that made all the difference in this classic of a football game, giving the Aggies a 31–30 victory and leaving the Bears with a broken heart that may not mend this season.

A year ago at Baylor Stadium, the Bruin defense gave Murray his worst game and the Bears won the contest. Playing under blue skies and a bright sun Saturday, with a huge crowd of 74,739 looking on, Murray repaid the debt and extracted a little interest to boot.

He threw three touchdown passes and sneaked a yard for another score. He completed 25 of 40 passes for 308 yards. He gave up not a single interception.

To get their 31 points, the Aggies had to travel 336 yards in a total of 50 plays. Murray personally accounted for 292 of those yards in 22 plays with his runs and passes.

He simply drove the Bears out of their minds.

And that was against a Baylor team, mind you, that played wonderfully well itself. At the finish line, the Bears had a little more yardage, a little more time of possession, and big advantage in rushing acreage.

They came within inches of victory—the inches they needed when they turned the ball over to the Aggies on fourth down at the A&M 1-yard line (make that the half-yard line) in the first quarter, the couple of inches they needed when John Simpleton caught a touchdown pass in the second quarter but then lost it when his foot came down right on the end zone line, and the couple of inches by which Thomas Everett missed an interception early in the third quarter when he had nothing but daylight in front of him.

They scored more points than any conference team has managed against the stouthearted Aggies since 1984. They almost snuffed out A&M's strong running game, limiting it to 83 yards in 37 plays. They held the Aggies to no first downs and a mere 23 yards in the first quarter.

But still they lost, and since the defeat was their second in conference play—indeed, their second in as many weeks—they very likely bowed out of a title chase they once thought they could win.

And the reason? Kevin Murray.

"On third down," said a drained, frustrated Grant Teaff, "Murray was just incredible. He escaped our pressure and did the job. It was a classic game, absolutely a sensational game. It's a game of inches, and really, that was the difference in the game."

A&M coach Jackie Sherrill said Murray "played the best game I've seen a quarterback play, and I've been around some great quarterbacks. Give Baylor a lot of credit. They are an outstanding football team."

The Bears had an excellent quarterback too. Cody Carlson completed 15 of 28 passes for 273 yards. He threw for one touchdown and ran for another, and it was his 58-yard run that set up still another Bruin score.

But he also was intercepted three times, and one of those Aggie thefts set up a field goal that helped spell the difference. "This game offered two of the best jobs of quarterbacking that you will see," said Teaff.

But no one was quite as good as Murray.

He would be rushed off his feet and still he would get his pass off with just a flick of the wrist—and more often

Kevin Murray takes the snap from center. Courtesy of Texas A&M University Athletics.

Thomas Everett. Courtesy of Baylor University Athletics.

than not, the pass would be on the mark. Twice he made incredible escapes to keep touchdown drives alive. Both came on third down. The first time, he got away from Bears who were all over him and ran for a first down. The second time, he did the same thing, only he completed a 22-yard pass to Shea Walker on that occasion.

As Thomas Everett said, "They hurt us on too many third-down conversions." And Murray made virtually all of those.

But it started off as if all the pain would belong to the Aggies.

After the two teams had exchanged fumbles early in the first quarter, Carlson threw a little screen pass to Randy Rutledge, and—bingo!—Randy turned the play into a 52-yard touchdown run. All those thousands of Aggies in the third-largest Kyle Field crowd in history suddenly got awfully quiet.

Having stomped 76 yards in just four plays to score a touchdown with 11:26 still left in the first quarter, the Bears hooked up and did a similar thing the next time they got the ball. That scoring drive went 64 yards in just five plays, and Matt Clark skirted right end for the final 2 yards, but the big one was a Carlson contribution. Faking an option pitchout, he kept the ball and out-legged the Aggie defense all the way to the A&M 2-yard line.

But then came what in retrospect was one of the game's major turning points. The Bears drove from the A&M 35 to the Aggie 1-yard line in six plays. Carlson's 32-yard completion to Leland Douglas was the play that gave the Bears a golden opportunity to take an early 21–0 lead. But on fourth down at the 1, Charles Perry drove at left guard and was stopped just short of the payoff window.

"I believe that was the turning point of the game for the defense. After that we were able to fly around the ball and make the big plays," said A&M linebacker Johnny Holland.

And sure enough, when Rod Harris fumbled a Baylor punt moments later, turning the ball over to the Bears on the A&M 7-yard line, Teaff's troops could get no closer than the Aggie 2 in three plays. So Terry Syler had to convert the opportunity into three points, giving Baylor a 17–0 advantage with 19 seconds still left in the first quarter.

At the end of the game, those 2 yards the Bears were unable to make also loomed exceedingly large.

In 15 minutes, the Bears had scored 17 points, rolled up 194 yards, and limited the Aggies to 15 plays that netted them fewer than 2 yards a play.

But now it was time for Murray.

Starting at his own 20, he pushed the Aggies 80 yards in 12 plays for their first touchdown, and on that drive he had seven completions for 76 yards, including a 5-yard touchdown pass to tight end Rod Bernstine. Bernstine, the league's leading receiver, wound up with seven catches for 81 yards. On that drive he also had an 18-yard catch, Keith Woodside had a 14-yarder, and Shea Walker an 11-yarder, but the play that made it all possible was that miraculous escape Murray made when it was third and 3 and he pulled away from two Bears and ran for 5 yards and a first down.

The next time the Aggies got the ball, they zoomed for 74 yards in just six plays, and one terrific third-down play did most of the damage—Murray on a third and 9 completing a pass to Rod Harris that quickly became a 68-yard bomb to the Baylor 5-yard line. Ron Francis managed to tackle the speeding Harris, staving off disaster for a moment. But three plays later, Murray sneaked a yard that made it 17–14.

Just before halftime, the Bears regained control long enough to drive 76 yards in eight plays to the Aggie 15. But after the touchdown pass to Simpson had just missed, Syler kicked a 32-yard field goal with six seconds left before intermission.

The Aggies ended Baylor's first two possessions in the third quarter with interceptions, and the second one, by Chet Brooks, set them up for a six-play, 28-yard drive that was culminated by Slater's 39-yard field goal.

Their lead narrowed to a mere three points, the Bears reacted by staging an impressive 75-yard, 12-play touchdown drive that included an 18-yard Carlson strike to David Davis and some strong running by Rutledge behind a line that featured two tight ends. Carlson got the final 3 yards on that drive himself, and Syler's kick made it a 27–17 game.

But again it was Murray to the rescue. "Maybe they ought to change the guy's name to Houdini," said Teaff admiringly. "Eight or nine times he made the crucial play. He must have had a jillion of them."

In directing the Aggies 74 yards in 10 plays for the touchdown that kept it close, he had completions of 22 yards to Walker, 8 yards to Harris, 23 yards to Bernstine, 11 yards to Tony Thompson, and finally 5 yards to Woodside for the score.

Baylor retaliated with a six-play, 55-yard drive that put the Bears in position for Mark Mahler to kick a 41-yard field goal with 9:29 left in the game. Most of that yardage was the product of a sensational 40-yard grab made by Simpson when two Aggies were guarding him tightly.

When the Aggie defense absolutely had to stop the Bears in the fourth quarter, it did. When the Baylor defense was asked to do the same, it couldn't.

Starting at his own 20, Murray got the touchdown the Aggies had to have in 16 plays. Six of those were completions, and two of them were big ones on the third down. And the last one—also a third-down play, after the Bears had thrown the Aggies from the Baylor 2 back to the 4-yard line—found Murray ignoring a heavy rush and getting his pass away just in the nick of time and Thompson bobbling the ball and then tucking it away securely in the end zone for the touchdown.

Slater's game-winning kick was almost automatic.

The Bears still had enough time, and the Aggies gave them a chance by twice putting the ball out of bounds on the kickoff. Forced to back up to his own 25 for the third kick, Slater's bouncer was returned 13 yards to the Baylor 41 by Scott Works. The clock gave the Bears plenty of time—three minutes and 43 seconds. All they needed was a drive that would put them in field goal range.

But they never got another first down.

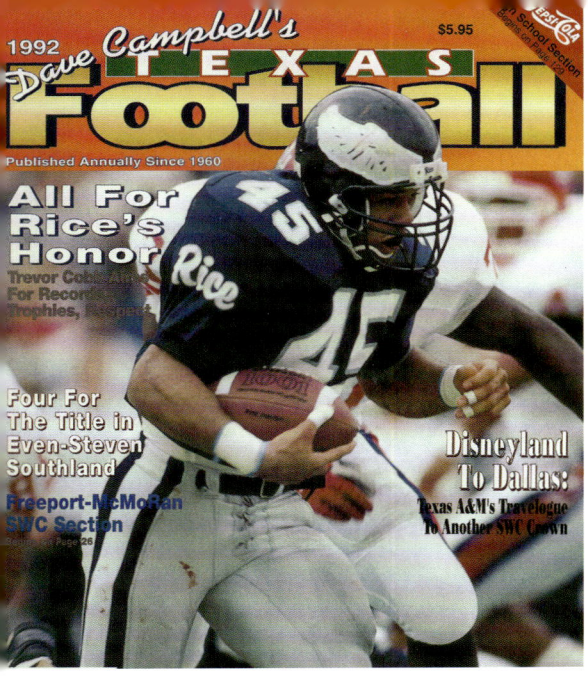

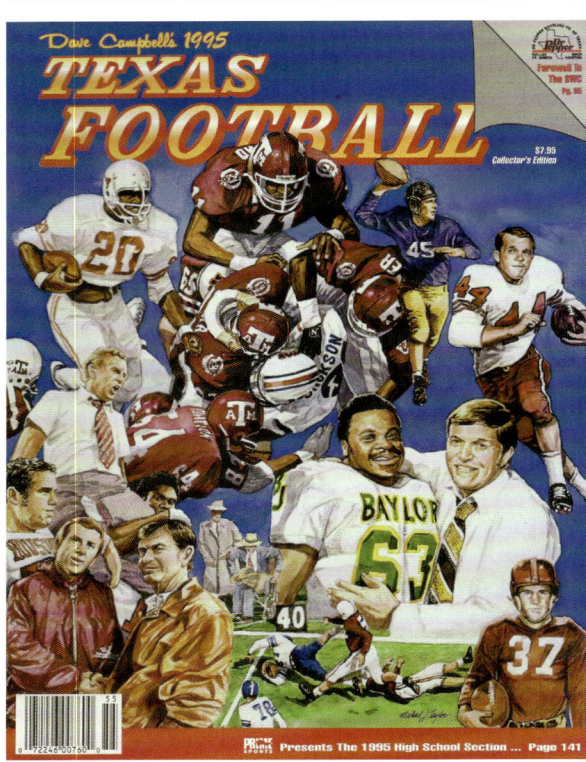

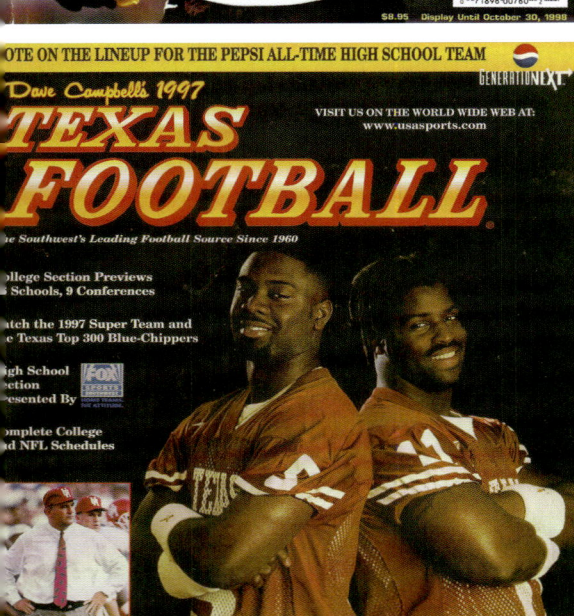
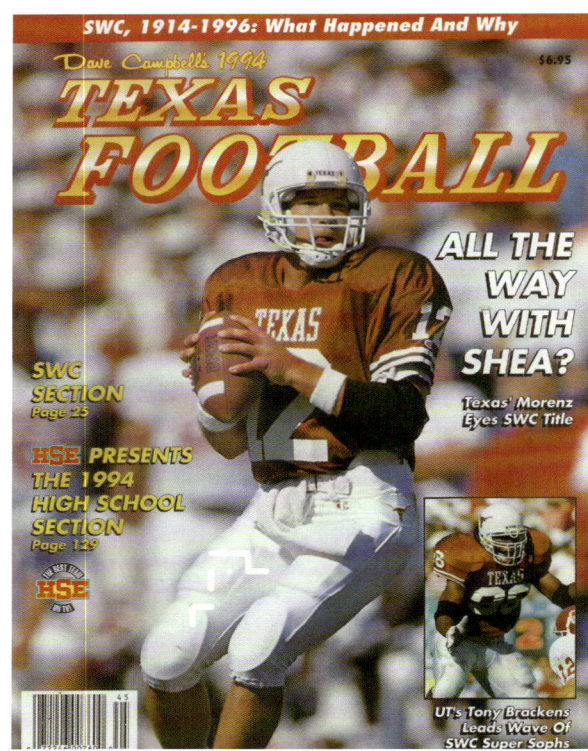
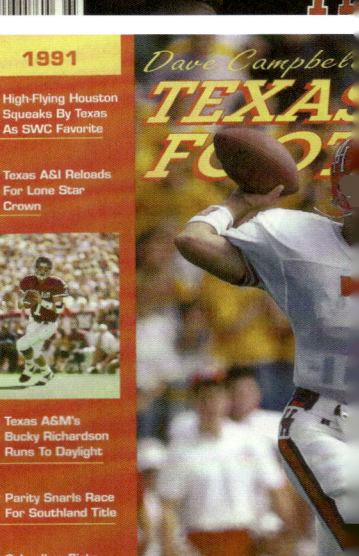
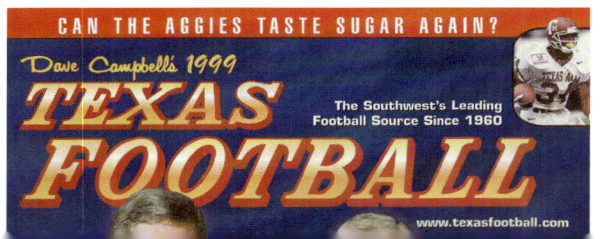

5
GOOD-BYE TO THE SOUTHWEST CONFERENCE
FROM THE 1990S TO THE NEW MILLENNIUM

For many reasons, the decade of the 1990s was a bittersweet time for Texas college football. On a personal note, I made the difficult decision to retire as sports editor of the *Waco Tribune-Herald* in 1993. Not too many people get a chance to spend 40 years doing a job they love, but that is exactly what I did. I wasn't getting any younger, and I finally decided it was time for me to step aside and focus on other pursuits. But that didn't make the decision any easier.

The year 1996 was the last for the Southwest Conference, and that is a final act that many folks are still mourning. However, the forces stacked against the conference, led by the sweeping changes in sports television coverage and the vast financial ramifications of that, finally became just too much to handle. When Arkansas departed for the SEC in 1990, it was the beginning of the end. Texas, Texas A&M, Baylor, and Texas Tech aligned with the former Big Eight to create the Big 12 in 1994, and soon after, SMU, TCU, and Rice moved to the Western Athletic Conference. Houston's departure to Conference USA completed the dissolution of what had at one time been one of the most dominant conferences in major college football. But even amid these sea changes, there was still a lot of great college football

I wrote the "On Second Thought" column for the Waco newspaper sports pages from 1953 until I retired from the paper in 1993.

Just a few of the issues we published through the years. *Dave Campbell's Texas Football* reaches more than 400,000 readers annually. Courtesy of the *Waco Tribune-Herald*.

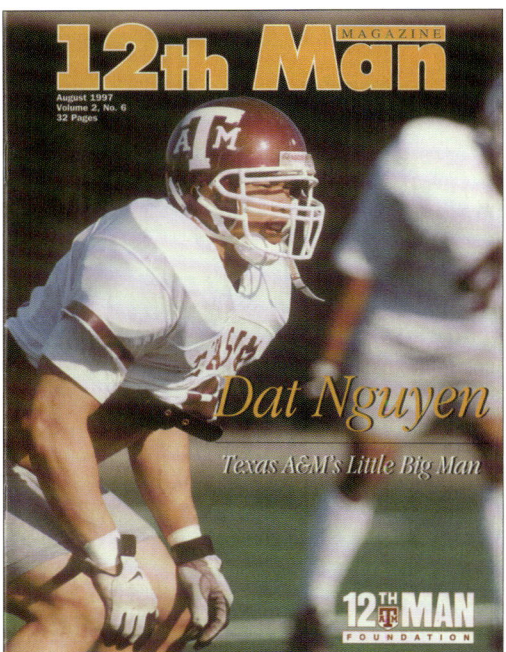

Dat Nguyen, Texas A&M defensive great who went on to a record-setting career with the Dallas Cowboys. Courtesy of *12th Man Magazine*.

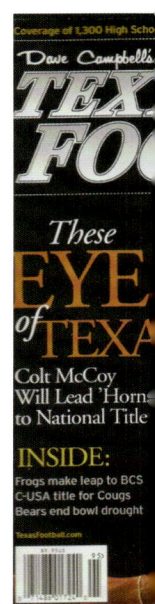
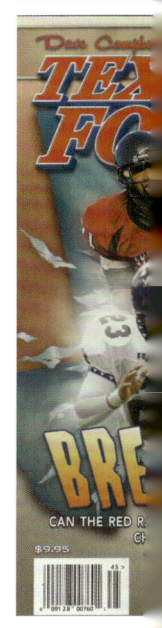

in the 1990s. After all, this was the era of R. C. Slocum's record-breaking home winning streak at Texas A&M and the "Wrecking Crew" defense.

The new millennium brought still more changes. In 2012, Texas A&M would opt to depart the Big 12 to join the SEC, soon followed by Missouri. This move would set up, among other things, the unforgettable game of November 10, 2012, when true freshman quarterback Johnny Manziel completed 24 of 31 passes for 253 yards—along with 92 yards gained on the ground—and led the Aggies to victory over the Crimson Tide, stunning the home crowd in Tuscaloosa on the way to a 29–24 win. Texas A&M was the only team to defeat Alabama that year, and Manziel's thrilling performance in this and other games would lead to his being the first ever freshman to win the Heisman Trophy.

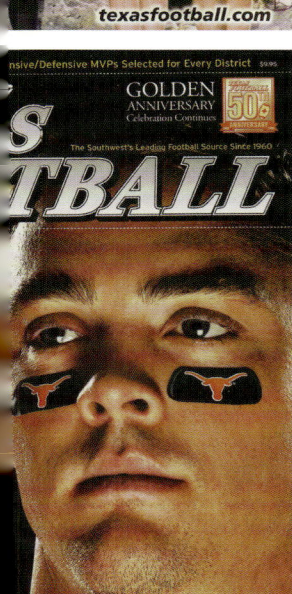
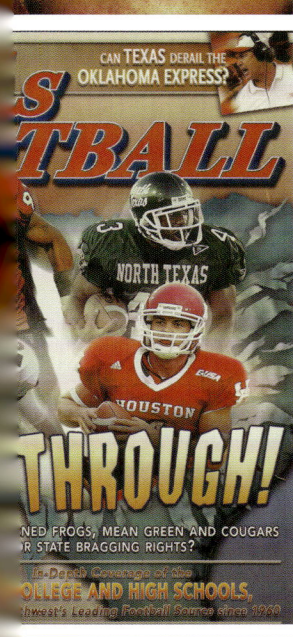
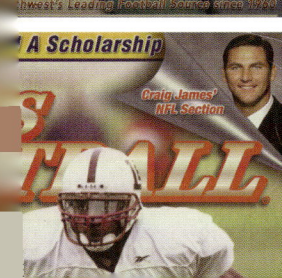

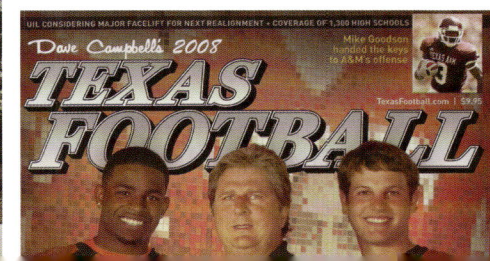

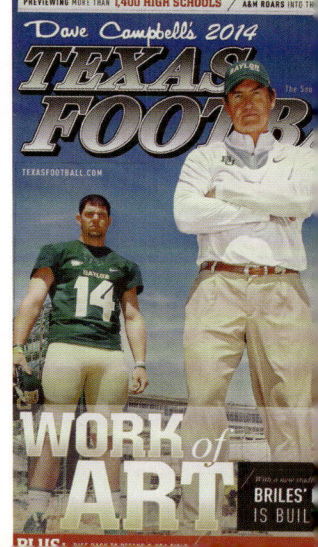

NOVEMBER 29, 1991

A&M DEVOURS LAST OF SWC: AGGIES MARCH OVER UT, 31–14

COLLEGE STATION, Tex.—It took them a week, but Cotton Bowl officials finally got No. 10 Texas A&M to accept their invitation Thursday night to host No. 3 Florida State in the New Year's Day classic.

Keven Smith's 73-yard punt return for a touchdown in the third quarter broke open a defensive battle and ignited Aggies to a 31–14 victory over the Texas Longhorns (5–6, 4–4).

The Aggies, who improved to 10–1, including 8–0 in the Southwest Conference, beat Southern Methodist 65–6 last week to clinch their 16th SWC title, but they didn't want to accept the Cotton Bowl offer until they played their archrivals from Austin.

"If we had accepted this last week and lost this week, it wouldn't have been the same," Aggies linebacker Jason Atkinson said.

Texas, the defending SWC champs who beat the Aggies 28–27 last year, fell to 5–6 and 4–4.

"It took me two months to get over the headache of losing to Texas last year, and this is the pain killer right here," Smith said. "I've been envisioning returning a punt all week. The last two weeks I've been trying, trying, trying to return one."

Texas A&M's defense, ranked first in the nation, held Texas in check in the first half and eased to a 10–7 halftime lead. The Aggies extended it to 17–7 on the first drive of the third period on Greg Hill's 2-yard run.

Smith gave the Aggies breathing room with 5:59 left in the third period when he fielded a punt, made a move to his right, and darted 73 yards for the touchdown. He also had a 71-yard punt return for a touchdown against Rice earlier this season.

"I'll never forget this," Atkinson said. "It's a family feeling the way we pulled together this year. We started celebrating after Kevin's punt return."

The Longhorns capitalized on an 18-yard interception return by Grady Cavness with a 3-yard touchdown run by Rodrick Walker with 8:44 to play.

Hill got his second touchdown on a 2-yard run with 3:03 to play.

The Aggies, quick starters all season, outscored the opposition 262–37 in the first half. But they had to struggle for their halftime lead against the Longhorn defense, ranked fourth in the nation.

"Coming in at the half, I thought our offense was a little frustrated," quarterback Bucky Richardson said. "But we just came out in the second half and made some plays. Tonight was a total team effort, and that's what it takes to win championships."

Linebacker Marcus Buckley fueled the Aggies' top-ranked defense in the first half with a 19-yard touchdown interception return, two sacks, and a fumble recovery.

Texas A&M's first score came on Texas' first offensive play, when Buckley blitzed through and caught a pass by Gardere in the Texas backfield. He ran untouched to score with 12:44 to go in the period.

The Aggies drove 44 yards in the second quarter to a 26-yard field goal by Terry Venetoulias and appeared headed for a 10–0 halftime lead until Richardson was chased out of the pocket and intercepted by Boone Powell with 1:51 to go in the half.

"You have to give their offense credit," Texas defensive end Shane Dronnett said. "We really shut them down in the first half, but in the second half, they sucked it up and did what they had to do. I like their chances against Florida State."

The Texas defense held the A&M offense to 55 first-half yards. The Aggies' offense came in game ranked No. 10 nationally and averaged 459 yards per game.

Kevin Smith (26) was a consensus All-American in 1991. He went on to play eight seasons with the Dallas Cowboys, where he collected three Super Bowl rings. Courtesy of Texas A&M University Athletics.

Bucky Richardson (7) rushed for more than 2,000 yards during his Aggie career, leading his team to three SWC championships. Courtesy of Texas A&M University Athletics.

NOVEMBER 22, 1992

BEAR DEFENSE FINALLY STOPS TEXAS, 21–20

WACO, Tex.—Coaching the final regular-season game of his long, illustrious stay at Baylor, Grant Teaff walked off the field a winner against Texas here Saturday, mainly because neither the charged-up Bears nor the football gods on high would permit it to be otherwise.

The final score favored Teaff's scrappy, intrepid troops, 21–20. It was a sweaty-palms affair all through the final moments—Texas trying desperately to break through, Baylor desperately trying to hang on, and the game officials making a few calls that left Longhorn fans livid.

Finally, with fewer than two minutes remaining, the Longhorns triggered a fourth-down play from the Baylor 41.

They needed 4 yards to get a first down and the chance to advance the few more steps they needed to get within kicker Scott Szeredy's field goal range—4 yards to stay in the hunt for a share of the SWC title.

They got 3 yards and about 30 inches.

The measuring stakes came out and went down, the Longhorns were that much short, and all those nervous Baylor fans in the stands suddenly erupted in jubilation.

Now they knew it was all over.

Now they knew the Bears had the Longhorn windpipe in a fist that was squeezing ever tighter. Now they knew the Bears had nailed down their sixth victory of the season, thus keeping Baylor in the bowl picture for at least a few more days.

No wonder Bruin fans in the crowd of 39,110 savored the moment.

Maybe they also cheered wildly at College Station. The Baylor victory, combined with the triumph the Texas Aggies scored over TCU, added up to an undisputed championship for Texas A&M.

Texas was left with a 6–4 record, but since only five of those victories came against Division I-A teams, the Longhorns now find themselves in a position of having to upend the unbeaten Aggies on Thanksgiving night even to qualify for bowl consideration.

The skies were weeping when Teaff's farewell game began at Floyd Casey Stadium, but when the coach walked off the field for the final time, he did so in bright sunshine.

"I guess it takes 21 years to get 21 points. I hadn't thought of that until now. Right now, I feel a lot of emotions," said Teaff, happy but emotionally spent.

DEFENSE FINALLY HELD

The Bears won because they got a touchdown pass and two touchdown runs from quarterback J. J. Joe and because their much-maligned, frequently fragile

J. J. Joe was the field commander for Baylor from 1990 to 1993. Courtesy of Baylor University Athletics.

defense twice refused to buckle in the last six minutes when to err even a little bit was to lose.

On the first occasion, end Matthew Pearson sacked UT's Peter Gardere for a 9-yard setback and took the Longhorns out of field goal range after they had gained possession on a futile fourth-down effort by the Bears at the Bears 39.

On the second occasion, the one that turned up only inches short, Trooper Taylor made surely the highest tackle of his Baylor career.

Texas' dangerous Phil Brown appeared to be on his way to a first down when Trooper sent him crashing to the earth.

Taylor was in the game only because Michael McFarland—"Our spiritual lead," Teaff calls him—was sidelined after suffering concussions in Baylor's two previous games.

"I knew I was going to leave it all on the field today," said the senior defensive back, and he did. He not

Grant Teaff received the Amos Alonzo Stagg Award in 2006. Courtesy of *Dave Campbell's Texas Football*.

only made that huge tackle; he also returned a kickoff 40 yards, enabling him to become the school's all-time record holder for career return yardage (1,063 steps).

UT MADE KEY ERRORS

While the Bears majored in big plays at opportune times, the Longhorns did a number of uncharacteristic things, like dropping touchdown passes and twice snapping the ball over their punter's head.

But the first of David Bearden's spectacular off-target snaps did not hurt them at all, and the second only cost them field position.

In the end, what cost them much was the fumble Adrian Walker lost at the Baylor 5-yard line after the Longhorns had marched 62 yards.

What also cost them, they complained, were the two Baylor fumbles they thought they should have had that the officials ruled were no fumbles at all.

"I don't know what was going on, but it [the officiating] was the worst I've ever seen," said UT sophomore defensive end Norman Watkins, a mighty man in defeat.

Teaff, who certainly knows a thing or two about bad calls going against his team, just smiled when asked about the officiating.

"I thought the officials did a great job," he said.

Neither offense was particularly productive. Texas finished with 295 yards, Baylor with 247. Both teams had been doing much better.

The Bears, who enjoyed excellent field position much of the afternoon, drove 55 yards in 11 plays the second time they got the ball.

Some hard running by Robert Strait (88 yards on 24 carries, tops for the afternoon) and a pass interference call against the Longhorns set up the score that gave Baylor a 7–0 lead.

MCKENZIE GETS 6

On the payoff play from the UT 11, J. J. rolled left, then threw back across the field to usually overlooked tight end Mike McKenzie for the touchdown.

Texas seized the momentum by blocking a Baylor punt a few moments later. Lance Gunn led a herd of Longhorns who broke through on Rhett Delaney and sent his kick skidding back toward the Bruin end zone.

Taking possession at the Baylor 18, Texas scored in two plays. Gardere's 17-yard pass to star freshman receiver Lovell Pinkney produced the touchdown, and Szeredy's kick made it a tie game.

The next time they got the ball, the visitors appeared on their way to a go-ahead score when

Albert Fontenot. Courtesy of Baylor University Athletics.

Adrian Walker's bobble wound up in Chris Lewis's hands at the Baylor 5.

The recovery saved the Bruin bacon but left them with their worst field position of the entire game.

So all they did was drive 95 yards in 12 plays for the score that put them back ahead to stay.

Nine of those yards came on a J. J. completion to Reggie Miller and another 9 came on a penalty. And the remainder came on power football, mostly Strait and Bradford Lewis banging away inside and J. J. keeping occasionally outside. J. J.'s final carry was an 8-yarder that scored the touchdown and gave Baylor a 14–7 halftime advantage.

TEXAS KEEPS KNOCKING

Baylor's Trey Weir missed a 48-yard field goal at the midpoint of the third quarter, and then Texas used Gardere's scrambling and a couple of nifty pass completions to drive 55 yards while setting up Szeredy's 31-yard field goal.

But it was a quarterback sack by Scotty Lewis and Albert Fontenot that made the Longhorns settle for the field goal. Give the Bruin defense another plus.

With their margin trimmed to 14–10, the Bears drove 56 yards in seven plays for their third touchdown. A 14-yard pass to McKenzie set it up, and J. J. scored it on a 1-yard sneak.

Texas answered that thrust in just five plays. Gardere found daylight up the middle on a quarterback draw and ran 19 yards for the touchdown that made it a 21–17 game.

The visitors came rushing back down the field on their next possession, driving to the Baylor 8 before they had to settle for another field goal.

So it was 21–20 with 8:05 left in the game, and Texas had the wind and the momentum, and when J. J. fumbled the snap on a fourth-and-inches play at the Baylor 39, Texas really had the momentum.

But the Baylor defense made the plays it had to make, and Grant Teaff was able to walk away with a victory he can remember for the rest of his life. At the finish, Baylor students came out of the stands and almost mobbed him.

A PARTING BOTH SWEET AND SORROWFUL

On the field, Baylor quarterback J. J. Joe was taking the snap and retreating a couple of steps and then dropping to one knee.

Baylor had a one-point lead over Texas, and the clock was running—30 seconds, 25, 20—and suddenly Baylor players from the bench were rushing onto the field, and a couple of them were grabbing their coach and lifting him up and taking him toward Texas coach John Mackovic, who was coming across the field to congratulate him.

WHAT A WAY TO GO

And that's the way the Grant Teaff era ended, with whoops of joy, with a victory ride, with congratulations, with a victory over an old and treasured rival that Baylor at one time in its history had forgotten how to beat.

Teaff not only beat the Longhorns here Saturday; he beat them 10 times in his last 19 tries, 4 times in his last 5 attempts.

Heck, he's almost made it a tradition. Baylor students and exes and partisans, remembering how it was before he arrived, remembering how it is now, almost mobbed him before he could make a few obligatory remarks for radio and TV.

A HUMAN WAVE

By the time all that had transpired, Teaff had been swept up and carried along to about the 25-yard line at the north end of the field. The band struck up "That Good Old Baylor Line." Arms reached skyward, giving the bear claw sign. A student carrying a huge yellow banner emblazoned with the bear claw was running hither and yon. At the north end, the goalposts were being twisted like a pretzel.

TEAFF'S FINAL GAME WAS A FAMILY AFFAIR

I thought Teaff would go with his players to the Baylor dressing room, but he came back to midfield and then approached the stands on the west side, where Baylor fans were on their feet, waiting, cheering.

The coach was dressed in a green rainsuit and Baylor cap. His face was flushed. He looked excited but drained. He waved to the fans still in the west stands. He waved twice. They were good-bye waves.

ALWAYS A TEAM

Then Teaff went to the sideline right in front of the Baylor bench. His wife, Donell, was there waiting. So were his daughters. And that was the way they left the field, arm in arm, the way they had planned it, win or lose.

"We're sort of a unique family," Grant later explained as he was making his traditional postgame visit to the press box. "We do things together," he said. "When we first came here, we were together. And when I walked off for the last time, I wanted us to walk off together—Donell, my daughters, my grandkids."

PRAISE ALL AROUND

By now, Teaff had changed into brown trousers and a coat, a yellow shirt, and a print tie. He answered the questions that came without pause. He praised the Longhorns, he praised what the Baylor-Texas rivalry has meant to both sides, he praised the Southwest Conference and the ongoing efforts to save it.

Grant Teaff (right) and Bear Bryant at the 1981 Cotton Bowl. Courtesy of Cotton Bowl Athletic Association / James D. Smith.

Teaff was inducted into the College Football Hall of Fame in 2001. Courtesy of Baylor University Athletics.

But mostly he praised his team.

"This football team has come along about as well as any I've ever coached. I'm so proud of this team," he said. "They've listened about as well and done the things I've asked about as well as any I've had.

"And they're special. They're my last team."

I thought maybe his emotions would get the best of him at that point—he can be an emotional man—but he remained dry-eyed.

What would he do Saturday night, the first night in 21 years that he had not had another season to contemplate?

When he left the press box, he said, he and his family were going to the Bear Club Room for some sort of preplanned affair.

"By 7 o'clock," he said, "I imagine my entire family, both sides of the family, will be eating dinner at my house. And then we'll probably sit down and watch a replay of the game.

"It'll be kind of fun."

"A GREAT 21 YEARS"

A longtime friend, Abilene sports columnist Bill Hart, shook Grant's hand and went back to his seat to complete his game story. "It's been a great 21 years," Hart said to nobody in particular.

A few yards away, Donell Teaff was watching, listening, smiling.

"This was perfect," she said. "I couldn't have scripted it any better."

NOVEMBER 27, 1992

A&M KNOCKS OUT TEXAS: AGGIES' 34–13 RUNAWAY KEEPS THEM IN TITLE PICTURE AND LEAVES LONGHORNS 6–5, OUT OF JOHN HANCOCK BOWL

MICHAEL A. LUTZ

AUSTIN, Tex.—Practical jokers recently dehorned the Texas Longhorns' midfield insignia on the Memorial Stadium turf. Fourth-ranked Texas A&M did the same thing Thursday night.

The Aggies, campaigning for the national championship, erupted with a 17-point second quarter, which included two touchdowns by Rodney Thomas, and survived Texas' explosive third quarter for a 34–13 victory.

Texas A&M (12–0, 7–0 Southwest Conference), which had won 21 straight regular-season games, remained one of three unbeaten, untied teams in the nation along with No. 1 Miami (10–0) and No. 2 Alabama (11–0).

The Aggies have won eight of the last games against the Longhorns but trail 64-30-5 in the series. A&M wrapped up its second straight SWC title last weekend and will be the host team in the Cotton Bowl on New Year's Day.

Texas (6–5, 4–3) ended its first season under coach John Mackovic, the school's 100th playing football. The Longhorns needed a victory over A&M for a berth in the Hancock Bowl on New Year's Eve.

The Aggies took a 17–3 halftime lead on a pair of 6-yard runs by Thomas and a 42-yard field goal by Terry Venetoulias, all in the second quarter, and threatened to make the game a rout.

But the Longhorns erupted in the third quarter with a 56-yard kickoff return by Mike Adams and a tricky 18-yard touchdown catch by quarterback Peter Gardere, who lateraled to wide receiver Darrick Duke and then took the return pass down the right sideline 28 seconds into the third quarter.

On A&M's next possession, Texas' Van Malone recovered a fumble that led to a 42-yard field goal by Scott Szeredy with 11:01 left in the period.

The rally merely woke up the Aggies, who took advantage of a fumble recovery by Steve Solari at the Texas 37 to set up a 28-yard field goal by Venetoulias. Moments later, Thomas scored his third touchdown on a 2-yard dive.

Workmen repaired the damaged Longhorn insignia before the game started, but the Longhorns couldn't keep pace with the Aggies.

Aaron Glenn put the final touches on the victory with a 95-yard interception return for a touchdown with 3:04 to play. The Longhorns had driven to A&M's 12.

Thomas put the Aggies ahead for good with 10:05 to go in the second quarter with a slicing run, streaking through a crease in the Texas defense and diving over the goal between two defenders. He scored again with 1:31 left in the half.

Adrian Walker, who had two fumbles in last week's loss to Baylor, fumbled with 54 seconds left in the half, and Venetoulias added a 42-yarder with two seconds left in the half.

Texas' only first-half points came on a 52-yard field goal by Szeredy, who tied his career best because he moved the spot of the ball up a yard just before the snap.

A crowd of 81,170 fell short of an expected record. The addition of 3,900 bleacher seats failed to break the stadium record of 83,053 for the Texas-Houston game.

Scott Szeredy prepares to launch a kickoff. Courtesy of University of Texas Athletics.

R. C. SLOCUM: A WINNER IN MORE WAYS THAN ONE

Football coach R. C. Slocum is the winningest coach in the long and storied history of football at Texas A&M University. And that is saying more than you might realize because the Texas Aggies have had quite a few football coaches in the many years of the football game—Charley Moran from 1909 to 1914, D. X. Bible from 1917 to 1928, Matty Bell from 1929 to 1933, Homer Norton from 1934 to 1947, Bear Bryant from 1954 to 1957, Gene Stallings from 1965 to 1971, and Jackie Sherrill from 1982 to 1988.

But when all is said and done, Slocum won more football games for Texas A&M's hundreds of thousands of football fans than any of the other coaches.

As a coach at Texas A&M when the Aggies were members of the old Southwest Conference, he compiled a record of 59-12-2. And then after the Aggies became members of the Big 12 Conference, he continued to win, pushing his final record at A&M to 123-47-2. He didn't win a national championship as Homer Norton did (1939) with All-American fullback John Kimbrough, All-SWC tackle Ernie Pannell, All-American guard Marshall Robnett, and All-SWC end James Sterling, but Slocum did win more championships than any Texas Aggie football coach in history—and without the likes of a John Kimbrough.

Side note: I was fortunate enough to get to see Kimbrough in what Jinx Tucker, my predecessor as sports editor of the *Waco Tribune-Herald*, called Kimbrough's "coming out party." That was in 1938. I was a boy scout at the time, and boy scouts were able to get in free to Baylor's home football games if they would help usher ticket holders to their seats. Thus I was able to see Texas A&M and fullback John Kimbrough play No. 17–ranked Baylor to a 6–6 tie that afternoon. In that Baylor homecoming game, the Bears were sparked by the All-SWC

R. C. Slocum recorded more wins than any other head coach at Texas A&M: 123 victories during his 13-year tenure. Courtesy of Texas Sports Hall of Fame.

players Sam Boyd and Billy Patterson, but the 1938 football season really belonged to TCU.

The Frogs were undefeated that season and then went to the Sugar Bowl and defeated Carnegie Tech, 15–7, to wrap up a perfect season and a national championship. Davey O'Brien, just 5-foot-7 and 150 pounds, won the Heisman Trophy that year. Then coach Homer Norton's Aggies did the same thing the following year, winding up a perfect season by defeating Tulane, 14–13, in the Sugar Bowl and nailing down a national championship. But Kimbrough finished only fifth in the voting for the Heisman that year and then second the following season to Michigan's Tom Harmon after A&M had lost to Texas, 7–0, in Austin in a monster upset.

But back to Slocum, a terrific coach in his own right. At final count, before retiring (after the 2002 season), Slocum had won *six* championships—three SWC titles, two Big 12 Conference South championships, and one (1998) Big 12 crown.

Here are some more facts and figures that you may have missed: Under Slocum, the Aggies finished out the 1990s with 94 victories, the most of any Division I football program in the state of Texas in *any* decade. After his last season at A&M (2002), he was the sixth-winningest active college football coach in the country, with a career record of 123-47-2, a .721 winning average.

Also, Slocum's 123 victories in his first 14 years ranks No. 8 all time, putting the Aggie coach in the company of such football greats as Barry Switzer of Oklahoma (137 wins), Tom Osborne of Nebraska (137), Steve Spurrier of Florida and South Carolina (132), Joe Paterno of Penn State (131), and Lavell Edwards of Brigham Young (129). Under his coaching tenure, the Aggies played in 11 bowl games, and 5 of those were New Year's Day bowls. And when the Aggies defeated Oklahoma State, 21–3, at Kyle Field, Slocum had reached the 100-victory mark. He had done so faster than any other active college head coach in the country.

Other memorable Slocum accomplishments: His Aggie-coached teams won 85 percent of their games at Kyle Field. They had a 29-game unbeaten streak in the SWC from 1990 to 1995 and a 22-game unbeaten streak at Kyle Field from 1996 to 2000. His teams were 30–1 against nonconference teams at Kyle Field. In Southwest Conference play, the Aggies once went four straight seasons without a conference defeat. And his winning percentage of .865 (44-6-2) is the *very best* in SWC history.

All this was accomplished by someone who attended Stark High School in Orange, Texas, where he was an all-district end. He then attended McNeese State University in nearby Lake Charles, Louisiana, where he was a four-year letterman, set school records as a pass receiver, and after completing his senior year, was named the team's most valuable player. In 2002 he was honored as a McNeese Distinguished Alumnus and in 2003 was inducted into the university's Athletics Hall of Fame.

He began his football coaching career at Lake Charles High School and then moved to Manhattan, Kansas, as an assistant coach at Kansas State during coach Vince Gibson's tenure. It was in 1972 that R. C. began his long relationship with Texas A&M and Aggie football, being hired as an assistant coach on new A&M head coach Emory Bellard's staff. He coached receivers initially and then moved to the defense, coaching defensive ends and then linebackers, and then he became the team's defensive coordinator.

In 1981 he left A&M to become defensive coordinator on the staff of Southern Cal's big-winning coach John Robinson. His defense led the Pac-10 Conference in 1982, and one of his linebackers, Chip Banks, was named on the All-America team.

But in 1982, Texas A&M startled all of college football by hiring Jackie Sherrill as its new head coach (at what, at the time, was considered an enormous salary), and Sherrill immediately brought Slocum back to Aggieland to take over the defense. In 1985 he was named the Aggies' assistant head coach, and when Sherrill left A&M, Slocum began a 14-year history of success, notable by conference championships, All-SWC choices, All–Big 12 and All-America selections and marked by the exploits of the team's great defensive "Wrecking Crew."

Now serving as special advisor to the president of Texas A&M, Slocum has served as president of the American Football Coaches Association and has been inducted into the Texas Sports Hall of Fame, the Texas A&M Athletic Hall of Fame, the Southeast Texas Coaches Hall of Fame, and the Museum of the Gulf Coast Sports Hall of Fame. Then in 2012, Slocum was inducted into the National Football Foundation College Football Hall of Fame, which many college football fans consider the ultimate honor for a coach.

He has also won the prized Touchdowner Award by the Houston Touchdown Club, the Robert Neyland Award, the Lifetime Achievement Award by the American Heart Association, and the Amos Alonzo Stagg Award, and several more as well. And in 2013, Slocum was inducted into the Horatio Alger Association of Distinguished Americans in a gala in Washington, DC.

He married Nel Jennings and they have three sons, all graduates of Texas A&M.

Courtesy of *Dave Campbell's Texas Football*.

NOVEMBER 29, 1992

A BIZARRE FINISH TO A BIZARRE SEASON

In their 93 years of football, the Baylor Bears have won their way to 15 bowls. They have done so by winning their final game of the season (most of the time) and by losing (on five occasions), and in 1948 they went to the Dixie Bowl after tying Rice in the finale.

They also have gone to bowls after winning big and winning narrowly, and in 1961 they were picked for the late and unlamented Gotham Bowl after losing their final game to Rice by two touchdowns.

But sports fans, what has developed this season is a new experience for the Bears. For the first time ever, they are, presumably, going to the John Hancock Bowl in El Paso, which has the reputation of being one of the better bowls on the crowded bowl calendar as far as entertainment for visitors is concerned. Former Texas Tech coach J. T. King always insisted that the Sun Bowl (which now comes disguised as the John Hancock) was the best bowl of them all, other than the Cotton Bowl.

The Bears are going after posting a 6–5 record—barely meeting NCAA minimum standards. But they went to the Gotham Bowl with a 5–5 mark (there were no minimums in those days).

And they are going after winning five of their last seven games, a commendable achievement that includes victories over ACC power Georgia Tech and old nemesis Texas.

HEAVYWEIGHTS FELL HARD

So in this zany season, which has seen such perennial powers as LSU, Clemson, and Oklahoma become well acquainted with sackcloth and ashes, there is no reason why mostly fast-finishing Baylor should not go to a bowl.

But the way they are getting there is a new experience.

They are getting there because the Houston Cougars took the Rice Owls apart feather by feather in an Astrodome showdown Saturday.

And also because the Texas Aggies on Thanksgiving night took the bowl-hopeful Longhorns apart horn by horn.

For Baylor to go bowling, both Texas and Rice had to lose. Both lost big time.

Texas lost to the Aggies for the eighth time in their last nine meetings. They lost by a score of 34–13. That's the most one-sided margin since 1985, when they lost by the score of 42–10.

Losing first to TCU, then Baylor, then A&M, Texas matched its worst production for November since 1956.

Welcome to the SWC, John Mackovic.

Rice lost to the Houston Cougars for the 11th time in their last 12 meetings, and while it could have been worse (it was 64–0 in 1989), it could hardly have been more painful.

Hoping to win the game that would send them to the John Hancock Bowl instead of Baylor and also put a grand climax on their finest season since 1963, the Owls got the shotgun treatment.

CALL 9-1-1! QUICK!

They got beat, 61–34. In the final moments, I kept expecting a call to go out for all the humane societies of Harris County to come rushing to the Astrodome. Or the Sierra Clubs. Or whichever clubs it is that have as their major goal the protection and preservation of that feathered fowl known as the owl.

(I also kept wondering how in the world Baylor lost to the team Houston routed.)

This was the season that finally put Rice above the .500 mark for the first time since the Jess Neely days (1963), and that is an accomplishment no one can take away from the 1992 Owls.

But they finally had put themselves into position to do so much more, and then it all turned to smoke.

"The Houston Cougars are what Darrell Royal once called the TCU Frogs—cockroaches," wryly observed one Trib staffer after Saturday's game. "It's not what they tote off; it's what they fall in and mess up."

Maybe so.

Regardless, it's Baylor that is going to El Paso, because in the SWC, only Baylor and Cotton Bowl–bound A&M qualified for bowl games this year. And they are going through their coaching staff in total transition—some going, some staying, some wondering who will be doing the coaching for this belated curtain call.

As noted earlier, this particular situation is an entirely new experience for the Bears. It might be unique for any SWC team.

JANUARY 1, 1993

BU SILENCES NOISEMAKERS / BEARS' FINAL SHOT IN WAR OF WORDS: YOU LOSE, 20–15

EL PASO, Tex.—Hey, guess what, those Fighting Baylor Bears did it again. Just as they did against Texas, they won Grant Teaff's final game as their head coach, only this New Year's Eve, victory was even sweeter.

In this one they got pushed around for two quarters and then came hurrying back in the second half to upset cocky Arizona, 20–15, in this colorful border city's 59th annual John Hancock (Sun) Bowl.

A crowd of 41,622, many of whom started out sitting under umbrellas because of a cold drizzle, saw the Bears beat the nation's No. 23–ranked team, which the oddsmakers had said would win by at least six points.

The way they had talked at various functions leading up to the game, the Wildcats probably thought they would win by twice or three times that margin.

"When we came in here last week, it became apparent that some people—not everybody, but some people—weren't giving our team or our conference a great deal of respect," said Teaff in the joyful dressing room. "I talked to the team about earning respect on the field, and that's what we tried to do today."

The Bears, determined to atone for their dreadful performance in the Copper Bowl a year ago, won the game by combining terrific plays by Melvin Bonner with two huge fourth-quarter fumble recoveries that set up a pair of field goals by Trey Weir and a goal-line stand that ought to be bronzed and mounted in the Baylor trophy case.

All that, mind you, against an out-of-this-world Arizona defense that had held 10 regular-season opponents to fewer than 20 points.

No. 1–ranked Miami scored only 8 points against the Wildcats. An undefeated Washington team that was ranked No. 1 at kickoff scored only 3.

Bonner, playing his final game in a Baylor uniform, scored 12 all by himself. He surely left a few pro scouts goggle-eyed.

Bonner caught a 61-yard touchdown pass—a tricky halfback pass thrown by freshman tailback Brandell Jackson—in the second quarter and then artfully turned a little J. J. Joe sideline pass into a bolt of lightning, a 69-yard touchdown strike on Baylor's second play of the second half.

Those two catches, plus three others he made for a net of 166 yards, left him clearly stamped as the game's most valuable player, and he was presented the C. M. Hendricks Trophy for his heroics.

Incidentally, that's a new Baylor bowl record for receiving yardage.

Bonner's second touchdown catch put the Bears ahead to stay with the second half only 50 seconds old.

But even his contributions might all have been in vain if the Baylor defense had not turned into a marvelous line of granite early in the fourth quarter.

Trailing by a point, the Wildcats drove from their own 48 to the Baylor 8, where it was first down and just that much yardage needed to give them the lead.

Tailback Ontiwaun Carter slammed up the middle to the 4. Tailback Chuck Levy then got the ball on a sweep to the right, and Le'Shai Maston dragged him down at the 3.

Third and still goal to go.

Arizona quarterback George Malauulu (at least half of the Wildcats seemed to have jawbreaker names—Ontiwaun, Malauulu, tackle Mike Heemsberger, center Mu Tugoai, tackle Joe Smigiel—and they didn't even permit center Hicham El-Mashtoub to make the trip) took one step back and then broke up the middle on a quarterback draw.

Melvin Bonner was drafted by the Denver Broncos in 1993. Courtesy of Baylor University Athletics.

He got to within 6 inches of the goal line.

Fourth and 6 inches, and everyone in the house knew it would be Malauulu again. And it was. And the Bears—the entire midsection plus the two safeties—were waiting for him.

Maston and Robbie Birleson were among those who got there in a hurry, refusing to yield even an inch, and the ball went over to the Bears.

"I thought I was over, but the zebras didn't think so," said Malauulu.

"We got a lot of breaks, and we played an all-around good game," observed Bruin quarterback J. J. Joe, who had his troubles but also some big plays.

There were still 12:13 left to play after that goal-line stand, but it clearly was the turning point.

The Bears managed to drive out of that hole—J. J. hit Bonner (who else?) on a pivotal third-down play from the 1, and a few plays later, Baylor's Rhett Delaney got off a 52-yard punt to the Arizona 12-yard line.

On their first play from there, the Wildcats, who never fumble, did just that.

Levy, trying to go inside, was hit hard by tackle Scotty Lewis, knocking him one way and the ball another.

Freshman linebacker Shelton Lewis, seeing his most action for Baylor all season, grabbed the loose pigskin and got down to the 8-yard line before fumbling out of bounds.

In three plays, the Bears lost 7 yards—that Arizona defense, led by the game's top lineman, middle guard Rob Waldrop, was all it was supposed to be, and never mind that the Bears scored 20 points—and Weir kicked a 32-yard field goal.

Then the Bears got lucky. Mike Chilton's short kickoff was returned to the Arizona 30, but the Wildcats were offsides.

So Chilton kicked again, and Levy came hurrying upfield for 16 yards—and then simply lost his grip on the ball. It flew into the hands of Bruin linebacker Chris Dull at the Arizona 22.

Three plays later, after the Wildcats had surrendered only 4 yards, Weir kicked a 35-yard field goal.

That gave the Bears a 20–13 margin, enough that Teaff felt safe in giving the Wildcats a safety with 31 seconds to play rather than let Delaney attempt a pressure-laden punt from deep in his own territory.

In the time remaining, Malauulu got the Wildcats to the Baylor 28, but the clock and the Bears stopped him there.

The quarterback and his favorite target, flanker Troy Dickey, both had outstanding games and set Arizona records for bowl competition.

Malauulu completed 20 of 38 passes for a whopping 292 yards and rushed for another 47. His 7-yard run on a quarterback draw in the second quarter produced Arizona's only touchdown of the game.

Dickey caught 9 of those passes for 108 yards. If Bonner hadn't been around, Dickey would have been sensational. But as it was, he was mainly a pain.

Other than Malauulu's scoring scamper and the late safety, the Wildcats got their points on 22- and 20-yard field goals by Steve McLaughlin, the first early in the game and the second just 40 seconds before halftime.

Arizona won most of the statistical battle. They managed 23 first downs, held the ball for 32:22 of the game's 60 minutes, averaged 5.1 yards per snap while rolling up 418 total yards, and both outrushed and outpassed the Bears.

They also got beat.

Arizona's first field goal was almost a gift. The Bears tried a fake punt at the end of their first possession, on fourth and 9 from their own 35, and the gamble blew up in their faces.

Keith Caldwell, taking a handoff from Delaney, was tackled 2 yards behind the line of scrimmage, and the Wildcats took over on the 33.

Eight plays later, after the Baylor defense produced an omen of things to come with a splendid goal-line stand, Arizona took a 3–0 lead on McLaughlin's 22-yarder.

On that stand, the Bears gave up only 2 yards on three plays after Arizona had first and goal at the 6.

The Wildcats pushed the Bears around only twice in the first half. They drove 65 yards in seven plays to get their touchdown, and they came right back with a 74-yard drive late in the half to get their second field goal.

In the second half, they seldom ran the ball effectively, and the Baylor pass defense just did not hold up. But those two fumble recoveries surely saved the day. Those, plus that huge goal-line stand.

"Give the credit to Coach Teaff and the Bears," summed up Arizona coach Dick Tomey. "They made the big plays with Bonner. They stopped us on the goal line and made the big plays in the fourth quarter."

And giving an admittedly "teared-up" Grant Teaff something special to remember for his last hurrah, they earned a full measure of respect. Right, Wildcats?

SEPTEMBER 26, 1993

FOURTH-QUARTER WONDERS TOP TECH, 28–26: DRAMATIC BEARS RALLY FROM 12 DOWN IN FINAL PERIOD TO WIN SWC OPENER

JERRY HILL

With the coolness of a riverboat gambler holding four aces, the Baylor Bears went into the fourth quarter of Saturday's showdown with Texas Tech as if there was never a doubt.

On a balmy day when the weather dial topped 90 degrees and the humidity was stifling, it was hard not to sweat. But the Bears never once panicked.

In a down-to-the wire finish that seems like a broken record, the J. J. Joe–led Bears erased a 12-point fourth-quarter deficit and opened the Southwest Conference season with a sweet 28–26 victory before an emotionally exhausted and physically drained crowd of 32,690 at Floyd Casey Stadium.

One of these days, the Bears are going to learn how to play the first three quarters like they do the last. But until that time, head coach Chuck Reedy will gladly take the gray hairs with the wins.

"Our feeling is that if we get into the fourth quarter with a chance, we're going to find a way to win," said Reedy, who is now 3–1 in his debut season. "I don't know how much more of this I can take. But if we can have seven more like that, we'll take it."

Spike Dykes left Midland Lee High School in 1984 to take the reins at Texas Tech as defensive coordinator. He became head coach in 1986. Courtesy of Texas Sports Hall of Fame.

While Baylor won its seventh straight home game, Spike Dykes's Red Raiders (1–3) suffered their third straight road loss to a 1992 bowl team. Despite rolling up 508 yards total offense, including 174 on the ground by bruising I-back Byron (Bam) Morris, Tech found a way to lose.

"It's hard to lose these kinds of close games," said Dykes, who has to face Top 25 teams Texas A&M and North Carolina State the next two weeks. "It takes a lot of wind out of your sails."

But Baylor seems to have its own patent on these opponent-deflating, fourth-quarter comebacks. Just ask Fresno State (42–39) and Utah State (28–24).

"I wasn't exactly sure how," said Joe, who hit 14 of 17 passes for 254 yards and two touchdowns, "but I just had a feeling we were going to win it.

"When you've got a young team like we do, it's like the fourth quarter is a signal to get that sense of urgency. It's like, 'Shoot, we got to start playing now.'"

What Baylor survived was the most potent offensive onslaught it has seen all year, better than even Fresno State or Colorado. Dangerous quarterback Robert Hall hit 15 of 24 passes for 250 yards, added 51 yards on the ground, and got plenty of help from his friend Morris.

But in a game that featured 960 yards offense—452 for the Bears—it was an opportunistic Baylor defense that provided the key to victory.

With the Bears on the ropes late in the third quarter, following their first and only turnover of the game, Pete Fredenburg's defense came up with a timely goal-line stand and held the Red Raiders to a 21-yard Jon Davis field goal.

And then in the pivotal fourth period, the Bears recovered Tech fumbles to start a Baylor touchdown drive and stop a Red Raider scoring threat.

"You have to give Pete Fredenburg and our other defensive coaches a lot of credit for bringing along a defense that has so many young players," Reedy said. "They've gotten better and better every week. And they came through when we needed it the most today."

That time came late in the third. After Baylor botched a fake field goal try from the Tech 24, the Red Raiders drove a painful stake to the heart with a 77-yard touchdown drive that gave them a 23–14 lead.

The payoff came on a memorable 44-yard run by Morris, who became well acquainted with each of Baylor's 11 defenders along the way. Each had a shot at the 240-pound running back, and all with the same results. He could have run another 100 yards if the refs had let him.

"I think he ran through 12 of our guys, didn't he?"

Tech receiver Lloyd Hill tries to snag a pass as Baylor's Phillip Kent comes in on defense. Courtesy of Texas Tech University Athletics.

posed Reedy after the game. "He's the best I've ever been around."

But the critical time for Baylor came when Joe fumbled a handoff exchange on the next offensive play. Shawn Jackson recovered to give the Red Raiders the ball at the Bears' 30.

Just 13 seconds after giving up a touchdown, the defense had to trot back on the field again to face a Tech offense that is all too lethal.

In three plays, the Red Raiders were knocking on the door at the 2-yard line. But that was when the young Baylor defense kicked it up a notch or two.

After throwing Byron Myles for a 1-yard loss, Malcolm Hamilton and Tony Tubbs combined to push Morris back another step on second down. And then, when Hall rolled to his left and lofted a pass to tight end Roger Corn, cornerback Kendrick Bell battled the ball away.

Somewhat regretfully, Tech settled on Davis's 21-yard field goal and a 26–14 lead with 2:37 left in the third quarter.

"I don't think you could say enough about the defense," said Reedy, "because we put them in the worst possible situation. They had just given up an 80-yard drive and had to go back on the field. That stand could have been the difference in the ball game."

When the final seconds of the third quarter ticked off the clock, the Baylor offense strolled confidently down to the other end of the field and finished off a 12-play, 74-yard drive that got the Bears back in the game.

Brandell Jackson did most of the preliminary work, rushing three times for 29 yards and adding 18 yards on a key fourth-down pass play. But it was John Henry who got the final call on a 3-yard touchdown run behind right guard David Leaks and tackle Fred Miller.

Jarvis Van Dyke, who was snubbed earlier on what would have been a 41-yard field goal attempt, booted the third of his four extra points to cut Tech's deficit to 26–21 with 13:03 left in the game.

Tech receiver Lloyd Hill had a dismal day with three drops and only three catches—far below his season average. But the All-American seemed to make up for his earlier miscues when he hauled in a pass from Hall for a 35-yard gainer into Baylor territory.

But at the tail end, with Hill running loose, linebacker Phillip Kent caught him from behind and stripped the ball with his right hand. Chris Lewis, with two game-winning fumble recoveries to his credit already, gave the Bears the ball back at their own 45-yard line.

With consecutive passes to Marvin Callies and Ben Bronson, Joe moved the Bears quickly down to the Red Raider 12-yard line. The Tech defense stiffened, but Henry picked up his second touchdown of the day and sixth of the season on fourth and 2 from the 4-yard line.

In a move that he would later second-guess, Reedy opted for a conversion kick and a 28–26 lead instead of going for two points and a field goal cushion for the Bears.

But with 9:14 still to play, Reedy had to figure neither team was through scoring. That was one of the few things he got wrong.

In a replay of the Fresno State game three weeks ago, Tech was driving for the winning score when disaster struck.

With a 43-yard pass from Hall to Donald Marshall, the Red Raiders moved inside the Baylor 20-yard line. But Marshall was flagged 15 yards for celebrating.

Morris, who had 174 yards rushing on 23 carries, made up for most of the penalty yardage with a 14-yard option run on first down. But on second down, with Hall looking for an open receiver, defensive end Lamone Alexander stripped the ball loose for Tech's fourth fumble of the day. Defensive tackle Charles Horton, Johnny on the spot, recovered back at the 27.

Thanks to another costly penalty—defensive holding on a third-and-9 play—Baylor kept the ball out of Tech's hands for the last five minutes and held on for their most important win of the year.

The Red Raiders took a 9–0 lead early on Hall's 19-yard touchdown pass to Jerod Fiebiger and a 22-yard field goal by Davis, but it could have been worse. Like they did in the third, the Bears held Tech to a field goal after a first and goal at the 6.

Baylor's offense moved the ball effectively most of the day, but its first score didn't come until the first-half clock was running out.

After Hamilton recovered a fumble by Connally ex Alton Crain at the Baylor 37, the Bears took just six plays to capitalize. Joe hooked up with Bronson on a 36-yard touchdown pass with 1:12 left that was a beauty to behold.

Joe put it where the Tech defensive back couldn't get it, and Bronson went diving into the end zone for the acrobatic catch and his first TD in a Baylor uniform. The extra point made it 9–7 at the half.

Tech regained the momentum in the third quarter when Hall hit Corn for a 3-yard TD pass that completed a six-play, 80-yard drive. Just 1:36 into the second half, the Red Raiders had a 16–7 lead.

Baylor's answer was another TD catch by Bronson, who had three receptions for 104 yards, as he beat Shawn Hurd for a 44-yard perfect strike from Joe and a 16–14 Tech lead.

With a chance to take the lead midway through the third quarter with a 41-yard field goal by Van Dyke, Reedy opted instead for a fake that came up woefully short. Fullback Robert Strait was stopped a good 2 yards short of the first-down markers.

"At the time, I felt like we needed a touchdown," Reedy said. "In a game like that, you figure you have to have touchdowns, not field goals. And I figured we had just as good a shot at making a first down as we did kicking a 41-yard field goal into a stiff crosswind."

And in the end, it didn't really matter. For the third time in four weeks, the play-it-to-the-wire Bears came up golden.

JANUARY 8, 2006

ROSE BOWL VICTORY HARKENS BACK TO '69

In more than a half century of covering college football games, I've seen literally hundreds of encounters that ranged from the dull to the routine to the spectacular to the absolutely unforgettable. On December 6, 1969, I saw Coach Darrell Royal's No. 1–ranked Texas beat Coach Frank Broyles's No. 2 Arkansas in a nail-biting showdown in Fayetteville and nail down the national championship. In the years since then, I have often tagged that "Big Shootout," as it was called, as the greatest football game I've ever seen.

Last Wednesday in the Rose Bowl in Pasadena, California, I saw its match. Indeed, maybe more than its match.

Maybe No. 2 Texas over unbeaten defending national champion Southern Cal, 41–38, rates a smidgeon higher than Texas over Arkansas, 15–14. It's close. Both were classics in the full meaning of the word.

There are obvious similarities, beginning with the fact that the Longhorns flew back to Austin carrying a national championship trophy with them. Both were games that had the national stage all to themselves and were hyped beyond all reason—and then actually lived up to their billing. That's rare.

The Texas-Arkansas game in 1969 had been moved to its special December date, after all other regular-season games had been played, in order to provide a final hurrah for college football's months-long celebration of its centennial season. But the Texas-USC game was played in the storied Rose Bowl, the grandpappy of all bowls, and it matched Southern Cal's 34-game winning streak against Texas' 19-game victory march, and it was the most talked-about showdown yet of these BCS season-ending extravaganzas, and it unfolded before a sellout crowd of 93,986. And what setting could be more compelling than that?

PROMINENT FIGURES

The 1969 clash boasted the presence of President Richard Nixon and the Secret Service and evangelist Billy Graham and every lawmaker in the country who could commandeer a ticket. The Rose Bowl battle was hardly lacking in celebrities (Dennis Quaid, Jim Belushi, Nick Lachey, Henry Winkler, Will Ferrell, Lance Armstrong, Matthew McConaughey, Roger Clemens . . . those names give you an idea).

Stretch limousines were there in profusion too. More than three hours before kickoff time, as we made our way along a crowded sidewalk and on a narrow street toward the big bowl itself, a white limo rolled slowly past us. One fan, clad in USC colors, hurried toward the vehicle, peered closely, then yelled, "My God, Britney Spears!" I think not, but the crowd laughed anyway.

That man who is now in the White House watched the game on television, and then George W. Bush telephoned his congratulations to UT coach Mack Brown at 6:00 a.m. the next morning. I'll bet he woke Mack up too.

"He told me he fell asleep in the third quarter," Brown later reported. "I told him we did too."

I have no idea what kind of TV ratings that 1969 game commanded, but they had to be huge. As for the Rose Bowl's ratings, they were the highest in the history of BCS championship games and the highest for any college game since the 1987 Fiesta Bowl, when Joe Paterno's Penn State team upset Jimmy Johnson's No. 1–ranked Miami Hurricanes.

In both cases, Texas had to win its national title on enemy grass—in icy Fayetteville in 1969 and in sunny Southern California last Wednesday.

THRILLING RALLIES

The Longhorns had to stage almost magical fourth-quarter comebacks to win both games. When the teams changed ends of the field for the last quarter in Fayetteville in 1969, Texas trailed by 14 points. In last Wednesday's game, the favored USC Trojans led by only a single point, 24–23, at the end of the third period, but their margin would grow to 12 points with 6:42 left to play when USC scored on a 22-yard pass to make it a 38–26 game.

And in both contests, Texas quarterbacks made the difference in the fourth quarter. In 1969, senior James Street, never a loser as a starting quarterback at UT, ran 42 yards for a touchdown on a play that was supposed to have been a pass, then he struggled into the end zone on a two-point conversion play following that first UT score to make it a 14–8 game. Then, late in the quarter, when the Longhorns' situation had become desperate, he completed an improbable fourth-down-and-3 pass from the Texas 43 to tight end Randy Peschel at the Arkansas 13 to set up the touchdown Jim Bertelsen scored two plays later. Texas' Happy Feller (that was his name, honest) then kicked the game-winning extra point.

As for the quarterback play in last Wednesday's game, well, two words tell you all you need to know: Vince Young. The play of Texas' junior wizard was out of sight, that's all.

Admittedly, he cut it a little thin. There were only 19 ticks left on the clock when he scored the second of his two fourth-quarter touchdowns that proved decisive. His first score came on a second-down, 17-yard run with 4:03 left, the second on a fourth-down 8-yarder to give UT a 39–38 lead. And he followed up on the second touchdown run with a two-point conversion to provide the final three-point margin.

When Vince then left the field for the last time, with victory all but assured, he had rushed for 200 yards (averaging 10.5 yards per rush) and passed for 267 yards (completing 30 of 40 passes), and he had left me convinced that I had just seen the greatest individual bowl performance my eyes had ever witnessed.

Heretofore, I have reserved that distinction for Rice's Dicky Maegle, who rushed for 265 yards and 3 touchdowns on just 11 carries against Alabama in the 1954 Cotton Bowl, the first Cotton Bowl game I ever covered. One of his TDs was on a 95-yard run that he never finished; Alabama's Tommy Lewis came off the bench to tackle the speeding, end zone–bound Maegle about midfield—remember?

Maegle was mind-boggling that first day of 1954. Vince Young was even better on the fourth day of 2006.

Vince was so good, his performance so riveting, his superiority over Trojan defenders wearing the cardinal and gold of USC so unbelievable that more than one voice in the press box after the game was wondering aloud if maybe another Heisman Trophy vote might not now be in order. In the first one, USC's Reggie Bush, was the runaway winner. Last Wednesday, Reggie was good, and so was USC quarterback Matt Leinart, the 2004 Heisman winner. But Vince was out of sight.

Vince made me glad I voted for him for the Heisman, with Bush second and Leinart third on my ballot, and anyone who doesn't believe that can consult my son-in-law Alan Carlson, who emailed my ballot for me.

I can also brag a bit that I picked seven-point underdog Texas to knock off the great Trojans. In a prekickoff press box conversation with the veteran of UT athletics, Bill Little, I told him Texas was going to win.

"The law of averages definitely is on your side," I said, "and bowl games are still made for upsets."

His reply: "Well, this is one of those deals where we can't lose. If they beat us, we will have just lost to the team they're now calling the greatest in the history of college football. And if we beat them . . ." He gave me a broad grin and winked. Then he added, "This morning the team was as relaxed and loose as I've seen them all year."

It was an omen of the way the Longhorns were to play, and never mind the fact that they fumbled away USC's first punt, setting up a Trojan touchdown.

Before the game, Darrell Royal, sitting one level

Texas quarterback Vince Young spearheaded the Longhorns' 2006 Rose Bowl victory over USC. Young was named offensive MVP of the game and teammate Michael Huff, safety, won the defensive honors. Courtesy of University of Texas Athletics.

below the writers in the press box, was asked to forecast the winner. Instead, he told us what Mack Brown had said when he was asked how this Texas team would fare against Royal's 1963 and 1969 national champions.

"Oh, we'd beat the daylights out of them," Brown replied. The scribe couldn't believe his ears. This was a real scoop. Then came Brown's next words: "You have to remember—those guys are 60 to 70 years old now. Yeah, we'd beat them easy."

Royal laughed again in telling the story. Then he turned serious and made his own prediction: "I think this one will be decided strictly by which quarterback has the hot hand," he said.

Vince Young's hand could not have been hotter.

"Their quarterback ran all over the place," summed up USC coach Pete Carroll after the game.

Added the Trojans' powerhouse runner LenDale White, "Vince did his thing tonight. There's no way to stop him."

If Vince decides to stick around UT for his senior season, get ready for more of the same in the national championship game next year.

NOVEMBER 11, 2012

BETTER BELIEVE IT: AGGIES PUT KINK INTO BCS WITH SHOCKER OVER NO. 1 ALABAMA, A&M PUTS AN END TO UNHAPPY TRADITION

KATE HAIROPOULOS

TUSCALOOSA, Ala.—Bryant-Denny Stadium roared. BCS No. 1 Alabama had been playing behind bold No. 15 Texas A&M all of this clear, crisp Saturday. But here, after a 54-yard pass put it at first and goal at the Aggies' 6, the Crimson Tide could restore order to college football, thank A&M for the gut check, and move on about its business of winning another national championship.

Except those irreverent Aggies—who had already exceeded expectations in their first year in the SEC—had no intention of playing their part. Not this time, not this bunch, who had blown losses and survived so much disappointment in previous years only to emerge stronger, remade with a new coaching staff and redshirt freshman quarterback Johnny Manziel.

A&M, clinging to a five-point lead, held 'Bama out of the end zone on three straight rushing plays, with quarterback A. J. McCarron finally getting to the 2 on a scramble. But on fourth and goal, A&M sophomore Deshazor Everett picked off McCarron to save the Aggies' lead with less than two minutes to play. A&M held on for its 29–24, turn-the-BCS-upside-down victory, which ranks among the program's most significant. Bama (9–1, 6–1 SEC) fell a week after first looking vulnerable in an emotional, last-minute win at LSU.

"Just give it all you got," senior linebacker Sean Porter said the Aggies were thinking on the fourth down. "This is how you win the game. This is what we'll be remembered by: Did we stop them? Or did we get scored on and lose the game like always?"

Those "like always" days may finally be a thing of the past. Kind of felt like it when the team belted out the "Aggie War Hymn" with the visiting fans afterward, singing at the top of their lungs.

"We did something great," junior defensive end Damontre Moore said.

A&M, which busted out to a 20–0 lead by the end of the first quarter on a 'Bama defense that had been giving up 9.1 points a game, improved to 8–2, 5–2. With nonconference opponent Sam Houston State up next and Missouri rounding out league play after, a potential BCS bid could be in the offing. Alabama's—and the SEC's—national title hopes may be on the ropes.

But the stock of A&M and Manziel is soaring. Manziel produced 345 total yards—going 24 of 31 for 253 yards passing and two TDs, along with 92 yards rushing. When the Tide forced A&M to rely on its passing game in the second half, bringing more pressure at Manziel, the Aggies executed. They gained 418 total yards, converting 11 of 18 third downs. Ryan Swope

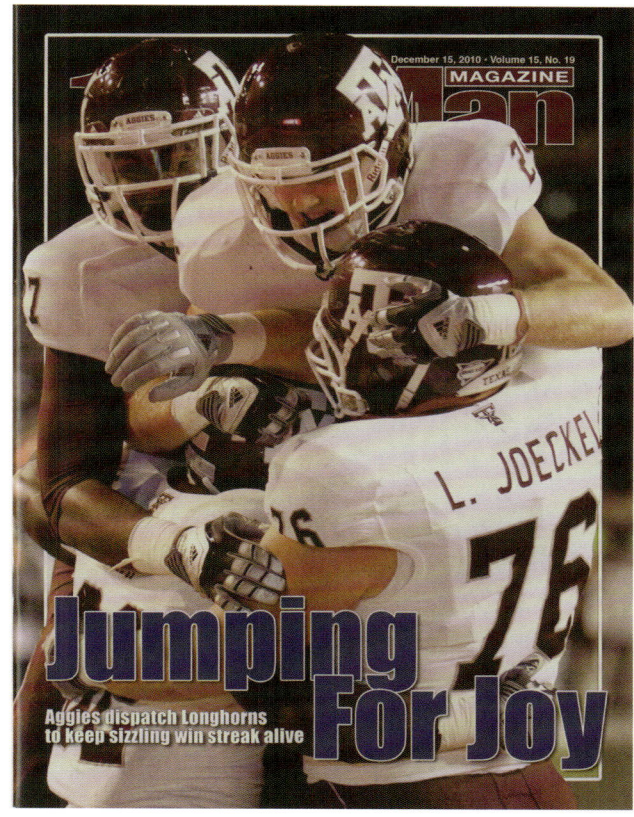

Ryan Swope (25) celebrates with Luke Joeckel (76) and other teammates after a big win over Texas. Courtesy of *12th Man Magazine*.

had 11 catches for 111 yards and a touchdown, and Mike Evans had 5 for 50 yards.

Manziel forced himself back into the discussion as a legitimate Heisman Trophy finalist, no matter that no freshman has ever won.

"He's been able to handle the moments better than most young guys," coach Kevin Sumlin said.

But as Sumlin stressed all week, A&M needed an all-around game to beat Alabama.

Manziel found Malcome Kennedy, who had one previous TD catch this season, for a 24-yard scoring pass with 8:37 left that put A&M up 29–17.

It came after Alabama's second of three turnovers, a fumble by T. J. Yeldon. McCarron also threw two picks, ending a streak of no interceptions that covered 291 attempts dating to last season. But he hit Amari Cooper for a 54-yard scoring pass with 2:28 to play. A&M went three and out, setting up the defense's final stand.

The Aggies were resilient throughout the second half, even after the second quarter, when Alabama surged back to pull within 20–14 before the break, grabbing back the momentum at home. Unlike A&M's two losses—to Florida and LSU—the Aggies were able to answer second-half adjustments. In an unforgettable way.

"There's no better way to go out senior year on the road," Swope said. "You've got to play with emotion when you're playing the No. 1 team in the country. . . . Guys played with heart tonight. It was unbelievable."

JANUARY 5, 2013

CAN'T BE BEAT: MANZIEL ELEVATES A&M WITH A PERFORMANCE THAT LEAVES OU REELING

KEVIN SHERRINGTON

ARLINGTON, Tex.—One of the debates about a Heisman Trophy candidate—and a bad one, at that—is what he's worth to his team. The only official requirement is to be "outstanding," a tough enough feat. But like it or not, it's not an MVP award.

If it's still the case you insist on making, though, Johnny Manziel obliged Friday.

Take Johnny Football out of the AT&T Cotton Bowl Classic, and Texas A&M not only doesn't beat Oklahoma by a whopping 41–13 before 87,025 at JerryWorld; the outcome might have been in jeopardy.

As for Manziel and what he means to his team—to his new league, to college football—there are no doubts.

Critics openly wondered if he could handle the sudden surge of fame and his offensive coordinator leaving him for Lubbock. He did Letterman's Top 10. He hammed it up with Leno. He hung with Rockets, mugged with LeBron, flirted with Megan Fox, teed it up with the Jonas Brothers.

And then he went out and played his best game yet.

So much for the Heisman hangover.

Manziel put the Aggies on his back in the first half, providing a slight lead despite the fact that the Sooners held the ball more than twice as long, then went wild on Oklahoma in the second.

He set classic records for total offense (516 yards), yards rushing by a quarterback (229), and defenders grasping at air (too many to count).

No other player in the storied, 77-year history of the classic—not Dickie Maegle, not Eddie Phillips, not Bo Jackson or Graham Harrell or Doug Flutie—had ever done what Manziel did.

No other player this season—not even Mantei Te'o or Collin Klein—comes close to his impact.

On any field, against any team, in any debate, there is only Johnny Football.

Best quarterback you've ever faced, Bob Stoops?

"Absolutely."

The Sooners couldn't do anything to stop him. If they dropped eight, he ran wild. If they rushed four, he ran wild.

He did the impossible Friday, especially for the Cotton Bowl folks: he kept a 28-point win interesting even if you weren't an Aggie.

On A&M's first touchdown, he dropped back, spun out of the pocket, looked, looked, looked . . . and took off. Watching him go, it reminded one of the classic line from Texas' Roy Williams about Vince Young and what it was like to play wide receiver to his quarterback.

"I'm gonna run my route," Williams said, "and he's gonna take off. And then I got blocking to do."

Fortunately for A&M, like Young, Manziel makes it

Courtesy of *Dave Campbell's Texas Football*.

Head coach Kevin Sumlin oversaw the Aggies' 2012 SEC debut. Courtesy of *12th Man Magazine*.

work. On the play in question, he wheels left, finds the sideline, slips past a seemingly sure tackle, tightropes a half dozen steps, skips just inside the pylon, and flashes a Superman pose.

Meanwhile, Bob Stoops is over on the sideline screaming at Mike Stoops, who looks like he's eight years old and back in Ohio getting it from his big brother.

Frankly, there was nothing the Stoops boys could do. Manziel is fast, but is he faster than all those Sooners? Stoops said he wasn't sure who'd win a track meet. But it's not just Manziel's speed. It's the nanosecond's hesitation, a side step, a change of direction, then he's back at top speed.

Consider a drive in the second quarter: Manziel drops back, starts up the middle, and swings right, Sooners sliding past him like cars on ice. No one's immune to the effect Manziel causes. He might have scored, in fact, but his teammates couldn't get out of the way fast enough.

Manziel isn't as pretty passing, but on occasion it can be startlingly effective.

Even when the results don't come out right, it can leave you shaking your head. Consider this: Spinning right out of a Sooner's grasp in the first half, he suddenly throws back to his right when he should have been dizzy. The ball hits Malcome Kennedy in the hands and bounces to the Sooners' Javon Harris, which, officially, goes down as Manziel's only miscue.

Of course, if you watched the game, you weren't buying that. If you watched the game, you realized that Ryan Swope is a nice possession receiver who has a good shot at playing in the pros. You could see Ben Malena is a pretty good running back. You could tell the offensive line is NFL caliber. But you might also recall that Ryan Tannehill played behind the same offensive line, and he didn't win much with it, and he plays on Sundays now.

For the moment, though, and as long as he chooses to remain an amateur, Saturdays belong to Johnny Football. Long may he reign.

I sold *Dave Campbell's Texas Football* in 1985, but I still enjoy signing copies when the new issues come out. One of my daughters asked me to autograph her copy of the 2014 edition. Courtesy of *Dave Campbell's Texas Football Magazine*.

DECEMBER 5, 2015

LONGHORNS UPSET BOWL-BOUND BEARS

I was so blind last Saturday that I couldn't see the handwriting on the wall.

I couldn't see that Baylor was going to get upset by 20-point underdog Texas and thus miss out on getting that delicious trip to the Sugar Bowl that they were in line for if they had just defeated Texas. Instead, they lost and wound up being chosen to play in the Russell Athletic Bowl based in Orlando, Florida.

Yes, they'll go to Orlando to play the 11–2 North Carolina Tar Heels. And here's the ironic part: the Tar Heels are coached by Larry Federa, a homegrown Texan who went to A&M Consolidated High School in College Station, then to Austin College in Sherman (where Kansas State's great coach Bill Snyder once ran the football program), and later became a graduate assistant at Baylor under Grant Teaff and later one of Baylor coach Chuck Reedy's top assistants.

And then to compound the irony, Federa later wound up as one of Oklahoma State's key offensive assistants and reportedly was considered for the Baylor job before Art Briles was chosen to head up the Baylor football program. Instead, Federa was tapped for a successful sojourn as head coach at Southern Mississippi and later for the head job at North Carolina. And as gridiron boss of the Tar Heels, he has brought that football program to national recognition.

In other words, like Briles at Baylor.

So now those two coaches will match teams, high-scoring offenses, and wits in Orlando, where Disney World is a prime attraction and Mickey Mouse hangs out. Small world, right?

But back to my blindness. Before last Saturday's game even started, I lost the lens out of one side of my glasses. I see things well enough close up; it's for distance that I need my glasses—like looking at a football game from the press box. That's distance. And that's tough.

But more than that, I was blinded by the situation: Baylor was overwhelmingly favored to defeat the visiting Texas Longhorns, and Baylor had been defeated only once at home in this the second year of football competition in their new stadium built alongside the rolling waters of the Brazos River ("the arms of God," the early day Spanish had called the Brazos). Baylor was set to sew up a trip to the Sugar Bowl as it did back in 1956, when it blew past Rice in old Baylor Stadium. I was sports editor of the *Waco Tribune-Herald* that year, and I covered that 46–13 victory over the Jess Neely–coached Owls in an era when neither Baylor football teams nor other football teams beat Neely-coached Owls by such a one-sided score.

Also last Saturday, I was blinded by what had happened to the Longhorns the Saturday before, when they went to Morgantown and lost to West Virginia, 38–20. This year's Baylor team had defeated West Virginia in Baylor's same McLane Stadium, 62–38. An easy victory.

Finally, at kickoff time, I didn't know that three is not enough.

The Bears had lost first-team quarterback Seth Russell in the Iowa State game and second-team quarterback Jarrett Stidham in Stillwater when they flattened Oklahoma State, 45–35, for the first time in ages. But Chris Johnson had immediately stepped up after Stidham suffered a broken ankle in the first half of that unforgettable Stillwater conquest. Johnson had played like he had been the starting QB all along.

To be sure, Johnson had been less than stellar in Baylor's next game played in Fort Worth when the rain was pouring down and the football was slick and heavy, like the gridiron itself. That's when the Bears lost to TCU in a second overtime. But last Saturday's game was going to be played in bright sunshine and in perfect football weather.

So I figured the Bears, with so much to play for, would win. I was totally wrong.

Johnson was knocked out of the game in the first quarter (concussion-like symptoms) when tackled by Texas safety P. J. Locke and never returned. Baylor tried to rally with swift sophomore wide receiver Lynx Hawthorne at quarterback (he had last played QB on a regular basis while a junior in high school at Refugio), and he didn't do badly. He ran for 66 yards in 10 tries and one TD and completed 10 of 22 passes. But alas, he also threw two interceptions (the Bears were guilty of four turnovers in all—usually a fatal number in a tight football game).

So Texas led from the get-go, 23–17, and if you still don't believe it, just ask the 48,095 fans who were there. Indeed, ask the Longhorns themselves. They know. They deserved to win. Nothing fluky about it.

As fullback Alex De La Torre told Chuck Carlton (*Dallas Morning News*) after the game, "We just came out and had nothing to lose. Why not go out, play your butt off, and go win?"

I should have known better. As my friend Hollis Biddle had told me all week, Texas "always" has talent. And they had handed the Oklahoma Sooners their lone loss of the season in Dallas, 24–17. But I should have known long before that what the Longhorns could do in an underdog role.

I can still remember what happened in 1937: Baylor was undefeated after six games and had already defeated the Texas Aggies in College Station and TCU in Waco at old Muny Stadium (TCU had Davey O'Brien and the makings of a Dutch Meyer–coached team that a year later would win college football's national championship). People all over the state assured one another that Baylor was going to the Rose Bowl as SMU had done two years earlier.

That season, the Longhorns, tutored by famed Hall of Fame coach D. X. Bible, had not won a single SWC game. It was at that Baylor-Texas game that my predecessor at the *Tribune-Herald*, Jinx Tucker, before going up to the press box, had seen a student representing the *Baylor Lariat* approach a well-known national broadcaster and ask him who he thought would win the game. And the famous broadcaster had brushed the student off, telling him, "Young man, I get paid for my opinions." Tucker, standing nearby and overhearing the conversation, had reached in his pocket, pulled out a penny, flipped it to the student, and said, "Here, kid, give him this and let's find out all he knows about football."

True story. So I should have known never to underrate the Longhorns. But obviously I forgot.

This 2015 Texas team came to Waco and seized the upper hand early and never trailed.

So it's off to Florida the Bears will go, and that's a bad trip or bowl, and certainly the Bears will face a worthy opponent. As Briles said Sunday, the Bears will go determined to win this one. "We'd certainly like to feel good for six months," he said, an oblique reference to last season's last-second loss to Michigan State in the Cotton Bowl.

In last Saturday's game, Baylor received the opening kickoff and rolled right down the field, despite being flagged for a holding penalty on the game's first play, leaving the Bears facing a first and 19. But they overcame that handicap. Johnson completed a 15-yard pass to Corey Coleman and then ran for 17 yards himself, and everyone must have thought, *Here go the Bears again.* That has become their mojo this season: get the football and score a touchdown right away.

But after carving out a first down at the Texas 39 on their first possession, the Bears were stopped. Three running plays left them needing about 30 inches to get a first down, and they gave the ball to Shock Lynwood for the fourth straight time. He hit the middle of the Longhorn defense that was braced for the play and gained nothing. As it turned out, Lynwood was ailing himself.

Texas took over and scored in three plays. Freshman Chris Warren had runs of 8 and 5 yards, and then junior quarterback Tyron Swoopes (6-foot-4, 244) fired a 57-yard pass to sophomore tight end Caleb Bluiett who was wide open. Bluiett galloped on for a touchdown, and the Longhorns were off to the races and making it look easy.

Bluiett started the season listed as a defensive end, so UT coach Charlie Strong is moving his players around, finding out which piece fits where best. Another talented Longhorn is senior Nick Rose, who regularly sends his kickoffs into or beyond the end zone (very few chances for long kickoff returns against Texas). Rose also booms long field goals. He kicked a 23-yard field goal at the 5:45 mark of the first quarter and then a 53-yarder in the second quarter. Texas also got seven more points from a 9-yard Swoopes run late in the first quarter and left the Bears in a 0–20 hole at halftime.

At halftime, it was time for the Bears to regroup and find the makings of a thrilling and perhaps winning comeback in the game's final 30 minutes. Give them full credit; they came close—closer than the final score indicates.

With Hawthorne now serving as the triggerman (and scoring one touchdown on an 8-yard run), coach Art Briles switched the Bears to a wildcat formation featuring swift and elusive Johnny Jefferson and power-running redshirt freshman Terence Williams. Williams is 6-foot-2, 220, and fast. And he delivered 42 yards on 11 carries. Sophomore Jefferson did even better, gaining 158 yards and scoring a touchdown (a 6.9-yard average). In turning to the wildcat formation, the Bears basically bet their chips on what the offensive line could do—and it did quite a bit, opening holes and enabling the Bears to make it a 17–20 game with 9:40 left on the clock.

But after the Bears had narrowed the gap to just three points, Texas answered as Charlie Strong wanted them to, driving 62 yards from the UT 19 to the Baylor 19 while using up 5:35 on the clock and leaving the Bears with fewer than four minutes to score a winning seven points. They tried. Jefferson got away on a 9-yard run to the Baylor 40 but fumbled at that point and Texas recovered. And neither team did much of consequence in the final 2:31 left to play.

The final stats showed Baylor with 29 first downs, Texas with 15; Baylor with 395 net rushing yards, Texas with 156; Baylor with 84 net yards overhead, Texas with 151. Turnovers (Baylor with four turnovers, Texas with zero) and the kicking game spelled the difference.

Jefferson led all ball carriers, totaling 158 yards. Hawthorne had 66, Williams 42, and Devin Chafin 38. Texas got important yardage overland from Warren (106 yards) and Swoopes (53), and Swoopes did the job overhead, completing 12 of 19 passes for 151 yards and a touchdown. So the kickers decided it. UT's Rose kicked three field goals; BU's Chris Callahan kicked one 24-yard field goal but missed a 40-yarder, and Spencer Evans missed a 54-yarder. Ultimately, those lost six points determined the outcome.

At the finish, Baylor's senior All-American offensive tackle Spencer Drango said something worth remembering: "I know there are some teams that would love to be 9–3 at this point," he told John Werner (*Waco Tribune-Herald*). "We still have the opportunity for a 10-win season. So the disappointing thing is sending the seniors out without a win in their last game here. But we're going to a bowl, a nice bowl, and we're excited to be a part of that."

MACK BROWN: A COACH FOR ALL SEASONS

I first met Mack Brown at the most unlikely of places. Mack Brown was the University of Texas' new football coach and was starting to make the rounds all over the state to meet alums and UT fans. That day he had come to Bell County's convention center in Belton, Texas, to meet the UT people in that area and tell them what he planned to do to restore UT football to its glory days.

As luck would have it, several Wacoans decided to make the trip to Belton and invited me to join them. Thus I was there when Mack talked to the crowd and outlined some of his plans, leaving the UT folk excited and eager for the season to hurry up and get there.

In the process of meeting people and shaking hands, he happened to bump into me. I guess he had heard of *Texas Football* magazine (after all, he had been the University of Oklahoma's offensive coordinator in 1984, so this wasn't his first trip to Texas; he knew all about the Red River Rivalry), and that day I found him friendly and very likeable. He had a gift for gab and a big smile. And over his years as the Longhorns' head football coach (1998–2013), win or lose, I never saw him change.

I saw Mack's Longhorns play when they were very good and when they were not that good. After the UT games played in Austin, I always found Mack to be very gracious, very friendly, and very accommodating, no matter which end of the score he came out on.

Their best game of all? Perhaps that would be a game played far removed from Austin. I was lucky enough to be able to go to the great Rose Bowl game when Texas defeated No. 1–ranked Southern Cal to win the 2005 college football championship. (Texas QB Vince Young had an unforgettable game, including his 18-yard run for a winning touchdown with 19 seconds remaining in the final quarter. Final score: Texas 41, USC 38, remember?)

The game I would put with it as the best UT football game I ever covered would be that unforgettable game of December 6, 1969, played in Fayetteville, Arkansas: No. 1 Texas versus No. 2 Arkansas, Darrell Royal versus Frank Broyles, the centennial year of college football, with Texas QB James Street versus Arkansas QB Bill Montgomery. UT won it, 15–14, on a bitterly cold afternoon because Royal, facing a fourth-and-3 challenge in his own end of the field, decided to call for a long pass instead of a punt. Street's pass to tight end Randy Peschel was complete, barely, and it put Texas on Arkansas' 8-yard line, and Texas went on from there to score the touchdown

Mack Brown guided the Texas Longhorns to victory over USC in the 2006 Rose Bowl, clinching the national championship. His teams beat Oklahoma seven times. Courtesy of University of Texas Athletics.

and two-point conversion that prompted US President Richard Nixon to visit the UT locker room after the game and present a special plaque to the UT team, pronouncing the Longhorns the national champions of 1969 college football.

I will never forget that game. However, to remove all doubt about deserving the national championship trophy, Texas had to go to Dallas three weeks later and defeat Notre Dame in another pulse pounder, 21–17, in the Cotton Bowl. Texas had to stage another fourth-quarter comeback to win that historic game. (Historic because Notre Dame had been refusing all bowl invitations since defeating Stanford in the Rose Bowl in 1925, but the Irish were persuaded they couldn't pass up that Cotton Bowl opportunity. After all, remember, it WAS college football's centennial year.)

And as luck would have it, I was president of the Football Writers of America that year, and the NCAA decided that the current and past presidents of the FWAA should make the selections, so I was able to be a part of that and also make a trip to New York City when Chevrolet decided to honor the team we had chosen. But that's another story.

Here's a side note: As far as I can remember, Texas has won five national championships—in 1963, 1969, 1970, 1977, and 2005, and I have covered them all. And if they had not suffered some key upsets (in 1984 by Georgia in the Cotton Bowl, 10–9; in 1964 by Arkansas in Austin, 14–13; and in 1961 by TCU, also in Austin, 6–0), I would have seen them win eight national college football crowns.

There are two other situations that I did not cover but that still *will* linger long in my 91-year-old memory. If an early first-quarter injury had not knocked UT quarterback Colt McCoy (shoulder injury) out of the game completely, I still believe Texas would have defeated Alabama in the Rose Bowl game following the 2009 football season. And then in 1941, a D. X. Bible–coached Longhorn team appeared to be in position to finish No. 1 in the national rankings (13 Longhorn players were pictured on the November 17 cover of *Life Magazine*). They were overwhelmingly favored to defeat Baylor in Waco but had to settle for a 7–7 tie, and then they lost to TCU, 14–7, the next Saturday in Austin. If not for these key defeats, Texas would have won 10 national football championships.

So Bible in 1941, Royal in 1961, UT coach Fred Akers in the 1977 and 1984 Cotton Bowl games, and Mack Brown in the 2010 Rose Bowl game all came tantalizingly close, only to lose those five games that went the other way.

Incidentally, while I did not personally see that 1941 Baylor-Texas game in Waco or the UT loss to TCU in Austin, I also can remember a then fully aroused Texas going to College Station and beating the Aggies on Kyle Field, 23–0, for the first time since 1923 and then closing out the season by drubbing a strong Oregon team in Austin, 71–7, on December 6. Twenty-four hours later, Japanese planes bombed Pearl Harbor. GIs like myself—14th Armored Division fighting in France and Germany—spent some of our idle hours in the next three years arguing about whether the 1941 Longhorns were the best college team ever or whether Minnesota or Ohio State or Tennessee or some other team was better. As for the Texas guys in my outfit, you know whose side we were on. But toward the end of the war, Army—with its Glenn Davis–Doc Blanchard combo—settled all that.

In my memory, Darrell Royal and Mack Brown will always be linked. Royal retired after the final game of the 1976 season (UT 29, Arkansas 12, played in Royal Memorial Stadium), and after writing our game stories that night, the sportswriters who were there covering the game all made it to the Villa Capri, where Royal always had his postgame press conferences. I was lucky enough to be there, taking notes, and the next day I wrote what I still believe was the best sports column I ever wrote.

Mack Brown became a part of the Texas football scene after coaches Fred Akers, David McWilliams, and John Mackovic had come and gone. I've had UT insiders tell me that it was after Royal had strongly recommended him that Brown was hired away from North Carolina, where he had been head coach of the Tar Heels for nine seasons.

Born in Cookeville, Tennessee, in 1951, Brown had played in college as a running back first at Vanderbilt and then Florida State and then had moved on to a number of coaching jobs in college: wide receivers coach at Southern Mississippi (1975–77), then the same at Memphis State (1978) and Iowa State (1979). Then he started moving up: offensive coordinator at Iowa State (1980–81), quarterbacks coach at LSU (1982), then head coach at Appalachian State (1983). When Oklahoma asked him to be the Sooners' offensive coordinator in 1984, he moved his family to Norman, and the Sooners finished 9-2-1 that season in the Big Eight Conference and won the league championship. That was the year Oklahoma tied Texas, 15-15, in the Red River Rivalry game.

Having played a key role in coaching a conference champion, Brown started receiving offers to become head coach at other well-known universities, and he took them—first at Tulane (1985–87) and then at North Carolina (1988–97).

And then in 1998, the University of Texas came calling.

Personally, I thought Mack was a great coach and recruiter and a very "approachable" person—some coaches aren't. His overall record speaks for itself—244–122, with one national championship in 2005; two Big 12 crowns in 2005 and 2009; and six Big 12 South Division titles (1999, 2001, 2002, 2005, 2008, 2009). He didn't win the title every year, but what coach does?

Mack Brown holds aloft the Rose Bowl trophy. Courtesy of University of Texas Athletics.

His peers and those who vote for such honors selected him to receive the Paul "Bear" Bryant Award in 2005, the Bobby Dodd Coach of the Year Award in 2008, and Big 12 Coach of the Year in 2005 and 2009. And he consistently led the Longhorns to a bowl game, not all of them the Rose Bowl or the New Year's Day Bowl, but in his era of high-powered football, few coaches do that.

Since leaving Texas, Mack has become one of the most knowledgeable and easy-on-the-ear football analysts (ESPN) on the various networks. To the best of my knowledge, he and his wife still live in Austin.

DECEMBER 29, 2015

BAYLOR UPSETS NORTH CAROLINA IN RUSSELL ATHLETIC BOWL WITH RECORD-SETTING GROUND GAME

There are upsets and then there are small upsets, big upsets, and unforgettable, unpredictable, hard-to-explain upsets. Mark the Baylor football team's 49–38 victory over the favored University of North Carolina Tar Heels as one of those upsets that few people expected and even fewer predicted. As a matter of fact, of those "experts" who make football predictions for a big-city newspaper that I read daily, there are eight or nine people who predict college football games (including bowl games) for that sports section. Before the Russell Athletic Bowl game was played, only one of those predictors said Baylor would win.

That was one in eight.

And why not? The Bears would be playing without their two top quarterbacks (junior Seth Russell, who was recovering from a broken bone in his neck, and gee-whiz true freshman Jarrett Stidham, who had suffered a broken bone in his foot), their national award–winning wide receiver Corey Coleman (post–regular season surgery from a hernia), their 1,000-yard running back Shock Linwood (broken ankle), and also their starting offensive right tackle Pat Colbert (torn shoulder muscle).

Missing those key elements, only those people who dote on long shots would have picked Baylor. And remember, they would be playing a North Carolina team that gave Atlantic Coast Conference champion Clemson about all it could handle in their big showdown, and remember how Clemson beat Big 12 Conference champion Oklahoma decisively (37–17) in their game in their College Football Playoff game in the Orange Bowl on New Year's Eve.

But those few who did believe the Bears would win and said so perhaps based their hunch on the belief that the Bears were fed up with losing bowl games. As Big 12 Conference football champions, they had lost the last two bowl games (to Central Florida in the Fiesta Bowl and Michigan State in the Cotton Bowl). And soothsayers also might have picked up on the clues presented in the second half of Baylor's season-ending loss to Texas.

And most important, those who thought the Bears would win must have been sold on the coaching genius of Baylor's Art Briles and what Briles and the Bears did in the second half against Texas. What they did in the Texas game was use their favored weapon (the forward pass) only sparingly and instead concentrated on their infantry; specifically, on the wildcat formation—or what we old-timers used to call the single wing.

Did the wildcat work in Orlando? Boy, did it work. It worked with gusto and then some. And as a result, the Bears, playing before a crowd of 40,418 plus an ESPN audience of millions, turned what had been shaping up as close game into a convincing victory.

Would you believe these figures? The Bears passed for a paltry 111 yards (probably the fewest passing yards the Bears have had since Briles arrived at Baylor), but they *rushed* for 645 yards, an all-time Baylor single-game rushing total. And sophomore Johnny Jefferson, moving up in Linwood's absence, rushed for an incredible 299 yards and three touchdowns (the most ever for the Russell Athletic Bowl, and he came within 9 yards of setting a new bowl rushing record for *any* bowl game ever).

"It was by far the best performance of my life," said Jefferson, a Killeen Shoemaker High School product. "We wanted to run the ball and pound it and see if they could stop us," he told John Werner (*Waco Tribune-Herald*) after the game.

The Tar Heels couldn't stop Johnny. They also couldn't stop junior Devin Chafin (161 yards) or sophomore Terence Williams (97 yards) or wideout-QB Lynx Hawthorne (63 yards), and they really didn't put any clamps on quarterback Chris Johnson (31 yards). Chafin

Johnny Jefferson (5) ran wild against UNC in the 2015 Russell Athletic Bowl. Courtesy of Baylor University, photograph by Robbie Rogers.

averaged 6.0 yards per carry, Williams 6.1, Hawthorne 9.0, and Jefferson a gaudy 13.0.

Is it any wonder that Jefferson was voted the game's MVP? Even the next day, listening to TV football analysts talk about the bowl game they were watching and discussing that game, they also were still talking about Baylor's Johnny Jefferson and what he had done in Orlando.

So it was a great night for the Bears and their fans everywhere, and it gave Coach Briles and his team plenty to think about and build on this spring.

And this spring, remember, they expect those two top quarterbacks to be healthy and raring to go and for Shock Linwood to be back along with all those other talented ball carriers—plus some proven and talented receivers, one veteran offensive lineman, and a number of experienced members of the defensive platoon.

And word has it that Baylor coaches have *not* been asleep at the wheel in their recruiting endeavors for next season. We'll get more of those particulars on signing day in early February, but already they've started restocking their lineup with some December signatures, including several highly rated juco recruits.

In the game in Orlando, the Tar Heels led only once. The first time they gained possession in the first quarter, they used the talents of their highly rated senior quarterback Marquise Williams (6-foot-2, 225, and fast) and the pass-snagging abilities of Ryan Switzer, Quinshad Davis, Kendrick Singleton, and Mack Hollins to drive 69 yards in 13 plays for their go-ahead points. Nick Weller kicked the extra point, and North Carolina had a 7–0 lead.

And I suspect about then that Tar Heel fans settled back in their seats and prepared to celebrate, expecting the deluge had just begun. Of course, they were in for a big surprise. Baylor immediately answered and kept answering.

The first answer found the Bears driving to the end zone in 13 plays for the equalizing TD (Hawthorne scored the touchdown on a 6-yard run). Then before the first quarter ended, the Bears moved ahead with a six-play, 83-yard thrust that featured a 37-yard run by Hawthorne to the Tar Heel 3-yard line, making it easy for Chafin to score the TD. At the end of that quarter, the Bears had already amassed 190 yards rushing (Jefferson had 90 by himself), a harbinger of things to come.

The Tar Heels came back with a 64-yard kickoff return and a nine-play, 26-yard drive to the BU 15, but at that point, the BU defense said, "That's far enough." So Weller kicked a 32-yard field goal.

Baylor answered with a 75-yard drive that included a roughing the punter penalty and reached the end zone with Jefferson's 11-yard scamper. Then when the Tar Heels tried to narrow the gap, Orion Stewart picked off one of Williams's passes and returned 24 yards to the BU 33. From that point, there went the Bears again, driving 67 yards in 10 plays to take a 28–10 lead. Jefferson got loose on a 27-yard run in scoring that touchdown.

The Tar Heels did finally get their attack working, driving 75 yards in 10 plays to make it a 28–17 game at halftime. Williams scored the touchdown himself with a 4-yard run.

Baylor used the remaining 35 seconds to drive to the North Carolina 20-yard line, but in the final couple of seconds, Chris Callahan missed a 37-yard field goal.

So at halftime, the Bears held a 28–17 upper hand and already had rushed for 358 yards—usually more than enough for a full game. They were still hungry, but so were the Tar Heels, and coach Larry Federa's team proved it by accepting the third-quarter kickoff and driving 75 yards in nine plays to score a touchdown and PAT that made it a 28–24 game.

The Bears still had plenty of work to do, and they did it. Although a pass interception thwarted their first effort (a 12-play, 68-yard drive to the Tar Heel 8), their defense got the ball back at the BU 39, and that time there was no stopping them. They drove 61 yards in eight plays to the payoff window (Chafin had runs of 14 and 17 yards, and Terence Williams scored the touchdown from 3 yards out), and Callahan made it a 35–24 game.

Then things really began to take their final shape. Although North Carolina's Elijah Hood immediately got loose on a 67-yard run to the BU 8-yard line (Xavien Howard finally stopped him), T. J. Logan got to the Baylor 1-yard line on the next two plays. But when Logan tried to reach the end zone on his next carry, Baylor's Aiavion Edwards forced him to fumble, and Orion Stewart recovered for the Bears in the end zone for a harmless touchback.

Then there went Jefferson—zip, zip, zip—80 yards for a touchdown and a 42–24 Baylor lead. And while the Tar Heels had enough time to score two more TDs and the Bears one, the verdict had been rendered. Baylor was going to fly home the winner—never mind that NC's Williams threw a 27-yard touchdown pass to 6-foot-6 wideout Bug Howard (that's his name in the game program, honest), Terence Williams scored on a 1-yard touchdown plunge for Baylor, and Williams threw a 7-yard TD pass to Kendrick Singleton in the final minutes of the game.

The final figures show that the Bears dominated just about everything that mattered: more first downs (38 to 28), more total offense (756 to 487), more time of possession (37:06 to 22:54), more total offense plays (102 to 72), more QB sacks (2 to 0), more third-down conversions (10 of 17 to 9 of 13) more fourth-down conversions (4 of 6 to 0 of 0), and more points off turnovers (14 to 0).

"I was hoping we would go out like this," BU's All-American offensive tackle Spencer Drango told the *Trib*'s John Werner. "I love this for this team and everybody involved. I'm glad the seniors could end our careers on a high note and go out with a bowl victory."

Federa, an A&M Consolidated High School grad, also an Austin College (in Sherman) grad and a former assistant coach at Baylor, summed up the game with these words: "I didn't think they'd run for 645 yards. Our guys weren't where they needed to be, and we missed tackles in the open field. But they did a good job of blocking up front. They basically ran it down our throats."

The Bears did what they needed to do on defense too. Edwards, a 6-foot-2, 200-pound junior linebacker, had a monster game; he was credited with a whopping 17 tackles (8 solo), including 1 sack, 2 tackles for loss, a forced fumble, and a pass interception. Both Stewart and Grant Campbell were in on 7 tackles, Chance Waz on 6, and Howard on 5, and linebacker Taylor Young had 4 stops and a QB sack.

And it was a happy team of Bears that flew back to Waco.

DECEMBER 27, 2016
BAYLOR WINS BOWL GAME

Somebody said it couldn't be done; actually, a whole lot of people, including the so-called experts, said that the Baylor Bears, losers of six straight football games, couldn't beat the Boise State Broncos in their Tuesday night (December 27) Cactus Bowl showdown in Phoenix, Arizona. After all, winning bowl games in Phoenix just seems to be what the Broncos do. They beat Oklahoma there (43–42 in double overtime) in the Fiesta Bowl in 2017, TCU (17–10) in 2010, and U of Arizona (38–30) in 2014.

Whether it is in the Cactus Bowl or the Fiesta Bowl, put Boise State in it and play the game in Phoenix, and the Broncos seem to find the weapons to win.

So they were seven-point favorites to beat the Bears two days after Christmas Day of 2016. Indeed, some of the Las Vegas tout sheets thought they would win by a bigger margin than that.

But they didn't. They didn't come close. Baylor led from wire to wire. It was 7–0 at the end of the first quarter, 14–6 at halftime, 24–6 at the end of the third quarter, and 31–12 when the final whistle sounded. By then, the 33,328 shocked spectators had been convinced—and likewise, ESPN's audience of millions.

It was a wild and topsy-turvy season for Baylor. The Bears began the season by winning their three nonconference games easily, then began their conference campaign by playing probably their best game (Baylor 35, Oklahoma State 24) of the regular season. They staged a monumental fourth-quarter comeback (45–42, with a field goal kicked in the last few seconds) to beat Iowa State in Ames, easily subdued Kansas (49–7) at homecoming, played Texas to a virtual draw in Austin before losing by one skinny point (35–34)—and then the bottom fell out, starting with the TCU game.

When they lost to eventual Big 12 Conference champion Oklahoma in Norman (45–24)—and lost their prize senior quarterback Seth Russell for the season in the process—defeats became the order of Saturday after Saturday. Interim head football coach Jim Grobe coached as well as anybody could, and better than anyone could have expected under the circumstances, but it didn't seem to matter.

That is, not until the West Virginia game, played on December 3 in Morgantown. In that season finale, the Bears lost by only a field goal (24–21), the closest they have played the Mountaineers on that team's gridiron since West Virginia became a member of the Big 12 Conference.

Maybe that was an omen most of us missed or ignored. But it certainly was there for all to see in Phoenix. The conclusion of this season was a reminder of how it was 12 months ago. After losing three of their last four regular-season games (to Oklahoma, TCU in double overtime, and then Texas by six points), the Bears bounced back with a big surprise, upsetting No. 10–ranked North Carolina, 49–38.

This was a game that proved the big-time talent of freshman quarterback Zach Smith, who threw for 375 yards and three touchdowns, of superswift receiver K. D. Cannon (14 receptions for whopping 226 yards and two TDs), and of sophomore tailback Terence Williams (25 carries for 103 yards). Both Smith and Williams will be back (there had been considerable talk that Smith was planning to transfer, but before the bowl game he said he will be back; if he had transferred, the Bears would not have had a proven golden arm on campus), but alas, Cannon announced after being named the game's outstanding offensive player that he now will opt for the NFL.

But tried-and-true linebacker Taylor Young, a 5-foot-10, 225-pound junior who was voted the game's outstanding defensive player after leading everybody with 17 tackles (12 solo), has indicated that he also will be back. In all, the Bears started nine underclassmen (that's

Baylor interim head coach Jim Grobe receives the traditional "Gatorade victory shower" as the Bears win the 2016 Cactus Bowl. Courtesy of Baylor University, photograph by Robbie Rogers.

including Cannon) on offense and seven on defense. Also, all but two of Baylor's backups for the bowl game will be back. New Baylor football coach Matt Rhule attended the game, so he saw the Bears make their final statement for this 2016 season, and it was an emphatic and ringing one.

The Bears started the game by staging a promising drive that moved 52 yards before Smith threw an interception—just about his only bad play of the game. The Broncos also were stymied on their first drive, then junior Travon Blanchard picked off one of Bronco QB Brett Rypien's passes and returned it 14 yards to the Baylor 19, and there went the Bears. They needed six plays to cover the 81 yards, including three passes: one to Chris Platt and two to Cannon—the first for 49 yards and then the next for 30 yards and the game's first touchdown. Chris Callahan's PAT was good, and the Bears were ahead to stay.

The Broncos put three points on the scoreboard early in the second quarter (57 yards in 17 plays before Tyler Rausa's 27-yarder was good). The Bears retaliated immediately with a five-play, 81-yard blow that featured Smith's 68-yard pass to Cannon that scored the touchdown. Callahan again kicked the extra point.

The Broncos surged back, reaching the Baylor 7-yard line. But Rypien again tried to get those final yards via the airways, and again a vigilant Bear, Orion Stewart, was there to intercept his fateful fling. And again the Bears answered with a long touchdown drive, 99 yards in 15 plays, with redshirt freshman JaMycal Hasty (in the entire game, he carried seven times and gained 34 yards) gaining the final 28 yards on three runs. Then Callahan did his thing again.

The Broncos had enough time left before halftime to drive 56 yards on 15 plays to kick their second field goal, that one a 26-yarder delivered by Tyler Rausa.

The Broncos produced nothing of real significance offensively in the third quarter, but the Bears refused to stay quiet. With 9:13 left before the fourth, they rolled 78 yards in 21 plays, overcoming two red flags along the way, and then called on Callahan for a 34-yard field goal that moved them into a 24–6 domination.

The fourth quarter saw Baylor strike first, surging 71 yards in 12 plays with Smith's 14-yard pass to Ishmael Zamora scoring the touchdown that moved Baylor further head, 31–6. Terence Williams did some productive running on that drive, and another Smith pass to

K. D. Cannon (9), caught 14 passes for 226 yards and two touchdowns in Baylor's 2016 Cactus Bowl victory over Boise State. Courtesy of Baylor University, photograph by Robbie Rogers.

Cannon also yielded a first down. A 15-yard unsportsmanlike penalty forced the Bears to kick off from their own 20 following the touchdown, but the Broncos were still stymied. The Baylor defense just refused to give much ground.

Finally, with 2:13 left in the game, Boise State did finally score a touchdown, driving 70 yards in five plays and reaching the Baylor end zone when Rypien completed a 28-yard pass to Cedrick Wilson. But fittingly, Boise State's try for a two-point conversion failed when Taylor Young intercepted Rypien's next pass in the end zone.

It was an unexpected and complete victory, marred only by that old bugaboo, penalties. Once again the Bears wound up leading the Power 5 Conference penalties. In the Cactus Bowl, they were called for infractions 11 times, resulting in 125 yards in lost yardage.

But on the positive side, the Bears led in first downs, 29 to 25; in net yards rushing, 140 to 83; in net yards passing, 375 to 305; and consequently in total yardage, 515 yards to 388 (although the losers actually ran more plays, 89 to Baylor's 83). The decisive difference was spelled out in Baylor's average per offensive play—6.2 for the Bears, 4.4 for the Broncos.

Other differences: Baylor lost no fumbles and intercepted two passes (no turnovers); the Broncos lost one fumble and suffered two interceptions (3 turnovers). The Bears averaged 48 yards for their two punts; Boise State averaged 41.3 yards for three punts. BU defenders came up with four sacks resulting in 28 yards of lost yardage for their opponents; Boise State sacked the Baylor quarterback only twice for 7 yards of lost yardage. The Bears scored 21 points off their opponents' turnovers; Baylor lost no points in that department.

So all in all, it was a complete victory for both the offense (meaning the offensive line) and the defense. Other than Taylor Young (who was all over the field), Baylor's defense was led by senior linebacker Aiavion Edwards (11 tackles, including 10 solo stops), freshman cornerback Grayland Arnold (9 stops), senior cornerback Orion Stewart (5 tackles, 1 QB sack, 2 tackles for loss, a fumble recovery, and an interception), redshirt freshman defensive end Tyrone Hunt (5 tackles, 2 QB sacks), and junior defensive end K. J. Smith (4 tackles, 1 QB sack).

And regarding recruiting, I saw Matt Rhule, new Baylor football coach (who personally saw the Bears beat Boise State from a vantage point in a suite at Chase Field in Phoenix), at the Baylor Lady Bear victory in their conference-opening 87–57 victory over Kansas State this past Thursday night and told him Baylor fans were rejoicing that he had persuaded Zach Smith to return for his sophomore season in 2017 (many Baylor insiders were telling me he planned to transfer).

"If Smith had transferred, you would have had no experienced quarterback to start the 2017 season," I pointed out. "But it would help if you could get another one as his backup, if Smith happened to get hurt early in the season."

But I quickly found out he was way ahead of me. "We're working hard to get three good ones," he said.

And so the book ends as it began: with my coverage of a Baylor football game. I guess I'll always be a Bears fan, deep down. After all, a 93-year-old habit is hard to break!

But of course, as I said at the start, I just love the game of football, period. Even though I never had the opportunity to compete on an official team, the weekly drama that plays out on Texas gridirons will never grow old to me. Each fall in tiny crossroads communities in farm and ranch country and in huge cities like Houston and Dallas, young men put on pads and helmets. They go out on the field of play, under the glare of the lights and amid the blaring of the bands, and do their best to make their coaches, parents, friends, teammates, and hometowns proud. The best of them go on to play at one of our state's fine colleges or universities in front of bigger, noisier crowds and against teams of other supremely gifted athletes.

Certainly, Texas football—at all levels—has been good to me too. I have been privileged to receive several awards and honors over the years just for doing what I love to do. In 2005, for example, the Texas High School Coaches Association honored me as the recipient of their Distinguished Service Award during their annual Hall of Honor banquet, where the association also recognized athletic director of the University Interscholastic League Charles Breithaupt and several others.

I was just about speechless. In my acceptance speech, I told them, "Of all the honors I have received over the years, the recognition you are giving me today will take a back seat to none."

Of course, I couldn't have done any of this by myself, and in my remarks, I also thanked Hollis Biddle, Jim Montgomery, and Al Ward, all of whom helped me start the magazine and keep it going during those early years. I reserved a few special words for my wife, Reba, who patiently put up with the use of her kitchen as the "layout room" when we were trying to get our publication off the ground.

And of course, I had to express my thanks to David Barron, the longtime managing editor of the *Waco Tribune-Herald*, who was such a tremendous help over the years. In his article for the special fiftieth anniversary edition of *Dave Campbell's Texas Football*, David wrote some very kind words about some of the things we've tried to do over the years to promote the sport and its players and coaches. And he closed with what he called his "favorite Dave Campbell memory":

> After arriving at the Rose Bowl before the Texas-USC game, I went to the TV booth to pay my respects to Keith Jackson, who was calling the final game of his career for ABC. Jackson asked me if I knew where Darrell Royal might be, and we tracked Royal down in a suite in the press box level.
>
> A few minutes later, I ran into Dave in the press box. I asked him to follow me, and we found Royal and Jackson. I walked back a few paces and marveled

Courtesy of the *Waco Tribune-Herald*.

at the scene: Dave Campbell, Keith Jackson, and Darrell Royal, chattering away as they prepared to watch what would become one of the greatest games in the history of college football. That day, as every day, was a good one to be at the stadium with Dave Campbell.

To be honest, I haven't had too many bad days at the stadium. The spectacle, the human interest, the emotion, the suspense, the grueling physical contest, the individual and team heroics—all of it combines in a way that captures my imagination like nothing else.

I hope you've enjoyed this personal tour through some of my favorite Texas college football memories. Most likely, as you've turned these pages, you've been reminded of some experiences of your own—memories centered on moments you've spent in a stadium, as a competitor or a fan, or transfixed in front of a television screen, agonizing or celebrating with your favorite team. I'm also pretty sure that many of the readers of this book can think of games and stories that I've left out. It probably can't be helped; I've lived a long time and seen a lot of football, but I haven't seen it all!

The fact is that feats of athletic skill have always inspired us. Since at least the time of the ancient contests in Greece, we have admired those who could run faster, jump higher, and throw farther. Not only that, but the experience of a common striving against a worthy opponent unites us, brings us together in the interest of the cherished goal of victory.

Texas college football captures that admiration, that striving. For the dedicated fan, it provides a thrill that can't be experienced anywhere else. And I guess that's why, as long as those young men don the pads and helmets and go out onto the field of play, people like me will be there to watch, to cheer, to appreciate, and to try to get it all down in writing so that others can remember that thrill for years to come.

INDEX

Page numbers in *italics* refer to figures.

Abercrombie, Walter, 200, 202–3
Adami, Buster, 118–19, 125
Adams, Don, 73–75, 81
Adams, Mike, 241
Adams, Willis, 194
Adkins, Herby, 60, 70, 73, 75
Akers, Fred, 177, 184–86, 191, *191*, 207, 209, 212, *213*, 216, 262
Akins, Marty, *154*, 154–55
Alexander, Lamone, 251
Allegre, Raúl, 205, 207–11, 213
Allen, Earl, 222
Allen, Grady, 115, 118–19, 121, 125
Allison, Rodney, 169–71
Amyett, Excell, 9–10
Anderson, Donny, 92, *92*, 191
Appleton, Scott, *84*, 87, 94, 96, 99–100
Armstrong, Ramon, 47
Arnold, Grayland, 269
Asberry, Wayne, 224
Aschenbeck, Harvey, 115, 119, 125
Atkins, Tennell, 159
Atkinson, Jason, 234
Auburn University, 224–26

Bailey, Pat, 50
Barnes, Joe, 145
Bass, Don, 167, 171
Baugh, Sam, 9, 191
Baylor Stadium, 50, 127, 165, 180
Baylor University, 1–4, 8–10, 13–15, 27–38, 44–46, 50–51, 57–60, 70, 81–83, 90–98, 105–7, 127, 141–45, 151–68, 180–81, 198–205, 227–29, 235–40, 242, 244–51, 258–61, 262, 264–70; team photo, *28*
Beaird, Steve, 154–59, *156*, 161, 163–65

Beall, Bill, 127
Beall, Junior, 27–28, 30–31, 35–37
Beam, Winston, 116
Bearden, David, 237
Beck, Ken, 41–42, 46
Becton, Paul, 106
Bedford, Vance, 211
Bedrick, Frank, 96
Bell, Kendrick, 250
Bellard, Emory, 187, *188*, 243
Belrose, Lester, 167
Benners, Fred, 50
Benson, Charles, 199, *199*
Benson, Leslie, 154
Bernstine, Rod, 225–26, 229
Berry, Don, 31, 33, 35–36
Berry, Powell, 58
Berry, Raymond, Jr., *7*
Bertelsen, Jim, 129–31, *130*, 136–37, 253
Bible, D. X., 260, 262
Birleson, Robbie, 247
Black, Mike, 142
Black, Tim, 154, 158
Blackwell, Alois, 167, 171–73, 179, *195*
Blackwood, Glenn, 183, 185
Blackwood, Lyle, 143
Blair, Dean, 57
Blair, Gary, 167–68
Blanch, George, 52–53, 56–57
Blanchard, Travon, 268
Bluiett, Caleb, 260
Blume, Les "Butch," 70
Bockhorn, Don, 156–57, 159
Boise State, 267–70
Bonner, Melvin, 246–48, *247*
Bostick, David, 159
Boston College, 221–23
Boyd, Sam, 11, 32–33, 37–38, *38*, 243
Braband, Randy, 150
Bradham, Steve, 195
Bradley, Bill, 112–14, 117–18, 120
Bradley, Elvis, 172–73
Bradshaw, Wesley, 155

Brame, Joel, 119
Branch, Clair, 52–53, 56, 59–60
Brannan, Mike, 201
Brannon, Buster, 46
Brewer, Robert, 212–14, 216
Bridgers, John, 57, 74, 90–92
Briles, Art, 258–60, 264–65
Brocato, C. A., 7
Brock, Jim, 23, 46–47, 68
Bronson, Ben, 251
Brooks, Chet, 229
Brooks, Leo, 119
Brothers, David, 180
Brown, Chuck, 166, 194
Brown, Jim, 39–40, *40*
Brown, Mack, 252, 254, 261–63, *262*, *263*
Brown, Phil, 236
Broyles, Frank, 20, 114, 128–29, 174–75, 177, 261
Brucks, George, 76, 80
Brupbacher, Ross, 115–16, 126
Bryant, Bob, 31, 53
Bryant, Domingo, 226
Bryant, Paul "Bear," *9*, 9–12, 20–27, *22*, 27, 41–44, 121–23, 126, *126*, 149–50, 201–2, 205, 212–14, 216, *239*
Bryant-Denny Stadium, 254
Bucek, Billy, 50
Buckley, Marcus, 234
Buckman, Tom, 115–16, 124, 126
Bucy, Flynn, 158, 167–68
Buell, Harold, 170
Buford, Maury, 199, *200*
Bull, Ronnie, 57–58, 60, 70, *71*, 72–75
Burk, Adrian, 50
Burk, Robert, 73
Burns, Ron, 154, 158–59, 168
Bush, Reggie, 253

Cactus Bowl, 267–70
Caldwell, Keith, 248

Callahan, Chris, 261, 266, 268
Callies, Marvin, 251
Campbell, Don, 90
Campbell, Earl, 135, 172, 182–92, *187*, *189*, *191*, *192*, 220
Campbell, Grant, 266
Campbell, Joe, 199
Campbell, Mike, 103, 131, 177
Campbell, Tim, 172
Campbell, Tom, 132–33, 136, 138–39
Candler, Jerry, 70
Cannon, K. D., 267–68, *269*
Carlen, Jim, 102, 139–40, 144
Carlisle, Duke, 76, 93–100, 103, *103*
Carlson, Cody, 227–29
Carter, Russell, 219, *219*
Cavender, Randy, 141
Cavness, Grady, 234
Chafin, Devin, 261, 264–66
Chipman, Marvin, 84
Choate, Carl, 72, 74–75, 81–82
Churchman, Ricky, 183
Claiborne, Jerry, 146
Clark, Darryl, 216
Clark, Matt, 228
Clark, Mike, 81–83
Clayborn, Raymond, 155, 169, 172–73
Clements, Joe, 18, 31–32
Coffee, Russell, 102–4
Colbert, Pat, 264
Coleman, Corey, 260, 264
Collins, Bobby, 217, *218*, 219
Collins, Jack, 55–57, *56*, 59–61, 63, *66*, 76, 78
Cones, Mark, 157
Conover, Al, *104*, 104–5
Conrad, Bobby, 41, 43–44, 46
Conradt, Mike, 141
Constanzo, Ted, 170, 172–73
Coody, Jerry, *3*, 3–4
Cook, Jerry, 77–78, 84

273

Cook, John, 68
Cook, Laney, 127
Cooper, Don, 17
Cooper, Larry, 53, 55–56, 59–60
Copeland, Morgan, 184
Coplin, Lennard, 166, 168, 171–73, 180
Cordaro, Mike, 169, 172–73
Corder, Dave, 90
Corley, Larry, 59, 74
Corn, Roger, 250–51
Cotten, Mike, 54–57, 60–61, 68–69, 76, 78
Cotton Bowl, 5–8, *7*, 39–40, 75–78, 98–105, 107–10, 123–26, 136, 149–51, 161–65, 178–80, 193–95, 201–5, 212–16, 221–26, 256–57, 262–63
Cotton Bowl Stadium, 54, 79, 88, 155, 205
Cozby, Terry, 157
Crain, Alton, 251
Crenshaw, Bobby, 95, 97
Crenwelge, Ted, 68
Crosby, Tony, 79, 93, 95, 97
Crow, Jim, 46
Crow, John David, 22, *22*, *24*, 24–25, 27–30, *29*, 41–42, *42*, 44–46, *45*
Crutcher, Tommy, 84
Culpepper, Pat, 68, *78*, 78–80, 84
Curtis, Chuck, 16–18, 23, 25, 39–40

Dale, Billy, 136
Dancer, Charles, *142*, 143
Dansby, Buddy, 58
Darnell, Ralph, 215
Davidson, Francis "Cotton," 3–4, *4*
Davis, Danny, 146, 165–68, *166*, 171–73, 178–79, *179*, 194–95, *195*
Davis, David, 229
Davis, Jon, 249–51
Davis, Rick, 149
Davis, Sonny, 57–58
Dawson, Larry, 49, 62
Dean, Mike, 154–55
DeAyala, Kiki, 207, *214*, 215
Defee, Richard, 106
DeGrazier, Tony, 8, 38
Delaney, Rhett, 237, 247–48
De La Torre, Alex, 259
Dial, Buddy, 43, *43*, 50
Dickerson, Eric, *209*, 209–11, 217, *217*, 219–20
Dickerson, Hank, 157
Dickson, Paul, 34
Dierking, Clarence, 3, *3*
Dike, Buddy, 39, 41–42, 48
Dixon, Joe, 97, *97*
Dodson, R. E., 62, 67
Doggett, Daryl, 127
Doke (Texas A&M), 53
Dooley, Vince, 108, 110
Douglas, Leland, 228
Dowdle, Mike, 49, 52–54, 60, 61–63
Drake, Dan, 142
Drango, Spencer, 261, 266
Dronnett, Shane, 234
Duke, Darrick, 241
Dull, Chris, 247
Dunlap, John, 157
Dupre, Charley, 27, 35–37
Dupre, Larry, 169

Dupre, L. G., 3–4
Dykes, Spike, 249, *249*
Ealey, Lester, 143
Ebensberger, Grady, 167, 195
Ebow, Mike, 159
Edwards, Aiavion, 266, 269
Ehrig, Bonnie, 118
Elkins, Lawrence, 82, 92–97, *94*
Ellington, Bill, 101–2, 105
Ellis, Tom, 104
Elston, Terry, 194
English, Doug, 152
Engram, Bryan, 17
Enis, Hunter, 49
Erben, Pete, 3
Erickson, Johnny, 83
Erxleben, Russell, 170, 172, 183–86, *188*
Evans, Jim, 57–60
Evans, Mike, 255
Evans, Spencer, 261
Everett, Deshazor, 255
Everett, Thomas, 227–28, *228*

Faulkner, Staley, 80
Federa, Larry, 258–59
Feller, Happy, 129–31, 136–37, 253
Ferguson, Ken, 80
Fiebiger, Jerod, 251
Field, Doak, 199, 203–4
Finney, Dick, 39–40, 48
Fisher, Mike, 202, 204
Fleming (SMU), 127
Fligg, Jack, 102
Floyd, Don, 47, 49, *49*
Floyd Casey Stadium, 236
Flutie, Doug, 148, 221–23
Foldberg, Hank, 83, *83*
Fondren, Walter, 17, *17*, 32
Fontenot, Albert, 238, *238*
Ford, Tommy, 78–80, *80*, 93–94, 96–97
Foster, Eddie, 173
Francis, Anthony, 166–67
Francis, Ron, 229
Franklin, Cleveland, 154, 159
Franklin, Eric, 226
Franklin, Tony, *181*
Frazier, Everett, 58, 60
Fredenburg, Pete, 249
Frongillo, John, 73
Fry, Hayden, 89, *89*, 106, 110, 127

Gallagher, Jack, 146
Galt, Bob, 122
Gannon (SMU), 90
Garcia, Eddie, 211
Gardere, Peter, 234, 236–38, 241
Gault, Billy, 49, 67
Gay, Richard, 42, 45–46
Gennusa, Ragan, 113, 120
Gentry, Dennis, 200–204
George, Donald, 61–62
George, Ernie, 103
Gibbs, Guy, 67
Gibbs, Sonny, *47*, 69, 84
Gibson, Pat, 108
Gilbert, Chris, 112–14, *113*, 117, 119–20
Gilmore, Jimmy, 49, 61–62
Glass, Bill, 32, *34*, 35–36, 38
Glasscock, Dale, 67
Glenn, Aaron, 241

Goehring, Allen, 53
Gonsoulin, Austin, 50–51, 58
Goodson, John, *206*, 209
Goodwin, Ronnie, 73, 75, 81–82, *82*
Gordon, Billy, 175
Gordon, Bobby, 34–35, 37
Goree, Roger, 142, *142*, 144
Gotham Bowl, 72–75, 244–45
Graham, William, 209, 211, 214–15
Grange, Red, *9*
Green, Gary, 168
Green, Jacob, 181
Greene, Johnny, 154
Greenwood, Vincent, 167, 171
Gremminger, Henry, *8*, 8–10
Grimes, Don, 144
Grobe, Jim, 267, *268*
Gurwitz, Bobby, 60

Hale, Lloyd, 28
Hall, Brian, 170
Hall, Luther, 52–56
Hall, Robert, 249–51
Hallbeck, Vern, 18
Hallman, Curley, 123, 125
Ham, Milton, 62, 66–68
Hamilton, Malcolm, 250–51
Hamilton, Norman, 17, 32, 39–40, 47
Hardin, Wayne, 99–100, 102–3
Hargett, Edd, 111, 114–21, 123–26, *124*
Hargett, George, 81, 83
Harkins, Pat, 118–19
Harlan, Herb, 74
Harper, Ray, 141
Harper, Sam, 164
Harpy (Baylor), 165
Harrell, Jeff, 216–17, 219
Harrington, Lee, 32, 35, 36
Harris, Barney, 114, *115*, 120, 123–24, 126
Harris, Marshall, 49, 61–63
Harris, Phil, 97–98, 100, 103
Harris, Rod, 228–29
Harrison, Jerry, 168
Harrison, Kenny, 158, *158*
Harrison, Randy, 195
Hartman, Alvin, 50
Hartman, Larry, 32
Harwerth, Bob, 52
Hasty, JaMycal, 268
Hatfield, Kenny, 172, 195
Hawthorne, Greg, 167
Hawthorne, Lynx, 259–61, 264–65
Hays, Ken, 70
Heath, Eddie, 189
Henderson, Bill, 46
Henderson, Scott, 139
Henry, John, 250
Herman, Tom, 148
Herskowitz, Mickey, 26, 121, 128
Hickman, Larry, 27, 30–32, 36–38, 46, 51
Hicks, Bill, 60, 73–75
Hicks, Bubba, 153–57, 161, 163
Higgins, Tom, 120
Hill, Greg, 234
Hill, King, 43, *43*
Hill, Lloyd, *250*, 250–51
Hillary (SMU), 89–90
Hilton, Carl, 222
Hixson, Chuck, 127

Hobbs, Bill, 111, 115, 117–21, 123–25
Hodge, David, 166–68, 173, 194
Hodge, Ken, 96
Hoffman, Dalton, 81, 92, 96–97
Holden, Sam, 111
Holland, Johnny, 224, 228
Holle, Eric, 207–8, 215
Holt, Radar, 204
Holub, E. J., *19*
Hooper, Billy, 8–10, 15, *15*
Hopkins, Wayne, 3–4
Horton, Charley, *14*, 32, 35, *45*, 45–46, 251
Hoskins, Cliff, 143, 145
Housley, Wendell, 114–16, 121, 123–24, 126
Housman, John, 166–68
Howard, Todd, 224
Howard, Xavien, 266
Howell, Steve, 167, 180–81
Huddleston, Billy, 9–12, *12*
Huff, Michael, *254*
Huggins (Baylor), 127
Huggins, Lide, 104–5
Humble, Weldon, 38
Humphrey, Buddy, 32–33, 35–36, 45–46, 50–51, *51*
Humphreys, Paul, 167
Hunt, Joel, 16
Hunt, Tyrone, 269
Hurd, Shawn, 251

Ingram, James, 72, 74, 92
Isaac, Larry, *170*, 171

Jackson, Alcy, *152*, 152–55, 159, 165
Jackson, Alfred, 182, 186–87
Jackson, Basil, 224
Jackson, Bo, 224–26
Jackson, Brandell, 246, 250
Jackson, Charley, 43
Jackson, Larry, 185
Jackson, Mark, 161–68
Jackson, Shawn, 250
James, Craig, 210–11, 220, *220*
Jefferson, Dwight, 183
Jefferson, Johnny, 260–61, 264–66, *265*
Jeffrey, Jay, 200, 202–4
Jeffrey, Neal, 141–43, 145, 152–59, 163–65
Jenkins, Dan, 48
Jernigan, Larry, 108–9
Jessup, Johnny, 97
Joe, J. J., *236*, 236–38, 246–51
Joeckel, Luke, *255*
John Hancock Bowl, 246–48
Johns, Freeman, 158
Johnson, Chipper, 127
Johnson, Chris, 259–60, 264
Johnson, Gary, 168, *168*
Johnson, Harry, 225
Johnson, Joe, 142, 158–59
Johnson, Johnnie, 183, 185
Johnson, Mike, 163–64
Johnston, Robert, 70, *71*
Jones, A. J. "Jam," 205–7, 210, 216
Jones, Allen, 3–4, 6, 9–10, 14
Jones, Bobby, 15, *15*, 30, 32, 33, 35–37
Jones, Dick, 62
Jones, Ivan, 119, 125
Jones, Johnny "Ham," 182, 184–87

Jones, Johnny "Lam," 169, *169*, 172–73, 187
Jones Stadium, 90, 198
Jordan, Lester, 110
Jordan, Mike, 127

Kachtik, Don, 9
Kaifes, Eric, 211
Keeling, Michael, 207
Kelcher, Louie, 155, *157*
Keller, Jim, 81–83
Kellogg, Gordon, 14
Kelly, Pay, 149
Kennedy, Malcome, 255, 257
Kennon, Garland, 32
Kent, Phillip, 153–55, 157–59, *250*, 251
Kettler, Elwood, 8–10
Kilgore, Brian, 143, 145, 159
Kimbrough, John, 123, 190, 242
King, Emmett, 193–95
King, J. T., 93, 140
King, Tony, 96–97
Kipp, Ken, 82
Knowles, Robert, 3
Kohlman, Mike, 82
Koy, Ernie, 85
Koy, Ted, 112, 117, 119–20, 130, 136–37
Kramer, Tommy, 146
Kristynik, David, 60, 62
Kristynik, Marvin, 99, 176
Krueger, Charley, *22*, *29*, 30, 42, 46
Krueger, Rolf, 115, 117, 119, 121, 125
Kubecks, Billy, 125
Kubin, Marvin, 68, 88
Kyle Field, 11, 21, 23, 44, 112, 118, 121, 186–87, 228, 243, 262

Lackey, Bobby, 49, 52–53, 55–57, 59–61
Lacy, Gary, 141, 143, 145
Lammons, Pete, 100
Landry, Gerald, 222–23
Lane, Bob, 73–74
Lasater, Marvin, 41, 47, 49, 62
Lavergne, Robert, 167, 173, 178
Layne, Rob, 112–14, 117–18
Leach, Bobby, 217, 220
Leaks, David, 250
Leaks, Roosevelt "Rosey," 143, 149–51, *153*, 191
LeBoeuf, Gordon, 57
Lee, Monte, 60, *60*, 68
Leiding, Jeff, 207, 209, *210*, 211, 215
Lesser, Bicky, 127
Lester, Danny, 129, 131–32
Letbetter, Clyde, 30, 33–36, *45*, 46
LeVias, Jerry, 105–7, *106*, 109–12, *112*
Lewis, Bradford, 238
Lewis, Chris, 238, 251
Lewis, Scotty, 238, 247
Lewis, Shelton, 247
Lilly, Bob, 49, 62, *67*
Linwood, Shock, 260, 265–66
Little, Bill, 253
Little, Donnie, 208, 212–14
Littlefield, Clyde, 188
Livingston, Mike, 105–7, 110–11
Locke, P. J., 259
Long, Bob, 111, 117–21, 124, 126
Love, Randy, 166, 194–95

Lowry, Alan, 149–51, *150*
Lucas, Tommy, 68, 80
Luce, Derrel, 142, 144, 158
Luck, Mike, 211, 213
Lucky, Bill, 3
Lunceford, Dave, 30, 32–33, 36, 38
Luttrell, Mike, 142–43
Lynch, Charles, 166, 168, 171, 173

Macicek, Marvin, 84
Mackovic, John, 238, 245
Magoffin, Tommy, 85
Mahler, Mark, 229
Majors, Johnny, 33, 35–37
Malena, Ben, 257
Malone, Van, 241
Mangrum, David, 202, 204
Mangum, Robert, 85
Mankin, Robert, 73–75
Manziel, Johnny, 255–57, *257*
Maples, Bobby, 95, 97
Maples, Butch, 70, 81
Marcontell, Jerry, *14*, 30, 32–33
Marks, Bobby, 41–43, 46
Marsh, Ed, 127
Marshall, Donald, 251
Martin, Abe, 15, *16*, 22–23, 25, 39, 41–42, 46–48, *47*, 68–69, 84
Martin, Arvie, 62
Martin, D. H., 113
Maston, Le'Shai, 246
Matocha, Bobby, 49
Matthews, Rudy, 84
Maxwell, Tommy, 114, *115*, 116–17, 119, 123–26
May, David, 140
McBath, Mark, 172–73
McClelland, Don, 45
McCloney, Maurice, 205, 211
McClooney (Texas), 207
McCoy, Colt, 262
McCutchen, Doug, 143, 145
McEachern, Randy, 182, 185–88
McFarland, Michael, 236
McGallion, Bubba, 146, *146*
McGeary, Max, 199–200
McGinniss, David, 143
McIlhenny, Lance, 208–11, *211*, 216–21
McIvor, Rick, 205, 207–8, 210–11
McKenzie, Mike, 237–38
McKinney, Mike, 119
McLane Stadium, 259
McLean, Dude, 121
McLeod, Buck, 58
McMichael, Steve, 183, 187
McMillian, Audrey, 222
McNeil, Gerald, 202–4
McNeil, Pat, 145, 154, 159, 161, 165
McVea, Warren, 147
McWilliams, David, 80
McWilliams, Perry, 79–80
Medlen (SMU), 107
Medlin, Ronnye, 105
Melancon, Terry, 149–50
Memorial Stadium, 16, 51, 68, 93, 96, 171–72, 174, 241
Mendoza, Chico, 39–40
Meredith, Don, *48*, 191
Meyer, Ron, 209
Miller, Earl, 32, 46
Miller, Fred, 250

Miller, Gene, 50
Miller, Ken, 41
Miller, Reggie, 238
Milstead, Charley, 45, 52–54, 58
Minter, Tommy, 57, 73–74
Mitchell, Bobby, 132
Mitchell, Leonard, 195
Moegle, Dicky, *5*, 5–7, *13*, 13–15, 109, 253
Moffett, Jim, 68
Mohr, Mark, 167
Molinare, Larry, 139
Montana, Joe, 135, 148, 193–95
Moore, Bill, 155
Moore, Damontre, 255
Moore, Gerry, 58
Moore, James, 83
Moreland, Harry, 49, 60–63
Moritz, Eldon, 76, 78
Morris, Byron "Bam," 249–51
Morris, Wayne, 158–59
Morrison, Lynn, 68
Moses, Bob, *76*, 76–77
Mosley, James, 143, 145
Motes, Ken, 107
Muennink, Jerry, 53, 60
Munson, Joe, 53
Murray, Kevin, 224–29, *225*, *228*
Myers, Danny, 32
Myles, Byron, 250
Mynatt, Lloyd, 69

Namath, Joe, 149
Napper, Charles, 140
Navy. *See* US Naval Academy (Navy)
Neely, Jess, 5, *5*, 13, 68, 70
Neely, Millard, 142
Nelms, Mike, 167–68
Nelson, Brian, 170
Nelson, Lindsey, *9*
Nelson, Shane, 167–68
Nesrsta, Horton, 15, 218
Nguyen, Dat, *232*
Nicklas, Pete, 73
Nikkel, John, 39–40
Nix, Ben, 85
Nobis, Tommy, *99*, *100*, 176
Norton, Homer, 242–43
Notre Dame, 136–38, 193–95, 262
Nunnally, Knox, *97*, 100, *100*

O'Brien, Davey, 50, 190, 243
O'Brien, Tillman, 53
O'Brient, Sammy, 224, 226
Odom, Johnny, 139
Odom, Lynn, 118
Oglesby, Robert, 173, 195
Oliver, Bobby, 30, 33, 35–36, 46
Oliver, John, 63
O'Neal, Steve, 116, 120, 125
Orange Bowl, 149
Orr, Terry, 213–14
Osborne, Roddy, 24–25, 27–28, *28*, 30, 41–46
Overton, Carroll, 32–34, 46

Padgett, Eddie, 78, *78*
Padgett, J. B., 53
Pannell, Ernie, 242
Pardee, Jack, 24, 27, 29–30, *30*, 148
Parkhurst (Texas A&M), 53
Parks, Dave, *91*

Partee, Dennis, 105–7, 109, 111
Paterno, Joe, 162
Patterson, Billy, 243
Patterson, Jack, 141, 160
Paul, Kenny, *13*
Pavliska, Billy, 58
Pearce, Dugan, 10, 27, 35, 38
Pearson, Matthew, 236
Peebles, Hart, 50
Peebles, Paul, 49, 61–62
Penn State, 161–65
Perez, Ines, 110–12
Perkins, Ken, 139–40
Perry, Charles, 228
Peschel, Randy, 117, 120, 129–33, 261
Peters, Bobby, 27, 30, 32, 35–36, 46
Peterson, Gerald, 17
Petty, Dan, 66
Philipp, Harold, 97–98
Phillips, Bill, 69
Phillips, Eddie, 140, 225
Pierce, Max, 67
Pierson, Mat, 223
Pinkney, Lovell, 237
Piper, Billy, 119
Piper, Jimmy, 125
Pittman, Jim, 103
Pitts, Hugh, 17, *18*
Platt, Chris, 268
Plumb, Ted, 72, 74–75
Plummer, Bobby, 68–69
Ply, Bobby, 57–58, 72, *73*, 74
Poage, Ray, 69, *77*, 78, 80, 83–85
Pollard, Harold, 18, 39–40
Polo Grounds, 72
Porter, Sean, 255
Powell, Boone, 234
Powell, Dee, 21
Presley, Mike, 155
Price, Ed, 31
Priddy, Merlin, 49
Purell, Greg, 223
Purvis, Bobby, 106

Quesenberry, Ken, 159, 162, 164

Rambo, Roy Lee, 61
Ramirez, Rene, 51–55, *55*, 60–63
Ramsey, Jones, 11, 19, 121, 177, 215
Randle, Floyd, 181
Ratliff, Harold, 26
Razorback Stadium, 129
Reed, Scooter, 155, 159, 181
Reedy, Chuck, 248–51
Reigels, Roy, 7–8
Rhule, Matt, 268–70
Rice University, 5–8, 13–15, 43–44, 50–51, 70, 160–61, 245; team photos, *6*, *71*
Richardson, Bucky, 234, *235*
Richardson, Harold, 111
Richardson, Mike, 109
Richey (SMU), 90
Riggs, Charlie, 111, 117, 119–20, 124
Rives, Don, *144*, 145
Roach, Walter, 46–47
Roach, William, 47
Roan, Oscar, 159, *159*
Roberts, Kelly, 75
Robertson, Ronnie, 157
Robinson, Carl, 207–8

INDEX ★ 275

Robinson, Ed, 143
Robnett, Marshall, 242
Roderick, John, 88–90
Rogers, Ronnie, 73, 83, 95
Rose, Nick, 260–61
Rose Bowl, 7–8, 252–54, 261–62
Royal, Darrell, 48, 54, 61, 68–69, 79, 85–88, *87*, 99, 102–3, 105, 113, 119–20, 121, 128–29, 132, 137–39, *138*, 147, 149, 152–53, 171–77, *175*, *176*, 253–54, 261–63
Russell, David, 78
Russell, Jack, 13
Russell, Seth, 259, 264, 267
Russell Athletic Bowl, 264–66
Rust, James, 95
Rutledge, Randy, 228–29
Ryan, Frank, 43–44

Saage, Reuben, 8, 30, 33, 35–37, *38*
Sadler, Billy, 143
Samford, Joe, 172
Sampleton, Lawrence, 205, *206*, 207, 213–14
Sarchet, Fred, 154
Sauer, George, 2, *2*, 10, 11
Savage, Paul, 142, 144
Saxton, James, 54–55, *56*, 61–63, 66–67, *67*, 69, 76, 78, 191
Schneider, Danny, 120
Scholtz, Bruce, 209, *210*, 215
Schott, Billy, 150–51, 153–54
Schriewer, Menan, 31
Schulte, Richard, 53
Schulz, Aubrey, 155, 157, 161
Sebastian, Don, 167
Senn, Perry, 142
Shaw, Chris, 32
Shearer, Brad, 173, *183*
Shepherd, Larry, 222
Sherrill, Jackie, 224, *225*, 227, 244
Shillingburg (Texas), 53
Shira, Charley, 102
Shirley, Bart, 62
Shofner, Del, 14, *14*, 30–41
Shofner, Jim, 48
Simmons, Bill, 50
Simpleton, John, 227
Simpson (Baylor), 229
Sims, Kenneth, 207–9, *210*, 215
Singletary, Mike, *197*, 199
Slater, Scott, 226–27, 229
Slaughter, Johnny, 154
Sloan, Steve, 147, 169
Slocum, R. C., 198, 242–44, *243*, *244*
Small, Ed, 113–14, 117
Smith, Charley, 3–4, 10, 14
Smith, Darrell, 180–81
Smith, Dave, 157
Smith, Donny, 69
Smith, Elmer, 26
Smith, Gary, 219
Smith, James Ray, 2, 2–4, 8–10
Smith, Kevin, 234, *235*
Smith, K. J., 269
Smith, Ralph, 104
Smith, Scott, 181
Smith, Tommy, 106

Smith, Zach, 267–70
SMU. *See* Southern Methodist University (SMU)
Sneed, Langford, 17
Snell, Frederick, 167
Solari, Steve, 241
Southall, Terry, 106–7
Southern Methodist University (SMU), 43, 88–90, 105–12, 127, 148, 155–59, 208–11, 216–21
Speyrer, Cotton, 137–39
Spikes, Jack, 47, 49, 62–63
Stabler, Kenny, 121, 123–26
Stallings, Gene, 11, 114, 117–24, *119*, *122*, 126, *126*
Stanley, Ronnie, 59–60, 72–73, 75
Staubach, Roger, 88–90, 98–100, *99*, 103, 105
Stegent, Larry, 114–16, 123–26
Steinmark, Fred, 136, 139
Sterling, James, 242
Stewart, Orion, 266, 268–69
Stewart, Tommy, 142
Stidham, Jarrett, 259, 264
Stockton, Tommy, 93, 95, 97
Stokes, Lonnie, 222
Stolhandske (Texas A&M), 53
Stone, Allen, 180–81
Stowe, Ron, 199, 203
Strait, Robert, 237–38, 251
Street, James, 129–33, *131*, 136–37, *137*, *138*, 253, 261
Strong, Charlie, 260–61
Stuart (Baylor), 127
Sugar Bowl, 33–38, 243
Sumlin, Kevin, 255, *257*
Sun Bowl. *See* John Hancock Bowl
Swink, Jim, 15–18, *17*, 22–26, 39–40, *40*, 47, 190
Swoopes, Tyron, 260–61
Swope, Ryan, *255*, 255–57
Syler, Terry, 229
Syracuse University, 39–40
Szeredy, Scott, 236–38, 241, *242*

Tabor, Tommy, 199, 202, 204
Talbert, Charley, 76, 97
Tannehill, Ryan, 257
Tate, Raymond, 222
Tate, Rodney, 205, 207, 211, 213
Tatum, Johnny, 17
Tausch, Terry, *206*, 207
Taylor, Billy, 170–71
Taylor, Ed, 142
Taylor, Fred, 46–48
Taylor, Hosea, 195
Taylor, Jim, *4*
Taylor, Kenneth, 181, 189
Taylor, Lance, 183
Taylor, Loyd, 25, 27–28, 30, 44, 46
Taylor, Trooper, 236–38
TCU. *See* Texas Christian University (TCU)
Teaff, Grant, 141, 144, 153, 155–57, *156*, 160, 160–61, *164*, 165, 167–68, 180, 198–202, 204–5, 227, 229, 235–40, *237*, *239*, *240*, 246–48
Terrell, Larry, 61

Terveen, Dede, 143
Texas A&M, 8–13, 18–30, 41–46, 51–54, 57–58, 81–83, 104, 110–12, 114–26, 180–81, 186–89, 224–29, 234–35, 241–45, 254–57
Texas Christian University (TCU), 15–18, 20–27, 39–42, 46–49, 60, 66–69, 83–85, 141–43, 243
Texas Stadium, 216, 220
Texas Tech, 18–19, 90–93, 139–40, 143–45, 147, 169–71, 198–201, 248–51
Thomas (SMU), 89–90
Thomas, Dyral, 166, 168, 173, 179
Thomas, Rodney, 241
Thompson, Arland, 167
Thompson, Ricky, 152, *152*, 154, 158–59, 162–65
Thompson, Ted, 158–59
Thompson, Tony, 229
Thornhill, Lynn, *111*
Tillman, Andre, 145, *145*
Tipton, Rell, 167
Todd, Don, 223
Tohill, Billy, 141
Toney, Anthony, 225–26
Townsend, Kenny, 141, 143
Tracey, John, 42, 52–53
Trammell, Dwayne, 142
Traylor, Doyle, 35–36, 46
Treadwell, Johnny, 77, 79, *80*, 84
Trull, Don, 70, 72–75, 81–82, *82*, 90–98, 101, 156, 191
Tubbs, Tony, 250
Tucker, Jinx, 242, 260
Turner, T. J., *222*, 223
Turnipseede, Tommy, 155

Underwood, Olen, 96
University of Alabama, 5–8, 122–26, 149–51, 201–5, 212–16, 254–56, 262
University of Arizona, 246–48
University of Arkansas, 114–16, 128–33, 174–75, 182–86, 216–21, 261–62
University of California–Berkeley, 1–4
University of Georgia, 107–10
University of Houston, 19, 146–48, 165–68, 171–73, 178, 193–95, 221–23, 245
University of Maryland, 178–80
University of Mississippi, 75–78
University of North Carolina, 264–66
University of Oklahoma, 54–57, 79–80, 112–14, 205–8, 256–57
University of Southern California, 252–54, 261
University of Tennessee, 33–38
University of Texas, 15–18, 31–33, 48–49, 51–56, 59–63, 66–69, 75–80, 83–88, 93–105, 112–14, 117–20, 129–33, 136–40, 147, 149–55, 169–75, 182–92, 205–16, 234–38, 241, 245, 252–54, 258–64
US Naval Academy (Navy), 88–90, 98–105
Utah State, 72

Van Dyke, Jarvis, 250–51
Venetoulias, Terry, 234, 241
Vick, Roger, 226

Wade, Tommy, 98
Wainscott, Loyd, 119
Walker, Adrian, 237–38, 241
Walker, Dale, 49
Walker, David, 180–81, 188–89
Walker, Doak, 190
Walker, Jimmy, 173
Walker, John, 206–7
Walker, Rodrick, 234
Walker, Shea, 229
Walls, Herkie, 212, 214
Ward, Al, 85–86
Ward, Lester, 199, 203
Warren, Chris, 260–61
Watkins, Norman, 237
Watson, Don, 9, 25, 27, 29–30, 121
Waz, Chance, 266
Weaver, DeWitt, 19
Weber, Mark, 208–9, 211
Weir, Trey, 238, 246–47
Welch, Jimmy, 32
Wesson, Ricky, 156, 158–59
West, Royce, 58
Whiddon, Eddie, 97
White, Allie, 46–48
White, Buddy, 70
White, Mac, 89–90, *108*, 108–9
Whitley, Wilson, *147*, 167, 171, 173
Whitmore, Bill, 14
Whitmore, Jack, 110–11
Whittier, Julius, 149
Whorton, Sonny, 70, 74
Wilder, Mike, 144
Wilkinson, Bud, 54
Willenborg, Jim, 81–82
Williams, Joe, 40
Williams, O'Day, 17, 25, 40
Williams, Roy, 256
Williams, Terence, 260–61, 264, 266–68
Williamson, Jim, 119
Wilson, Billy, 141, 143, 145
Wilson, Gene, 143, 145
Wilson, Jackie, 208, 211, 218
Wilson, Tom, *91*
Wineburg, Ken, 17–18, 39
Witcher, Albert, 57, *58*
Womack, Delano, 17
Woodard, George, 181, 188
Woodside, Keith, 225–26
Worster, Steve, 137, 140, 191
Wright, Elmo, 148, *148*
Wuensch, Bobby, 140
Wyatt, Jay, 166–67, 193

Yeoman, Bill, *146*, 146–48, *147*, *148*, 166, 171, 173, 178–80, 191, 193, 221–23
Young, Taylor, 266–67, 269
Young, Thomas Earl, 199, 203–4
Young, Vince, 253–54, *254*, 256, 261

Zamora, Ishmael, 268
Zunker, Coy, 142, 144